MODERNITY
AND
MASS CULTURE

EDITED BY

James Naremore and
Patrick Brantlinger

MODERNITY
AND
MASS CULTURE

INDIANA UNIVERSITY PRESS
Bloomington & Indianapolis

The paper used in this publication meets the minimum requirements of American National Standard for Information Sciences—Permanence of Paper for Printed Library Materials, ANSI Z39.48-1984.

⊗™

Manufactured in the United States of America

Library of Congress Cataloging-in-Publication Data

Modernity and mass culture / edited by James Naremore and Patrick
   Brantlinger.
     p.   cm.
   Includes index.
   ISBN 0-253-33968-5 (cloth). — ISBN 0-253-20627-8 (pbk.)
     1. Arts, Modern—20th century.   2. Arts and society—History—20th
   century.   I. Naremore, James.   II. Brantlinger, Patrick, date.
   NX456.M65   1991
   700'.1'030904—dc20   90-41881
                                                                CIP

1 2 3 4 5   95 94 93 92 91

CONTENTS

Acknowledgments

We would like to thank Professor Mary Burgan and the Department of English at Indiana University for sponsoring a lecture series in 1988–89. Several other programs cosponsored the event: Film Studies, Victorian Studies, Women's Studies, and Horizons of Knowledge. We would also like to thank Jeffrey Sumler for his editorial assistance.

Some of the essays have been previously published. We acknowledge the following journals: *Poetics Today* 9, no. 2 (1988), Richard Ohmann, "History and Literary History: The Case of Mass Culture"; *New Formations* 2 (1989), Peter Wollen, "Cinema/Americanism/the Robot"; *Cinema Journal* 28 (Summer 1989), Barbara Klinger, "Digressions at the Movies: Reception and Mass Culture"; *American Literary History* (Fall 1990), Devon Hodges and Janice L. Doane, "Undoing Feminism: From the Preoedipal to Postfeminism in Anne Rice's Vampire Novels"; *International Labor and Working Class History* (Fall 1989), Michael Denning, "The End of Mass Culture."

The Editors

Modernity
and
Mass Culture

Introduction:
Six Artistic Cultures

James Naremore and Patrick Brantlinger

Most of the essays assembled for this volume were delivered at Indiana University during 1988 and 1989, in a series of lectures entitled "The Theory and Interpretation of Mass Culture." The contributors addressed a wide range of phenomena, including advertising, avant-garde art, movies, television, best-selling novels, and postmodernist theory. Taken together, their work represents a variety of concerns in the growing academic movement known as "cultural studies."

The cultural studies movement resists definition, as if it were miming the decentered and appropriative quality of the formations it investigates. We might say that it comprises a leftist mode of analysis with at least three important precursors: the British culture-and-society debates, which began at the start of the nineteenth century and culminated in the work of Raymond Williams; the critical theory of the Frankfurt School; and the more recent conjuncture of Roland Barthes's semiology, Louis Althusser's Marxism, and Jacques Lacan's psychoanalysis. The founding texts of cultural studies would certainly include Barthes's *Mythologies* (1957), but the movement takes its specific character from the writing published by members of the Birmingham Centre for Contemporary Cultural Studies under the direction first of Richard Hoggart and then of Stuart Hall. During the past two decades such writing has been strongly influenced by radical feminism and theories of social difference; still more recently, it has become interested in forms of popular reception, and has argued forcefully against the overly deterministic or apocalyptic tone of much previous cultural criticism. In general, it occupies a sort of middle ground between post-structuralism and humanism; thus it is based on a dynamic model of the social subject, and it shows a marked interest in the work of Antonio Gramsci, Michel Foucault, Michel de Certeau, and Pierre Bourdieu, along with the British cultural theorists.

The phrase "mass culture," which guided our original conception of the lecture series, is equally difficult to pin down; we used it reluctantly, aware that it connotes an authoritarian theory of the media. In general terms, it involves a double inflection, derived from the "dual revolutions" of the late eighteenth century: on the one hand it points to the culture of the masses, or the majority of people most of the time; on the other it points to culture mass-produced by industrial techniques. But Shakespeare wrote dramas that have been reprinted, translated, staged, filmed, adapted, and televised countless times in virtually every context. Are *Hamlet* and *Othello* examples of mass culture? Conversely, certain anonymous sayings, jokes, songs, games, and rituals have come through the ages without benefit of votes or factories. Are these also examples of mass culture? Given the overlapping, often contradictory meanings of both "mass" and "culture," sharp definitions aren't possible. We can only say that meanings of the phrase tend to circulate around the fairly recent processes of democratization and industrialization. Democracy and technology are crucial factors in every major cultural development of the past two centuries. Romanticism, modernism, and postmodernism are all responses to these intertwined processes; to speak of such ideologies is to engage at some level with a supposed antithesis or "other," usually designated as belonging to the masses or to the mainstream.

However we define mass culture, it isn't a recent development. Why hasn't it always been on the academic agenda? The history of mass-produced literature extends back at least to the late 1700s, which alone might have made it an important object of study. And "mass" suggests a ubiquity that might have made mass culture a major focus of several academic disciplines. Indeed, one way to define mass culture is as everything that members of an industrialized society share with all the other members. Anything not universally shared may be less than "mass," an aspect of a "minority" or "sub"-culture. An immigrant to the United States may not speak English, but will nevertheless hear rock music, watch TV, see billboards, travel on freeways, eat fast foods, shop at Sears or K-Mart.

Perhaps its very ubiquity has rendered mass culture invisible to the established academic disciplines. But it is often the most visual and also visible forms of culture—ads, sports, television—that are most clearly "mass," experienced by the largest numbers of people. Its academic *in*visibility must therefore spring from other causes. With or without industrialization, the culture of "the masses"—the most common, ordinary, everyday culture shared by most people most of the time—has perhaps always been viewed antagonistically by intellectuals. As long ago as 500 B.C. Heraclitus condemned the majority for their inability to value "the best," which he identified with the singular or unique. The majority resent excellence and prefer the commonplace—this was also to be Nietzsche's theme 2400 years later. Ironically, like Plato after him, Heraclitus included poetry in his version of mass culture: the majority "follow the bards and use the multitude as their teacher, not realizing that there are many bad but few good. For the best choose one thing over all others, immortal glory among mortals, while the many are glutted like beasts."[1]

The scorn Heraclitus expresses is not merely the learned aristocrat's for the values of commoners and slaves; it derives also from the philosopher's or intellectual's assumption that the highest values adhere to that which is invisible, to ideas and ideals, whereas the majority understand only that which is visible, material, tangible ("the many are glutted like beasts"). The supposedly cultured or civilized person responds to more than his or her physical needs and pleasures; the supposedly ordinary person is bound to the physical. Resistance to the serious study of *visible* cultural objects such as films and photographs begins here, with the ancient belief that the sources of value are unseen, hidden from all but the enlightened few. Whatever has seemed both mainly material and common has through the ages also seemed "low," debased, or else surface or superficial—and therefore not worthy of scholarly attention.

Most intellectual responses to mass culture have been negative. As Williams demonstrated in *Culture and Society*, the American and French Revolutions gave a new urgency to debates about "the masses" in relation to culture. The democratization of culture was either a threat or a promise, depending on one's politics. Edmund Burke feared that "learning" was being "trampled under the hooves of a swinish multitude," while Tom Paine celebrated the overthrow of "force and fraud" and the future enlightenment of the common people. Even those who shared Paine's radicalism, however, often found it difficult to share his optimism about the cultural prospects of democracy. Whatever the ultimate outcome, the masses were at last on the stage of history, perhaps in the leading role. But because they did not necessarily behave the way intellectuals predicted or wanted, their apparent lack of the right sort of enlightenment or culture generated theories of ideology, most famously in the writings of Marx and Engels. They sought to explain why the masses adhered to beliefs that, as it seemed, prevented them from recognizing their true class interests and their solidarity with other workers. To greater or lesser extent, many workers seemed to accept the new capitalist order as inevitable, natural. Ideology as "false consciousness" was the key to explaining why most workers (however grudgingly) put up with their class subordination and exploitation.

In every historical form of social existence, Marx and Engels declared, "the ideas of the ruling class are . . . the ruling ideas: i.e., the class which is the ruling *material* force of society, is at the same time its ruling *intellectual* force."[2] This famous assertion can be understood as an early version of conspiratorial or manipulative theories of mass culture as well as of ideology (today often virtually synonymous terms). One highly influential version is Theodor Adorno and Max Horkheimer's theory of the "culture industry" as the tragic culmination of "the dialectic of Enlightenment." "The man with leisure has to accept what the culture manufacturers offer him."[3] These "manufacturers" are the new rulers, enforcing the regime of industrial capitalism through the ideological reproduction of "the man with leisure" or the pacified consumer—the uniform "mass man" himself. Foreshadowing Althusser's structuralist-Marxist account of the reproduction of the "subject" of "Ideology" by "Ideology," Adorno and Horkheimer argue that the ultimate product of the culture industry isn't movies, newspapers, and ads, but the pseudo-individuals who consume these commodities. Through such mass media as film and radio,

> the might of industrial society is lodged in men's minds. The entertainments manufacturers know that their products will be consumed with alertness even when the customer is distraught, for each of them is a model of the huge economic machinery which has always sustained the masses, whether at work or at leisure—which is akin to work. From every sound film and every broadcast program the social effect can be inferred which is exclusive to none but is shared by all alike. The culture industry as a whole has molded men as a type unfailingly reproduced in every product. (Adorno and Horkheimer, 127).

In the growing perfection and dissemination of the mass media, Adorno and Horkheimer see only the death of authentic selfhood, the reverse transubstantiation of the "subject of history" into the subjugated or disintegrated individual, but also the death of all possibilities of resistance and freedom: the culture industry conquers everything, even its own managers and rulers.

But negative theories of mass culture as ideology imposed from above must be qualified on several counts. First, who rules the rulers? Marx and Engels did not exactly mean that members of the ruling class consciously choose the ideologies they then consciously impose on subordinate classes: the rulers themselves are under the sway of ideology. On the contrary, "the mode of production of material life conditions the social, political and intellectual life process in general" (*Marx-Engels Reader*, 4). The entire ensemble of material or economic forces determines the consciousness of rulers as well as ruled. On the basis of "the economic foundation" rises "the entire immense superstructure"—culture, including everything from the arts to institutions of church and state that are not primarily economic. Second, although Adorno and Horkheimer believed that the culture industry was eliminating all chances for resistance and radical change, Marx and Engels did not claim so much for their version of ideology. Radicalisms, rebellions, and occasionally revolutions were the stuff of working-class history in the nineteenth century. The mass man whose life was (according to the culture industry theory) a mere reflection of the movies and advertising had not yet appeared. Third, and perhaps most importantly for later theories of the mass media, it isn't clear that the ideology the media disseminate is all of a piece—that it is uniform, standardized, or "mass" in the sense of devoid of internal cracks and contradictions. As several of the essays in this volume contend, people construct diverse, often contradictory meanings out of what seem to be the uniform products of the mass media.

Perhaps, as Williams insisted, there are no "masses"—"there are only ways of seeing [other] people as masses."[4] Both the uniform mass man, zombified creature of the culture industry, and the enlightened worker, member of the revolutionary masses, may be exceptional rather than "mass." Certainly the masses as revolutionary force did not develop as Marx and Engels hoped, except sporadically. Toward the end of the nineteenth century, the rise of labor parties, starting with the German Social Democratic Party in the 1870s, sharpened the Marxist identification of the masses with the industrial proletariat preparing to shake off its chains. But this definition was blurred by another—the masses as the anonymous, apparently classless "crowd," the indiscriminate urban conglomeration. The masses in the first sense threatened upper-class hegemony through revolution; the masses in the second sense—frightening to Marxists as well as to reactionaries—threatened class distinctions through entropy or apathy, overwhelming social boundaries by sheer numbers and blunting the weapons of socialism in the process. Besides the population explosion which made nineteenth-century urban growth rates enormous, the factors that contributed to this second meaning are summed up in the phrase "consumer society," characterized by a sharpening separation between the spheres of production and consumption from about 1870 forward.

The proletarian masses of the Marxist tradition were identified with work or production. But the masses of modern consumer society were large numbers of people on holiday or after work, crowding the stadiums, the music halls, the tourist resorts. Increased leisure and rising expectations about living standards, the proliferation of consumer goods, large-scale advertising campaigns, widespread dependence on credit, and the appearance of the first department stores were the mass cultural reflexes or symptoms of the "second Industrial Revolution."[5]

The development of consumer society was reflected as well in the series of new techniques and inventions that underlie the electronic mass media. The cinema was the most spectacular of these; through the entrepreneurship of Thomas Edison, the Lumières, and others, it rapidly became a new type of mass entertainment, which by 1914 was "the most widely distributed cultural form that there had ever been."[6] Other communications devices—the transoceanic cablegram, the linotype, the typewriter, the telephone, the phonograph, the wireless, inexpensive photographic equipment—were nearly as spectacular as cinema. Each of these devices made the instant transmission and sometimes mass reproduction of messages possible, although it was a matter of debate as to whether messages thus transmitted gained or lost in accuracy, value, truth, or beauty. The very shift in emphasis from production to consumption, although involving increased leisure and prosperity for many, called forth feelings of guilt and decadence. To the puritanical (whether religious or political), time off and fun could never be worthwhile goals of work: taverns, music halls, and cinemas were all dens of iniquity. Even the telephone inspired protest from those who worried that it threatened privacy or was no substitute for face-to-face dialogue. Anxiety was also expressed about the wireless and ca-blegrams, as when, in *The Psychology of Jingoism* (1901), John Hobson de-clared that the latter were "the ideal mode of suggestion" for manipulating "the general mind" by playing upon "the common pulse of passion which sways . . . members of a crowd."[7] And if mass "suggestion" could be an effect of cablegrams, to many it seemed even more clearly an effect of film. In 1913 Louis Haugmard declared that " 'the masses' are like a grown-up child who demands a picture album to leaf through in order to forget his miseries." Cinema was a "circus" or daydream world which gave only the illusion of putting the masses in direct touch with reality. "Through it the charmed masses will learn not to think anymore. . . . "[8] Similarly, in the same year Robert Donald told the British Institute of Journalists that the cinema and phonograph would make people "too lazy to read, and news will be laid on to the house or office just as gas or water now is."[9]

Ironically, the "age of cinema" saw the achievement of nearly universal literacy in most industrialized nations. But the entry of the working and lower middle classes into the political arena sharpened perennial questions about what the masses were or were not reading. At the heart of many paradoxical, turn-of-the-century complaints about mass literacy as a new social problem rather than solution lies a concern with the allegedly ne-farious effects of the "sensational" press. The warmongering "yellow jour-nalism" of the United States was matched by the imperialistic "new journalism" of Britain, and similar developments characterized press his-tory in France and Germany. "Yellow journalism" was widely held to have sparked the Spanish-American War, while Hobson blamed the jingoism that helped fuel the Boer War largely on "a biased, enslaved, and poisoned press."[10]

With yet another political crisis in mind, the Boxer Rebellion in China in 1900, the British historian G. M. Trevelyan denied that the "yellow peril" was as much a threat to European civilization as the "white peril," con-sisting of "the uniform modern man," creature of "the great cities." "By modern machinery . . . moulded for good or for evil with a rapidity of change unknown at any previous epoch," the "white peril" was also moulded by what it read:

> Journals, magazines, and the continued spawn of bad novels, constitute our
> national culture, for it is on these that the vast majority of all classes employ

their power of reading. How does it concern our culture that Shakespeare, Milton, Ruskin, in times gone by wrote in our language, if for all the countless weary ages to come the hordes that we breed and send out to swamp the world shall browse with ever-increasing appetite on the thin swollen stuff that commerce has now learnt to supply for England's spiritual and mental food?[11]

Nothing seemed more nightmarish to Trevelyan than the "uprooting of taste and reason by the printing press," except the threat of its readers swamping the world. Foreshadowing José Ortega y Gassett's "revolt of the masses," the "white peril" of 1900 was already on the march, a barbarian invasion from the heart of civilization, manufacturing and consuming enormous quantities of journalistic "nonsense" and "vulgarity" to spur itself on.

While even mass literacy could inspire fear and loathing, for many the new communications techniques radiated a utopian promise of ultimate democratic enlightenment. Against Haugmard's dire assessment of the influence of cinema on the mass mind can be ranged countless expressions of optimism. Hugo Münsterberg believed that "the greatest mission" of "the photoplay" would be the "esthetic cultivation" of the masses.[12] Edison thought that cinema would bring about the perfection of education: "I intend to do away with books in the school. . . . When we get the moving-pictures in the school, the child will be so interested that he will hurry to get there before the bell rings, because it's the natural way to teach, through the eye."[13] Even more extravagantly, Henry Hopwood ended his book *Living Pictures*(1899) by assimilating the celluloid gaze to an omniscient gaze, God as the supreme viewer of the ultimate motion picture: "So a . . . record of the earth's history in its slightest details is continually streaming off into the eternal void, and, granted an eye capable . . . one universal perception extending through infinity would embrace . . . an eternal and universal living picture of all past events."[14]

Extreme euphoria and extreme despair seem as much products of the mass media as movies or commercials. The tension between these extremes is evident in many of the responses to mass culture in literary and artistic modernism and avant-garde movements. It shows itself clearly in the well-known debates between Walter Benjamin and Adorno, and it pervades the revised version of Benjamin's seminal essay, "The Work of Art in the Age of Mechanical Reproduction." Benjamin celebrates the destruction of artistic "aura" by photographic montage, and he brilliantly reveals the revolutionary implications of the new Soviet cinema and the collages of John Heartfield. In one of his most amusing footnotes, he quotes Aldous Huxley on the proliferation of "trash" in the modern media, adding his own brief comment: "This mode of observation is obviously not progressive." At the same time, however, Benjamin seems to regret the possible disintegration of *Kultur*. He recognizes that a new kind of "false aura" is possible in the movies, and even though he cheerfully predicts the end of the "theology of art," in the epilogue to his essay he observes that the fascists are using films to aestheticize horror.[15]

The conflict between Benjamin and Adorno (seen clearly in Adorno's essay, "On the Fetish-Character in Music," written in 1938) continues to replay itself, animating debates over art and culture down to the present day. On the one hand are those who find a transforming, liberating potential in new technologies; on the other are those who fear that the mass media will create passive, one-dimensional audiences. Perhaps both camps are correct, since, as Fredric Jameson has remarked, every form of technological progress seems to entail catastrophe.[16] In any case, a good way to sort out the issues at stake in modern cultural criticism is to view the media in relation to a larger configuration, which we've only hinted at up to now. The following cultural typology provides such a configuration. It says relatively little about the exact relationship between social formations and artistic production, but it provides the basis for a more extended analysis that would bring those and other issues into play.

Far from congealing into a mass, Western society in the early decades of the twentieth century seems to have split into an unsettled mixture of at least six artistic cultures, each producing different kinds of images, stories, music, and what Carl Schorske calls "intellectual objects." These same cultures appear also to have generated ideologies, reading practices, and forms of subjectivity through which art can be received or understood. Let us quickly add that there is good reason to doubt whether all the cultures have actually existed. If they are real, they partake of one another, sometimes overlapping, blurring together, or speaking dialogically—and sometimes, like figures on a chessboard, living in antagonistic relation. They could be described as mental constructs, or, in Foucault's language, as discursive fields. But even if they're only ideas, they constitute a network of real social power; and because their names occur frequently in the writings of historians and theorists, they have a certain heuristic value. At the risk of appearing glib or simplistic, we list them here, providing a brief commentary on each:

1. *High art.* In Europe, the idea of high art received its fullest expression in the courtly *civilité* of the Renaissance. By the time of the Enlightenment, however, it had become a bourgeois phenomenon, in the sense intended by Horkheimer, who once remarked that "there is no other thought properly speaking than in cities."[17] Although it took root in ecclesiastical circles and at court, the culture of high art was disseminated in the growing European capitals, where it had the effect of mapping empires, forging national identities, and subtly maintaining the authority of aristocrats over their most powerful subjects. By the nineteenth century, with the industrial

revolution and the spread of democracy, it was harnessed to an ideology of progressive education, deriving its rationale from texts like Matthew Arnold's *Culture and Anarchy*. In the twentieth century, it underwent still further transformations, providing an agenda for welfare-capitalist institutions such as the BBC in England.

Matthew Arnold and his descendants (including F. R. Leavis, Robert Hutchins, and Allan Bloom) have usually argued that high art transcends the values of any particular social class. Until recently, they've located its qualities in a series of largely male European writers who create "touchstones," a "great tradition," or simply "great books." Academic departments of humanities were designed to study these canonical works, at the same time providing a haven from commerce and industry—an apolitical retreat, where intellectual curiosity, scholarship, and the contemplation of masterpieces could advance civilization.

In the 1960s, '70s, and '80s, the canon of high or academic art became much more diversified, open to women and people of color, and even capable of including such things as Hollywood movies. Regardless of its social origins or the medium in which it has appeared, however, high art is usually something of a literary phenomenon, given sanction and authority by the written word. It inevitably possesses both classical and romantic aspects, pointing simultaneously toward the need to master a tradition and toward the need to develop free and autonomous individuals. It also promotes two attitudes toward the meaning of culture: on the one hand, an optimistic feeling of "sweetness and light," and on the other, a pessimistic but sublime recognition of a tragic human condition. These contradictory tendencies are often in conflict, but they're alike in their fundamental idealism and their deep hostility toward the vulgar marketplace. In other words, the ideology of high art has an asymmetrical relation to the modern economy: it belongs in some sense to a hegemonic order, but its opposition to Philistinism means that it can't be described *simply* as "bourgeois" or "capitalist." As Alan Sinfield and others have pointed out, it frequently serves as a "banner of dissidence" for alienated intellectuals— a rallying point for members of an internally divided middle class.[18]

2. *Modernist art.* Modernist art develops out of high culture but is sharply critical, even deconstructive, of certain high-culture values. It originates in the orientalism and the art-for-art's-sake movements of the late nineteenth century, and it always cultivates what Adorno (a modernist himself) described as an "autonomous" social role. Artistically, the early modernists were proponents of a media-specific formalism; politically, they were opposed to any social organization—whether industrial capitalism or state socialism—that would prevent artists from functioning as unacknowledged legislators, or as members of a philosophical elite. (Some of the modernists, especially the theorists of the Frankfurt School, could also be understood

as ecologists *avant la lettre* because of their fears of what the factory system would do to nature.) Aggressively individualistic, contemptuous of bourgeois realism, and sometimes nostalgic for pre-industrial society, they seemed at once reactionary and new. In English literature, for example, the quintessential modernist texts are Joyce's *Ulysses* and Eliot's *The Waste Land*—both of them "experimental" montages, mixing the artifacts of urban mass culture with fragments of classical literature, encouraging belief in the transcendent value of their own sophisticated craft.

Because of its roots in high culture, modernism quickly achieved canonical status in universities; nevertheless, it has a potentially scandalous effect. The modernists were profoundly influenced by Nietzsche, Marx, Freud, and the second industrial revolution. As a result, throughout the 1920s their art frequently resembled category 3, listed below. To see how threatening they could become, one need only consider the problematic status of the subject in Virginia Woolf's *To the Lighthouse*, or the tissue of quotations, collages, pastiches, and parodies in Joyce and early Eliot. Partly for this reason, modernism never established a comfortable home in the empirical, humanistic environment of England, and in the decades before and after World War II, it lost some of its iconoclastic spirit and jazz-age vitality. What remained was a contempt for certain fractions of the bourgeoisie and a growing fear of state power; thus the 1930s and '40s in England were characterized by literary jeremiads against liberal progress and technocracy—Waugh's *A Handful of Dust*, Greene's *Brighton Rock*, Huxley's *Brave New World*, Orwell's *1984*. Elsewhere, varieties of formalist or "experimental" modernism continued to flourish—in Latin American painting, for example, and especially in the French nouveau-roman. Meanwhile, in the academy, the works of the first generation of modernists provided the conceptual basis for the most influential postwar developments in literary theory, including such apparently different movements as the new criticism and post-structuralism.

3. *Avant-garde art.* Cultural historians often equate modernism and the avant-garde, but recent critics—including Peter Bürger, Andreas Huyssen, and Martin Jay—have persuasively argued that the two terms ought to be kept distinct.[19] In its most aggressive form, what Bürger describes as the "historical avant-garde" was a radicalized and largely political movement of the 1920s that used technology as a weapon against the institution of high art. Generally speaking, whereas modernism tended to be critical of industrial society, the avant-garde welcomed machines and celebrated their utopian potential; hence the well-known debates between Adorno and Benjamin, representing the modernist and avant-garde wings of left German culture in the 1920s.[20]

The favorite devices of the avant-garde have always been automatic writing, performance, *bricolage*, and any technique of *détournement* that problematizes the authority of autonomous art. Above all, the avant-garde wants to promote what Roland Barthes called the provisional "text" over the commodified "work." The definitive examples of such practice are Marcel Duchamp's ready-mades, although the early avant-garde cultural formations—including Berlin Dada, French Surrealism, and Italian Futurism—provide equally important instances. The films of Dizga Vertov and some of the theatrical productions of Brecht and Piscator are the most celebrated expressions of the Marxist avant-garde, and in the United States, Andy Warhol might be described as a paradoxical variant of the type. Some historians would argue that Warhol and the Pop movement represent a decisive break with the old cultural categories; even so, Warhol shares at least one familiar strategy with the historical avant-garde: the use of mechanical reproduction to undermine the epistemology of museums and art galleries. (Where this collection of essays is concerned, Robert Ray's paper represents an avant-garde practice within the sphere of pedagogy and academic criticism.)

4. *Folk art.* The binary opposite of high art—and hence its virtual creation—folk art is agrarian or pre-industrial, belonging chiefly to peasants. In twentieth-century America it hardly survives, except perhaps in music and stories composed by southern blacks or Appalachian coal miners, in murals painted by Chicanos, or in artifacts produced by Native Americans. Not surprisingly, a leading motif of cultural theory during the first half of the century was a lament over how folk art was being destroyed by modernization. This lament was especially strong in the Frankfurt School's Weberian analysis of the American media, and it was echoed by a number of modernist American intellectuals of the 1940s, especially by Dwight Macdonald, Clement Greenburg, and James Agee. Agee, for example, wrote a controversial piece for the *Partisan Review* in 1944, in which he argued that the "folk tradition" had been utterly bourgeoisified by celebrity artists like Hazel Scott, Paul Robeson, Duke Ellington, and Walt Disney.[21]

In Europe, folk art has a more distinctive identity, although it often seems a figment of high-culture imagination. Perhaps because the "folk" are subject to academic preservation and analysis, and perhaps because they often perform their rituals for the benefit of tourists, recent theorists have become deeply skeptical of them. For instance, Roger Chartier contends that entrenched beliefs about the reading habits of eighteenth-century French farmers are nothing more than the *topoi* of pastoral ideology, imposed from above by anthropologists; and Jean Baudrillard claims that "primitive" societies are merely "simulacra," designed to give the postindustrial world a myth of origins.[22] Even if we were to avoid such problems by defining folk art more broadly, as the popular expression of any disenfranchised, semiliterate group in modern society (such as subway graffiti or punk fashion), it couldn't be analyzed except in an official, legitimate discourse; hence it would be framed and represented by something other than itself.

5. *Popular art.* This highly politicized category is sometimes associated with a more or less proletarian audience that, in the words of Pierre Bourdieu, has not "acquired legitimate culture in the legitimate manner."[23] It connotes the world of sports, circus, fairgrounds, nickelodeons or penny arcades, early jazz, early rock 'n' roll, comic strips, and certain kinds of down-market theater or film—a hazy terrain that resists most attempts at definition, although it's usually described as earthy and excessive.

In a study of early British music halls, Stuart Hall and Paddy Whannel have argued that popular art differs from folk art in depending on a star system and a professionalized type of performance; in other words, popular art transforms the folk "community" into an urban "audience."[24] More recently, however, Hall and other theorists have used "popular" in a quite different fashion, signaling their belief that potentially dominated social groups have the power to resist hegemonic control. The most influential of these theorists, Michel de Certeau, has defined the whole of popular culture as "combinatory or utilizing modes of consumption . . . a way of thinking invested in a way of acting, an art of combination which cannot be disassociated from an art of using."[25] For de Certeau, *bricolage* is not merely a technique of primitive cultures or of avant-garde artists, but also an adaptive strategy employed by modern consumers—a sort of "Browning movement" that circulates across social formations. As he puts it, "this cultural activity of the nonproducers of culture, an activity that is unsigned, unreadable, and unsymbolized, remains the only possible one for all those who nevertheless buy and pay for the showy products through which a productivist economy articulates itself" (xvii). Most contemporary accounts of popular culture (such as those of John Fiske, who is represented in this book) have accepted de Certeau's argument, and have therefore been more concerned with reception than with production. In these writings, the term "popular" operates in dialectical relation to industrial and state power, and it inevitably blurs over into the next category.

6. *Mass art.* All the other types of art have European origins and definitive practitioners or theorists on the continent. Mass art, however, seems particularly American. In fact, as Peter Wollen indicates in the essay he contributes to our volume, the very word "Americanism" was used by both Gramsci and the Frankfurt School to signify the concept of assembly-line manufacture and consumer culture. Intellectuals may have expressed anxieties about the masses as far back as classical antiquity, but the terms "mass art" and "mass culture" were coined in the decades immediately before and after World War II, with the rise of Hollywood talking pictures,

American network radio, and Henry Luce's empire of slick-paper magazines filled with photography. These were the institutions comprising what Horkheimer and Adorno labeled the culture industry—the manufacturers of *Kitsch*, a German word meaning "trash" or "rubbish." And indeed, throughout the middle decades of the century, mass art was produced by a Fordist, vertically integrated factory system, its regularized products designed to appeal to as many social classes or class fractions as possible. Capital-intensive and assembled according to complex divisions of labor, it was usually rationalized by its producers as entertainment rather than as art. By its very nature it devalued "originality" and "individuality"— two keywords of high culture—and was supervised by committees or boards of executives.

Despite its industrial basis, however, twentieth-century mass art has allowed and selectively encouraged certain kinds of experiment. In its relatively brief history, it has absorbed material from all five of the cultural categories listed above, and has employed the finest artists from every sphere. It has even appropriated the ideology of romantic individualism, which it uses to promote a star system. During the 1970s and '80s, it was reorganized by multinational, conglomerate capitalism, and in the age of electronics it has become so pervasive that the other cultures now tend to represent themselves through its technology. A vast, "leaky" form of production, it makes use of everything from home videos to high literature. Even so, intellectuals have always charged that its message is totalitarian. Thus in the 1960s, filmmaker Jean-Luc Godard termed the American and Soviet movie studios "Nixon-Paramount" and "Paramount-Mosfilm," as if the industrial leviathans of the West and East had become Tweedledum and Tweedledee.

We could have reduced this list of six cultures to a familar high/low opposition: the first three categories are the domain of those who have what Bourdieu calls "cultural capital," whereas the last three are accessible to the general population. Then, too, we could have devised a more elaborate typology, using different ideas of cultural determination. For example, we've avoided "postmodernism," a term that suggests late-capitalist modes of production, decentered forms of reception, and eclectic borrowings from older styles. (We shall say more about this term in a moment.) We've also avoided *Tendenz*art and such politico-stylistic concepts as "social realism" or "classical narrative," which can be subsumed within the larger realms. In this last regard, notice that each of the categories has *both* left-wing and right-wing manifestations, and can't be described with the usual political language; Adorno and Eliot, for example, were proponents of modernism, but their politics were antithetical. By the same token, none of the various cultural categories can claim to embody a "correct" moral or social position; judged on the basis of the historical record, high culture is no more or less patriarchal and racist than mass culture. Moreover, few artists have actually labeled themselves with one of the six terms we've employed: Alfred Tennyson didn't claim to write high art; James Joyce never used the word "modernism"; Tristan Tzara wouldn't have declared membership in the avant-garde; Leadbelly didn't think of himself as a folk performer; Marie Lloyd never billed herself as a working-class star; and L. B. Mayer would hardly have said that *Grand Hotel* was mass art.

Some artists are especially difficult to classify. Where, for example, shall we place a writer like Edgar Allan Poe? This problem is exacerbated by the fact that artists who seem to belong to one culture at a given point in history can later be adopted by another culture. During the first two decades of the century, D. W. Griffith was regarded as a popular or mass artist; by the 1950s, his early films were displayed in museums and discussed in the language of high art. In the 1880s, James McNeill Whistler's "Arrangement in Grey and Black" was considered an advanced form of European modernism; sixty years later, reproductions of that same painting, popularly known as "Whistler's Mother," had become the cultural equivalent of calendar art, or of the familiar images of Norman Rockwell. In the mid-1920s, Virginia Woolf was recognized by a coterie audience as a "stream of consciousness" novelist and as the coeditor of the Hogarth Press; but by 1937, when her historical novel *The Years* was published in the United States, she had become a best-selling author whose face appeared on the cover of *Time* magazine.

Even when artistic objects are determined by the ideology of a specific culture, they usually contain material drawn from a variety of sources. Every text is "heteroglossic," and some texts contain a rich enough mixture of elements to be used in a variety of circumstances—a phenomenon that's especially noticeable in the performing arts, where nearly anything can be adapted to suit different audiences. Consider, as one minor example, the American history of *"Moritat,"* a song written by Bertolt Brecht and Kurt Weill for the 1928 Berlin production of *Die Dreigroschenoper*. The song originates in the modernist and avant-garde movements of prewar Germany, and it was influenced by popular Weimar cabaret. It was given its first English lyrics by Gifford Cochran and Jerrold Krinsky, and was performed for twelve shows in the 1933 Broadway version of *The Threepenny Opera*. Marc Blitzstein later wrote his own translation of the song, entitled "Mack the Knife," which was presented in a successful concert performance at Brandeis University in 1952. Blitzstein's version of *The Threepenny Opera* had a long run on Christopher Street in New York's Greenwich Village, where it developed a cult following. Eventually, the show became a staple of academic and off-Broadway drama; meanwhile, "Mack the Knife" was recorded in the United States in 1954 by Lotte Lenya. In 1957, Louis Armstrong, a so-called "folk" or popular performer who had crossed over into mass culture, recorded a skat version of "Mack the Knife," containing improvised lyrics. In 1959, Bobby Darrin performed a swinging, Vegas-style rendition that became the best-selling record in the United States for nine consecutive weeks. And in the late 1980s, Darrin's arrangement of the song—its title changed to "Mac the Night"—was used in a major advertising campaign for McDonald's hamburgers.

This may sound like a simple story of resistant culture being absorbed by the mainstream, but the situation is more complex. In the first place, there's no objective reason to claim that any of the famous American recordings of "Mack the Knife" is artistically better than the others. (Brecht himself rather liked the Louis Armstrong version, and Bobby Darrin's rendition has considerable virtues of its own.) In the second place, the recordings can take on different implications in different circumstances. For instance, not long after the success of Darrin's record, the comedian Ernie Kovacs used the original Lotte Lenya version of "Mack the Knife" as background music for a surreal TV skit. Kovacs's absurdly funny routine, which was repeated many times on American networks, restored some of the sinister implications of the original tune and at the same time divested Lenya's record of the high-art connotations it had begun to acquire.

We now live in a world of global electronic communication, where texts are constantly metamorphosed and recycled. In such an environment, Walter Benjamin seems our contemporary, if only because he points to the way words, images, or simulacra can move easily across reading formations and historical conjunctures. But cultural meaning is always already unstable, as "Mack the Knife" illustrates. The original Brecht/Weill song, after all, was a mixture of modernist, avant-garde, and popular ingredients, and it could be easily appropriated by a variety of performers. At the same time, the history of the song also suggests that the meaning of a text can't be reduced completely to its mode of reception, or to whatever reading strategy its audience might adopt. In this respect, Adorno is as relevant as Benjamin. He would doubtless remind us that in most cases where "Mack the Knife" has been put to different uses, it has entered different "relations of production," and its form has changed slightly.

Perhaps the most important thing to be said about the six artistic cultures is that even if they exist in some "real" fashion beyond intellectual and academic discourse, none of them is unchanging or complete unto itself. Culture, like language, is forever in a condition that Raymond Williams described as "emergent," and its various forms are constantly subject to transformation, combination, and dissolution. Nevertheless, most cultural theory and a great deal of artistic practice in the twentieth century could be described as an attempt to defend one of the first five categories we've named against the encroachments of a hypostatized mass art—or, conversely, as an attempt to wrest power from mass art on behalf of one of the other categories.

A classic case in point is Dwight Macdonald's well-known essay of the

1950s, "A Theory of Mass Culture," in which mass art serves both as a threat and (unbeknownst to Macdonald) as a kind of foil against which "high art," "folk art," "popular art," and "vangard art" can define themselves.[26] Borrowing much of his argument from *The Dialectic of Enlightenment*, Macdonald describes mass art as a dynamic process that plunders the other cultures. It does this, he claims, in both the USA and the USSR, the only difference being that American artists devote themselves to "entertainment," while Russians are concerned with "propaganda and pedagogy" (60). He compares these twin versions of mass culture to a "caterpillar" who destroys a leaf, and to an "improvident" miner who extracts riches from the land and puts nothing back; elsewhere, he makes the products of the culture industry seem like a monstrosity from a low-budget, 1950s horror movie—a "spreading ooze" or synthetic blob, against which we can briefly see the outlines of more authentic arts (73). The chief problem, he says, is that mass art (promulgated by big-time show business, academia, and the State) "mixes and scrambles everything together, producing what might be called homogenized culture" (62). For Macdonald, this homogenization is especially evident in what happened to movies during his own lifetime: individual artists such as Griffith, Stroheim, and Chaplin were supplanted by the studio system; and when the sound film arrived, "Broadway and Hollywood drew closer together," engulfing America in middlebrow *Kitsch* (64–65).

Looked at today, Macdonald may seem quaint. A typical cold-war liberal, he's anxious to preserve the boundaries between types of art, and he fails to recognize that every artistic culture borrows indiscriminately from every other culture in order to survive. He has a romantic belief in the powers of the individual, and he clearly has elitist tastes. Few people nowadays would agree with him about specific works of art; since his essay was written, several generations of intellectuals have grown up experiencing the products of the culture industry, and while these intellectuals sometimes make fine aesthetic judgments, they're disinclined to observe rigid distinctions between high and low forms. Indeed the very objects Macdonald derides—including such things as the novels of Dashiell Hammett and the films of classic Hollywood—have now become canonical works or cultural treasures guarded by preservationists.

Nevertheless, certain of Macdonald's arguments aren't easy to dismiss. At the very least, they're revealingly symptomatic of the period when his essay was written. To appreciate this fact, we need only recall a big-budget movie released by Hollywood in 1953—the same year when "A Theory of Mass Culture" was published. MGM's *The Band Wagon*, directed by Vincente Minnelli and starring Fred Astaire, makes systematic use of the cultural categories Macdonald describes—often parodying them, and always requiring that they serve the purpose of "entertainment." As Geoffrey Nowell-Smith points out in a footnote to the essay he has written for this volume (and as he elaborates further in an unpublished lecture), *The Band Wagon* is a virtual melting-pot of artistic discourses, all of them controlled by the ruling ideology of MGM in the early fifties.[27] It might even be regarded as Hollywood's answer to Macdonald, or perhaps as the culture industry's specific contribution to the widespread midcentury belief in such things as highcult, midcult, and masscult.

It's worth pausing here to recall a few scenes from the film. Early on, Astaire performs a number entitled "When There's a Shine on Your Shoes," accompanied by a popular artist named LeRoy Daniels—an actual shoe-shine man, who until this moment had plied his trade on the streets of Los Angeles. In the next major sequence, Astaire goes to a theater, where he encounters a modernist director who wants to stage a musical version of *Faust*. When Astaire reluctantly agrees to star in this dubious enterprise, he is teamed with a ballerina. As we might expect, the musical lays an egg in out-of-town tryouts. To save the show, Astaire himself steps in as director; he raises capital by selling his personal collection of fine European paintings, and he completely revises the concept of the production, turning it into a light entertainment called *The Band Wagon*. In the final third of the movie, Broadway and Hollywood coalesce, and we see a series of musical numbers representing a smash hit. Among them is "Louisiana Hayride," which might be described as MGM's notion of folk art.

Interestingly, *The Band Wagon*'s climactic number is an extended dance narrative entitled "The Girl Hunt Ballet," which, as Minnelli tells us in his autobiography, was intended as a parody of Mickey Spillane.[28] We should remember that in 1953, Spillane was the most successful writer in America, his six volumes having sold a total of thirteen million copies; indeed, he was such a significant figure that Dwight Macdonald devoted several paragraphs to him. According to Macdonald, the depredations wrought by years of *Kitsch* could be seen in the history of detective fiction, which had begun with ratiocinative heroes like Sherlock Holmes only to end with stupid gumshoes like Mike Hammer. Dashiell Hammett had inaugurated what Macdonald calls a "sensational" style, and this led to Spillane's fiction, where the search for the criminal was a "mere excuse for the minute description of scenes of bloodshed, brutality, lust, and alcoholism" (68). Almost as if it were taking Macdonald's essay as a guide, *The Band Wagon* comments humorously on the same phenomenon, transforming the hard-boiled detective into a dancer, exchanging Spillane's prose for Michael Kidd's choreography, and filling the mise-en-scène with allusions to the Hollywood film noir. Here and everywhere else, however, the film aims its cultural borrowings toward the justification of its own status as an artistic commodity. As Jane Fuer has pointed out, *The Band Wagon* is a brilliant instance of "conservative self-reflexivity."[29] Its overriding purpose is summed up perfectly by its concluding song, "That's Entertainment," which tells us that the whole world's a stage, and that everything on the stage ought to be entertaining. Even *Hamlet* is only a tale of how "the ghost and the prince meet / and everyone ends in mincemeat." Entertainment, moreover, is downright patriotic: "Hip, Hip, Hooray," Astaire and the rest of the cast proclaim, "it's the American way—that's entertainment!"

Viewed in these terms, *The Band Wagon* seems to confirm Macdonald's dire analysis of American life. Even so, many historians now regard the film as something of a masterpiece. One reason why (certainly not the only reason) is that today's style of "legitimate" cultural discrimination has less in common with Macdonald than with Susan Sontag, a symptomatic theorist of the 1960s, whose early work contributed to the development of what would later become known as a "postmodern" aesthetic. Sontag's influential book, *Against Interpretation* (1966), was designed as an attack on the cultural modernism of figures like Macdonald, whom she equated with the great tradition of "Jewish moral seriousness."[30] Over against the Hebraism of the New York intellectuals, she posed the Hellenism of Oscar Wilde; more significantly, she used movies and pop music to challenge the "conventionally accepted boundaries" between high and low culture, as well as the artistic distinction between "unique and mass-produced objects" (297). In her concluding essay, she announced the birth of a "new (potentially unitary) sensibility" through which "the feeling (or sensation) given off by a Rauschenberg painting might be like that of a song by the Supremes." Seen from the vantage of this sensibility, Sontag wrote, "The brio and elegance of Budd Boetticher's *The Rise and Fall of Legs Diamond* or the singing style of Dionne Warwick can be appreciated as a complex and pleasureable event. They are experienced without condescension" (303).

But experienced, one might ask, by whom? Despite the egalitarian implications of Sontag's argument, she was addressing an audience of high-culture or traditional intellectuals. In effect, she was advocating a form of reading that would enable an elite to make counterraids on mass culture, thus *reversing* the process Macdonald had described. Consider Sontag's famous essay, "Notes on Camp," which offers an implicit and somewhat rarified justification for objects like *The Band Wagon*. "Camp," she remarks, "is the answer to the problem: how to be a dandy in the age of mass culture" (288). Fred Astaire is of course an answer to that same problem, and he might be seen as a quintessential camp artist. Notice also that where camp taste is concerned, mass culture becomes more interesting when it's slightly out of date. As Andrew Ross has observed, the camp effect depends not only on an aristocratic, theatrical sense of refinement and irony—qualities we can feel to some degree in all of Vincente Minnelli's films—but also on a sense of nostalgia and disempowerment. Camp is made possible, Ross argues, whenever "the products . . . of a much earlier mode of production, which has lost its power to dominate cultural meanings, become available, in the present, for redefinition according to contemporary modes of taste."[31] Seen in this way, *The Band Wagon* achieves its status (both as a canonical work within film studies and as an object of camp affection) at least partly because its particular form of entertainment has long passed from the scene.

In fact, the classic Hollywood musical was already ending as *The Band Wagon* was being produced, and a sense of nostalgia is inscribed everywhere in the film. In 1953, Lowes Incorporated, the parent company of MGM, had been ordered by the Supreme Court to divest itself of theater chains. The vertical integration of the movies was being challenged, television was changing the face of America, and Fred Astaire was growing old. Hence, even in its own day, *The Band Wagon* was a deliberate form of commercial aestheticism—an ode to what Ross calls a "disempowered mode of production" (139). A new movie industry, designed to achieve a more spectacular integration of leisure-time activities, would emerge over the next few decades, forging strong ties with every form of commodity culture. During the transitional period, the United States also underwent a number of social upheavals, and there was sometimes a space for critical modernism within the mainstream cinema. Think of the vivid contrast between *The Band Wagon* and Robert Altman's 1975 film, *Nashville*, which uses the "country music" capitol as a metaphor for America. In the essay he has written for this collection, Christopher Anderson notes that the final scenes of Altman's movie are as relentlessly pessimistic as anything the Frankfurt School ever wrote; in color and wide screen, they depict a city where pseudo folk-performers gather in front of a plaster-of-paris Parthenon to sing mindless, protofascist tunes to the anonymous masses. Even so, nowadays you can see *Nashville* broadcast on TV, in a reduced format and interspersed with commercials.

Television has clearly made the old cultural debates, as well as the arguments about camp and canonicity, seem problematic. In the postmodern era, the distinction between public and private space, which was always threatened by the industrial revolution, has virtually disappeared, and with it many of the distinctions between categories of culture or forms of art. (Interestingly, the Edison laboratories at the beginning of the century never wanted to invent a movie camera; what they were trying to achieve was a phonograph with pictures—a forerunner of the TV set.) As David E. James has put it, the age of TV has fulfilled the Wagnerian dream of the *Gesamtkunstwerk*: "The commodities produced by and around 'The Victory Tour,' Madonna's tour, or the Pope's tour; by the protean roles of Andy Warhol or Malcolm McLaren, Cher or Ronald Reagan; by the Olympics or the Euro-Vision song contest or the presidential elections . . . manifest an unprecedentedly consolidated integration of one medium with another and of art with social reality."[32] Meanwhile, Hollywood's blockbuster films rely on a dense intertextuality, uniting highbrow and lowbrow, spinning off into a variety of products. *Batman* (1989), for example, is an explicitly Wagnerian melodrama, joining comic book with film noir, award-winning actor with comedian, pop singer with classic orchestral score, high tech with retro style. The film alludes to the cinema's official art gallery—including such pictures as *Metropolis* and *Vertigo*—and at the same time allows the villainous joker to momentarily become an avant-garde performance artist: he enters the Gotham City Museum and spraypaints the masterpieces, preserving only a single modernist work by Francis Bacon.

We might say, in the language of Michael Denning's essay at the end of our collection, that we live in a world in which "mass culture has won; there is nothing else." But this doesn't mean that the dystopia predicted by intellectuals has at last arrived. The media remain what they've always been: a "social arena," where ideas and practices struggle, sometimes on unequal ground. Since at least the mid-1960s, even TV has regarded its customers as belonging to one or more "markets" rather than to an undifferentiated mass. In a lively history of the American TV sitcom, David Marc has observed that culture "has become too large and diversified a business to be identified with any one of its market constituencies. . . . [It] has a high end, a low end, and a vast sagging middle, to be sure, but this is the same marketing configuration that challenges automobile manufacturers, shoe companies, the makers of artificial breakfast drinks, or any other industry doing large-scale business in an advanced capitalist society."[33] As a result, the "postmodern condition," which is usually explained as a merging of the old artistic types, offers many cases of appropriation, reappropriation, and revision, indicating that the tension between cultural discourses still exists, and still has potential strength. There are also certain older texts that can't be fully absorbed into the mainstream. A striking recent instance is the appearance of a short, colorized version of Buñuel and Dali's surrealist film, *Un Chien Andalou*, on MTV. Buñuel, who described his film in 1929 as a "desperate appeal to murder," might have approved of the MTV colorization and the use of the original musical themes (a mix of Wagner and an Argentine tango). He would also appreciate the fact that music videos, like television commercials, are inherently surrealistic. But surely he would lament MTV's omission of the anticlerical passages in his film; and he would profoundly regret the loss of his most famous image—a razor slicing an eyeball.

Bizarre as the example of *Un Chien Andalou* may seem, it's symptomatic of a process that has a long history. We need only recall the various uses to which Shakespeare has been put to realize that all cultures are adept at "performing" texts in different ways. Contemporary developments have simply made us intensely aware of the formal exchange and the potential for conflict between cultural discourses. The old categories, never so clear or secure as their proponents often claimed, haven't ceased to exert influence; they've simply become more suspect and permeable, and the struggles over meaning have become more visible.

The process of appropriation and resistance, together with many of the other themes we've been discussing, is taken up in greater detail in the essays that follow. Rather than characterize these papers, we'll let them speak for themselves. We should note, however, that they weren't selected to illustrate different methods or approaches to the study of cultural modernity. Ultimately, they're all concerned with the same issues, even though they sometimes disagree. In addition to the essays mentioned above by Anderson, Denning, Fiske, Nowell-Smith, Ray, and Wollen, the collection also includes Richard Ohmann on advertising and popular narrative in the nineteenth century; Barbara Klinger on extratextual determinants of meaning; Devon Hodges and Janice L. Doane on Anne Rice's vampire fiction; Lynne Joyrich on "Moonlighting"; Stephen Watt on Baudrillard; and Jim Collins on retro-style. Implicit in these writings—as everywhere in the theory and practice of art at the end of the twentieth century— are familiar questions about the relationship between technology and democracy. Will the traditional discourses of culture be absorbed into a "mass," or will they reform into new configurations? Should we fear the media, or expect that, if guided by different social and economic priorities, they will lead to a more open and creative society? Such questions contain traces of old debates, but they also point toward new problems, and toward the emergent forms of a changing culture.

Notes

1. Heraclitus, *On the Universe* (with Hippocrates), trans. W. H. S. Jones (New York: Loeb Classics, 1931), p. 505.
2. Karl Marx and Friedrich Engels, from *The German Ideology*, in *The Marx-Engels Reader*, ed. Robert Tucker, 2d ed. (New York: Norton, 1978), p. 172.
3. Theodor Adorno and Max Horkheimer, *Dialectic of Enlightenment* (New York: Seabury, 1972 [1944]), p. 124.
4. Raymond Williams, *Culture and Society 1780–1950* (New York: Columbia University Press, 1983), p. 300.
5. For the second industrial revolution and the emergence of "consumer society" see, among others, Geoffrey Barraclough, *An Introduction to Modern History* (Harmondsworth: Penguin, 1967), pp. 43–64, and Rosilind Williams, *Dream Worlds: Mass Consumption in Late Nineteenth-Century France* (Berkeley: University of California Press, 1982).
6. Raymond Williams, "British Film History: New Perspectives," in James Curran and Vincent Porter, eds., *British Cinema History* (Totowa, NJ: Barnes and Noble, 1983), p. 11.
7. John Hobson, *The Psychology of Jingoism* (London: Grant Richards, 1901), p. 11.
8. Louis Haugmard quoted by Rosilind Williams, *Dream Worlds*, pp. 80–83.

9. Robert Donald quoted by Alan J. Lee, *The Origins of the Popular Press in England, 1855–1914* (London: Croom Helm, 1976), pp. 216–17.

10. Hobson, *Psychology of Jingoism*, p. 125.

11. G. M. Trevelyan, "The White Peril," *Nineteenth Century* 50 (December 1901), pp. 1049–50.

12. Hugo Münsterberg, *The Film: A Psychological Study* (New York: Dover, 1970 [1916]), p. 11.

13. Thomas A. Edison quoted by Charles Brewer, "The Widening Field of the Moving-Picture," *Century Magazine* 86 (May 1913), p. 72.

14. Henry V. Hopwood, *Living Pictures: Their History, Photo-Production and Practical Working* (New York: Arno Press, 1970), p. 234.

15. Walter Benjamin, "The Work of Art in the Age of Mechanical Reproduction," in *Illuminations* (New York: Schocken Books, 1969).

16. Fredric Jameson, "Postmodernism or the Cultural Logic of Late Capitalism," *New Left Review* 146 (July/August, 1984), p. 86.

17. Max Horkheimer quoted by Martin Jay, *The Dialectical Imagination* (Boston: Little, Brown, 1973), p. 258.

18. Alan Sinfield, *Literature, Politics, and Culture in Postwar Britain* (Berkeley: University of California Press, 1989), p. 41.

19. Peter Bürger, *Theory of the Avant-Garde* (Minneapolis: University of Minnesota Press, 1984); Martin Jay, *Fin-de-Siècle Socialism* (New York: Routledge, 1988); Andreas Huyssen, *After the Great Divide* (Bloomington: Indiana University Press, 1986). For a discussion of the relationship between technology and the aesthetics of modernism, see Hugh Kenner, *The Mechanic Muse* (New York: Oxford, 1987). See also James Knapp, *Literary Modernism: The Transformation of Work* (Evanston, Ill.: Northwestern University Press, 1988).

20. A useful account of these and other debates within German Marxism is Ronald Taylor, ed., *Aesthetics and Politics: Debates between Bloch, Lukacs, Brecht, Benjamin, Adorno* (London: Verso, 1980). See also the afterword by Fredric Jameson in this edition.

21. James Agee, "Folk Art," in *Agee on Film* (New York: McDowell, Obolensky, 1958), pp. 404–10.

22. Roger Chartier, *Cultural History*, trans. Lydia G. Cochrane (Ithaca: Cornell University Press, 1988); Jean Baudrillard, *Simulations*, trans. Paul Foss, Paul Patton, and Phillip Beitchman (New York: Semiotext(e), 1983).

23. Pierre Bourdieu, *Distinction: A Social Critique of the Judgement of Taste*, trans. Richard Nice (Cambridge: Harvard University Press, 1986).

24. Stuart Hall and Paddy Whannel, *The Popular Arts* (New York: Pantheon, 1965).

25. Michel de Certeau, *The Practice of Everyday Life*, trans. Stephen Rendell (Berkeley: University of California Press, 1984), p. xv.

26. An early version of Macdonald's essay, entitled "A Theory of Popular Culture," was published in 1944 in *Politics Today*. In 1953, Macdonald revised and expanded his argument, changing the title of the paper and making it less sympathetic to Marxism. The version discussed here was published orginally in *Diogenes*, No. 3 (Summer 1953). It is reprinted in *Mass Culture: The Popular Arts in America*, ed. Bernard Rosenberg and David Manning White (Glencoe, Ill.: The Free Press, 1958), pp. 59–73. All quotations are from this volume.

27. Geoffrey Nowell-Smith, "The Band Wagon" (unpublished lecture).

28. Vincente Minnelli, with Hector Acre, *I Remember It Well* (New York: Doubleday, 1974), pp. 269–72.

29. Jane Feuer, *The Hollywood Musical* (Bloomington: Indiana University Press, 1982), p. 102.

30. Susan Sontag, *Against Interpretation* (New York: Dell, 1966), p. 290. Sontag concludes her book by observing that the sensibility of the late twentieth century is "defiantly pluralistic; it is dedicated both to an excruciating seriousness and to fun and wit and nostalgia. It is also extremely history conscious." Contrast this cheerful assessment with the gloom and pessimism of Fredric Jameson, who believes that postmodernism is "schizophrenic" and "incapable of dealing with time and history." See "Postmodernism and Consumer Society," in Hal Foster, ed., *The Anti-Aesthetic* (Port Townsend, Wa.: The Bay Press, 1983), pp. 111–25.

31. Andrew Ross, *No Respect: Intellectuals and Popular Culture* (New York: Routledge, 1989), p. 139.

32. David E. James, "Rock and Roll in Representations of the Invasion of Vietnam," *Representations*, No. 29 (Winter 1990), p. 78–79.

33. David Marc, *Comic Visions: Television Comedy and American Culture* (Boston: Unwin Hyman, 1989), p. 1.

ONE

History and Literary History:
The Case of Mass Culture

Richard Ohmann

I intend a straightforward exposition, although my subject is messy enough. I will offer readings of two simple texts; one is an ad for Quaker Oats and the other a story I will soon outline. Both appeared in the same issue of a popular American magazine in 1895. I argue that a reader cannot adequately understand either without grasping its relation to the other and to the ensemble of historical forces that brought them together.

As for the story, I hope not to distort it much in compression; it is only about three thousand words long. It is called "On the Way North" and was written by Juliet Wilbor Tompkins. I quote the two opening sentences to give you a feeling for its tone:

> The train strolled along as only a Southern train can, stopping to pick flowers and admire views and take an unnecessary number of drinks. Why should you hurry when you have barely a dozen people in your three cars, and the down train will keep you waiting anywhere from half an hour to half a day at the switch?

The third sentence introduces the hero, a "young man from the North," impatient with the train's progress; and the fourth gives us his name and his way of thinking about himself: "Gardiner Forrest—of New York City, thank goodness!" Having entered his mind, we stay there through the next paragraph and find his thoughts occupied with an unnamed "she," the "nicest, jolliest girl in the world," whom he ardently wishes on the pokey train with him, and free of the watchful scrutiny of her chaperone aunt.

Incident rapidly ensues. A conductor enters the nearly empty car, seeking the help of a "negro nurse" there, for a lady who has fainted in the forward car. The nurse deposits a white baby she is caring for next to Forrest, to his dismay, and rushes off. A dialogue follows, of which this exchange is typical: "The baby leaned towards him and said distinctly,

'Papa!' 'Good heavens!' ejaculated Forrest. 'Do you want to start a scandal? I'm not your papa. You have made a mistake.' " The infant threatens to cry and Forrest takes it onto his lap, not noticing that the train has made a stop "and that a tall girl, evidently of the North, was staring at him in utter amazement from the door of the car." *We* are scarcely amazed to discover that this is the "she" of Forrest's longings. Her name is Amy Baramore, and she indeed proves to be a jolly girl who banters with Forrest and talks baby talk to the baby: "I didn't know how dear they were," she says.

They devise a scheme for its entertainment. Forrest will tell a story in "straight ahead English," and Miss Baramore will translate into baby talk. The story serves as a veiled communication between the two adults. It is about a poor boy—obviously young Forrest himself—who lives next to a rich girl (obviously Miss Baramore) and is too ashamed of his "shabby back yard" and "disgracefully unpatched" trousers to do more than gaze at her over the fence. Amy's "translation" makes it clear that she likes him in spite of his "poor patches." A delicious bond of intimacy has begun to grow between the two. "Her lips twitched a little, then their eyes met, and they both laughed."

At this point the conductor brings news that the nurse is still needed in the forward car and that the train will be on a switch for quite a while, so they may alight if they wish. They choose to sit on the rear platform of the empty car at the rear of the train where they exchange more tender information: in sum, each had been romantically interested in the other for a few days when they were both in St. Augustine, but he had left early because he wrongly thought that a certain very rich Mr. Douglas had the inside track to her affections. We and Forrest now learn that Amy, unlike her watchful Aunt Emma, rates character above wealth in potential husbands.

Before Forrest can digest this welcome news, adventure interrupts the idyll. The train has gone on, leaving the empty car on the isolated siding. How to get the baby back to its presumably distraught nurse? They reject the idea of walking to the next station (too slow) and Forrest proposes a bold strategy: release the brakes and roll several miles to the valley town. Amy barely hesitates; all her concern is for the "baby in her lap," and they begin to coast. Suddenly the grade becomes much steeper: "Forrest's heart leaped as he looked first at the descent before him and then at Amy beside him, for there was real danger." He races to the rear brake, she bravely holds the front one, and they ride out the peril. Returning, "he flung his arm around her to steady her. Their eyes met, and it was all said without words." As they reach safety, Forrest "stooped and kissed her," saying, "You're dead game, Amy."

The denouement is quick. They declare their engagement, coyly using the baby as an intermediary. Amy reveals that the rich Mr. Douglas had proposed to her and that she had declined; that she had felt an attraction to Forrest that was confirmed when she saw how "dear" he was with the baby. One more false fright and they are at the station. The train is delayed there by "the daily hot box." The nurse and the conductor never even noticed that the rear car was missing. The ferocious Aunt Emma is there, "inspecting Forrest through her lorgnon" and tut-tutting, but without power now to harm the betrothed couple. Baby has the last word: Amy notes that "But for him it might never have happened" and wonders what they might give him. " 'Dindin!' suggested the little Napoleon."

The story is slight and conventional. It demands little interpretation and hardly calls criticism into play. Nonetheless, I will offer a few critical comments of a traditional sort to establish points of reference to which I will return later in the discussion.

The plot moves Gardiner Forrest and Amy Baramore from unspoken longing, to veiled declarations of interest in one another, to a wordless embrace, to an understanding then briefly realized in fuller verbal intimacy. The Aristotelian "action" (or motive) of the story is, roughly, "To give words to the heart's desire and fulfill it in marriage." That can happen only after Forrest shows himself to be amateurishly tender with the baby as well as resourceful in a crisis, and after Amy shows herself to be "dead game" in the face of physical danger. Character, so revealed and enacted, manifests their rightness for each other. I would also mark how the couple are stranded in an asocial space, almost a wilderness—"blue outlines of the hills, rising above the thick tangle of woods in which they stood"—and how, passing the test of character there, they return deservedly to the social world and to the socially defined relation of betrothal. I would tie the story to the structure of literature through Northrop Frye's scheme, remarking that we have here in nearly perfect miniature the mythos of comedy, complete with tyrannical old order, blocking characters, even the green world and the city. And I might situate the story in American literary history by setting its breezy dialogue and relaxed, accepting narrative voice against the formality of a genteel narrative voice, now falling into disuse. More might be said, but probably few would sense the need for even this much.

The Quaker Oats ad (Figure 1) requires still less interpretation. Its verbal rhetoric is direct enough, with the appeal to a reader's prudence, taste and sagacity. Where its text exhorts, its image offers; yet the pitch is much the same in text and image, for the Quaker figure projects seriousness, reliability and robust health, even without the aid of his scroll and its message of purity, making a semantic link with "Wholesome" in the text. One might wonder about the connection between herrings and cereal, or indeed about that between Quakers and oats. These lacunae suggest either incoherence in the message or a reader-viewer who will know how to supply the needed tissue of meaning, a reader initiated into this discourse. The ad itself cannot

1. *Munsey's Magazine*, October 1895.

tell us which of these hypotheses is correct, though historical hindsight will surely incline us toward the latter.

But how are we to fill in the much wider gap between the Quaker Oats ad and "On the Way North"? How do they belong in the same bundle of signs, *Munsey's Magazine* of October 1895? Is there *any* connection beyond that of physical proximity? I mean to problematize what may seem unproblematic. In spite of the ubiquity of such odd conjunctions now, there is nothing inevitable about them. Indeed, they were nowhere to be found 150 years before this issue of *Munsey's* appeared; they were unusual before the Civil War; and they were uncommon even in the early 1880s.

There are no breakfasts in the story or even any commodities. There is no love or danger in the cereal ad. The story makes no sales appeal. The ad may be read as implying a sort of narrative (if you go to the store and buy Quaker Oats, you will be satisfied) but, apart from the happy ending, this plot has nothing in common with that of "On the Way North." The only connection I can easily spot is in the register and tone of the two voices that address us in ad and story. Both are casual, familiar, a bit coy.

To bring these two cultural productions closer, we will have to look for a different kind of connection than structural similarity. I believe we can locate such a connection only in a broad social process "outside" the magazine, where meaning emerges from historical change. I will now briskly indicate the kind of change I think most pertinent, before returning to the ad and the story. I refer *my* story of historical change, first, to production.

Let me characterize the middle decades of the American nineteenth century as the epoch of competitive capitalism or entrepreneurial capitalism. As industrial production approached and then surpassed the magnitude of farm production, the men who organized it followed straightforward procedures. Find the capital needed, build the factory, stock it with machines, buy the raw materials, hire workers, produce the goods, convey them to jobbers and wholesalers for distribution, realize profits (if any), and—more often than not—reinvest those profits in further productive capacity. Firms were small by later standards. Price competition was intense.

The invisible hand worked busily. Production became more and more efficient, and total product grew. By the end of the century the process had accelerated to an extraordinary rate. Between 1865 and 1900, roughly speaking, the value of manufactured goods increased sevenfold, the number of factories quadrupled, the number of industrial workers tripled, and industrial capital increased fourfold. As the figures suggest, production changed utterly, bringing a host of other changes, like the great movement from country to city.

The brilliant success of the system also generated dangers and failures. The boom-and-bust cycle intensified: there were three major depressions between 1870 and 1900. As companies fought for markets, naturally many of them lost out in the competition. Bankruptcies were endemic; individual businessmen felt—and were—able to do little to alleviate chaos and risk. Pools, gentlemen's agreements, price-fixing arrangements of every legal and illegal kind, failed to stabilize the environment of capital accumulation. And toward the end of the century, after reaching its highest level in American history, the rate of profit began to fall. Capitalism was triumphant; capitalism was in profound crisis.

What gave it new life and created our world was a new kind of social formation sometimes called advanced capitalism or late capitalism, but for which I use the Marxist term, monopoly capitalism. Its characteristic unit is the giant, vertically integrated corporation, a form that emerged with great rapidity in the 1890s. Such a corporation brought the entire economic process within its compass, from raw materials through production through marketing. Rather than simply producing the goods and hoping they would sell, it tried to coordinate making with selling and to guarantee that what the machines turned out would find buyers, thus eliminating a main source of uncertainty and risk. Let me make this more concrete through the homely example of Quaker Oats, one of the early innovators.

Through the 1860s and 1870s, producers of oats perfected machines for milling and "cutting" the grain. In 1882 Henry P. Crowell, one of the leaders, built a mill that took it through a continuous process from grading and cleaning to packaging, all under one roof. By then, production of rolled oats was twice the demand and makers faced the usual choice: cut prices until some lost out in the competition, or leave the machines idle much of the time and lose the advantage of low marginal cost accruing from a large capital investment. Crowell hit on a third possibility: increase demand. Oats were virtually unknown as a breakfast food, and Crowell set out to promote that use of the cereal, simultaneously changing the form of distribution. Oats had always been shipped in bulk: barrels a grocer would dip into for individual customers. One of Crowell's competitors had begun selling the product in individual sacks. Crowell took a further step and put oats into two-pound cartons like the one the Quaker is holding in the ad. (A machine for producing such cartons had been perfected in the 1870s.) He also put the Quaker on the package and registered him as a *trademark*, the first for a cereal.

I will return to that part of the story, but first a word about the corporate aftermath. In 1888, Crowell and his six leading competitors merged their operations into the American Cereal Company, one of the first large, vertically integrated corporations. It established offices around the United States and abroad, where its people scheduled the flow of packaged oats to jobbers, taking much more direct control of distribution than formerly. At the other end of the process, it employed fieldmen to purchase oats from farmers, and buyers on the Chicago commodity exchange. It developed the multilevel table of organization characteristic of the modern corporation, to organize and monitor this complex of making and selling.

From its position of dominance, the company now looked almost directly into the American home. There, if it actually had had corporate eyes, it would have seen a very different configuration of spaces and practices than was common fifty years earlier. I will characterize it with brutal simplification by saying that it was now an urban or suburban home rather than a farmhouse; that it was more a place for recuperation from work, for child-rearing, and for much-simplified tasks of cooking, sewing, etc., than the center of an elaborate and nearly self-sufficient home production; that the men of the house went out to sell their labor power in the market, while home was the domain of the women; and that the women, too, went out into the market, not to sell labor power but to buy the commodities which were increasingly the basis of survival. These homes were, then, *ready* for Crowell's idea. He did not so much create a need (the common charge against advertising) as show housewives how a generalized and very real historical need—itself created by the new factory production that Quaker Oats instanced—might be narrowed and met through purchase and use of a particular kind of commodity.

To effect the necessary connection between home and corporation, Crowell placed his package in local stores and its image in a thousand places where it could register upon the eye and emotions of the housewife. In short, he turned to advertising: on billboards, in streetcars, in newspapers, on calendars, on fences, on blotters, in cookbooks and so on. In 1890 he undertook a coordinated national *campaign*. The old military word now assumed a new commercial meaning: an assault on the consciousness of the *consumer* (another new sense for an older word). And Crowell turned to a new kind of institution to plan and execute his campaign: an advertising *agency*. Specifically, sometime before 1894 he engaged the Paul E. Derrick agency, which opened an office in London that year to spread the Quaker Oats image and message abroad. In 1894, Derrick also took the Quaker image off the box, enlarged and varied it, and put it in magazine ads like the one displayed here. Meanwhile, as almost every mind in the country absorbed and retained the image and the idea of purchase, the four-color package carried recipes to instruct the housewife in creative and caring *use* of the new product. The new bond between corporation and home was secure.[1]

Before taking a fresh look at the ad and story which were my point of departure, I must turn to one more part of this historical transformation. How did the Derrick agency hit on magazines as a medium, and on *Munsey's* in particular, which had begun publishing only four years earlier? Until the late 1880s, general monthly magazines were a rather sleepy genre; none had a circulation of more than 250,000 or so and, with their cover prices of 25¢ or 35¢, they were too expensive for a much broader audience, as well as too genteel in content. With a few exceptions (*Century*, *Cosmopolitan*), they carried little or no advertising. This began to change around 1890. Publishers of general monthlies, perhaps taking a hint from more commercial women's magazines (notably the *Ladies' Home Journal*) and the so-called "story papers," reconsidered their prejudice against advertising and sought to enlarge their circulations. The big break came in 1893. In the midst of that year's financial panic, S. S. McClure came out with his new magazine, at an unprecedented cover price of 15¢. *Cosmopolitan* quickly dropped *its* price to 12½¢. And in October, Frank Munsey, with a great deal of publicity, lowered his single issue price from 25¢ to 10¢—a figure that soon became standard but not before *Munsey's* had taken a quick lead in the competition.

Munsey's gamble and his one-man war against the American News Company's distribution monopoly instantly paid off. The circulation of his dying magazine went from 20,000 to 60,000 in two months, passed 200,000 in six, and was close to 600,000 in two years, when the issue I am discussing appeared.[2] Munsey had "invented" the general mass circulation magazine, with luck, desperation, and genius, and in tandem with his competitors. They and he created a cultural industry of quite new dimensions which was not just a matter of size. They had reached a wider and *different* audience, not previously included in this form of culture. Most important, they had hit on a business formula new to national media: sell the magazine for less than its cost of production, build a huge circulation and make your profit on advertising revenues. In other words, they were no longer dealers in their physical product and became dealers in groups of *consumers*. What they came to sell, like radio and television later on, was *us*—or more precisely, our attention. This appears to be a development of world-historical importance: the invention of the mind industry or, more commonly, of mass culture.

So *Munsey's Magazine* was a perfect vehicle for the Quaker Oats ad in 1895. The 600,000 imprints of the ad passed in front of still more pairs of eyes, all over the country. It was in the company of many hundred other ads, most of them, like the ones on the accompanying page, for inexpensive items of housekeeping or personal care. The October 1895 issue carried 78 pages of ads, with its 128 pages of editorial matter. (Soon the former would outweigh the latter.) The contents of the magazine drew readers into the milieu of the ads with a mix of light fiction, articles, celebrity gossip, art and theater news, sports, semiclad women, and dozens of photoengravings of artwork and famous people. This mix was as forward looking as the commodities in the ads.

We are now in a position to think again about relations of the Quaker Oats ad to Tompkins's story. Most obviously, the ad *paid for* the story and probably for a good deal more. At Frank Munsey's famous rate of a dollar per page per thousand of circulation, he would have received $600 for the ad space, and I doubt that Miss Tompkins got more than $50 for her story. Reciprocally, "On the Way North" helped bring the reader's attention into proximity with the image of the wise Quaker. Furthermore, this silent interaction of ad and story was part of a complex, new, and intensifying historical process, with many agents not discernable on the page or even deducible from it.

In the context of this history, we can read the ad more "thickly." For just a few examples:

1. The Quaker is *already* known to the viewer; his image reinforces many previous impressions and barely requires interpretation. This is a discourse of repetition.
2. His relation to oatmeal is arbitrary and conventional; signifier and signified hang together almost as with a common noun of the language.
3. Yet the signifier retains its own aura of meaning: solidity, respectability, thrift, honesty, etc., and all this slides over as a secondary aura for the product.
4. Both that aura and the explicit message—"pure," "wholesome"— make historical sense in mediating a new relationship of individual, corporation, and name-brand product. People were only now learning to depend on commodities produced at a distance by strangers. *Trust* was necessary but had to be funded over time.
5. One means toward that end was linking the new product to old and familiar things: the Quaker himself; and the proverb with its wisdom from time out of mind and from an oral tradition in sharp contradiction to the industrial and commercial relations that actually surround the ad. Thus herrings and breakfast cereal turn out to have a most intimate and dialectical connection, a simultaneity and exchange of old and new.
6. The *new* figures here as the product itself, in its mentioned and novel use as a breakfast food; as the manufactured package (in silent opposition to the unbranded barrel of oats): and in the legend at the bottom of the page, now understandable as insistent praise for a new way of buying things.
7. Modernity also expresses itself through two *absences*: nowhere do we find the name or address of the corporation (cf. the other three, more old-fashioned ads in Figure 2) or of the ad agency. The voice that invokes and constitutes "you" comes from no identifiable source; it materializes out of the opaque space of monopoly capital.
8. Yet it speaks to you in an amiable, familiar, personal though authoritative voice. An imaginary social relation effaces the real ones that populate the historical stage, just beyond the ad. The ad in a way refers to that stage and cannot be understood apart from it; yet it mutes, distorts, or denies most of its connections to the historical process.

2. *Munsey's Magazine*, October 1895.

These principles of reference and meaning structure a microlanguage, that of modern advertising. As I have said, ads like this were a recent historical innovation. But already by 1895 the adman addresses the reader as a knowing participant in the discourse: able to assume the strange role of "you"; able to become the consumer to whom the Quaker offers his product; able to decipher the relation of image to text and of both to product;

savvy in the oppositions of old and new that organize the ad's appeal. That tacit knowledge was necessary in 1895 for quick interpretation of the ad. Presumably, most readers had it: they had acquired a new kind of literacy. I conjecture that they were also learning to collaborate in a kind of tacit *ignorance*—of the social relations being effaced by advertising: relations of labor and making, of corporation and consumer, of ad agency and cultural production. The "magic system," as Raymond Williams calls it, was in place.[3]

I will now turn again to "On the Way North" (in a more conjectural way because fiction is more mediated persuasion than advertising) and will posit some ways of re-reading the literary features I mentioned earlier. Later, I will dwell a bit more on their ensemble.

Against the historical emergence of monopoly capital, I read what I called the Aristotelian motive of the story—to give words to the heart's desire and to fulfill it in marriage—as validating the personal, internal self, by confirming its feelings through the preverbal understanding of another person, then by making those feelings at home in the social medium of language and finally by projecting them toward a marriage that will keep the private self intact even while giving it institutional embodiment. Nothing new about that, of course: much the same could be said of a Jane Austen novel. But the utopian impulse grows more urgent and its fictional realization less grounded, in a context of impersonal corporations, bureaucracies and great cities. Perhaps that explains why the test that proves affection and equal worth occurs in a natural setting away from other people, certainly away from economic life, yet in an archetypal product of the industrial system, the railroad car, cut loose from the control of its inept corporate master and tamed by individual courage and cunning. (That the dual test of worth moves toward obliterating the differences between the sexes—*he* holds the baby; *she* joins in a bold adventure—seems to contest the separation of spheres and of gender roles and to affirm the ideal of the "new woman" which was ascendent in the nineties.)

I see the offhand, colloquial style of the story as much akin to the voice of the Quaker Oats ad, eradicating the distance that print interposes and proclaiming a kind of generalized neighborliness and affability which weighs in against the thoroughly corporate transaction in which the reader is engaged.

I could spell out and defend each of these rather gnomically stated interpretive claims but instead, I want to spend a few paragraphs on the comic plot, which gives shape to Tompkins's story. It is of course unabashedly traditional, hardly a feature out of place. (That's one reason the story can be told so brusquely: we all know it already.)

Yet this rendering of the myth also strains *against* tradition, by highlighting and historically referencing that part of the mythos that identifies the marriage or feast at the end with a freer social order. Aunt Emma is not just Holdfast, *the* tyrant; she figures a particular nineteenth-century generation seen as checking the evolution of the new woman—a girl "you liked to travel with," who can handle herself outside the home and away from chaperonage, being a good sport and making alliances on her own. The shadowy Mr. Douglas, the other blocking character, is not just a seemingly advantaged rival in love; he represents a retrograde upper class, out of touch with *work*. (Forrest was in St. Augustine on "business"; Douglas was there to play on his yacht; to Amy he represents a brougham and a maid, not a person active in the world.) Forrest—a "rising young lawyer, who hasn't risen yet"—is obviously putting a lot of distance between himself and that dingy back yard, by strenuous effort and a technical rationality that comes forward right at the beginning of the story, when the impatient young man reads "his paper down to the last 'Wanted,' and calculate[s] in the margin" how much money the railroad is losing on the nearly empty car. This technical rationality, of course, is what later conquers the runaway car and wins Amy's kiss.

Forrest is the socially mobile individual, whose power and ambition have affinities with and a clear place in the new corporate order. And, one more point, Tompkins aligns him with the North (where his marriage and future will take place) and its commercial center, and makes the South stand for a backwater that has never learned corporate efficiency. A "lazy, slipshod, good for nothing country," he calls it, when he discovers that the train has left the car on the siding.

In short, the marriage of Forrest and Amy may be read as harmoniously conjoining the age-old myth of comedy and the new epoch of monopoly capital, much as the ad links a new market relation to folk wisdom and a seventeenth-century Quaker. I might add that if Amy Baramore really does have to forgo the services of a maid for this love match (and who can doubt that such deprivation will soon end?), she will herself run a modern household, efficiently preparing modern breakfasts with wholesome Quaker Oats. The story glances forward toward an urban nuclear family. Neither partner has visible parents, and Aunt Emma will surely not be there to transmit generational skills and technique in kitchen or sewing room. *That* role has been deeded over to the outside expert and the neighborly voice of the ad man.

That is how I would jointly read these two productions of the mind industry, under the sign of progress. But there is another stage in the argument. To reference the narratives and icons of mass culture to epochal change is necessary but not sufficient. I have so far left *conflict* out of my picture, as if change were an uncontested linear process in which all participated equally. Speaking of the crises that businessmen faced toward the end of the century, I left out the deepening antagonism between capital and labor. The emergent industrial system was not kind to its workers. All-but-total class warfare erupted in 1877, 1885, 1892 and 1894, in close synchrony with the cycle of depressions, because capitalists generally responded to bad times with wage cuts and layoffs. Thus, in addition to the other pressures on competitive capitalism, there was the persistent threat of rebellion from below.

Eventually, the productive power of the system would help to ease that conflict, partly as a result of the very flow of cheap, name-brand commodities to consumer markets of which I spoke earlier. Even in the late 1890s, many workers could buy Quaker Oats and Wool Soap, though few could yet afford the more expensive household goods.

But the opposition of capital and labor relaxed somewhat in the new social order at least as much for another reason. A new class was rapidly growing *between* capital and labor, distinct from the old petty bourgeoisie. It included the middle managers who proliferated in the new integrated corporations, upper-level office workers, professors in the fast-growing universities, service professionals who helped moderate the worst consequences of inequality and urban decay, government bureaucrats, doctors, lawyers, engineers, and so on. By the 1890s, most of these groups were busy forming organizations, setting professional or business standards, regulating admission to their ranks: in short, becoming a self conscious stratum of society. Barbara and John Ehrenreich dubbed it the Professional-Managerial Class (PMC) and argued that, toward the end of the century, it came to occupy a complex position in partial antagonism to and partial alliance with both the ruling class and the working class. It associated itself with science, technique, efficiency and the rational analysis and management of society.[4]

I argue that the primary audience of the mass circulation magazines was just this class, along with those who had reasonable or unreasonable hopes of joining it. I cannot prove that; reader surveys and market research by publishers and advertising agencies were still in their infancy in the nineties. But certainly some of the publishers *thought* they were reaching a moderately well-off group of educated and semi-educated, urban and suburban, upwardly mobile people and they pressed such claims on potential advertisers.

Certainly the contents of the magazines imply such a readership, as I suggest by taking a final interpretive pass at "On the Way North." Not only is Gardiner Forrest oriented toward the dynamic and progressive future, but he is moving into it as a young professional, a lawyer. He comes from humble origins and is entering the business world, evidently with some university education in his background. He is sharply differentiated from Mr. Douglas ("Croesus, Jr., and his yacht") by having to work for a living, from Aunt Emma by the haughtiness and conservatism of her manners and by her class-bound views on matrimony, and from Amy herself by the contrast in their childhood backyards and present circumstances. Clearly the comic resolution of the story spreads its utopian goodwill not only over modernity and the free bourgeois self, but over the future of Forrest's class as well. It does so through an unequivocal triumph of this class hero's values and capabilities over those of the upper class. Forrest takes "the jolliest girl in the world" away from her socially natural mate and his inherited money. Amy herself, free spirit and new woman, defects from her class in favor of a husband who can both handle a child and stop a railroad car: the domestic and heroic virtues seem a manifestation of the same abilities that enable him to rise through law and business. And Aunt Emma shrinks into powerlessness.

In short, a third reading of the comic plot, this time foregrounding the dynamics of class, suggests that the aura of its benign fulfillment confers ideological blessings not only on a vague doctrine of progress and a new economic order, but more specifically on the project and prospects of an emergent class. "They lived happily ever after," the unwritten final sentence in every story of this kind, refers to more than the fortunate couple; it applies also to the future of the lawyers, businessmen, planners, and mediators for whom Gardiner Forrest stands and whose values bask in the glow of requited love.

Let me briefly annotate the other literary features of "On the Way North," against this third interpretive grid. Evidently the "motive" of the story gains much of its appeal from the fact that when desire breaks into speech, the words overcome a silence imposed partly by class exclusions on the one side (Aunt Emma would condemn any relation more intimate than "casual acquaintance" between Gardiner and Amy), and by class timidity on the other (he "wouldn't stand much of a chance"). That the forbidden words issue first in the oblique mode of baby talk and with reference to a childhood misunderstanding, signifies that this particular class boundary is an artifact of the adult social world and its unfair distinctions, which the forthcoming marriage will nullify.

The test of character occurs in a space and a situation where such distinctions have no power and where timeless virtues like boldness and ingenuity take precedence. That Forrest should turn out to possess those traits, along with class-specific ones like pragmatism and technical rationality, aligns the latter with the hero myth and so *naturalizes* them. (I would note in passing that the hero's name, while impeccably Anglo-Saxon and indeed highbrow, blatantly asserts his affinity with the natural; while the heroine's first name, invoking the classless feminine role of beloved, negates her uncompromisingly aristocratic surname.)

The narrative voice of the story also naturalizes the outlook of the PMC. It is a knowing, confident voice that takes its values as unproblematic and uncontested. Thus the narrator and the reader strike an amused alliance with Northern, technical superiority, in a clause like "the daily hot box had not been omitted." Mock heroic prose ("The two eyed each other in silence a few minutes, each measuring his man") glides effortlessly into genuine heroic ("Forrest's heart leaped," "there was real danger," "a sharp whistle . . . made his heart contract with a fear that was not for himself"), with no self-consciousness of how the first tone might imply criticism of the cliches in the second. Nor is there any felt contradiction between the narrator's tacit praise for Amy's masculine "calm directness" of speech and her coy conspiracy in Amy's feminine *indirectness*, as she bends over "the sleeping baby, who would have seen something if he had been awake." The narration effortlessly draws upon a variety of registers and codes, as a social group might do which felt itself liberated by culture and privilege from any one class rhetoric. (The same kind of stylistic mobility is present, though less comfortably managed, in the voice of the ads in Figures 1 and 2: "nor imagine . . . " versus "Sweet and wholesome"; "FOR STYLE AND FIT" versus "Correct the figure to the latest fashionable contour"; "Woolens will not shrink if Wool Soap is used in the laundry" versus *"Buy a bar at your dealers."*) The voice proclaims its freedom from traditional manner or conventional restraint.

In general, read as taking part in a discourse of class, the story manages to announce on behalf of the PMC its own recognition as darling of history, yet also to annul any thought of irreconcilable conflict. True, Forrest defeats Aunt Emma and Mr. Douglas, but that Amy should marry him shows the class rivalry to be bridgeable; that she should *love* him discloses that PMC charms can win over progressive members of the upper class.

It would be convenient for my argument if Gardiner Forrest had managed along the way North to stave off a rebellion of railroad workers and earn their gratitude and respect. Failing such aid to the critic from Tompkins, I must be satisfied that the ineffectual workers ("one of the wheels, at which men were still tinkering") blend in harmlessly with the backward, pastoral scene and that the conductor—a labor aristocrat—is suitably inept and properly amiable toward Forrest. Forrest's managerial talents hold center stage; were *he* to run the railroad, defective brakes would not stay long unrepaired, and there would be no daily hot boxes. But mainly, the working class is an absence here, offering no obstacle in fact or imagination to the PMC thrust. Even racial conflict is nullified by the complacence of the nurse, who, with "only a slight negro accent," is clearly on the way toward integration—quite an augury of social peace. In the early days of Jim Crow and just one year after the Pullman Strike, this happy PMC dream pushes racism and class warfare beyond the field of vision.[5]

I claim that this way of reading "On the Way North" does not look *behind* or *through* the text to "background" conditions but reconstructs meanings that were "there" in the text for properly schooled contemporaries. Like the Quaker Oats ad, the story called tacit knowledge of old and new into play and also of class-based values and ideas. An interpretive strategy not grounded in such knowledge and in such habits of decoding would have given the reader an experience of the story almost drained of tension, affect, and satisfaction. Surely there were such readers in 1895; just as surely, readers literate in the codes of popular fiction were in the majority, or Frank Munsey's formulas would not have won a mass audience for his magazine. The story resembles the ad, too, in that its code demands some areas of what I called tacit ignorance. For any reader who puzzled about the relations between Mr. Douglas's old wealth and Gardiner Forrest's "business," or who understood the railroad as indexing the Great Upheaval and the Pullman Strike, or who read North-South coordinates as evocations of slavery and civil war, Tompkins's idyll would collapse into incoherence or into reprehensible silliness.

Even so, mine is a rather heavy reading of a light story. If anyone were to enter that as an objection, I would reply, first, that the formulas of mass culture work as smoothly as they do, in part because they incorporate dense historical understandings and reduce them to comfortable ideology. They offer possibilities of meaning that seem untroubled and uncontested. That is generally the case because cultural producers like Munsey must deliver to advertisers not simply the attention of many readers but attention of a certain quality. Readers must feel broadly content with their place in the world, so that the flow of their anxieties may be channeled into smaller concerns like the need for a healthy breakfast or for a laundry soap that won't shrink clothes—worries that may be allayed by purchasing commodities.

For mass culture at its inception was a discourse inseparable from the circulation of commodities. It was also a discourse carried on especially among members of the PMC and aspirants to it, a sharing of commercial messages and cultural practices that helped define the class, while bathing it in self-congratulation. There is no way adequately to read the popular literature of this period without building that historical process into its understanding.

In closing, I want to situate the kind of literary history I have tried to mobilize here by acknowledging two ways in which it is old fashioned. First, I have privileged a version of what really happened in history and used it to explain and interpret the texts at hand. Some recent theorists would object that my story of capitalist crisis and transformation can itself be no more than a distillation of other texts, and that it and they have no epistemological priority over texts like "On the Way North." For such thinkers, history dissolves into a parity of infinitely many structures, with no center except language and at that a language severed from its capacity for reference or action. This is a history without causes or agents; to the extent that it admits of change at all, it attributes change to something like the random collision of molecules. I have no philosophical reply to what Perry Anderson nicely calls this "megalomania of the signifier,"[6] nor do I think there is one. Rather, a person who wants to do causal history must take Jonathan Culler's advice and ignore deconstruction—not kick the stone in useless refutation like Dr. Johnson, but adopt the double consciousness of Hume when he repaired from his skeptical labors to dinner and backgammon.[7] Ignoring deconstruction won't make it go away but neither will ignoring history stop it from happening or perhaps from doing us in, unless we intervene as if it had causes and we might be agents.

Having opted for causes, one must make the more vexed and interesting decision which causes to take as most deeply determinative. In assigning priority to forces and relations of production I have committed myself to a second premise some think old fashioned. I think that commitment right, though I recognize the vulnerability of traditional conceptions of base and superstructure, because there is no way to account adequately for mass culture (or for much else) without seeing that the needs and projects of capital counted more powerfully than those of housewives in reshaping the markets for breakfast food and culture. Still, the needs of housewives set limits to what capitalists could do. I hope that by acknowledging those limits and giving weight to the projects of intermediaries like admen, magazine publishers, writers and the PMC, I have drawn a sketch of the cultural process complex enough to be exempt from the charge of vulgarity. Henry Crowell and his peers couldn't have built monopoly capital without Paul Derrick, Frank Munsey, Juliet Wilbor Tompkins, and *their* peers, many of whom had little interest in enriching the American Cereal Company. But if their aspirations had not harmonized with his, he could have found other, structurally similar ways to achieve his ends. That proposition doesn't work the other way around. Hegemony is the diffusion of power, not its equalization.

Notes

1. See Arthur F. Marquette, *Brands, Trademarks and Goodwill: The Story of the Quaker Oats Company* (New York: McGraw-Hill, 1967); Alfred D. Chandler, Jr., *The Visible Hand: The Managerial Revolution in American Business* (Cambridge: Harvard University Press, 1977), 294; Daniel Pope, *The Making of Modern Advertising* (New York: Basic Books, 1983), 54–55; Frank Presbrey, *The History and Development of Advertising* (New York: Doubleday, Doran, 1929), 107–406; and Michael Schudson, *Advertising, the Uneasy Persuasion: Its Dubious Impact on American Society* (New York: Basic Books, 1984), 64–66.

2. Theodore Peterson, *Magazines in the Twentieth Century* (Urbana: University of Illinois Press, 1956), 7–9.

3. Raymond Williams, *Problems in Materialism and Culture* (London: Verso, 1980), 170–95.

4. Barbara Ehrenreich and John Ehrenreich, "The Professional-Managerial Class," in *Between Capital and Labor*, ed. Pat Walker (Boston: South End Press, 1979), 12–27; Robert H. Wiebe, *The Search for Order, 1877–1920* (New York: Hill and Wang, 1967), 111–32.

5. Juliet Wilbor Tompkins was a recent graduate of Vassar College. I don't know if she came from wealth, but she headed straight for the kind of PMC career to which college education was increasingly adapted. In 1897 she became an associate editor at *Munsey's*. Frank Munsey himself was a farmer's son; in 1895, at age 41, he had several entrepreneurial failures behind him and was just beginning his rise to great wealth. His work as editor, publisher and writer put him squarely in a PMC context at this time. His prescriptions for fiction stressed the dynamic: "stories, not dialect sketches, not washed out studies of effete human nature, not weak tales of sickly sentimentality, not 'pretty' writing" (George Britt, *Forty Years—Forty Millions: The Career of Frank A. Munsey* [New York: Farrar & Rinehart, 1935], 98). This was a repudiation of upper-class culture as presented by the elite monthlies.

6. Perry Anderson, *In the Tracks of Historical Materialism* (Chicago: University of Chicago Press, 1984), 46, 48.

7. Jonathan Culler, *On Deconstruction: Theory and Criticism after Structuralism* (Ithaca: Cornell University Press, 1982), 130; M. H. Abrams, "Construing and Deconstruing," in *Romanticism and Contemporary Criticism*, ed. Morris Eaves and Michael Fischer (Ithaca: Cornell University Press, 1986), 132–33.

TWO

<hr>

Cinema/Americanism/the Robot

Peter Wollen

If, in the early years of the century, Orientalism was crucial to the emergence of modern art (fashion, ballet, decorative art),[1] the period of consolidation was marked by Americanism (cinema, architecture, applied art). Filmmakers and theorists of culture looked to the work of Griffith and Chaplin. Architects sang the praises of the silo and the skyscraper. The cult of jazz swept across Europe.[2] Oskar Schlemmer observed that, at the Bauhaus: "The artistic climate here cannot support anything that is not the latest, the most modern, up-to-the-minute, Dadaism, circus, variety, jazz, hectic pace, movies, America, airplanes, the automobile. Those are the terms in which people here think."[3]

In 1929 Pirandello wrote that "Americanism is swamping us. I think that a new beacon of civilization has been lit over there." In Berlin, he thought that "the structure of the city itself offered no resistance," whereas in Paris, "Americanism is as strident and jarring as the make-up on the face of an ageing *femme du monde*."[4] In fact, the further east you looked in Europe, the more intense was the cult of Americanism (Germany, the USSR) while in the west (Britain, France) the cult was much weaker. Gramsci explained the discrepancy succinctly: the further east you went in Europe, the more completely the traditional ruling class had been swept away.

In the Soviet Union, Americanism had a pronounced utopian ring. The avant-garde stage company, Feks, issued a typical proclamation: "Yesterday, European culture. Today, American technology. Production and industry under the star-spangled banner. Either Americanization or arranging the funeral ceremonies."[5] Under the influence of Frederick Taylor's work-study experiments, Gastev set up the institute for the Scientific Organization of Work and the Mechanization of Man.[6] Mayakovsky hymned the Brooklyn Bridge and Douglas Fairbanks and Mary Pickford were mobbed throughout a triumphant tour of the Soviet Union.[7] There, as elsewhere, Americanization stood for true modernity, the liquidation of stifling traditions and shackling life-styles and work-habits.

On a simple level, there was a fascination with movies, soaring towers, powerful machines, and speeding automobiles. But behind this was a growing recognition that the USA was providing the world with a new model of industrialism. Taylor was the pioneer of what we now know as ergonomics. By observation, photographic recording, and experiment, he broke down the physical gestures of workers to find which were the most efficient, in time and expenditure of labor power, for any particular job. These model gestures then became a standard for all workers, to be instilled by coercion or by habit. All would perform the same maximally efficient, radically simplified movements. Taylor's *Principles of Scientific Management*, published in 1911, heralded a new epoch in which the worker would become as predictable, regulated, and effective as the machine itself.[8]

By the time of Taylor's death in 1915 the assembly line at Henry Ford's factory in Highland Park, Detroit, was fully in operation after two years of experiment. Fordism meant more than the mass production of standardized objects. It meant a new form of organization of production. This involved bringing together three principal elements. First, a hierarchy of standardized segmented and subsegmented parts, all interchangeable, plus a parallel hierarchy of machine tools (themselves made up from standardized parts) which both formed and assembled the parts into the finished product. Second, a fully Taylorized workforce, themselves performing segmented and standardized repeated actions (a de-skilled labor force, controlled by an elite of engineers, supervisors, and designers). Third, a continuous, sequential assembly line, with a tempo determined by time and work studies, which transferred the parts through the whole process, designed so that the worker never had to move, even to stoop to pick something up. In effect, Fordism turned the factory into a kind of supermachine in its own right, with both human and mechanical parts.[9]

In the 1920s Fordism became a worldview, whether extolled, feared, or satirized. Matthew Josephson, editor of the avant-garde magazine *Broom*, wrote there in 1923: "Mr. Ford, ladies and gentlemen, is not a human creature. He is a principle, or better, a relentless process. Away with waste and competitive capitalism. Our bread, butter, tables, chairs, beds, houses, and also our homebrew shall be made in Ford factories. There shall be one great Powerhouse for the entire land, and ultimately a greater one for the whole world. Mr. Ford, ladies and gentlemen, is not a man." He went on: "Let him *assemble* us all into his machine. Let us be *properly* assembled. Let us all function unanimously. Let the wheels turn more swiftly."[10] Fordism became a vision, not only of greater productivity, necessary for the development of capitalism, but of a new model of social organization, with universal implications.

Thus, one of the most favorable accounts of Fordism was that given by Gramsci in his prison notebooks.[11] Gramsci unreservedly welcomed the advent of Fordism. He saw it as a necessary and desirable restructuring not only of the capitalist system but of the working class itself. At one point Gramsci asks himself, in view of the high labor turnover at the Ford plant, despite high wages, whether this does not indicate that Fordism is a "malignant phenomenon which must be fought against through trade union action and through legislation." But Gramsci decides for Fordism. "It seems possible to reply that the Ford method is rational, that is, that it should be generalized; but that a long process is needed for this, during which a change must take place in social conditions and in the way of life and habits of individuals." The keyword here, of course, is "rational."

Gramsci comes to a positive conclusion about Fordism despite his recognition that the old "psycho-physical nexus" of work involved "a certain active participation of intelligence, imagination and initiative on the part of the worker," whereas the de-skilled Taylorized and Fordized worker finds labor reduced "exclusively to the mechanical, physical aspect." Indeed, Gramsci goes much further in his approval of Fordism. "A forced selection will inevitably take place; a part of the old working class will be pitilessly eliminated from the world of labour, and perhaps from the world *tout court*"(!). The transformation of Italian society demanded, through a "passive revolution," the march of reason through the working class.

Perhaps the most memorable image of the "elimination" of the irrational is the forced removal of Charlie Chaplin from the factory to the lunatic asylum in *Modern Times*.[12] Chaplin proves unable to acquire the new psycho-physical habits required under Fordism. He runs amok, unable to stop performing his segmented mechanical action even when away from the assembly line. Demented by the speed-up of the line and relentless video-surveillance, he throws himself into the machine itself, being swallowed up in it, and then after his release goes on compulsively tightening bolts everywhere inside and outside the factory, including bolt-like objects such as noses and buttons on women's clothing. The image of incorporation into the machine is inverted when Chaplin is clamped into an automatic feeding machine that crams bolts into his mouth instead of lunch. The machine too runs amok, defying its designer.

In *Journey to the End of the Night*, Céline describes the experience of his hero as a worker on the Ford assembly line in Detroit: "One lived in a sort of suspense between stupefaction and frenzy."[13] It is exactly this world Chaplin captures in his mime. Céline's hero too is thrown back into the lumpen world, a reject. "I even felt shamed into making an effort to go back to work. Nothing, however, came of my heroic little gesture. I went as far as the factory gates, but on this boundary line I stood rooted and the thought of all those machines whirring away in wait for me irrevocably quashed my wish for work." In any case, it turns out that he has already been replaced by a machine, within three weeks of leaving.

From Gramsci's point of view both Chaplin's and Céline's heroes lacked the self-discipline necessary to transfer from the old to the new working class. Gramsci argues for a new puritanism, a kind of phase two of Weber's Protestant ethic, extended from the bourgeoisie to the workers. " 'Puritanical' initiatives simply have the purpose of preserving, outside of work, a certain psycho-physical equilibrium which prevents the physiological collapse of the worker, exhausted by the new method of production. This equilibrium can only be something purely external and mechanical, but it can become internalized if it is proposed by the worker himself, and not imposed from the outside, if it is proposed by a new form of society."

Gramsci identifies with Henry Ford's support of Prohibition and even approves his monitoring the private lives of his workers. For Gramsci, as for Ford, the question of sexuality is intimately involved with that of labor. Gramsci sees the new labor discipline as a blow against sexual promiscuity. The new (assumed-to-be-male) worker will want (in the words of Horace) *"venerem facilem parabilemque,"* easy and accessible sex, a woman to return home to, "sure and unfailing." "It might seem that in this way the sexual function has been mechanized, but in reality we are dealing with the growth of a new form of sexual union, shorn of the bright and dazzling colour of the romantic tinsel typical of the petit bourgeois and the Bohemian layabout. The exaltation of passion cannot be reconciled with the timed movements of productive motions connected with a fully perfected automatism."

Gramsci saw the 1920s as a period of sexual crisis. On the one hand, "the institutions connected with sexual life" had been profoundly shaken by the war and the demand for an end to sexual repression when peace returned. On the other hand, the demand for sexual liberation "came into conflict with the necessities of the new methods of work" imposed by "Taylorism and rationalization in general." In this conflict, Gramsci felt constrained to come down on the side of reason "against the element of 'animality' in man." Gramsci's vision of a new monogamy is really one which extends the "order, exactitude and precision" of the machine and the assembly line to the sphere of private life. Just as the industrial economy needs a stable labor force, "a permanently well-adjusted complex," so too domestic life must be stable and well adjusted. The workforce of a factory, Gramsci argued, is itself like "a machine which cannot, without considerable loss, be taken to pieces too often and renewed with single parts." The wife waiting at home becomes another such permanent machine part.

Sexual passion is seen as an excess which must be expelled from the rational system of advanced industrial civilization, inconsistent with "order, exactitude and precision." In 1932, contemporaneously with Gramsci's writings on Fordism, Rudolf Carnap published a notorious article on "The Elimination of Metaphysics through Logical Analysis of Language" in the journal of the Vienna Circle, *Erkenntnis.*[14] Metaphysics was the philosophical waste to be expelled from the realm of reason, the realm of emotion rather than cognition, nonsense rather than meaning. Carnap's philosophical project, as R. S. Cohen has pointed out, was "conceptualized parallel with the technological demands of modern industry."[15] Its criteria were indeed order, exactitude, and precision, particularly in segmentation and subsegmentation. In his reply to Strawson's "natural language" critique, Carnap noted: "A natural language is like a crude primitive pocketknife, very useful for a hundred different purposes. But for certain specific purposes, special tools are more efficient, e.g., chisels, cutting-machines, and finally the microtome."[16] Standardized artificial symbols, terms, and protocols function like philosophical machine-tools, shaping the useful and excising the waste.

A parallel project of standardization can be seen in the contemporaneous development of the "Isotype" by Otto Neurath, one of the leaders of the Vienna Circle and a colleague of Carnap.[17] In the late 1920s Neurath began work on designing an international picture language for graphic communication. This consisted of a basic vocabulary of graphic signs and a number of rules for combining them. They show simplified silhouetted figures of people and objects, somewhat similar to Léger's standardized figures of the 1920s, developed during his *Esprit Nouveau* period. Indeed, both Léger and Neurath were influenced by Egyptian art.[18]

The standard Isotype signs were combined into complex charts and diagrams in order to convey information visually with immediacy and clarity. Thus a chart showing automobile production in 1929 contrasts five identical silhouette workmen and fifty-five identical silhouette automobiles for the USA with eight workmen and only seven cars for Europe. The rows of standardized human figures are immediately reminiscent of the factory discipline under which the real workers worked on the assembly line, as well as Carnap's arithmetization of syntax. (The whole chart also graphically illustrates the impact of Fordism and the European lag which gave rise to the voluntaristic upsurge of Americanism.)

The members of the Vienna Circle saw their work as part of an overriding project of "rational socialism" and "scientific humanism." They saw market forces as irrational and wasteful and favored conscious, scientific planning. Neurath was militantly within the Austro-Marxist tradition. In the Soviet Union too socialism became identified with planning and industrialization on a Fordist model. As Asya Lacis put it in conversation with Walter Benjamin: "Gradually she had realized what was going on here [in the Soviet Union]: the conversion of revolutionary effort into technological effort."[19] In the Soviet Union, of course, the lag behind the United States was also an incentive towards "Americanization" in a revised Fordist form, however parodic this may now appear.

The Fordist vision expounded in different ways by Gramsci, the Vienna Circle, and Stalinist productivism contrasts starkly with Aldous Huxley's critique in his 1932 science fiction novel *Brave New World*.[20] Huxley imagines a future in which Fordism has become a world system, having absorbed both American capitalism and Soviet communism. Ford is invoked in place of God as the founder of a new secular religion and his book *My Life and*

Work (bound in surrogate leather) has become a new Bible. The whole of society, on a global scale, is now organized on Fordist principles, though Huxley envisages these as supplemented by developments in genetic engineering, pharmacological regulation of the psyche and new forms of state-controlled mass media. The imperatives of a "rationalized" technology rule throughout the system.

However, in Huxley's dystopia the workers do not return to stable monogamous families as they do in Gramsci's matching Utopia. Instead monogamy and the family unit have been eliminated and replaced, for human reproduction, by genetic technology. For sex there is a compulsory pattern of short-term relationships with a series of different partners. It is frowned on to spend too long with any one partner. Thus the need for *venerem facilem parabilemque* is organized on lines which demand interchangeability of parts. Huxley associates this pattern of sexual behavior with Freud. "Our Ford—or Our Freud, as for some inscrutable reason, he chose to call himself whenever he spoke of psychological matters—our Freud had been the first to reveal the appalling dangers of family life."

For Huxley, it is the family which is counterposed to the machine—especially the mother. Mothers, he notes, give rise to "every kind of perversion from sadism to chastity." His anti-hero, the Savage, is born anomalously to a mother and brought up by her (though he lacks a father). As a result, he is characterized precisely by sadistic impulses and a flight into chastity in his relations with women.[21] Like Gramsci, Huxley sees the passions as a threat to the well-regulated social mechanism. Where they differ is that Gramsci sees the family, albeit transformed, as a complement to the machine, whereas Huxley sees it as radically other, necessarily beyond the control of the system. For Huxley the "savage" threat of sexuality-out-of-control is family-generated (especially mother-generated) whereas for Gramsci it comes from the "animality" of the drives, to be regulated through the agency of the family.

The problem of the machine and sexuality is vividly expressed in the imagery and literature about robots which springs up during the 1920s. The robot is, of course, a metaphorical extension of the position of the worker in a Taylorist and Fordist system, like that of the clone in *Brave New World*. The term was coined by the Czech writer, Karel Capek, in 1917, from the Czech word for "serf," implying "forced labor." In 1920 Capek wrote his robot play, *R.U.R.*[22] The R.U.R. company (Rossum's Universal Robots) mass-produces artificial humanoids and sells them all over the world as cheap labor. The orderly running of the factory is disturbed by the arrival of a visitor from the Humanity League, Henrietta Glory. She wants to improve the oppressive conditions of robot "life." The factory managers and engineers resist this, putting forward a series of different ideas on the role played and benefits provided by robots, but in the end she seductively persuades one to alter the design (they are all of them in love with her!). As a result of the alteration the robots reach a new level of self-consciousness and begin to revolt. Eventually they take over the factory and the whole world, destroying humanity.

The robots are simplified and ergonomically improved models of humans. "A working machine must not want to play the fiddle, must not feel happy, must not do a whole lot of other things. A petrol motor must not have tassels or ornaments, Miss Glory. And to manufacture artificial workers is the same thing as to manufacture motors." Thus emotions are rejected as unnecessary and consequently equated with ornaments. The robots feel neither pleasure nor pain: they have neither libido nor affect. They have no fear of death but go immediately to the stamping-mill to be destroyed when ordered. They have no enjoyments and feel no sorrow. They have no childhood: "From a technical point of view, the whole of childhood is sheer stupidity."

On the other hand, they are superior to humans in many ways: "Nature hasn't the least notion of modern engineering. The human machine was terribly imperfect. It had to be replaced sooner or later," since, after all, "the product of an engineer is technically at a higher pitch than a product of nature." The robots have astonishing memories and can repeat whole encyclopaedias word for word with complete accuracy, but "they never think of anything new." They are stronger than humans, more intelligent (in task-oriented ways), more reliable, more punctual, and so on. In short, they have been designed as ideal mechanical slaves, inexpensive, capable, and obedient.

Occasionally robots do go wrong. "Something like epilepsy, you know. We call it robot's cramp. They'll suddenly sling down everything they're holding, stand still, gnash their teeth—and then they have to go to the stamping-mill." When the extra quality of "sensitivity" is added, it joins with this tendency to malfunction to produce organized revolt. Led by the librarian robot, Radius, who has a larger brain than the others, the robots begin to demand power for themselves. The first signs of "humanity" are hatred and the will-to-power. As they mutate they claim sovereignty and wreak destruction. "I don't want any master. I know everything for myself. I want to be master over people"—and eventually to kill people. Robots trained as soldiers turn on their human overlords and declare war.

Revolutionary committees of robots set up soviets and issue manifestos: "Robots of the world. We, the first national organization of Rossum's Universal Robots, proclaim man as an enemy and an outlaw in the Universe. Robots of the world, we enjoin you to murder mankind. Spare no men. Spare no women. Save factories, railways, machines, mines and raw materials. Destroy the rest. Then return to work. Work must not be stopped." The underlying fantasy is that of the Terror and the Bolshevik Revolution, of class warfare carried through to the extreme without pity or restraint. Only one man is spared. Alquist, a Tolstoyan, who has argued for the dignity and virtue of toil. Victorious, the robots continue to work harder and harder in an orgy of senseless productivity.

It is as though the robots, in the main part of the play, are projections of human sadism and aggression which have become, so to speak, sedimented in machines. The whole of Fordist civilization, seen together with the industrialization of war, is oriented towards death. The aggression which is turned on humanity by the robots originates in humanity itself, in the splitting-off and overvaluation of a will-to-power in the whole enterprise of Fordism and modern capitalism. Thus the phenomenon of technology-out-of-control, which is the central fear of *R.U.R.*, is simply another aspect of a perverse turn from love to hate, from natural reproduction to mechanical sterility. It is as if the technology itself is an externalization of the sadism and chastity of Huxley's Savage.

For Capek there were two "deep structures" underlying the metaphor of the robot, presented symbolically in the two contrasting worldviews of Old and Young Rossum, the father and son inventors of the robots. For Capek, Old Rossum "is no more or less than a typical representative of the scientific materialism of the last century."[23] He wishes to create an artificial man in order to prove God unnecessary. Thus, paradoxically, he is both a scientist and a magus, a creator of golems. In contrast, Young Rossum is a modern scientist, untroubled by metaphysical ideas; scientific experiment is for him the road to industrial production, he is not concerned to prove but to manufacture. Young Rossum, then, is a pragmatic engineer. His invention of the industrial robot takes place on the anniversary of the discovery of the United States. He is the exponent of Americanism.

As we have seen, the central idea of "Americanism" was provided by Fordism. Ford stood for the mass rather than the individual. He provided one standard and constant manufactured object—the Model T. "I thought that it was up to me as the designer to make the car so completely simple that no one could fail to understand it."[24] It was to be a basic, "generic" car, reduced to functional essentials. "We made no provision for the purely 'pleasure car,' " according to Ford. If the Model T gave any pleasure, this was to be purely a by-product. It was to have no unnecessary decoration or ornament. "Start with an article that suits and then study to find ways of eliminating the entirely useless parts"—like the cockade on a coachman's hat. And it was to be black. "Any customer can have a car painted any color that he wants as long as it is black." (When Chanel launched her "little black dress" in 1926, *Vogue* wrote: "Here is a Ford signed 'Chanel.' ")[25]

Capek's robots followed the same pattern as the Model T. They were all identical in appearance, like women wearing their Chanel "uniform" or like the cars rolling off the assembly line. Young Rossum's motto might have been, as was said of Chanel, "Lop it off"—reduce, be functional. The difference between Old and Young Rossum reflected the distinction between two epochs of technology and of the economy. The difference between the fantastic automaton and the industrial robot was like that between the magic horse of folklore and the Ford car. When Vaucanson made his famous automaton of a duck in 1738 he tried to imitate a real duck exactly. A single wing contained more than four hundred articulated parts and the duck could walk, quack, splash about, and even eat, digest, and excrete food.[26] It was intended as a marvel rather than an object of use.

Earlier versions of robots were, as Capek points out, semimagical beings. "To create a Homunculus is a medieval idea: to bring it in line with the present century this creation must be undertaken on the principle of mass-production." Beyond that, the robots themselves become the masses, standing in for the human masses of the great industrial cities. The ideal robots of the nineteenth century were still conceptualized as individuals, unique artifacts with a personal relationship to their maker: Frankenstein's monster, Spalanzani's Olympia, Edison's Future Eve.[27] They were essentially craft products—experimental prototypes or customized luxury goods.

In these instances, the dialectic between human and machine is mapped onto that between parent and child and also—quite explicitly in the case of Olympia and Hadaly (the Future Eve)—that between male lover and female love-object. Caught up in the circulation of desire, the automaton becomes both philosophical toy and sexual fetish or surrogate. Thus Edison in Villiers de L'Isle Adam's *The Future Eve* is both magus (though American) and marriage-broker (even "idealized" procurer and pimp). His project is the technical realization of the ideal object of masculine desire. The real task of creation is not simply to create a human being, but to create woman *for man*. In the twentieth century, this project reached a point of delirium with two modern artists, Kokoschka and Bellmer, both of whom had dolls manufactured for their personal gratification. Kokoschka took his (a life-sized replica of his ex-lover, made by her dressmaker, Hermine Moos) for excursions in his carriage, for meals in restaurants, where he insisted a place be laid for her, and to the theatre where she sat in the seat next to his. Bellmer, who knew of Kokoschka's doll, crafted a whole series of dolls, which he arranged in provocative postures and photographed. They became famous after they were publicized as "surrealist objects" in the magazine *Minotaure* and were later categorized as "bachelor machines."[28]

Unlike other puppets and robots, Hadaly is not entirely a "bachelor machine" because she is given a surrogate "mother" who is co-creator of the "soul" through her occult influence on the recorded *voice* given to Hadaly. Thus the ideal receives the necessary "maternal" input; the robot is intrinsically as well as contingently feminized. It is important to note this because, as both Raymond Bellour and Annette Michelson point out,[29] the Ideal which Edison produces, the perfect facsimile of image and sound, is a prefiguration of the cinema—still to be invented at the time the book was written, "the artificial living through illusion.""There's no doubt that within a few years, models like this one will be fabricated by the thousands: the first manufacturer who picks up this idea will be able to start the first factory for the production of Ideals." In a word, Hollywood.

In fact, not only does the gynoid prefigure the cinema, she comes to figure in it. Hadaly prefigures the False Maria, the robot vamp of Fritz Lang's *Metropolis*,[30] which combines the thematic of *The Figure Eve* with that of *R.U.R.* (as well as Kaiser's *Gas*). The robot-maker, Rotwang, is a magus of the same type as Old Rossum and Edison. Like them, he is a scientist magician, whose roots are in medieval times but whose technical resources are ultramodern. *Metropolis* sets the primordial drama of the creation of a female robot in a setting of industrial production and enslaved masses. At the same time, the robot is part of the personal project of Rotwang, the instrument of his desire. Through her seductive powers she will bring his sexual rival, Fredersen, to destruction, along with his industrial empire of Metropolis.

As Andreas Huyssen has shown, the film revolves around the displacement of the fear of technology-out-of-control on to that of (female) sexuality-out-of-control.[31] When the anarcho-hysteric flood of female sexuality is tamed and the (robot) witch who provoked it burned at the stake, then the owner and minder of the machines can be reconciled and progress through technology assured. The heart brings the hands and the head (body and mind, labor and capital) together, once the force of female sexuality has been eliminated. The robot vamp, unlike Hadaly, has not transcended her sterility through the maternal gift of a "soul." She is completely outside the sphere of the good mother, the True Maria, and utterly opposed to it. She is the incarnation of destructive sexuality, seductive and spellbinding.

Thus technology and sexuality are condensed in the figure of the robot Maria. Libido and the drives are represented in the first part of the film by the industrial machinery of the underground city which swallows up and destroys the human workers who are presented as its slaves. The destructive power of the technology is represented by the terrifying image of Moloch, the cannibal who devours his own children.[32] These sadistic and aggressive paternal drives must be counteracted by a nurturing maternal libido if catastrophe is to be averted. This is achieved through the agency of the True Maria, who is a spiritualized and desexualized mother-figure. Her victory over the False Maria, who urges the workers to destroy the machines in a frenzy of autocastration and infanticide, allows the paternal aggression projected into the industrial apparatus to be sublimated and controlled. The family is reconstituted symbolically and thus both pro-

3. *Metropolis* (Fritz Lang, 1926).

ductivity and social harmony are assured without further danger. For this to happen the aggression and destructiveness of the False Maria's phallic female sexuality have first to have been vanquished.

The False Maria, like Hadaly, is a creature whose physiognomy is itself a masquerade, a facsimile transferred from a model, the True Maria. These robot women, as Patricia Mellencamp has pointed out, are literally "special effects,"[33] natural on the outside, but mechanical within. The False Maria is herself "false" and holds sway, as a witch, over the "false" realms of superstition and rhetoric, emotive suasion.

In the figure of her creator, Rotwang, we see an unusually clear case of the way in which "scientific materialism" and "medieval magic" are linked on the terrain of sex. On the one hand, sex subsumes the realm of sensation and the body (hence, as the opposite of the spiritual, it is materialistic) and yet, on the other hand, it is irrational, disordered, and compulsive (hence, as the opposite of the rational, it is occult and magical, a seduction from the truth). Sex is associated with matter, the carnal and the sensual, but also with enchantment, mesmerism, and weird powers. Thus eros falls outside the sphere of logos in two conflicting ways. Again, we might be reminded of Carnap. First, the scientific—the meaningful—must be separated from the meaningless and, worse, from the pseudo-meaningful or metaphysical. The master-image used by Carnap was that of music ("Metaphysicians are musicians without musical talent")[34] but we can easily make the parallel between music and sex.

The linking category between "music" and "metaphysics," sex and witchcraft, is that of "passion." The False Maria exists in the realm of the mechanical and the spectacular. She falls outside the sphere of the natural and the spiritual, the sphere of motherhood. At the same time, her role as enchantress and spellbinder puts her outside the reach of patriarchal order and reason. She distracts and diverts the mesmerized masses and thus endangers the mastery of the father. Not until she is destroyed, therefore, can a naturalized and spiritualized technology be secured, the danger of mass hysteria finally averted. The connection with Gramsci's fear of sexual excess is clear: sexuality-out-of-control is the main threat to the rationality of technology. For Gramsci, too, feminism is identified with the True Maria rather than the False ("unhealthy 'feministic' deviations in the worst sense of the word"). The True Maria contains pleasure within the private sphere, whereas the False Maria carries it into the public sphere—Yoshiwara, the site of spectacle (music and sexual display).

Cinema has always been open to the same double charge: on the one hand, a mechanical copy and, on the other, a diverting spectacle, like Hadaly or the False Maria, an "electrical-mechanical spectacle," as El Lissitsky put it.[35] Cinema too can be condemned as a simulacrum, a masquerade, a display which bewitches the passions and the mind. In 1935 Walter Benjamin completed his famous essay on "The Work of Art in the Age of Mechanical Reproduction."[36] Here Benjamin defends film against both lines of attack, tackling the question of the "copy" and of "diversion" head on, while at the same time trying to enlist cinema on the side of technological reason, to the exclusion of enchantment and sensual pleasure (unless "fused" with instruction). His essay is the high point of the modernist theory of cinema, resolute in its insistence that art must be industrialized if it is to be truly modern; that is, to reach and respond to the needs of the masses.

It is important to realize that for Benjamin "copy" and "distraction" are subsidiary concepts to that of the "masses." It is mass production that produces the copy, the standardized product, and mass consumption that produces "diversion" or "distraction." His modernist transformation of aesthetics is founded on the postulate of Fordism, capitalist production in its most contemporary form. Just as the Model T replaces the customized coach or car, so the copy replaces the original. The scandal of Benjamin's approach was that this involved reversing the traditional terms of discussion. For Benjamin, the copy becomes associated with the true and the original with the false. Exhibition value, brought to dominance by the copy, brings the masses close to reality, whereas cult value, the province of the original, required contemplation at a distance, to be rewarded by a spiritual, rather than a secular and real, experience. Thus the decay of the "aura," the special quality of cult-value, is part of the general decay of magic, theology, and metaphysics.

Benjamin associates the filmmaker, the artist working with modern technology, with the surgeon (a technician using an "endonasal perspective procedure" or a laryngoscope) whereas the painter, the traditional artist, is associated with the magician, the shamanistic healer with his spells and mystical laying-on of hands. The modern is the impersonal and the standardized. Thus Benjamin notes the "increasing importance of statistics" in the sphere of theory, the translation of human behavior into abstract numerical values. He explains at some length how the artificial means of film production can paradoxically bring us closer to reality. "The equipment-free aspect of reality here has become the height of artifice; the sight of immediate reality has become an orchid in the land of technology." We are reminded, perhaps, of Carnap's insistence that an artificial language is necessary to the scientific representation of the world.

For Benjamin this whole approach meant a rejection of the "poetic politics" associated with the surrealists who had long been a major influence on his work. In his 1929 essay on surrealism he endorses the surrealist project: "To win the energies of intoxication for the revolution," i.e. the energies of the marvellous, the passionate, the ecstatic.[37] But he insists that to serve the revolution these energies must be welded to the life of the masses, a life dominated by the norms of modern industry and urban life. This means taking the surrealist moments of "illumination" (dreams, drugs, telepathy, etc.) outside the realm of private experience and rendering them public and "profane." For Benjamin, this could be envisaged as a kind of dream-sociology, a recapturing of lost configurations of fragmentary images of urban life, webs of affinity and correspondence, which, by restoring to memory what was lost to everyday experience, could also suggest the lineaments of a hoped-for future, the goal of a "poetic politics."

However, as time went on, and Benjamin felt himself constrained to identify more closely with communism as the only hope of defeating fascism, so he began to shift still further away from a surrealist conception of politics. He became much more critical of the romantic idealism which characterized the surrealist project and began to doubt that surrealist ideas of magic and the mysterious could ever take a profane rather than a spiritual form. He concluded his lecture on "The Author as Producer" with the words, addressed to Aragon (whose *Paris Peasant* had once deeply influenced him): "The more exactly he is thus informed on his position in the process of production, the less it will occur to him to lay claim to 'spiritual' qualities. The spirit that holds forth in the name of fascism *must* disappear. The spirit that, in opposing it, trusts in its own miraculous powers *will* disappear. For the revolutionary struggle is not between capitalism and spirit, but between capitalism and proletariat."[38]

As he turned away from surrealism, so he moved closer to Brecht, whom he had come to know. Behind Brecht stood the tradition of Soviet constructivism and avant-gardism which had, in turn, influenced Brecht and in which Benjamin had long shown an enthusiastic interest. Brecht, of course, was much closer to mechanical materialism than Benjamin—he argued in favor of behaviorism and logical positivism—and it seems clear that he pulled Benjamin some way in this direction. Brecht's whole thought revolved around the antinomies between feeling and reason, individual and collective, psychology and action, each of which can be mapped onto the other. In his famous afterword to *Mahagonny* two sets of antinomies are listed side by side, culminating in "feeling" versus "reason."[39] In the very next paragraph there is an onslaught against witchcraft, hypnosis, intoxication, and fog (whose unstated opposites are science, reason, sobriety, and clarity). A little further on and we find magicians who are seeking to keep their (bourgeois) audience spellbound. All these pairs of contraries can be detected in the structure of the "work of art" essay.

The link between the concept of the "copy" and that of "distraction" is effected in a curious way, through another couplet, drawn from nineteenth-century psychology and aesthetics, that of the "optical" and the "tactile." Benjamin reserves the realm of the "optical" for the original image (*bild*), while the copy (*abbild*) is assigned to the realm of the "tactile." The image demands contemplation, absorbed attention, a fixed gaze. It is always at a distance, to-be-looked-at. The copy, on the other hand, is always close, it can be handled, touched, and manipulated. Moreover, the whole mode of apperception of modern life is "tactile." Here Benjamin turns to a concept which becomes ever more important to him, that of "shock." He conceives of life in the city as an unending series of shocks, which act on us like physical blows—to use a favorite image—like being jostled in a crowd. The copy, because it is both ubiquitous and transient (unlike the image, unique and permanent), jostles us in a crowd of other copies.

In a later essay, finished in 1939, "On Some Motifs in Baudelaire,"[40] Benjamin describes how "the shock experience which the passer-by has in the crowd corresponds to what the worker 'experiences' at his machine." He quotes Marx on the division and de-skilling of labor under conditions of capitalist production, the way in which workers learn to coordinate "their own movements with the uniformly constant movements of an automaton" and subject their own volition to the objectified will of the machine. It is clear, I think, that this reading of Marx is performed retroactively, a method of reading fundamental to Benjamin, tracing at the beginning of modernism the ulterior lineaments of Fordism. Benjamin associates the cinema particularly closely with the experience of the masses. Film provides a series of shocks, sudden shifts in camera position, discontinuities in time and space, close-ups and bird's-eye views, changes in the tempo of editing and the scale of objects. "There came a day when a new and urgent need for stimuli was met by the film. In a film, perception in the form of shocks was established as a formal principle. That which determines the rhythm of production on a conveyor belt is the basis of the rhythm of reception in film."

Benjamin turned the concept of "distraction" upside down. Instead of seeing it as antagonistic to thought and reason, he argued that it was supportive of reason. He did this in two ways. First, he argued that film, through its technique of shocks, instilled new habits in the masses, new modes of apperception. These, in turn, were necessary to the masses at the present turning point in history when the human apparatus of perception was confronted with a multitude of new demands and new tasks. Thus cinema, in a sense, was fulfilling the role of fitting the masses for the new and progressive forms of production which were being introduced. Here, of course, Benjamin is on the same ground as Gramsci, in looking for a new kind of psycho-physical complex in the worker. Shock (instead of being a shock of juxtaposition, suggesting new and hitherto secret affinities, as with surrealist montage) has become a form of training and film a form of training manual.[41]

Gramsci, in fact, went even further than Benjamin and argued that Taylorized work could itself be potentially liberating. "Once the process of adaptation has been completed, what really happens is that the brain of the worker, far from being mummified, reaches a state of complete freedom. The only thing that is completely mechanized is the physical gesture: the memory, reduced to simple gestures repeated at an intense rhythm, 'nestles' in the muscular and nervous centres and leaves the brain free and unencumbered for other occupations." Just as, when we walk, we can synchronize our physical movements automatically and still "think whatever we choose," so the new worker, instead of being a "trained gorilla" (Taylor's unfortunate phrase), can become a free intellectual.[42]

Gramsci reaches this conclusion after considering the case of the skilled typesetter, which he sees as a prototype of mechanized work processes. The compositor, he argues, has to learn to isolate the symbols of a text from its "often fascinating intellectual content." In the same way, the worker on the assembly line performs a series of symbolic operations without any regard for their meaning. As Ehrenburg put it, in his brilliant novel *The Life of the Automobile*, "The worker doesn't know what an automobile is. He doesn't know what an engine is. He takes a bolt and tightens a nut. . . . Upwards to the right, half a turn and then down. He does this eight hours in a row. He does it all his life. And that's all he ever does."[43] Benjamin compares the drudgery of the assembly line worker to that of a gambler: the endless repetition of futile, empty gestures, none of which has any meaning. "They live their lives as automatons and resemble Bergson's fictitious characters who have completely liquidated their memories."[44]

Fordism introduces an industrial regime, for the worker, of pure signifiers. Medieval copyists, Gramsci observed, became interested in the texts they were copying and consequently made mistakes, interpolating glosses and comments, distracted by the signifieds. "He was a bad scribe because in reality he was 'remaking' the text." When copying was mechanized through printing this led to a mechanization of the labor process, a suppression of the signified. The Ford worker carries out a single symbolic operation. The assembly line proceeds like an algorithm, carrying out a predetermined sequence of formalized instructions. Meaning is suspended until the process is completed and there is an output which can be interpreted—in the case of the Ford factory, a fully assembled automobile with a meaning for its purchaser. Gramsci's argument was that this very formalization, this reduction of work to a series of empty signifiers, made it possible to think about something else, left a space for other signifieds.

Benjamin attempted a similar paradoxical reconciliation of "distraction" with "reason" in his final observation that "film makes cult-value recede into the background not only by putting the public in this position of critic, but also by the fact that at the movies the position requires no attention. The public is an examiner, but an absent-minded one." Benjamin, in fact, deploys two concepts of "criticism." The first is drawn largely from Brecht. The example which Benjamin gives is of "a group of newspaper boys leaning on their bicycles and discussing a bicycle race." In the cinema it is "inherent in the technology," as it is with sports, that "everybody who witnesses its accomplishments is something of an expert." As early as 1922 Brecht had been arguing for a "smoker's theatre" whose audience would be like that at a boxing match. In his notes to *The Threepenny Opera*, he called for "a theatre full of experts, just as one has sporting arenas full of experts."[45] Benjamin's contribution to this dubious view was to link the expertise to the possibility of interchanging spectators with performers, in line with the theories of Vertov and Tretyakov about proletarian art.

But Benjamin has a second concept of expertise, also taken from Brecht, but very different in its implications. This is the idea that a segment of film is like a vocational aptitude test or a scientific investigation of human behavior. "The act of reaching for a lighter or a spoon is familiar routine, yet we hardly know what really goes on between hand and metal, not to mention how this fluctuates with our moods," but these ordinary actions can be brought into our cognitive scope by the film camera (shades of Taylor and his chronophotography of work gestures!). Brecht was interested in the possibility of building up an archive of gestures on film and used film to record gestures during rehearsals for stage performances. Benjamin seems to assimilate this both to the screen test and the related vocational aptitude test, as if unaware of the concession he is making to "scientific management" in the Taylorist sense.

As Benjamin moves away from a fascination with the "fragment," the detail of dream-kitsch, the waste product of the economy which reveals more than it seems to tell, towards an obsession with the "segment," the detail isolated for scientific analysis, we can sense very clearly the affinity between his thought and that of Gramsci. It is not only in the residues of surrealism or "mysticism" that distance Benjamin from Brecht (indeed both share, at this point, a number of "mystical" beliefs—in sports, physicalist psychology, and so on) but the absence of politics. In the "work of art" essay, as in Gramsci's *Fordism and Americanism*, politics is subsumed in an uncritical acceptance both of technology and, more important, of new technology-related forms of production. The progressive status of Fordism is taken for granted, with very perfunctory argument. Moreover, this leads both of them to take the mechanization of the worker at least as a necessity and even, explicitly for Gramsci, a desideratum.

In Huxley's *Brave New World*, film production is a division of "Emotional Engineering," a central part of the regulation of leisure. Films have evolved into pan-sensory experiences, "feelies," which enable the spectators to experience in exact detail all that is felt by the characters in the spectacle—"every hair on the bearskin rug." Instead of training the workers for the world of repressive labor, they channel the repressed impulses which might otherwise erupt subversively. They are a force of stability. " 'Stability,' said the Controller, 'stability. No civilization without social stability. No social stability without individual stability.' "[46] Thus the role of the feelies, of emotional engineering, is to ensure that the release of pent-up sexuality in leisure never gets out of control, never becomes impassioned. "Wheels must turn steadily, but cannot turn untended. There must be men to tend them, men as steady as the wheels upon their axles, sane men, obedient men, steady in contentment."

Huxley's vision of the feelies reads strangely like a logical extension of the Aristotelian "theatre of pleasure" which Brecht denounces in the name of epic theatre, "theatre of instruction": "the pleasure grows in proportion to the degree of unreality"[47]—unreality, that is, expressed in a stupendously totalizing illusionism. The sensual pleasure and emotional experience provided in the sphere of "distraction" compensate for the lack of pleasure and loss of affect suffered in the sphere of labor. A carefully regulated new "soul" is added to the new Fordized body, a kitsch soul for a machine body. Huxley emphasizes that the central feature of the feelie is the kiss. Cinema supplies vicarious eroticism, divorced from pain or tragedy, stability guaranteed by the "happy end." Throughout the book, this model of "distraction" and spectacle is counterposed to Shakespeare's plays and to sacred ceremonies—the Hopi snake-dance and the *penitentes* of

Acoma.[48] Huxley's alternative is not the epic drama of Brecht and Benjamin but a theatre of tragedy and ritual.

A third model is put forward by Siegfried Kracauer in his extraordinary essay on "The Mass Ornament."[49] Kracauer's central image of art in the age of the engineer is that of the Tiller Girls, an American dance troupe which represented for 1920s Berlin the acme of a form of popular entertainment replicated throughout the world, in live shows and on film.[50] Kracauer is quite clear that the Tiller Girls are a reflection of Fordism. "Everyone goes through the necessary motions at the conveyor belt. . . . It is conceived according to rational principles which the Taylor system takes to its logical conclusion. The hands in the factory correspond to the legs of the Tiller Girls. . . . The mass ornament is the aesthetic reflex of the rationality aspired to by the prevailing economic system."

In 1931, after the crash, Kracauer looked back on the Tiller Girls in another essay, "Girls and crisis."[51] "In that postwar era, in which prosperity appeared limitless and which could scarcely conceive of unemployment, the Girls were artificially manufactured in the USA and exported to Europe by the dozen. Not only were they American products; at the same time they demonstrated the greatness of American production. . . . When they formed an undulating snake, they radiantly illustrated the virtues of the conveyor belt; when they tapped their feet in fast tempo, it sounded like *business, business*; when they kicked their legs with mathematical precision, they joyously affirmed the progress of rationalization; and when they kept repeating the same movements without ever interrupting their routine, one envisioned an uninterrupted chain of autos gliding from the factories into the world."

The mass ornament mirrors the production process of Fordism: a series of formal operations carried out on meaningless parts ("Arms, thighs and other segments are the smallest components of the composition"). These operations produce abstract patterns using the same movements as machines: lines, rotations, repetitions. The Tiller Girls are like Neurath's Isotypes, marshalled in identical lines (as also, Kracauer points out, are the spectators). Kracauer argues that, in the mass ornament, the female body and its component parts are de-eroticized; the body becomes a pure signifier "which no longer has erotic meaning." The apparently human (and sexual) elements are transformed into "mere building blocks, nothing more." For Kracauer this dehumanization appeared as a return to abstract nature, objectification, but it would surely be more accurate to see it as a process of abstract symbolization.

The Tiller Girls reduced the erotic to a set of formal operations, just as logic reduced the rational to a set of formal operations. Indeed the operations and procedure of logic have not simply been formalized but also mechanized. The first steps to this were taken during the early 1930s and it is striking how the early projects for reasoning machines follow the model of the Fordist assembly line. Alan Turing's idea developed through imagining a standardized worker (or "computer") placed before an endlessly moving line (or tape).[52] The procedures performed by the "computer" are "to be split up into 'simple operations' which are so elementary that it is not easy to imagine them further divided," and which are themselves reduced to a minimum number. "We may now construct a machine to do the work of this computer," i.e. segmented tasks on a moving line. Post, in his parallel speculation, was even more explicit. A "worker" would be operating on an endless line of "boxes" moving in front of him. He was limited to five simple operations. Thus the computer, the reasoning machine dreamed of by Leibniz, is finally realized on the model of the assembly line, processing not material commodities but abstract units of information.

Kracauer suggests a way of going beyond the antagonism between Benjamin and Huxley, the endorsement or repudiation of "distraction" as a functional element within the Fordist system. Kracauer, like Benjamin, rejected the option of going back to traditional forms of art. The way forward "leads directly through the mass ornament, not away from it." But he thought that "distraction," though a necessary step in the right direction, could provide only a partial answer. Its value lay precisely in the "emptiness and externality" which were also its limits. The mass ornament exemplified a one-sided, purely formal rationality. It was not a "full" reason, "concerned with bringing truth into the world."[53] Kracauer opposed attempts to add an extrinsic content or "truth" to the abstract form of the mass ornament. This could only spiritualize or mythologize it in a reactionary way (as Leni Riefenstahl was to do in *Triumph of the Will*). The problem was how to develop a new content, a truth-bearing content, from within formal reason, intrinsically. His dream was of a Fordist rationality that would not be dehumanizing.

The question we must ask is, perhaps, even more difficult than Kracauer imagined. On the one hand, within the sphere of reason, formal processes of computation, algorithms for the manipulation of symbols, and so on, are separated and cut off from cognitive states, from intentions, wishes, values, and desires, from the world. And, on the other hand, both the assembly line worker and the Tiller Girl are subjected to a segmentation and formalization of the body itself. The problem is that of reintegrating reason not only with truth, but also with the body. The Tiller Girls offered the spectacle of (female) bodies in movement, duplicating the alienated form of the Fordist labor process, its instrumental rationality. What form of bodily movement would correspond to a process of production which displayed a different, transformed rationality—and, of course, a transformed gender division and sexuality?

At the very end of his life, disillusioned by the Hitler-Stalin pact, Benjamin began to rethink many of the basic assumptions of the 1930s. In his "Theses on the Philosophy of History,"[54] his last writing before his death, he looked back sadly: "Nothing has corrupted the German working class so much as the notion that it was moving with the current. It regarded technological developments as the fall of the stream with which it thought it was moving. From there it was but a step to the illusion that the factory work which was supposed to tend towards technological progress constituted a political achievement. The old Protestant work ethic was resurrected among German workers in a secularized form." Benjamin goes on to contrast this with the formalized utopian conceptions of Fourier, the dream of a new kind of relationship between humanity, technology, and nature. This would require a new reason, not the instrumental reason of utility and the machine as tool but, we might speculate, an ornamental reason in which the "magic force" of the Tiller Girls (no longer Girls) was directed to a new form of mass art (for mass art's sake) with the same technical and formal rigor but with a resituated hedonism and transformed eroticism.

By the time when Benjamin was writing "The Work of Art in the Age of Mechanical Reproduction," Fordism was already entering a new phase. Continued increases in production made it necessary to increase consumption. Fordism brought with it advertising, packaging, variety marketing, annual changes in model. In the motor industry itself the change was initiated by General Motors, who, under the leadership of Alfred Sloan, introduced styling into automobile design, changing the superstructure, add-ons, and "look" of their cars every year. Customers were encouraged to trade in their old model in part-exchange for a new one chosen from a range of new models with new looks, launched each year in a blaze of publicity. Fordism gave way to Sloanism.[55] It was no longer possible just to manufacture one basic car, as Ford had done with the Model T. The market (basically the farm market) was exhausted and new markets had to be developed. Thus marketing began to dominate the production process itself.

This process reached its "golden age" in the "consumer society" of the long postwar boom. Indeed, once again "Americanism" became identified with the image of the automobile—but now the ornate dream-car, the pink Cadillac with tail fins and scallops, the car celebrated by Chuck Berry in his classic rock 'n' roll lyrics. This was the car attacked by Vance Packard in *The Waste Makers* precisely for being dysfunctional, a monstrous, gas-guzzling, badly engineered fantasy contraption.[56] Packard excoriated "pink dinosaurism" and called for a return to historic values: "Or better still the motorcar makers might try copying some of the features of the Model A Ford, perhaps the most rugged motorcar ever built." The Model A, with its "straightforward frame," was "still getting daily use in North America three decades after it was built."

Packard's attacks signalled the beginning of the end for Fordism. From being the symbol of instrumental reason in industry, the automobile had become a byword for waste and ornamentalism. The economy and culture of the west entered a period of crisis, the decline of Fordism, as consumerism reached the limits possible within the old system. A long transitional period during the 1960s and 1970s finally led to the introduction of a new post-Fordist economy. The first signs of this were already visible in the 1950s, with the beginnings of automation. At that time, automation was seen primarily as a way of rationalizing still further the existing Fordist structures of industry. In reality, we can now see that it prefigured much more sweeping changes in the economy. The rationality of the computer and of robotics turned out to be significantly different from the rationality of the Highland Park assembly line.

Post-Fordism brought three main developments.[57] First, the rise of whole new industries made possible by advances in electronics. Second, the use of new technology in the manufacture and design of old products, the upgrading of old industries. Third, a systemic shift from the object as commodity to information as a commodity. These changes were associated with the shift from smokestack to Sunbelt industry, from the manufacturing to the service sector, and with an international shift in the relations between center and periphery: a more polycentric world economy accompanied by the appearance of a new periphery within the major western countries, a marginalization of whole zones and sectors. One result of this, of course, was the demotion of the automobile industry, the relegation of Detroit itself to the periphery of American industry.

The communications industry, on the other hand, moved to the center. Benjamin, writing in the 1930s, was celebrating what was still primarily a nineteenth-century technology. The Lumière brothers, like their American counterpart, Edison, or like Henry Ford himself, were typical inventor-entrepreneurs of the period. While it is true that the infant electronics industry had already made its contribution to the coming of sound in the cinema, this was overlooked by Benjamin, who was a protagonist of the silent cinema. Like many avant-garde theorists, he distrusted sound film. Today, we are living in a transformed world in which the cinema itself is fast becoming archaic—an age, not so much of "mechanical reproduction" as "electronic intertextuality." The electronic revolution that began with sound accelerated with magnetic tape and spread into the technology of images with video and television. Now we are moving into an epoch of digitalized image storage and high-definition electronic media (HDTV).

Most important of all, the invention of the computer, beyond Benjamin's imagination, has transformed the whole field of image production. We are now in the first phase of the period of video-computer integration. In the 1920s Vertov described the camera as a mechanical eye; now it is the mechanical eye of an electronic brain. Indeed, the camera itself has been transformed. It is now simply one option within a whole range of sensors and information recording devices, some visual, some nonvisual. Images can be produced with X-rays, night vision, thermal, magnetic, electronic spin, and a host of other kinds of sensor. The camera (film or video) is simply the one which most closely approximates "natural vision." Sensors are no longer hand-held or mounted on tripods, with humans attached to them, looking down viewfinders. Their motion and action can be remote-controlled. They can circle the earth in satellites or transmit from within the human body.

New theories of the image and the media began to appear in the late 1950s and early 1960s, culminating in the work of Marshall McLuhan.[58] Indeed, McLuhan put himself forward explicitly as the theorist of the end of Fordism, a process which—like Gramsci—he saw as the culmination of a logic implicit in typography and the invention of the printing press. Fordism was the end of the Gutenberg era: "the breaking-up of every kind of experience into uniform units in order to produce faster action and change of form." Fundamentally, McLuhan, like Huxley or Céline, was an opponent of Fordism who saw, in the advent of the new electronic technology of the media, the possibility of superseding it and reconstructing, on a new basis, the old pre-Fordist (indeed, pre-Gutenberg) "community" in the form of the "global village."

The extraordinary achievement of McLuhan was to break out of the terms of the polemics for and against technology (Benjamin vs. Heidegger) by fusing romantic reaction with futurist technolatry. With McLuhan you get aspects of both Benjamin and Heidegger. Like Benjamin he privileges the tactile over the visual and dreams of the creation through technology of a radically new kind of human being. But like Heidegger he sees the new human being in a quasi-mystical way as a return to origins (back beyond mass production, beyond printing, even further, beyond the alphabet), to a world without separation, a world of perpetual now-ness. Whatever the incoherence and, indeed, idiocy of many of McLuhan's prophecies and pronouncements, his underlying vision still exerts its fascination.

McLuhan was a visionary writing when the first impact of vast changes was being felt, projecting his own fantasies and hopes onto the new technologies he could partially foresee. We now have a much clearer idea of where those media technologies are leading. Old distinctions are beginning to blur and lose their meaning as the technologies of image production and reproduction begin to merge. The computer with its capacity for manipulation and simulation becomes part of an integrated system with both the old and new recording technologies. We can sum up the main characteristics of the new systems as follows.

(1) Access to a data base of stored images in the electronic memory. This opens up the possibility of recycling the contents of a vast image bank, an archive from which images can be taken and recontextualized at will.

The image bank is more immediate and directly accessible than the "real world"; it is intra-systemic, whereas the "real world" is extra-systemic.

(2) Immediate manipulation—matting, combination, distortion, alteration, etc.—of available images. Images from different sources can be combined together. With motion-control cameras linked by computer, moving imagery from the "real world" can be combined with other imagery, also from the real world or from the archive, so that there are no discrepancies in speed, point-of-view in movement, perspective, or lighting.

(3) Generation of images by the computer. The computer can be used to produce animated imagery. Once images are produced they can be stored, retrieved, rotated, textured, etc. The computer can also generate text and consequently opens up new possibilities for the combination of text with image. Computer-generated imagery can itself be combined with other images.

(4) Simulation of the "real world" by the computer. Thus, in Helmut Costard's film *Real Time*, we see computer programmers who produce a visual display of a landscape out of nonvisual, numerical data. Currently simulations, even the most advanced, such as landscape images in flight simulators, are still relatively sparse and schematic. The next areas to be developed include the use of fractal geometry to produce irregular and chaotic forms (also recursive, so that they can be zoomed into without loss of detail) such as we find in nature; improvements in texturing to give greater variation in the surface quality and "look" of objects; physiognomic analysis to permit the simulation of expressive human facial movements and other types of gesture.

(5) Combinations of all the above. Thus imaging can combine the characteristics of the documentary, the studio film, special effects, the animated film, and the compilation film. The beginnings of this hybrid imaging can already be seen in many music videos. But this is only a beginning. For instance, we can imagine films in which Charlie Chaplin meets Marilyn Monroe, once their images have been digitalized and the problems of texturing and physiognomic analysis are solved. They can be taken out of the archive to star in new films with new stories and settings.

(6) Further areas of development include holographs and other types of 3-D imagery; interactivity and other types of spectator-image interface; multiscreen systems; new types of transmission and reception, such as optical fiber. These will change not only the nature of imagery but also its patterns of use, as new types and situations of display are introduced. Computer-video imagery could become as ubiquitous as print and photographic imagery is now.

To a lesser or greater degree, the new systems of imagery will be *heterogeneous palimpsests*. They will combine a number of different types of image (as well as other kinds of sign) and they will refer not only, or even primarily, to the "real world" (the extra-textual), but also to the existing archive of images and texts from which they borrow (the inter-textual). This does not mean that we will all live in a "global village" or a ubiquitous "simulacrum" controlled by a totalizing master code. In effect, these versions of the future (McLuhan, Baudrillard) are projections of a loss of faith in human reason, a revolt against "modernity" conceived of as the elevation of instrumental reason to an absolute. McLuhan's optimistic version sees the new technology as heralding the end of western analytical reason (homogeneous, standardized, linear) and the dawn of a new age, a return to lost pre-Gutenberg values. In contrast, Baudrillard's pessimistic version sees the new technology as an extension of analytical reason, digitalization as the final culmination of a process of alienation.

The problem of finding an appropriate aesthetic for the new media is aggravated by the philosophical abyss which has opened up between a logicist rationalism and an anti-logical metaphysics (or "post-metaphysics"). As we have seen, this split reflects conflicting attitudes to Fordism and the rationality of modern technology and industry. On the whole, aesthetics has been set firmly against Fordism and logicism, in the Romantic tradition, with the outstanding exception of writers such as Benjamin or Brecht, who hoped for a meeting of art and science, mediated by the industrialization of art on "rational" grounds. Yet the concept of "reason" at issue here has been a very limited one. In effect, the great advances in logic made possible by Boole's *Mathematical Analysis of Logic* in 1847 transformed not just logic, but the whole of philosophy, cutting aesthetics definitively adrift.[59]

The long-term effect of Boole's work, followed by that of Frege, Russell, and so on, has been to reject art as the sphere of fiction, metaphor, vagueness, nonsense, wordplay, etc., all of which fall outside the scope of logical semantics. Conversely, anti-logicist philosophers such as Heidegger proceeded to privilege art and aestheticize philosophy, at the expense of clarity and precision of meaning, running the danger of setting art against analytical reason.[60] The way forward, therefore, must depend on a critique of logicism which is not itself anti-logicist, and a critique of aesthetics which is not itself anti-art. Logic and aesthetics both have their place in the realm of reason.

The first requirement is the development of a *heterogeneous* theory of meaning, open rather than closed, involving different types of sign, and bringing semantics together with hermeneutics, reference with metaphor. The second is a specific (formal) theory of *intertextual* meaning, the way in which recontextualization changes meaning, the double, hybrid coding involved in quoting, plagiarizing, grafting and so on, the back and forth of meaning between texts. Both these projects entail a reconsideration of the logical form of meaning. In the last resort, both logic and aesthetics are concerned with form. The computer is itself, of course, the end-product of the triumphal march of mathematical logic. It would be ironic if the formalism of machine code was used to generate new artistic forms which themselves made possible the transformation of reason, closing the gap between logic and aesthetics.

Notes

1. This article is the companion piece to my "Fashion/Orientalism/the body," *New Formations* 1 (1987).
2. The first jazz band to reach Europe was the Original Dixieland Jazz Band which toured in 1918. For a fascinating account of the impact jazz made in the Soviet Union see Frederick Starr, *Red and Hot* (Oxford: Oxford University Press, 1983). As for England, Clive Bell protests against the jazz cult in his "Plus de jazz," in *Since Cezanne* (New York: Harcourt, Brace, 1922). On "Amerikanismus," see John Willet, *The New Sobriety* (London: Thames and Hudson, 1978).
3. Schlemmer is cited in Willet, *The New Sobriety*.
4. Pirandello is cited in Antonio Gramsci, "Americanism and Fordism," in *Prison Notebooks* (London: Lawrence and Wishart, 1971).
5. Mario Verdone and Barthelemy Amengual, *Le Feks* (Paris: 1970). Feks stood for Factory of the Eccentric Actor.
6. The best short account of Taylor's work and influence is in Siegfried Giedion, *Mechanization Takes Command* (Oxford: Oxford University Press, 1948). Giedion reproduces examples of chronophotography by Taylor's disciple, Frank B. Gilbreth, which can be compared with those used by Gastev, shown in René Fülöpp-Miller, *The Mind and Face of Bolshevism* (London: Alfred A. Knopf, 1927). For Taylor see also the portrait in John Dos Passos, *The Big Money* (New York: Modern Library, 1936); and for Gastev, Christina Lodder, *Russian Constructivism* (New Haven: Yale University Press, 1983).
7. See Sergei Komarov's astonishing film, *Mary Pickford's Kiss* (USSR, 1927).
8. Frederick Taylor, *Principles of Scientific Management* (New York: Harper, 1911).
9. For Fordism, see Henry Ford, *My Life and Work* (London: W. Heinemann, 1924). The concept of Fordism as an economic system of production is developed in Emma Rothschild, *Paradise Lost: The Decline of the Auto-Industrial Age* (New York: Random House, 1973); Michel Aglietta, *A Theory of Capitalist Regulation*, trans. David Fernbach (London: New Left Books, 1979); and Alain Lipietz, *Mirages and Miracles*, trans. David Macey (London: Verso, 1987).
10. Matthew Josephson, "Made in America," *Broom* 2 (June 1922). Cited in Dickram Tashjian, *Skyscraper Primitives* (Middletown: Wesleyan University Press, 1975).
11. Gramsci, *Prison Notebooks*. The preface to the English edition contains a detailed bibliographic account of the notebooks by the editors, Quintin Hoare and Geoffrey Nowell-Smith.
12. Chaplin describes the origin of *Modern Times* (USA, 1936) in *My Autobiography* (New York: Simon and Schuster, 1964): "Then I remembered an interview I had with a bright young reporter on the New York *World*. Hearing that I was visiting Detroit, he had told me of the factory-belt system there—a harrowing story of big industry luring health young men off the farms who, after four or five years of the belt system, became nervous wrecks."
13. Louis-Ferdinand Céline, *Journey to the End of the Night*, trans. Ralph Mannheim (New York: New Directions, 1983).

14. Rudolf Carnap, "The Elimination of Metaphysics through Logical Analysis of Language," in *Logical Positivism*, ed. A. J. Ayer (Glencoe: Free Press, 1959). This essay was largely directed against Heidegger's inaugural address at Freiburg University, published in 1930 under the title "What Is Metaphysics?" See Martin Heidegger, *Basic Writings*, ed. David Farrell Krell (New York: Harper and Row, 1977).

15. R. S. Cohen, "Dialectical Materialism and Carnap's Logical Empiricism," in *The Philosophy of Rudolf Carnap*, ed. Paul Arthur Schilpp (LaSalle: Open Court, 1963).

16. Rudolf Carnap, "P. F. Strawson on Linguistic Naturalism," ibid.

17. See Otto Neurath, *International Picture Language* (Reading, 1980) and *Graphic Communication through ISOTYPE*, ed. Michael Twyman (Reading, 1975). Neurath's text is written in Basic English. I am indebted to Victor Burgin for these references.

18. See Neurath, *International Picture Language*, and Christopher Green, "Léger and L'esprit nouveau," *Léger and Purist Paris*, Tate Gallery catalogue (London, 1970). Green points out that the Egyptian rooms at the Louvre were reopened at the pertinent time for them to have influenced Léger.

19. Walter Benjamin, *Moscow Diary*, ed. Gary Smith, trans. Richard Sieburth (Cambridge: Harvard University Press, 1986). Benjamin sought a way between the Scylla of Carnap and the Charybdis of Heidegger.

20. Aldous Huxley, *Brave New World* (London: Chatto and Windus, 1932). Theodor Adorno wrote an important critique of Huxley's book, "Aldous Huxley and Utopia," in *Prisms*, trans. Shierry and Samuel Weber (Cambridge: MIT Press, 1967).

21. Among the sources for Huxley's vision of the Savage were William Seabrook's accounts of his travels. When Seabrook was a neighbor of Huxley in Sanary, Huxley noted that "the rumour has gone round the village that he beats his lady friend" (letter to the Vicomte de Noailles, November 1932, in *Letters of Aldous Huxley*, ed. Grover Smith [London: Chatto and Windus, 1969]). For further details of Seabrook and sadomasochism, see Vève A. Clark et al., *The Legend of Maya Deren* (New York: Anthology of Film Archives, Film Culture, 1984) and Man Ray, *Self Portrait* (New York: Little Brown 1963).

22. Karel Capek, *R. U. R.* (New York: Samuel French, 1923). On robots, John Cohen, *Human Robots in Myth and Science* (South Brunswick, NJ: A. S. Barnes, 1967) and his later *The Lineaments of the Mind* (San Francisco: W. H. Freeman, 1980).

23. Capek, *R. U. R.*

24. Ford, *Life and Work*.

25. Cited in Edmonde Charles-Roux, *Chanel and Her World* (London: Vendome Press, 1981).

26. See Reichardt, *Robots*, and Cohen, *Human Robots*.

27. Mary Shelley, *Frankenstein* (Oxford: Oxford University Press, 1969); E. T. A. Hoffmann, "The Sandman," in *Tales of Hoffmann* (London: Penguin, 1982); Villiers de L'Isle Adam, *L'Eve Future* (Paris, 1922). Hadaly is the robot in *L'Eve Future*.

28. See Frank Whitford, *Oscar Kokoschka: A Life* (New York: Atheneum, 1986); Peter Webb, *Hans Bellmer* (New York: Quartet Books, 1985); and *Hans Bellmer, Photographe*, Center Georges Pompidou catalogue (Paris, 1983).

29. Raymond Bellour, "Ideal Hadaly," *Camera Obscura* 15 (Fall 1986). Annette Michelson, "On the Eve of the Future: The Reasonable Facsimile and the Philosophical Toy," *October* 29 (1984), reprinted in *October: The First Decade 1976–1986*, ed. Annette Michelson et al. (Cambridge: MIT Press, 1987).

30. Fritz Lang, *Metropolis* (London: Lorimer, 1973). See also Fritz Lang, *Metropolis: Images d'un Tournage* (Paris, 1985).

31. Andreas Huyssen, *After the Great Divide* (Bloomington: Indiana University Press, 1986).

32. Roger Dadoun, "Metropolis: Mother City—'Mittler'—Hitler," *Camera Ob-*

scura 15 (Fall 1986). Sigmund Freud, "The Uncanny," *Standard Edition*, vol. 27 (London: The Hogarth Press, 1955).

33. Patricia Mellencamp, "Oedipus and the Robot in *Metropolis*," *Enclitic* 5, no. 1 (Spring 1981).

34. Rudolf Carnap, "The Elimination of Metaphysics."

35. El Lissitsky, "The Electrical-Mechanical Spectacle," *Form* 3 (1966). See also "Americanism in European Architecture," in Sophie Lissitsky-Küppers, *El Lissitsky* (London: Thames and Hudson, 1968).

36. Walter Benjamin, "The Work of Art in the Age of Mechanical Reproduction," in *Illuminations*, trans. Harry Zohn (New York: Schocken, 1968). See also Susan Buck-Morse, *The Origin of Negative Dialectics* (New York: Macmillan, 1977).

37. Walter Benjamin, "Surrealism," in *One Way Street* (London: New Left Books, 1979).

38. Walter Benjamin, "The Author as Producer," in *Reflections*, ed. Peter Demetz (New York: Harcourt, Brace, Jovanovich, 1978). See also Louis Aragon, *Paris Paysan* (London: 1971).

39. Bertolt Brecht, Afterword to *Mahagonny*. Brecht's liking for logical positivism did not please Benjamin. For how they avoided a quarrel on this subject, see Benjamin, "Conversations with Brecht," in *Reflections*.

40. Walter Benjamin, "On Some Motifs in Baudelaire," in *Illuminations*.

41. Benjamin, "The Work of Art in the Age of Mechanical Reproduction."

42. According to Céline, the doctor at Highland Park "confided to us that what they really wanted was chimpanzees." See Louis-Ferdinand Céline, "La Medecine chez Ford," *Oeuvres Complètes*, vol. 1 (Paris, 1962).

43. Ilya Ehrenburg, *The Life of the Automobile* (New York: Urizen Books, 1976).

44. Benjamin, "On Some Motifs in Baudelaire."

45. Bertolt Brecht, Notes on the *Threepenny Opera*.

46. Huxley's negative attitude towards "stability" parallels Gramsci's positive attitude to "equilibrium."

47. Brecht, Afterword to *Mahagonny*.

48. For Huxley's own observation of American Indian ceremonies, see Sybille Bedford, *Aldous Huxley* (London: Chatto and Windus, 1973).

49. Siegfried Kracauer, "The Mass Ornament," *New German Critique* 5 (Spring 1975).

50. Kracauer was mistaken in thinking that the Tiller Girls were an American troupe. They were in fact English. See Derek and Julia Parker, *The Natural History of the Chorus Girl* (Indianapolis: Bobbs-Merrill, 1975).

51. Siegfried Kracauer, "Girls und Krise," *Frankfurter Zeitung* 27 (May 1931). See also Patrice Petro, "Modernity and Mass Culture in Weimar," *New German Critique* 40 (Winter 1987); and Sabine Hake, "Girls and Crisis: The Other Side of Diversion," in the same issue, which also contains Miriam Hansen, "Benjamin, Cinema and Experience." These three articles are indispensable contributions to these debates.

52. See Andrew Hodges, *Alan Turing: The Enigma of Intelligence* (New York: Simon and Schuster, 1983).

53. Kracauer, "The Mass Ornament."

54. Walter Benjamin, "Theses on the Philosophy of History," in *Illuminations*.

55. See Rothschild, *Paradise Lost*.

56. Vance Packard, *The Waste Makers* (New York: D. McKay, 1960). See also Stephen Bayley, *Sex, Drink and Fast Cars* (New York: Pantheon, 1986).

57. See Aglietta, *A Theory of Capitalist Regulation*, and Lipietz, *Mirages and Miracles*.

58. Marshall McLuhan, *The Gutenberg Galaxy* (London: Routledge and Kegan

Paul, 1962) and *Understanding Media* (London: Routledge and Kegan Paul, 1964). See also Jonathan Miller, *McLuhan* (New York: Viking, 1971).

59. George Boole, *The Mathematical Analysis of Logic* (Oxford: Blackwell, 1948). Boole was the first to produce a workable calculus of logic on the model of algebra. He is thus the founder of modern symbolic logic.

60. For Heidegger's comment on "the electronic brain" as the irresistible outcome of logic, see Martin Heidegger, *What Is Called Thinking* (New York: Harper and Row, 1968).

THREE

On Kiri Te Kanawa, Judy Garland, and the Culture Industry

Geoffrey Nowell-Smith

The idea for the book I am now writing crystallized in my mind one evening a couple of years ago. I had idly switched on the TV and found myself watching the end of a concert from the Royal Festival Hall on BBC 2. The performer was the soprano Dame Kiri Te Kanawa, and she was just launching into an encore—an arrangement, in classical mode, of the Martin and Blane song "Have Yourself a Merry Little Christmas" from the MGM musical *Meet Me in St. Louis.* Her voice was rich and pure, with a controlled vibrato, and she sang the song straight, with no ironic inflections, occasionally raising her eyes to heaven to express tender emotion. The Festival Hall was filled to capacity, and the audience was loving it. I found it grotesque.

Watching it, my mind was inevitably drawn back to a memory of the film, directed by Vincente Minnelli in 1944, where the song is sung by Judy Garland in a dramatic context filled with desperate pathos. It is near Christmastime, 1903, in the city of St. Louis, in the run-up to the World's Fair. The father of the Smith family has rather whimsically decided, in order to further his career, to decamp to New York taking his reluctant family with him. This, therefore, will be the last Christmas the family will spend together in the house in St. Louis where the children have all grown up together. It is against this background that the second of the four Smith daughters, Esther (Judy Garland), sings to her youngest sister, Tootie (Margaret O'Brien), about a Christmas that they won't actually have because the looming shadow of the move to New York will make it a sad, nostalgic occasion, very different from the good cheer evoked by the words of the song.

To check my memory, I went out and got a video. In the film, the song is sung over four shots—a two-shot of Esther and Tootie, a close-up of Esther singing, a close-up of Tootie listening, and a return to the setup of the two-shot. These shots are not isolated from the action of the film. The opening two-shot starts by concluding some dialogue about how Tootie can take all her toys to New York but not her snow people; the background music changes from "The First Noel" to a new tune which has been adumbrated on the soundtrack but not heard properly before, and then Judy/Esther starts to sing, winding Tootie's musical box the while. Only in the next shot, the close-up of Esther, is the audience offered the simple spectacle of someone singing, because the shot after that reaffirms the dramatic context by showing Tootie listening intently, with a single tear running down her cheek. Then in the fourth shot, Esther finishes her song and almost immediately Tootie turns round and moves toward camera. This shot is then beautifully matched on action to one showing her running from the room. Esther follows—we are now on shot six—and then (shot seven) we see Tootie beating off the heads of her snow people with a walking stick. The musical number is thus totally integrated into a drama which it barely interrupts. It provides a deceptive moment of calm before the amazing—and to me still very frightening, however many times I watch it—explosion of violence when Tootie decapitates the snow statues. As for the singing, it has tremendous power and restraint; nothing is forced. There is pathos, irony, variety, all balanced to the needs of the narrative. What conceivable value, I asked myself, can there be in tearing this song out of its context and putting it on an artistic pedestal?

My immediate temptation, on comparing the film and concert versions, was to launch into a tirade against the insipid decadence of so-called high culture, in contrast to the vitality of popular forms, of which the MGM musical is one. This is one of my favorite tirades, and my friends are stoically tolerant of it. But the more I thought about it the less appropriate it seemed as a reaction. For a start, it seemed wrong to compare a good example of one mode with a poor example of another. More importantly, I was not sure that the examples were indeed from opposite modes. It is not actually obvious that the MGM musical is, in a simple and uncontroversial way, a "popular" form, whereas what classical musicians call a popsicle would belong, however undeservedly, with "high" art. The high versus popular contrast, as I have argued elsewhere,[1] is misleading at the best of times, but particularly so in a case like this, where we are dealing with two different ways of reaching a large, middlebrow audience, separated by forty years and two distinct cultural histories on opposite sides of the Atlantic Ocean.

What the contrast in singing styles exemplifies, it seemed to me, is not so much the opposition of two cultures as a set of differences between two culture-producing apparatuses. There is a place for the opposition high/popular culture within this set, but it is not a determining one. If a single factor could be isolated as determining, it would have to be the technology—though not the technology in a pure state, but as applied within the overall apparatus.

Let us go back to consider the differences between the Garland and Te

Kanawa versions of the song. First of all, the intensity: Te Kanawa is a belter. She has been expensively and elaborately trained to produce maximum decibels with minimum distortion (in hi-fi jargon), in order to be heard at great distances in large auditoria. The democracy of the nineteenth-century opera house or concert hall dictated that the singer's voice had to be audible to all, though of course it sounded better from the more expensive seats. Audible, too, does not mean comprehensible. To obtain power, singers like to produce an uninterrupted stream of sound; consonantal blocks which impede the flow tend to get swallowed up. Except in the singing of lieder and art songs, where there is a focus on the words, classical singing turns the human voice, or rather the human body, into a musical instrument, producing sound rather than speech. It is the relation of the body to sheer sound that gives operatic, and in some cases sacred, music its erotic charge.

The microphone and associated technologies add little to operatic and concert-hall performance. If anything, they diminish it. Recording has not been without its effect, economic in particular, on classical music, and it is worth recalling that the first ever "golden disc" was of Enrico Caruso singing "Vesti la giubba" from Leoncavallo's *I pagliacci*. But a record of Caruso is no more than precisely that—a record, a piece of evidence that this man once sang that song. Opera lives in live, unassisted performance alone. Recording loses the sensual thrill, and adds nothing else except perhaps a chance to study the otherwise incomprehensible words from a text while listening.

By contrast, British and American popular song in the first half of the twentieth century were very dependent on the way words were delivered. Unlike operatic and concert music, popular song asks to be understood. Its verbal content as well as its sound is addressed—though in different ways and to different degrees—to a listening audience. Furthermore, it adapted to recording and amplification. Recording and amplification gave a boost to styles that didn't need trained technique and didn't need to be belted out. Singers and their instrumental or orchestral backing could be rebalanced so that the singer did not have to strain to produce sound and could be listened to without effort in a variety of circumstances. In particular it enabled intimate vocal and performance styles to be projected in nonintimate surroundings or carried over from, say, a nightclub ambience to that of domestic listening. This was not a sudden or overnight revolution. Early recording techniques, both acoustic and, when it came, electric were inflexible, and such flexibility as they had was not immediately exploited. It took time, experiment, and cautious adaptation to circumstance before records and sound tracks emancipated themselves from their origin as registration of preexisting sound and became methods of production as well as reproduction.

At least until 1950, the transformations brought about by recording and amplification were more radical in the cinema than in broadcasting and the music industry. Discs, radio, and even early television were mainly a matter of taking sound from one presentational context—concert, music hall, honky-tonk, nightclub, ringside—and representing them in a smaller, more domestic one, while the impact of amplification on live music was not really felt until the arrival of rock 'n' roll. The cinema was really the first place where electric sound was applied on a large scale and where different types and sources of sound had to be merged for presentation in a public space. Unlike records, music for the cinema had to be scaled up as well as down and adapted to visual scale changes as well as other aspects of film narrative.

When Judy Garland performs "Have Yourself . . . " in *Meet Me in St. Louis,* she is not singing live to camera. In line with regular practice for musical numbers, she is predubbed and miming to her own recorded voice. There is a barely noticeable disparity between how she looks to be singing—almost conversationally—and the sound of her voice, which is more powerful than the lip movements and facial expression suggest. How this disparity is experienced depends on the circumstances of viewing. On a video her voice comes across as implausibly strong. In the cinema—and of course the film was made for the cinema, though it is rarely shown theatrically any more—the strength of the voice seems natural: it is a voice pitched at the level needed to fill the theater, and as such has its own rightness. The contradiction between the diegetic (dramatic) setting—a child's bedroom—and the reception context can be expected to pass unnoticed in the way other implausibilities of scale (effects of shot changes for example) normally do when the audience is absorbed in a dramatic narrative.

Although it may pass unnoticed, as part of the general cinematic illusion, the extra intensity of the singing is in fact necessary—necessary precisely to the maintenance of the illusion itself. For the audience has to be held, simultaneously, to speech and to song. Speech flows into song, and then out again as the drama is resumed. The transition must be imperceptible; but once the song is fully entered into, it is a *song* that the audience is listening to, and the mode, temporarily, is lyric rather than dramatic. Or rather it is both lyric and dramatic, since the drama—Esther comforting Tootie and Tootie listening and not being comforted—is not suspended but held in check. The imperceptible transition from speech to song, and from dramatic to lyric, is a hallmark of the fully developed film musical and the MGM musical in particular. Minnelli is probably the greatest exponent of these transitions and he, together with Fred Astaire, Gene Kelly, and Stanley Donen, can also share the credit for a parallel achievement in creating smooth transitions from ordinary body movement into dance. It is also, we may note in passing, very much of a piece with the rest of Hollywood cinematic practice (with "invisible" editing, for example) and has as its direct opposite the theatrical practice of Brecht, who regarded smooth transitions into song from "sober speech" (*nüchterne Rede*) as anathema to the canons of epic theater.

Judy Garland's performance of the song, and indeed throughout the film, is quite extraordinary, and it is intended as no disparagement to point out that it is, of course, not autonomous. Its terms are given for it by the apparatus she was employed to serve. The apparatus in question is, on one level, that of the film industry, which was by 1944 heavily integrated into American industry and finance capital as a whole. On another level it is the institution "entertainment," which is an ideological construct uniting the consumption of culture-industry products such as movies with various other, less industrialized activities such as music-making or watching and playing games. The trend throughout the twentieth century, however, has been a steady encroachment of capitalism into these areas of life so that even the most self-active forms of entertainment involve the consumption of products emanating from what are now called leisure industries, of which the cinema is a part.

In the case which concerns us here (relatively primitive by today's standards) the point of conjunction between capitalist industry and the ideological concept of entertainment is provided by Metro-Goldwyn-Mayer and specifically by its musicals. For it was MGM more than any other film studio which most clearly articulated entertainment as an artistic goal (and source of profit).[2] MGM, however, must not be thought of just as a producer, making films for general public delectation. It was a part of a vertically integrated combine, which both produced, distributed, and exhibited films. The combine's films were made in the first instance for the combine's theaters. In capitalist economic terms (i.e., levels of investment and profitability and consequent management decisions) it can be said that the purpose of MGM (the production arm) was to fill the theaters owned and run by Loew's (the exhibition arm) and to do so by producing films whose distinctive appeal would bring patrons back into Loew's theaters rather than those of the rival chains. The MGM studio style was at least in part a function of Loew's need for a brand-name product to retail. In the studio logo preceding each film, the circle with the motto "ars gratia artis" is propaganda for how the studio wished to be seen; the power lies with the lion—*Löwe*, or Loew—erupting from inside the circle.

The hallmarks of the MGM studio style have often been remarked on: the visibility of production values, expressed most notably through the art direction; the flamboyant use of color (MGM originally had its own color process, but eventually bowed to the supremacy of Technicolor, which it exploited with particular zeal); certain conservative, cultured, and middle-class values, with a deliberate admixture of popular and folk elements. With the move from operetta to the musical proper, MGM made it clear that it was not in the business of passing on high culture's reach-me-downs. It sought rather to give refinement to the popular.

So let us now ask the question "What's a nice girl like you doing in a place like that?" Or: "What is a classical and operatic singer like Kiri Te Kanawa, who made her reputation on Mozart and Mahler and sang in St. Paul's Cathedral for the wedding of the Prince and Princess of Wales, doing with a musical comedy number, and singing it as if it were a concert aria by Handel?"

The answer relates on the one hand to the singer's personal profile and on the other hand to the operations of television. A quick look at the record catalogs establishes that this particular singer has recorded a number of albums from the pop and sub-classical repertory, including one called "Kiri Sings Gershwin" and an operatic version alongside José Carreras of Leonard Bernstein's *West Side Story* conducted by the composer himself. "Have Yourself a Merry Little Christmas" is a simple addition to an already full repertory of songs which adapt easily to concert treatment, and in which concert treatment covers up for an absence of subtlety in the style, an absence which could not be concealed if the singer was dealing with something from the classical repertory proper or, on the other hand, if the singing style was not classical but popular.

On the other side, what is visible is an operation by British public television to reconcile cultural service with the need to achieve viable ratings. Popular concert music has always had very large radio audiences in Britain, where it has profited, along with other forms of music, from advances in sound technology; and it is now getting large audiences on the BBC's second television channel, even though sound quality on TV remains poor. In the early days, and at least until the 1950s, the BBC used to distinguish between "serious" music—i.e., music which called for attentive listening and included jazz as well as classical—and "light" music, which was distinguished from the serious kind by being less demanding and belonged in the category of entertainment.[3] This distinction no longer operates. Music is now more of a continuum, and almost all types of music are represented on both radio and television, though the most demanding forms of twentieth-century music are relegated to a single radio channel (Radio 3, formerly known as the Third Programme). The BBC is, however, very heavily committed, economically as well as ideologically, to the popularity of "serious" music. If the paternalistic ethos of giving people what is good for them no longer reigns supreme, it remains the case that the rationale for the present structure is dependent on there being sizable audiences for music other than the most easily consumable pop. This involves a complex negotiation of various categories of taste and a considerable investment in the popularization of forms of music whose popularity cannot be taken for granted. This investment, regarded by its critics as a nonproductive vestige of the paternalist ethos, has proved very effective, and advances in TV and video technology, such as the introduction of stereo sound and HDTV, can only serve to confirm its effectivity further.

Watching Kiri Te Kanawa on BBC 2, therefore, in anonymous company with a million or so other people, was an experience of the operation of the culture industry in very much the same way as watching Judy Garland in *Meet Me in St. Louis*. Behind the performance stands a high level of industrial investment: investment in the show, in the machinery of reproduction, in the institution, in the profile of the artist. The difference lies in the effect the investment is designed to produce. Put in the crudest terms, Judy is marketed as Nature, Kiri is marketed as Art. In the case of Judy Garland (and of the MGM product in general) Nature is, of course, transfigured, while in that of Kiri Te Kanawa (and arguably of many BBC products) Art is to a certain extent debased. But in each case we are dealing with a "product"—a song performance—which has taken shape within an industrial complex to serve the ends of that complex.

"Movies and radio," wrote Theodor Adorno and Max Horkheimer forty years ago, "need no longer pretend to be art. The truth that they are just business is made into an ideology in order to justify the rubbish they deliberately produce."[4] Unfortunately the truth is more complicated. Movies, radio, and now television, do indeed pretend to be art, and this is often the most deceptive thing they do, bombarding audiences with products which fetishize the signifiers of artisticness. The word for this fetishism is *Kitsch*.

At the same time, what the culture industries produce is by no means always rubbish. They also produce art, and often do so precisely under the banner of business. Where Adorno and Horkheimer were right, however, was in detecting a *tendency* in the development of the culture industry which, if unopposed, could easily reduce artistic production to the level of commodity production in general. Where they were wrong was in not seeing that this leveling tendency was no more than that—a tendency within the development of capitalist production which was subject to the operation of many countervailing factors both within and without the capitalist mode of production itself.

The "tendential law" on which Adorno and Horkheimer based their dystopian predictions involves two main assumptions about the operation of capitalist economies. The first is that these economies tend to expand— either into further corners of the globe or into different areas of social and economic life. The second is that this expansion can be made profitable in a systematic way. Capitalists always seek the maximum rate of profit, but, since they are all seeking it at the same time and in the same market, they end up settling for an average rate of profit, with some nudging ahead and some falling behind. For an expansion into culture to be achieved, the culture industry must provide a rate of return across the board comparable to that of other branches of industry.

The growth of the film and music industries in the twenties and thirties is a classic case of these assumptions being partially verified. Industrial and finance capital advanced into areas which were previously organized in a preindustrial manner. They attempted to impose as far as possible the textbook rules of commodity production and exchange. Corporations competed with each other in the classic manner, sometimes by undercutting each other in the market, sometimes (as with MGM) adopting strategies of nonprice competitiveness—that is, offering a better, or at least distinctive, product for the same price. These capitalistic operations succeeded in creating an industry where none previously existed and in producing returns on capital sufficient to satisfy major investors.

But there were always limits to the success of these operations. There were limits to the ways products could be standardized and profits equalized. Capitalists found themselves competing for a resource which was neither abundant nor scarce but seemingly aleatory—talent. Of course plenty of examples can be cited, from the music industry in particular, of talentless "artists" producing standardized performances which reaped comfortable and secure profits for their backers. But the general rule was that there was no rule. It was in the nature of the product, and the popular demand for it, that the requisite talent could not be produced to order. In the desperate search for distinctiveness of product, the laws of average costs and average profits went out of the window. Stars, in particular, could not be mechanically produced nor, if they came into being, controlled. They were expensive, unpredictable, rebellious, creating a level of risk for their employers which would not be acceptable in other branches of industry.

Nor could the public be controlled. However much the industry tried to standardize, to offer new films or new songs which were different from but similar to the old so that customers could reliably be sold predictable modifications of a standard product, the formulas never satisfied for long. Since the fifties, profits have only been maintained by gambling on a slate of products. Film and record companies (and book publishers too) sign up a number of projects and individual artists in the hope that one at least will produce a hit. For the rate of profit to be maintained, this hit has to outweigh losses made elsewhere on the slate.

The difficulty of guaranteeing profits by ordinary managerial methods means that the culture industry has to grant large measures of autonomy to independent entrepreneurs and even to artists—an autonomy that is unusual even in the most flexible companies in other branches of capitalism. It also has to be sensitive to fluctuations of taste and to the workings of a taste-forming machine which it does not itself control. Of course the industry would like to control the machine, and has attempted to do so since the beginning of the century, when film companies hit on the idea of publishing magazines to review their own productions. But attempts to control the market have only ever been partially successful. The industry therefore has to chase the market and bow to the demands, not just of popular taste but of those parts of the taste-forming machine, which represent more traditional criteria of what is good and what is not.

From this derives an irony, which is that the culture industry can often be happier with art—or what passes for art—than with items of acknowledged junk culture like game shows and pop singles. The virtues claimed for art, such as permanence, are also those that appeal to investors, particularly if a deal can be struck whereby private or state patrons pay for innovation and experiment, while publishing, video, and record companies collect the profits on safe investment. The division, typical of the middle half of the century, between a popular culture which was increasingly industrialized, and a "high" culture which clung to a preindustrial independence, has now broken down. High culture artifacts may still be produced in preindustrial ways—with oil paints or violins rather than computer graphics or synthesizers—but their reproduction is industrial, through records, videos, process photography, and lithoprinting. In a way this is a throwback to the early days of the culture industry—to "Vesti la giubba," indeed. What is new is that it is not new, but now, seventy years on, takes the form of a repackaging of the old: old masters retouched with the airbrush. The conservative critique of the culture industry—and some "left" critique as well—has focused on the way it has marginalized art and displaced it with commercial pap. This critique seems to me misplaced. Living art may well be marginal, thriving only in the interstices of society untouched by the culture industry. But what has replaced it in the mainstream is not just the novelty of popular culture. All too often, the replacement for living art is dead art. Not art produced by artists who are now dead, for there is nothing wrong with that; but art which is a simulacrum of itself. I do not think the culture industry can be accused of killing art: but it can be blamed for embalming the corpse.

Notes

1. Geoffrey Nowell-Smith, "Popular Culture," *New Formations* 2 (Summer 1987), pp. 79–90.
2. One can think forward to *The Band Wagon* (1953), also directed by Vincente Minnelli, and in particular the song "That's Entertainment" featured in the film, and to the subsequent withdrawal of MGM from film production, the release of the compilation *That's Entertainment* as film and record album, etc.

3. See Simon Frith, "The Pleasures of the Hearth—The Making of BBC Light Entertainment," originally in *Formations of Pleasure* (London: Routledge and Kegan Paul, 1983), reprinted in *Music for Pleasure* (Cambridge: Polity Press, 1988), pp. 24–44.

4. Theodor Adorno and Max Horkheimer, "The Culture Industry: Enlightenment as Mass Deception," in *Dialectic of Enlightenment* (New York: Herder and Herder, 1972; translation of *Dialektik der Aufklärung*, first published in German in 1947). If I am not mistaken, the book was actually written in 1944—the year that *Meet Me in St. Louis* was made.

FOUR

Hollywood in the Home:
TV and the End of the Studio System

Christopher Anderson

The transformation of the American motion picture industry following World War II has been perceived as a rupture, a crisis so grave that it forced the major studios to abandon or adulterate many of the practices that had constituted the Hollywood studio system since the industry's shift to sound films in the late 1920s. For those who worked within the film industry, the decade of the 1950s frequently has been depicted as the decline and fall of an empire, a time of confusion in New York boardrooms and panic on Hollywood backlots. Screenwriter Robert Ardrey has described a lunch-room scene in the exclusive Green Room at the Warner Bros. commissary during this era. Fresh from examining the latest sagging box-office figures, Jack Warner, an elegantly suntanned autocrat, burst into the dining room, screaming and jabbing at contract writers and producers as they ate their lunches. "I can do without you! And you! And you! I can do without you!" he exclaimed as he strode defiantly among the tables. Suddenly face to face with Jerry Wald, by far the studio's most successful producer, Warner paused for an instant and then shouted, "I can *almost* do without you!"[1]

While such tales of temporary madness are probably apocryphal, they have fascinated fans, scholars, and even those who participated in the events. When formerly powerful industry leaders such as Darryl Zanuck, Louis B. Mayer, and David O. Selznick were displaced during the industrial reorganization of the 1950s, they saw their enforced exile in epic terms, as a barbaric attack on Hollywood's glorious tradition. Selznick, in a letter to his friend and former partner, John Hay Whitney, depicted the 1950s as the movie industry's dark ages: "Our old stomping ground, what is laughingly known as the motion picture industry, is very mixed up and unhappy. Whatever the weakness of the old and rugged pioneers, who are all disappearing from the scene almost simultaneously—what a hardy race they were!—their successors are pygmies by comparison. There is no leadership; all is chaos. . . . "[2] Until recently, this epic version of Hollywood's fall has been accepted and perpetuated even by media scholars. In his history of

American broadcasting, for instance, Erik Barnouw echoes Selznick's sentiment by characterizing 1950s Hollywood as "Panicsville." Film historian Robert Sklar goes further; he not only describes the film industry's "crisis" and "collapse" during the 1950s, but actually pronounces the death of Hollywood, a death which he dramatically attributes to suicide.[3]

Frequently, television played the primary antagonist in the mythic version of Hollywood's postwar transformation. Tales of Jack Warner's early animosity toward television are legendary. Studio personnel claim that during the early fifties Warner delivered a stern edict to producers working on motion pictures at Warner Bros., forbidding television sets from the decor of Warners films.[4] From our vantage point in a world saturated by television, it's hard to believe that a TV set could trigger such desperate measures from one of Hollywood's most venerable movie moguls, yet Warner's animosity toward the industry's competitor was not a sentiment that he alone felt. Throughout this period, industry trade papers debated whether television would ultimately reveal itself as friend or foe of the movie studios.[5] As television charged toward its unprecedented expansion following World War II, revenues throughout the motion picture industry plunged dramatically. Warner Bros. suffered among the worst losses, with net profits falling from a record $22 million in 1947 to $2.9 million in 1953— a decrease of nearly 90 percent in just six years.[6] Although television was not the sole cause of this decline, one can appreciate Jack Warner's reported hostility toward a medium that threatened to displace the motion picture as the preeminent cultural commodity in twentieth-century America.

Beginning in the late 1940s, however, many independent producers and smaller studios embraced the opportunity to produce films for television.[7] Long excluded from the lucrative profits guaranteed by the major studios' restrictive system of distribution and exhibition, independent telefilm producers viewed TV as an open market, a new exhibition outlet beyond the stifling grasp of the major studios. Although the future of the telefilm business was far from certain during the early 1950s, the atmosphere of opportunity among Hollywood's independent producers was similar to that of the film industry's earliest days, before the major studios dominated the business. Independent TV production companies were formed by a varied cast of entrepreneurs: emigrés from the major studios (Jerry Fairbanks), former B-movie makers (Hal Roach, Jr.), radio syndicators (F. W. Ziv), talent agencies (MCA), real-estate investors (Lou Snader), oilmen (Jack Wrather), and, most prominently, actors (Bing Crosby, Jack Webb, Lucille Ball and Desi Arnaz). In 1951, Ball and Arnaz's Desilu Productions delivered the first telefilm series to have a national impact, the situation comedy *I Love Lucy*. Webb's Mark VII Productions followed later that season with the first successful crime series shot on film, *Dragnet*. Within a year *I Love Lucy* and *Dragnet* stood atop the network ratings as the most popular series on television.

By mid-decade even old-guard Hollywood leaders launched themselves into television production. The month of October 1954 stands out as a key transitional moment for Hollywood's major powers and their relations with the television industry. Early in the month, Columbia Pictures became the first major studio to produce episodic TV series when its television subsidiary, Screen Gems, premiered *The Adventures of Rin Tin Tin* on ABC and *Father Knows Best* on CBS. Within three days in late October, two of the film industry's top independent producers, David O. Selznick and Walt Disney, joined the movement into network television. Selznick made Hollywood's most auspicious debut with a two-hour celebration of electricity and American enterprise titled *Light's Diamond Jubilee*. Sponsored by the electrical industry, this program capped a yearlong celebration of Thomas Edison's "invention" of the incandescent light bulb seventy-five years earlier. On the night of 24 October, regular viewers of NBC's *Colgate Comedy Hour*, CBS's *Toast of the Town*, ABC's *Flight #7*, and the beleaguered DuMont network's *Rocky King, Detective*, found their favorite programs preempted. No matter where viewers flipped their dials, they couldn't escape Selznick's extravaganza, which was broadcast on virtually every existing TV station. In a year in which television viewers found themselves deluged by so-called "spectacular,"one-of-a-kind programming, *Light's Diamond Jubilee* was still unique. Selznick, the movie industry's most famous independent producer, a man whose name had become virtually synonymous with Hollywood spectacle after blockbusters like *Gone with the Wind* (1939), *Rebecca* (1940), and *Duel in the Sun* (1946), made his initial foray into network television surrounded by such impressive talent as directors King Vidor and William Wellman, writer Ben Hecht, actors Joseph Cotten, Helen Hayes, Thomas Mitchell, Lauren Bacall, and David Niven, and an unlikely performer in a commercial broadcast, President Dwight D. Eisenhower.

Selznick's venture may have caused the biggest splash, but Disney's premiere was no less eagerly anticipated. Disney had garnered a reputation as the maestro of family entertainment. His series, *Disneyland*, promised not only to deliver what *Time* described as "the true touch of enchantment" to American homes, but also to allow viewers to witness the embodiment of "Walt's dream," the Disneyland amusement park. In its review of the week's TV fare, *Time* recognized that the productions by Selznick and Disney could be considered milestones in the relations between movies and television. "The two best TV shows of last week—and perhaps of this year," the magazine reported, "originated in Hollywood and were created by veteran moviemakers."[8] Inspired by Disney's successful TV series, Warner Bros., Twentieth Century–Fox, and MGM initiated television production during the 1955 season.

The emergence of Hollywood's most acclaimed independent producers and major studios as suppliers of TV programming exemplifies one of the most significant trends in the transformation of the Hollywood studio system: the convergence of the motion picture and television industries during the 1950s. In turn, the integration of these media points toward more general corporate trends that have given shape to the contemporary film and television industries and to American popular culture since World War II. Diversification into related fields, the consolidation of capital through corporate mergers, technological developments, and advanced marketing techniques have led to the increased interpenetration of media industries and media texts in an age of digital reproduction and multinational conglomerates. Clearly, the motion picture industry experienced changes during the 1950s, but to depict this transformation as an era of chaos or the demise of the studio system, or to view it in isolation from developments in such related fields as recording, publishing, advertising, or broadcasting, obscures more important issues. How and why does an established mode of cultural production like the Hollywood studio system undergo change? What relation do the economic practices and narrative strategies established in the studio system have to those of television and the "New Hollywood" that has developed since media conglomerates gained control of the motion picture industry? How do cultural institutions, such as those of the movie and television industries, interact in practice? How has this interaction affected the texts produced by these media and the social relations that the media make possible?

To answer these questions, we should begin by noting that although the motion picture industry experienced changes during the 1950s, these weren't necessarily the seismic shifts described in the epic accounts of the industry's demise. A number of converging forces propelled the industry into its postwar slump: the 1948 consent decree that ordered the major studios to divest their theater chains, heightened competition for the public's leisure and entertainment spending, demographic shifts in postwar American society, restricted foreign markets, and increased production costs in the industry.[9] By the mid-1950s, the studio system as a mode of production largely had given way to independent production. As one consequence of the structural change in the production and financing of theatrical feature films that occurred after World War II, the major studios adjusted their corporate strategies to create highly differentiated feature films that were financed, produced, and distributed individually. Meanwhile, the studios phased out the standardized production of the moderate-to low-budget, formulaic films that had sustained the industry by providing a dependable means for meeting the fixed expense of studio overhead and the screen-time demands of exhibitors. With the rise of television, however, the studios discovered a new rationale for their standardized productions—supplying television programs to the major networks. By shifting their mass production efforts into series television, a number of the major Hollywood studios were able to capitalize on *aspects* of the studio system even as the system itself changed.[10]

Considering that all of the major studios entered the field of television production by the late 1950s, therefore, it comes as a surprise to realize just how fully most historians have neglected interaction between the film and broadcasting industries. Film historians pay scant attention to television production by the major studios. Broadcast historians discriminate against the rise of the telefilm industry by privileging the so-called "Golden Age" of television, the period dominated by live programming produced in New York. In these terms, the development of the filmed television series marked the ultimate commodification of television narrative, the origin of TV's headlong plunge into the mediocrity of the 1960s' "Vast Wasteland."[11] The assumption that the "Golden Age," with its prestigious anthology dramas and live comedies, somehow represented television's early, unfulfilled promise has dominated writing about 1950s TV programming. This vision of paradise lost fails to recognize, however, that "Golden Age" programming represented less the potential future of network television than the dying gasps of residual cultural practices held over from network radio, vaudeville, and the legitimate theater. At its best, as Laurence Bergreen has remarked, the "Golden Age" was really just "a charmed interval before the networks became truly national."[12]

Still, as far as the majority of scholars and critics are concerned, the filmed television series that replaced live prime-time programming are mostly disreputable cultural products without hope of critical redemption. During an era in which critics like Dwight Macdonald denounced most expressions of "mass" culture as parasitic, cancerous growths threatening the vitality of "authentic" culture, a program like *Cheyenne*, with its aesthetic ambitions tempered by a demand for regular, thundering gunfights, stood little chance of passing muster among the arbiters of taste. In the intervening years, this widespread aesthetic judgment, more than any other factor, has accounted for the scholarly neglect of the telefilm series. Restricted by the meager budgets that advertising revenue could support during the television networks' first decade of national broadcasting, these series displayed production values that made Hollywood's most impoverished B-movies look extravagant by comparison. Indeed, early telefilm series were bargain-basement knockoffs of the movie industry's cheapest productions. These series copied the most common and least esteemed action genres—westerns, crime, science fiction, exotic adventures—or adopted radio series formats like the situation comedy. Although early telefilm series introduced narrative strategies and production practices that still characterize much of prime-time television, they have received a critical and scholarly neglect equal to that of B-movies, but without offering the B-movie's potential for recuperation by auteurist critics. With only a few exceptions, the critical discourse surrounding 1950s filmed TV series treats them either as kitsch or as the spontaneous eruption of concerns circulating throughout the era's culture.

Although dozens of books are devoted to the movie studios, Hollywood television production companies active before 1970 have merited only one published history—a monograph that accompanied the Museum of Broadcasting's 1986 retrospective for Columbia's TV subsidiary, Screen Gems.[13] The other major telefilm producers of the 1950s and 1960s—Warner Bros., MGM, Twentieth Century–Fox's TCF-TV, MCA's Revue, Four Star, Desilu, and Ziv—exist as terra incognita for media scholars. During the past decade, however, a number of scholars have paved the way for the study of telefilm production by examining the role of the motion picture industry— the corporations, trade organizations, and unions—in the convergence of the movie and television industries. Initially, this convergence was depicted according to a master narrative, a classical three-act structure which charts the film industry's initial disdain for television, followed by open antagonism after TV's early success, concluding with the industry's final resolution to adapt to the demands of television. One early article succinctly represents this narrative structure, with its movement from conflict to resolution, as a tale of "complacency, competition, cooperation."[14]

More recently, though, historians have demonstrated that this influential master narrative contradicts many of the events in the interaction of the two media. It assumes that the motion picture and television industries were initially separate, autonomous economic structures that merged only after a protracted period of competition. It also suggests that there was a rational, linear progression to this convergence, in which the movie industry survived by finally submitting to the demands of a competitive medium and a new economic order. In contrast, recent historians have demonstrated that the motion picture and broadcasting industries have maintained a symbiotic relationship not only since the 1950s, but since the founding of national broadcast radio networks during the late 1920s. While the form of these interactions has been conditioned by shifting relations of social and economic power, motion pictures and the broadcast media have been interlocked economically and textually for decades during which media scholars have maintained them as conceptually distinct categories.[15]

Indeed, one could say that the general public—as well as industry practice—recognized the interpenetration of these media long before media scholars. Will Rogers, the top-ranked box-office star of the early 1930s, was also one of radio's most prominent performers. Similarly, director Cecil B. DeMille's period of greatest box-office success coincided with his appearance as the host of *Lux Radio Theater* beginning in 1936. From 1935 until 1957, every film directed by DeMille appeared among the ten top-grossing films of its year.[16] In his memoirs, DeMille recalled the radio show as "the experience which brought me closer to the American people than anything else I have ever done." By offering Hollywood's most popular stars in condensed audio adaptations of contemporary feature films, *Lux Radio Theater* developed into one of the greatest promotional devices ever imagined by any studio's marketing department, a program that attracted thirty million moviegoing listeners each week. DeMille, always one of the industry's great showmen, relished the seeming ubiquity of a nationally broadcast program:

> I liked the big [ratings] numbers but what the Lux program meant to me cannot be measured by any numbers. It meant families in Maine and Kansas and Idaho finishing the dishes or the schoolwork or the evening chores in time to gather around their radios. It meant the shut-ins, the invalid, the blind, the very young, and the very old who had no other taste of the theater. It meant people, not in the masses, but individuals, who did me the honor of inviting me into their homes; people for whom I was no longer a name filtered through the wordage of press agents, but a person whom they knew.[17]

Lost in reverie over the prospect of Hollywood crossing the threshold into the American home, DeMille failed to mention that the Lux radio program transformed him into a highly marketable commodity recognized by millions of Americans—and not merely by the poor invalids imprisoned in their homes and unable to attend DeMille films, but also by the millions of ambulatory Americans eager to march to the box office and purchase a ticket for the latest DeMille feature. DeMille's signature statement, "This is Cecil B. DeMille saying goodnight to you from Hollywood," virtually identified the director with everything represented by the word "Hollywood," transforming his name into a trademark that was tantamount to the very notion of the Hollywood director.[18]

At the height of network radio in the 1940s, Hollywood celebrities appeared regularly on their own programs or on those like *Lux Radio Theater* designed to promote feature films. Bob Hope and Bing Crosby consistently dominated the rankings of movie and radio stars. It is no coincidence that Hope, Crosby, and DeMille all were under contract to Paramount, the studio most committed to establishing economic ties with the broadcasting industry. Together, the films of these radio celebrities accounted for two-thirds of Paramount's top-grossing films during the 1940s, the studio's most profitable decade during the studio era.[19] These figures alone suggest that if scholars had ever attempted systematically to account for the popularity of the American cinema during the studio era, it would have been difficult to overlook the relations between motion pictures and broadcasting for so long. Unlike media scholars, audiences have never been shackled to a single medium.

One explanation for this oversight by scholars is that these media have been defined too narrowly. Instead of being viewed as related sets of practices, motion pictures and broadcasting have been depicted as economic structures, as modes of production and distribution, or as immanently defined groups of texts. Such definitions construct these media as manageable, closed systems, but they obscure the convergence of historical conditions and material practices that constitute commercial motion pictures and broadcasting in the United States. In cinema studies, for example, most historical and critical research has focused primarily on feature films and feature film production. Until recently, the related activities of the major studios (promotional practices, exhibition practices, financial diversification) and the related texts produced by the studios (cartoons, newsreels, short subjects, serials, promotional films, industrial films) were treated solely as context, as miscellany. It was frequently through these subsidiary practices, however, that the studio system intersected with related media and with other social institutions.[20]

If relations between the motion picture and broadcasting industries have been depicted as openly antagonistic, it is due in part to the fact that American movies frequently have lobbed satirical bombshells at television, especially during the period when relations between the media were taking shape. Emerging from Hollywood's tradition of liberalism, the cinema's critique of television first appeared in 1950s satires like *It's Always Fair Weather* (1955), *A Face in the Crowd* (1957), and *Will Success Spoil Rock Hunter?* (1957), and continues to the present with films like *Nashville* (1975), *Network* (1977), and *Robocop* (1987). In its surprisingly elitist echoes of the 1950s "mass culture" debate, this relatively consistent representation of television seems more a product of the Frankfurt School than Tinsel Town. Television, as depicted in these films, is a merchant of false consciousness, a medium irredeemably compromised by its devotion to advertising. Television is an electronic medicine show whose obsession with the commodification of art and experience has corrupted and undermined traditional moral and aesthetic values. In effect, these values are identified with the cinema by the very fact that motion pictures have the ability to reveal television's corrosive influence on them.

The films mentioned above construct a position of moral superiority for the cinema by representing the medium's epistemological superiority over television. A virtual meditation on commercial culture, *Nashville* provides a particularly clear example of this process. As Colin MacCabe has noted, one of the organizing discourses in *Nashville* can be described as "cinema's ability to make visible what is invisible to television." Through a variety of narrative strategies, the film "constantly insists on the opposition between the knowledgeable position we occupy as viewer in the cinema compared with the ignorance of the television audience."[21] Running throughout the films mentioned above, this discourse implies that television's inferiority to motion pictures results not from inherent technological differences between the media, but because television's commercialism leaves it without access to the "real"—unmediated, authentic social experience. Television has been seduced and distracted by the alluring image of commodities. Consequently, the television spectator is identified with the passive consumer whose identity exists only in response to commodities.

Such high-minded rejection of commercial broadcasting began in the movie industry during the days of radio. David O. Selznick, for example, was eager to use commercial radio when it could benefit his organization, but he hoped to maintain a respectable distance from the medium's image of blatant hucksterism. For Selznick, the advertising industry's fascination with the superficial was a constant source of cynical amusement. In 1938, while Selznick was courting Orson Welles, he wrote a letter of congratulations to the Campbell Soup Company, sponsor of *Campbell's Playhouse*, a radio program on which Welles regularly performed and directed. In response to Selznick's kind words, Campbell executive J. E. McLaughlin concluded his letter with a plug that reinforced Selznick's disdain for advertisers. "Naturally, it is our hope," McLaughlin wrote, "that you enjoy Campbell's Soup in your home just as much as you enjoy the *Campbell's Playhouse* programs and we assure you we shall continue to exert every effort to [earn] your approval for both." Appalled by the crassness of the plug, and by its reminder of the true spirit of commercial radio, Selznick circulated the letter among his staff, saying that it would "have a special place in my files" and adding sardonically, "Have you tried Campbell's chicken soup with noodles? The rich, warm flavor makes one think of Orson Welles."[22]

Selznick's response actually provides a superb insight into the movie industry's frequent discursive efforts to argue its superiority over broadcasting. Selznick's ironic transposition—in which Welles's identity is sublimated within the product he endorses—raises an important question about the relationship between the programs that fill a broadcast schedule and the advertisements that provide the economic basis of commercial broadcasting. At the time, radio advertising exploited a distinction between the spheres of art and commerce in which the aesthetic or expressive function of broadcasting appeared to have primacy over the commercial. Broadcast industry discourse argued, therefore, that the consumer purchased the advertised product due to what Erik Barnouw describes as the " 'gratitude factor'—the osmosis of affection and trust from the program to the product."[23] Within this conception, the advertisements themselves existed in a parasitical relationship to the "host" program. As Selznick recognized, however, commercial broadcasting's insistent emphasis on the commodity form actually signifies that commerce takes precedence over the aesthetic function. Programs provide a suitable context for advertising, not vice versa. While the medium's aesthetic function is never entirely erased by its commercial function, program and product interweave to construct a mutual identification that is impossible to unravel. Therefore, while an impressive Orson Welles radio program may lead a consumer to purchase

Campbell's Soup, a can of Campbell's Soup also serves as a metonymic representation of Welles's artistic identity. This tendency toward blurring the distinction between the program and the advertised products was supported by textual practices during the radio era in which "integrated" advertisements were woven into the narrative and listeners were encouraged explicitly to identify performers with a sponsor's product. Introducing himself weekly as Bob "Pepsodent" Hope, for instance, radio's most popular comedian became the personification of his sponsor's product, "a walking Pepsodent commercial."[24]

Obviously, the Hollywood studios were involved in an equally commercial enterprise, but the industry denied its commercial function by implying that, in contrast to broadcasting, the cinema existed in an autonomous sphere outside the corrupting influence of the marketplace. This ideological fantasy is best expressed by MGM's famous slogan, *ars gratia artis*. Along with the studio's unmistakable roaring lion, MGM's assertion of artistic autonomy served as the trademark for the aesthetic commodity that MGM marketed—feature films that carried the connotation of aesthetic quality. The irony of an entertainment corporation advancing the doctrine of art for art's sake is absurdly obvious. As Theodor Adorno has noted, however, the disavowal of commercial impulses recurs throughout modern mass culture:

> Vestiges of the aesthetic claiming to be something autonomous, a world unto itself, remain even within the most trivial product of mass culture. In fact, the present rigid division of art into autonomous and commercial aspects is itself largely a function of commercialization. It was hardly accidental that the slogan *l'art pour l'art* was coined in the Paris of the first half of the nineteenth century, when literature really became large-scale business for the first time.[25]

Thus, the studios attempted to locate their products within an autonomous aesthetic sphere, in part, as a marketing strategy designed to differentiate their product from that of a competing industry. This practice continued even after the major studios began to produce television programming, because the studios still hoped to construct a different exchange value for their theatrical and television product.

The motion picture industry's argument for its superiority over broadcasting was never entirely coherent because the industry could never comfortably deny that it also marketed a commodity. Yet the industry actually constructed another marker of its difference from broadcasting by emphasizing that, while cinematic texts were commercial products, they were at least uncompromised by *external* commercial discourses. This argument acknowledges that the motion picture is a commodity, but suggests that at least the medium is not a vehicle for marketing other commodities. In a sense, the motion picture industry imagined the cinematic text as being intransitive—bounded, complete, closed to external commercial discourses; while the broadcasting text is transitive—little more than a delivery service for greedy advertisers. Taken together, the motion picture industry's contradictory efforts to argue the autonomy and superiority of the cinema obscure three important factors: first, motion pictures never have been entirely free of "extraneous" commercial discourses; second, since the rise of commercial broadcasting, the motion picture industry never has been autonomous from the broadcasting industry; and third, the movie industry always has exploited broadcasting's commercial imperatives for its own promotional purposes.

In his article "The Carole Lombard in Macy's Window," Charles Eckert traces the simultaneous rise of consumer culture and the commercial cinema during the early decades of the twentieth century. Far from existing in an autonomous aesthetic sphere, argues Eckert, the development of the American cinema during the studio era can only be understood "in terms of the almost incestuous hegemony that characterized Hollywood's relations with vast reaches of the American economy by the mid-1930s." Indeed, cinematic narrative quickly assumed a central role in encouraging the commodity fetishism that serves as a basis for consumer society. Eckert explains:

> When the first movie cameraman shot the first street scene that included a shop sign or a labeled product . . . all of the elements of a new advertising form were implicit. . . . The short dramas and comedies of the first decade of this century, especially those that pictured the contemporary lifestyles of the middle and upper classes, presented innumerable opportunities for product and brand-name tie-ins. But more than this, they functioned as living display windows for all that they contained; windows that were occupied by marvelous mannequins and swathed in a fetish-inducing ambiance of music and emotion.[26]

Mary Ann Doane has extended Eckert's "display window" metaphor to suggest the extent to which the cinema's claim to aesthetic autonomy was a fiction. "The film frame functions, in this context," she argues, "not as a 'window on the world' as in the Bazinian formulation, but as a quite specific kind of window—a shop window."[27]

The motion picture industry had the opportunity to exploit the cinema's capacity for showcasing products by becoming an advertiser-supported medium and producing explicitly sponsored films. Warner Bros. tested the idea in the early 1930s when its short-subject division produced "sponsored moving pictures" such as *On the Slopes of the Andes* for the A & P grocery chain and *Graduation Day in Bugland* for Listerine. Although Warners had contracts to produce a dozen other films, exhibitors pressured the studio to cancel its plans.[28] This conflict between the studio and exhibitors established a recurring pattern in the movie industry's relations with advertisers and broadcasters. Although the studios were eager to generate revenue in any manner possible, exhibitors wanted to differentiate their product from commercial broadcasting and, therefore, resisted the presence of advertising in movie theaters. Thus, it was generally exhibitor pressure, and not a moral position, that kept the cinema from becoming, at least in part, a commercial advertising medium.

In place of explicitly sponsored films that might unleash exhibitor anger, Warner Bros. and other studios established a more sublimated form of advertising that still exists in the industry. According to Eckert,

> the keystone of this method was a contractual agreement with a large established manufacturer. If the product would seem blatantly displayed if shown in a film—a bottle of Coca Cola, for instance—the contract provided merely for a magazine and newspaper campaign that would employ pictures and endorsements of stars. . . . There were other products, however, that could be prominently displayed in films without arousing criticism, except from the knowledgeable. Warners' tie-up with General Electric and General Motors provided both for the use of Warners' stars in magazine advertisements and for the display of the appliances and autos in films.[29]

Eckert describes two primary strategies through which the cinema promoted consumption of related products—showcasing products within films and exploiting promotional "tie-ups" through print and radio advertising—both of which introduce external commercial discourses into the seemingly closed cinema narrative. Warner Bros. soon institutionalized these practices by organizing a special department to facilitate interaction with commercial sponsors. From these examples, it becomes clear that Hollywood studios had established extensive relationships with advertisers and had proven their willingness to allow external commercial discourses into their apparently autonomous narratives long before they began producing specifically for television. Hollywood's commercial messages may have been less explicit than those of broadcasting, but they were no less influential in the rise of American consumer culture.

The motion picture industry's presentation of products within its narratives and adoption of commercial tie-ups provides an early example of the convergence between movies and related media. As this relationship blurred the boundaries between narrative and advertising discourses, it aimed to promote an ideology in which the consumption of commodities is centered primarily in the home and the institution of the family. The impulse of manufacturers and advertisers to cultivate the home as the primary arena of consumption also led Hollywood into the American home via the domestic medium of television. Indeed, Laura Mulvey argues that the cultural shift from the public exhibition of movies to the domestic reception of television during the 1950s coincides with "the triumph of the home as point of consumption in the capitalist circulation of commodities."[30] Measuring the significance of this development for American culture, Nick Browne writes, "The commercial development of television in the post–World War II years as a mechanism for reaching into the household represents a singularly significant moment in the development of the American economy and culture. Through television, American business has represented, penetrated, and constructed the family with an eye to its aptitude for consumption and moved to complete its organization of the libidinal economy of the desiring and consuming subject."[31] While Browne's formulation overestimates both the coherence and the influence of marketing strategies aimed at the family in the 1950s, he is correct in suggesting that television provided the crucial link in the postwar reconfiguration of American political, economic, social, and cultural institutions.

After deciding to enter television production, the motion picture industry invested in the discursive construction of television as a domestic medium. In announcing Warner Bros.'s decision to produce television programming, for instance, Harry Warner took great pains to distinguish the Warner TV product from its theatrical features. He did not make distinctions over their relative budgets, production values, narrative strategies, or stars; instead, he emphasized the divergent social functions of the two media. Warners TV, he proclaimed, would emphasize the educational aspects of television which "can accomplish social good that sound films have failed to accomplish. . . . In my opinion, proper programs can unite families— father, mother, children—at home, rather than separate them as the search for amusement and 'a good time' has done in the past."[32] It is both amusing and revealing that Harry Warner, a man who made his fortune with the motion picture, would immediately adopt the modern discourse of public and private spheres, imagining the new privatized medium of television as the entertaining savior of the American family, while figuring the motion picture and other public amusements as forces of corruption. Although Warner Bros. ultimately employed many strategies to differentiate studio features and TV programs, this statement suggests that Edward Buscombe is correct when he writes that "the consequences for television of the enormous ideological and economic investment in the construction of the family and domestic life during the latter part of the 20th century can scarcely be overestimated."[33]

From the example of Cecil B. DeMille's radio show to the emergence of TV production at Warners (and onward to the present era of cable and home video), the movie industry has sought through the electronic media to plant traces of Hollywood in the American home. Whether it meant displaying consumer goods in cinematic narratives, marketing ancillary products based on movie characters, promoting feature films through broadcasting, or exhibiting its own films and series on TV, the motion picture industry consistently has demonstrated an interest in colonizing the domestic sphere, a trend that Buscombe describes as "the privatization of consumption in general and of entertainment in particular."[34] By shifting into television production, therefore, the major studios participated in the most influential social and cultural trends of the postwar years, while reinforcing tendencies that the industry had always cultivated.

Walt Disney provided the model for the major studio's emergence in television production because he was the producer most adept at employing the changing conditions in the entertainment industry to construct and exploit the "family audience" around the axis of television. Although events leading up to 1955 had convinced executives of the major studios that television should be a necessary element in the industry's new economic strategies, no major studio took decisive steps until Disney's triumph in television during the 1954–1955 season. Indeed, more than any single event, Disney's success convinced the major studios that they could at last reap profits by introducing their product into the new medium. "I'm not sure just where the initiative started," Warner Bros. executive Benjamin Kalmenson later explained when recounting the origins of Warners TV, "but as a result of the success Mr. Disney was having with a feature motion picture called *20,000 Leagues under the Sea*, I personally felt that his ability to exploit his pictures on television was of great value, and began to wonder why we couldn't do likewise."[35] Disney's emergence in television set the terms for the initial interaction between the major studios and the networks, not only providing a precedent for the deals that Warner Bros., Twentieth Century–Fox, and MGM would negotiate during 1955, but also establishing a format for the programs that the studios initially would produce.

It was not the Disney television program itself, however, that fascinated the Hollywood studios. The revenue generated by the series was relatively insignificant, and the episodes themselves were little more than a collection of the B-films, short subjects, travelogues, and ephemera that the studios were purging from their production schedules. What made the major studio executives take notice was the unexpected boost that the program provided to the box-office returns for Disney features. While the major studios had been able to rationalize the production of motion pictures during the studio system, they had never been able to bring the same sort of predictability to the marketing of these pictures. They had never developed a system which could guarantee that the variety of promotional efforts used to exploit a film, communicated through a number of media, actually reached a film's entire potential audience. The emergence of national network radio, with a signal that penetrated both socioeconomic and geographic boundaries, had provided the most efficient means for promoting films. But Disney's video success story made it apparent that television, like radio before, had become a national medium by 1954. With the expanded audience it could become the most effective marketing device ever imagined by the movie industry.

The Disney studio was the first motion picture production company fully to appreciate the substantial opportunities made possible by the new broadcast medium's capabilities, the scope of its signal, the access it provided to the American home. Television served as the cornerstone on which Disney mounted a burgeoning postwar entertainment empire. By 1953, Walt Disney and his brother, Roy, had decided that the less restrictive industry conditions emerging from the 1948 Paramount decree, along with the rapid expansion of a new and affluent youth market, would provide a conducive environment for the growth of a restructured Disney company, an independent production firm transformed into a diversified, integrated communications organization. Beginning in 1953, the Disney corporation ceased production on its unprofitable cartoon short subjects, cut back on animated features, and shifted its production emphasis to live-action movies. In the two years that followed, Disney built the Disneyland amusement park, established its own distribution company, Buena Vista, enlarged its trademark merchandising concerns, and began producing the TV series, *Disneyland* and *The Mickey Mouse Club*.[36]

As Walt admitted, the Disney studio was "never much interested" in radio, but television, with its ability to display the visual appeal of Disney products, was another matter entirely. After having produced successful Christmas TV specials in 1950 and 1951—both designed to promote the release of feature films—Walt proposed in 1953 that his company make a television series for NBC.[37] Before the company would produce a television series, however, Walt insisted that the network purchase not only the series, but a one-third share in the studio's ambitious project, the Disneyland amusement park. The significance of this proposition should not be underestimated. In uniting the TV program and the amusement park, Disney made one of the most influential commercial decisions in postwar American culture. Building upon the lucrative character merchandising market that the Disney company had joined in the early 1930s, the company now intended to weave its products throughout the American mass media in a strategy of "total merchandising," spinning a vast commercial web that would enable the studio fully to capitalize on the 1950s expansion in the commodification of leisure. Television programs, movies, amusement parks, books, comic books, clothing, and toys—anything imprinted with the name of Disney—would combine to form a self-perpetuating system, a complete fusion of promotion and entertainment in which each Disney product—from *Snow White* to a ride on the Matterhorn—would advertise all Disney products. And television would serve as the beacon to draw the American public to the domain of Disney. "We wanted to start off running," Walt later recalled. "The [amusement park] investment was going to be too big to wait for a slow buildup. We needed terrific initial impact and television seemed the answer."[38]

Although NBC balked at the thought of investing in the amusement park business, ABC quickly jumped at the offer. Anxious to attract advertisers by acquiring more prestigious programming, the third-place network gambled on Disney, committing $2 million for a fifty-two-week series (with a seven-year renewal option) and purchasing a thirty-five percent share in the park for $500,000. Without even a prospective format for the series, ABC invoked the Disney reputation alone to sell the program under a joint-sponsorship package to American Motors, the American Dairy Association, and Derby Food. The twenty original episodes of the program were sold at $65,000 each; the network time was billed at $70,000 per hour. Once the network became competitive with NBC and CBS during the late 1950s, Leonard Goldenson consistently referred to this deal as the network's "turning point." Indeed, *Disneyland* attracted nearly half of the network's advertising billings during 1954, the final year during which the network operated at a loss.[39]

Examined closely, the program itself was a fascinating concoction. Although Walt Disney repeatedly assured the press that *Disneyland*, the TV series, would stand on its own terms as entertainment, the program functioned primarily as promotion for Disney products. As William Boddy has noted, *Disneyland* "was unprecedented in both the number of re-runs per season, the number of commercial breaks per hour, and the amount of each program devoted to direct promotion of Disney's feature films, comic books, trademark merchandise, and new amusement park."[40] The studio actually invested extremely little capital in the series. The contract with ABC called for only twenty original episodes, with each of these episodes repeated once, and twelve of them broadcast a third time during the summer. Instead of producing twenty episodes of new television programming, Disney used the deal as an opportunity to capitalize on products already amortized during previous theatrical releases. Still, the studio recognized that it would not turn a profit from its first year in television. There were production costs in preparing the theatrical product for television (editing for time restrictions to construct compilation episodes, filming Walt's introductory appearances) and in producing its limited amount of original programming. But these costs generally were defrayed throughout the studio's various operations. The three hour-long episodes of the Davy Crockett series, for instance, cost $600,000—over three times the industry standard for telefilm production—and yet, during that year alone, the cost was spread across two separate network broadcasts and a theatrical release. By employing up to eighty percent of the studio's production staff, the television operations also enabled the Disney studio to meet the overhead costs of remaining at full productivity. In addition, all costs not covered by the network's payments were charged to the studio's promotion budget.[41]

It has been claimed that one-fifth to one-third of each *Disneyland* episode was devoted directly to studio promotion, but in fact the entire series carefully blurred any distinction between promotion and entertainment.

Indeed, *Disneyland* capitalized on the unspoken recognition that the commercial broadcast media had dissolved the distinction between advertising and entertainment. *Disneyland*'s identification of the amusement park and the TV series, an analogy emphasized by the program's title, was confirmed when both the series and the park were divided into four familiar movie industry genres: Fantasyland (animated cartoons), Adventureland (action-adventure), Frontierland (western), and Tomorrowland (science fiction). The episodes broadcast within these categories were introduced by Walt himself, and generally consisted of truncated versions of Disney animated and live-action features (*Alice in Wonderland* [1951], *Treasure Island* [1950]), compilations of animated short subjects, the studio's True-Life Adventure series of dramatized nature films, or short films produced as outright promotions for Disney features. One such episode, "Operation Undersea," provided a behind-the-scenes glimpse at the making of *20,000 Leagues under the Sea* (1954) just one week before the film was released to theaters.[42] This episode was later followed by a True-Life Adventure, "Monsters of the Deep," which essentially served as another advertisement for the theatrical release. Although it is not generally remembered, during the first three years of *Disneyland*, the Disney studio produced only one narrative film made specifically for the series—the three-part Davy Crockett serial which took the nation by storm during that first season, delivering larger ratings each time it was aired.[43] Yet no one seemed concerned that *Disneyland* was pure Hollywood ballyhoo. During the show's initial season, viewers made *Disneyland* the first ABC program ever to finish among the season's ten top-rated programs.[44] Because the series delivered viewers like no program in ABC history, even the advertising industry didn't mind Disney's self-promotion. The trade magazine *Sponsor* applauded Disney's skills at blending entertainment and promotion, quoting an unnamed ABC executive who quipped, "Never before have so many people made so little objection to so much selling."[45] Through its Emmy awards, the television industry offered its own approval of Disney's venture, nominating Walt as TV's "Most Outstanding New Personality" and honoring the promotional film, "Operation Undersea," as TV's Best Documentary.[46]

For Hollywood's major studios, the most telling detail in the entire Disney phenomenon was the surprising performance of the studio's feature films. By releasing its features through its own distribution company, Buena Vista, and by timing the release dates to coincide with simultaneous promotion on the television program, Disney emerged as the top-grossing independent production company of 1955. Undoubtedly aided by its exposure on the TV series, *20,000 Leagues under the Sea* grossed $8 million—the largest sum ever reached by a Disney film. It finished the year as the industry's fourth highest-grossing film and became the first Disney film ever to crack the list of twenty all-time top-grossing films. In addition, Disney's new animated feature, *Lady and the Tramp*, pulled in $6.5 million—

the largest figure for any of Disney's animated films after a single release. Even its first feature-length True-Life Adventure Series production, *The Vanishing Prairie*, grossed a respectable $1.8 million. As though the box-office returns on these features alone weren't proof of TV's marketing potential, Disney edited together the three Davy Crockett episodes from the TV series and released them as a single feature during the summer of 1955, making another $2 million at the box office on a film that *Variety* accurately described as nothing more than a typical "program oater."[47] The Disney studio had tapped into a rich promotional vein by integrating its various activities around television and the family audience.

Perhaps the program's most significant accomplishment, however, was the fanatical interest it generated in the Disneyland amusement park. Without the growth of national network television and the privileged access it provided to the American family, Disney would not have gambled on the park. "I saw that if I was ever going to have my park," Disney explained, "here, at last, was a way to tell millions of people about it—with TV."[48] Disney needed television not simply to publicize the park, but to position it properly as a new type of suburban amusement, a bourgeois park designed to provide edifying thrills for baby-boom families instead of cheap thrills for the urban masses. To distinguish his park from such decaying relics as Luna Park and Coney Island, Disney assured the public that any amusement experienced in his park would be tempered by middle-class educational values. Disneyland wouldn't be another park trading in the temporal gratifications of the flesh, but a popular monument to human knowledge, a "permanent world's fair" built around familiar Disney characters and a number of unifying pro-social goals, including educating the public about history and science.[49] Just as it hooked American television viewers with the serialized story of Davy Crockett, the *Disneyland* series bound up its audience in the ongoing story of what came to be mythologized as "Walt's dream." With Walt as on-screen narrator, the series, in effect, narrated the construction of Disney's amusement park, making the project a matter of continued concern for the show's viewers by narrativizing the construction and certifying it as the crowning accomplishment of an American entrepreneurial genius in a league with Thomas Edison and Henry Ford. No less than three entire episodes, and portions of others, were devoted to the process of conceiving, building, and inaugurating the park. The premiere episode of the series was an introduction titled "The Disneyland Story." A later episode, "A Progress Report," updated the audience on the construction, while a concluding episode, broadcast after the series had been in re-runs for four months, enabled home viewers to experience the park's opening ceremonies (which were hosted by Disney and Ronald Reagan).[50]

By constructing a story around the events of the park's development, and by creating an analogy between the TV program and the park, the

Disney organization provided a narrative framework for the experience of Disneyland. Television made the entire Disney operation more enticing by fashioning it as a narrative experience which the family TV audience could enhance—and actually perform—by visiting the park. Here again Disney shrewdly perceived television's ability to link diverse cultural practices that intersected in the domestic sphere of the family. In effect, Walt identified the program with the park in order to create an inhabitable text, one that would never be complete for a television-viewing family until they had taken full advantage of the postwar boom in automobile travel and tourism to make a pilgrimage to the park itself. A trip to Disneyland offered the family viewer a chance to perform in the Disneyland narrative, to provide unity and closure through personal experience, to witness the "aura" to which television's reproductive apparatus only could allude. In a sense, Disney succeeded by exploiting the quest for authentic experience that has become central to the culture of modernity. In fact, tourism, as Dean MacCannell suggests, is based on the modern quest for authenticity, the belief that authentic experience exists somewhere outside the realm of daily experience in industrial society.[51] While Walter Benjamin predicted that mass reproduction would diminish the aura surrounding works of art, Disney seems to have recognized that the mass media instead could intensify the desire for authenticity by invoking a sublime, unmediated experience that is forever absent, just beyond the grasp. As a tourist attraction, Disneyland became the destination of an exotic journey anchored firmly by the family home, which served not only as the origin and terminus of the journey, but also as the site of the television set that would confirm the social meaning of the vacation experience. A father visiting the park expressed something of this sentiment. "Disneyland may be just another damned amusement park," he explained, "but to my kids it's the Taj Mahal, Niagara Falls, Sherwood Forest, and Davy Crockett all rolled into one. After years of sitting in front of the television set, the youngsters are sure it's a fairyland before they ever get there."[52] In the first six months alone, one million paying customers passed through the gates at Disneyland. After the first full year of operation the park had grossed $10 million, one-third of the corporation's revenue for the year, and more than any Disney feature had ever grossed during its initial release.[53]

Disney's concept of "total merchandising" clearly shaped the type of text which his company produced for television. Whereas traditional notions of textuality assume that a text is discrete, unified, and autonomous, with a centripetal structure that pulls the viewer inside, Disney's television texts were, from the outset, fragmented, propelled by a centrifugal force that guided the viewer away from the immediate experience toward a more comprehensive—and contradictory—sense of textuality, one that encouraged the consumption of further Disney texts, further Disney products, further Disney experiences. At its greatest extreme, Disney's notion of "total merchandising" encourages a type of "total textuality" in which the totalizing function of narrative, with its movement toward ideological closure, is displaced into a more comprehensive narrative of consumption. No single text can satisfy a viewer; no individual text feels sufficiently complete. At this point, when virtually every Disney text triggers the desire to consume other Disney texts and Disney products, the line that divides narrative and advertising is utterly erased. As I have suggested, however, the distinction between narrative and advertising was never entirely clear in the motion picture industry. By turning to television production, Disney merely exploited a tendency that had long existed in the industry, a desire to plant traces of Hollywood in the American home. In so doing, Disney provided the model of economic and textual integration that has characterized the development of the American media since the 1950s. When Hollywood's major studios turned to television production, they followed Disney's example, producing remarkably similar programs in the hope of exploiting television's promise as a promotional medium that provided access to the postwar family audience. For the motion picture industry, therefore, the shift to television production was less a moment of "crisis" and "panic" than the most significant stage in the process of consolidation that dissolved the distinctions between movies and television following World War II and produced what we now recognize as the integrated leisure industries that characterize the "New Hollywood."

Notes

1. Described in Erik Barnouw, *A History of American Broadcasting*, vol. 2 (New York: Oxford University Press, 1968),291.

2. David O. Selznick to John Hay Whitney, personal correspondence, 7 August 1958. David O. Selznick Archives, Harry Ransom Humanities Research Center, University of Texas, Austin, Texas. All further references to Selznick correspondence are from this source.

3. Barnouw, *History of American Broadcasting*, 290–92; Robert Sklar, *Movie-Made America* (New York: Vintage Books, 1975), 268, 283–86.

4. William T. Orr, personal interview, Beverly Hills, California, 28 October 1986. Other studios established similar rules. A 1949 memo at MGM reportedly prohibited mention of the word "television" in that studio's feature films. See "Hollywood in a Television Boom," *Broadcasting*, 26 October 1959, 88.

5. For a discussion of this debate, see Milton MacKaye, "The Big Brawl: Hollywood versus Television," *Saturday Evening Post*, 19 January 1952, 17–18; 26 January 1952, 30; 2 February 1952, 30.

6. Warner Bros. Pictures, Inc., *Annual Report*, 1947–1953, Warner Bros. Pictures Archives, Department of Special Collections, University Library, University of Southern California, Los Angeles, California.

7. See William Lafferty, " 'No Attempt at Artiness, Profundity, or Significance':

Fireside Theater and the Rise of Filmed Television Programming," *Cinema Journal* 27, no. 1 (Fall 1987): 23–46.

8. "The Week in Review," *Time*, 8 November 1954, 95.

9. For a discussion of this period in the film industry, see Tino Balio, ed., *The American Film Industry*, revised edition (Madison: University of Wisconsin Press, 1985), 401–38; Janet Staiger, "Individualism versus Collectivism," *Screen* 24, no. 4–5 (July-August 1983): 68–79.

10. Warner Bros., for example, maintained term contracts with actors, directors, producers, and technicians, continued regular studio operations, and guaranteed a steady supply of product that was financed, produced, and owned by the studio until the entire studio was sold in 1967.

11. See Ross Wetzsteon, "Get Television Out of Hollywood," *Channels of Communication*, September-October 1981, 41–45.

12. Laurence Bergreen, *Look Now, Pay Later: The Rise of Network Broadcasting* (New York: Mentor Books, 1980), 194.

13. *Columbia Pictures Television: The Studio and the Creative Process* (New York: Museum of Broadcasting, 1987).

14. Lawrence L. Murray, "Complacency, Competition, Cooperation: The Film Industry Responds to the Challenge of Television," *Journal of Popular Film* 6, no. 1 (1977): 47–68.

15. For example, see William Boddy, "The Studios Move into Prime Time: Hollywood and the Television Industry in the 1950s," *Cinema Journal* 24, no. 4 (Summer 1985): 23–37; Edward Buscombe, "Thinking It Differently: Television and the Film Industry, *Quarterly Review of Film Studies* 9, no. 3 (Summer 1984): 196–203; Douglas Gomery, "Failed Opportunities: The Integration of the Motion Picture and TV Industries," *Quarterly Review of Film Studies* 9, no. 3 (Summer 1984): 219–28; Richard B. Jewell, "Hollywood and Radio: Competition and Partnership in the '30s," *Historical Journal of Film, Radio and Television* 4, no. 2 (1984): 125–41; and Robert Vianello, "The Rise of the Telefilm and the Networks' Hegemony over the Motion Picture Industry," *Quarterly Review of Film Studies* 9, no. 3 (Summer 1984): 204–18.

16. Douglas Gomery, *The Hollywood Studio System* (New York: St. Martin's Press, 1986), 42.

17. Cecil B. DeMille, *The Autobiography of Cecil B. DeMille* (Edgewood Cliffs, N.J.: Prentice-Hall, 1959), 347.

18. For a more extensive description of the program, see Bernard Lucich, "*The Lux Radio Theater*," in *American Broadcasting: A Sourcebook on the History of Radio and Television*, ed. Lawrence W. Lichty and Malachi C. Topping (New York: Hastings House, 1975), 391–94.

19. Gomery, *The Hollywood Studio System*, 42–44. For a discussion of Paramount's early ties to the broadcasting industry, see Jonathon Buchsbaum, "Zukor Buys Protection: The Paramount Stock Purchases of 1929," *Cine-Tracts* 2 (Summer/Fall 1979): 49–62.

20. By ignoring until recently the connections between film and television, film scholars have participated in the cultural construction of the cinema's superiority to television and have contributed to the general dismissal of television as a disreputable cultural form. Considering that film studies itself has only emerged from the stigma of cultural disreputability within the past two decades, this blindness is difficult to explain, but it has frequently mirrored the discourse used by the media industries.

21. Colin MacCabe, "The Discursive and the Ideological in Film: Notes on the Conditions of Political Intervention," *Screen* 19, no. 4 (Winter 1978–1979): 38, 37.

22. David O. Selznick to John Hay Whitney and Katherine Brown, personal correspondence, 4 January 1939. So astonished was Selznick that he told Welles of the letter at the celebration welcoming Welles to Hollywood, later mailing him a copy as proof. Welles sent a jovial note in response: "I am appalled . . . at the enclosed communication received by you from my clients, the makers of Campbell's soups, and promise faithfully to boycott both tomato and chicken gumbo, from this time forth. I trust you will join me in this." Orson Welles to David O. Selznick, personal correspondence, 2 August 1939; David O. Selznick to Orson Welles, personal correspondence, 5 August 1939.

23. Erik Barnouw, *The Sponsor: Notes on a Modern Potentate* (New York: Oxford University Press, 1978), 47.

24. Bergreen, *Look Now, Pay Later*, 66. Radio soap operas often quite ingeniously blurred the distinction between the narrative and the commercial message. See Robert C. Allen, *Speaking of Soap Operas* (Chapel Hill, N.C.: University of North Carolina Press, 1985), 112–14, 161. It should be noted also that in early television variety series the commercials were often presented as musical production numbers that were integrated into the program.

25. Theodor W. Adorno, "Television and the Patterns of Mass Culture," in *Mass Culture: The Popular Arts in America*, ed. Bernard Rosenberg and David Manning White (New York: The Free Press, 1957), 474–75.

26. Charles Eckert, "The Carole Lombard in Macy's Window," *Quarterly Review of Film Studies* 3, no. 1 (Winter 1978): 4.

27. Mary Ann Doane, *The Desire to Desire: The Woman's Film of the 1940s* (Bloomington: Indiana University Press, 1987), 24. Jane Gaines inverts the metaphor to analyze the relationship between shop windows, motion pictures, and consumer culture. See "The Queen Christina Tie-Ups: Convergence of Show Window and Screen," *Quarterly Review of Film & Video* 11, no. 1 (1989): 35–60.

28. Eckert, "Carole Lombard," 11–13.

29. Ibid., 14–15.

30. Laura Mulvey, "Melodrama In and Out of the Home," in *High Theory/Low Culture: Analyzing Popular Television and Film*, ed. Colin MacCabe (New York: St. Martin's Press, 1986), 98.

31. Nick Browne, "The Political Economy of the Television (Super) Text," in *Television: The Critical View*, fourth edition, ed. Horace Newcomb (New York: Oxford University Press, 1987), 597.

32. Thomas F. Brady, "New Hollywood Enterprise," *New York Times*, 9 January 1949, 11, 5.

33. Buscombe, "Thinking It Differently," 201.

34. Ibid.

35. Benjamin Kalmenson, Testimony, United States v. 20th Century–Fox, et al., 31 October 1955. Warner Bros. Pictures Archives, Theater Collection, Firestone Library, Princeton University, Princeton, New Jersey.

36. John McDonald, "Now the Bankers Come to Disney," *Fortune*, May 1966, 141, 224; Richard Shickel, *The Disney Version* (New York: Simon and Schuster, 1968), 308–16; "Disney's Live-Action Profits," *Business Week*, 24 July 1965, 78.

37. Frank Orme, "Disney: 'How Old Is a Child?' " *Television*, December 1954, 37; "Disney 'Not Yet Ready' For TV," *Variety*, 23 May 1951, 5; "Disney's 7-Year ABC-TV Deal," *Variety*, 21 February 1954, 41.

38. "The Wide World of Walt Disney," *Newsweek*, 31 December 1962, 49–51; "The Mouse that Turned to Gold," *Business Week*, 9 July 1955, 74. The origins of Disney's character merchandising are described in "The Mighty Mouse," *Time*, 25 October

1948, 96–98. For a more detailed discussion of the Disney corporation's use of character merchandising in relation to other TV producers of the early 1950s, see "He'll Double as a Top-Notch Salesman," *Business Week*, 21 March 1953, 43–44.

39. "The abc of ABC," *Forbes*, 15 June 1959, 17; Spencer Klan, "ABC-Paramount Moves In," *Fortune*, April 1957, 242; Albert R. Kroeger, "Miracle Worker of West 66th Street," *Television*, February 1961, 66; "Corporate Health, Gains in Radio-TV Theme of AB-UPT Stockholders Meeting," *Broadcasting–Telecasting*, 21 May 1956, 64; Frank Orme, "TV's Most Important Show," *Television*, June 1955, 32.

40. Boddy, "The Studios Move into Prime Time," 31–32.

41. Orme, "How Old Is a Child?" 37, 72.

42. Critics within both the movie and television industries referred sarcastically to this episode as "The Long, Long Trailer." See "A Wonderful World: Growing Impact of the Disney Art," *Newsweek*, 18 April 1955, 62–63.

43. "Disneyland Repeats Getting Bigger Audiences than First Time Around," *Variety*, 20 April 1955, 32. A complete filmography of Disney television programs through 1967 appears in Leonard Maltin, *The Disney Films*, second edition (New York: Crown Publishers, 1984), 321–26. For an examination of the Disneyland-inspired Davy Crockett phenomenon that swept through American culture beginning in 1954, see Margaret Jane King, *The Davy Crockett Craze: A Case Study in Popular Culture*, Ph.D. dissertation, University of Hawaii, 1976.

44. Tim Brooks and Earle Marsh, *The Complete Directory to Prime Time Network TV Shows*, third edition (New York: Ballantine Books, 1985), 1031. Disneyland remained among the top fifteen programs through 1957, and then fell from the top twenty until it shifted to NBC—and color broadcasts—in 1961.

45. Charles Sinclair, "Should Hollywood Get It for Free?" *Sponsor*, 8 August 1955, 102.

46. Maltin, *The Disney Films*, 315.

47. "Disney Parlays Romp Home," *Variety*, 30 November 1955, 3; "All-Time Top Grossing Films," *Variety*, 4 January 1956, 84. At the time, *20,000 Leagues under the Sea* was the nineteenth highest-grossing film of all time.

48. Schickel, *The Disney Version*, 313.

49. "Father Goose," *Time*, 27 December 1954, 42; "Tinker Bell, Mary Poppins, Cold Cash," *Newsweek*, 12 July 1965, 74.

50. For an account of the opening ceremonies, see Bob Chandler, "Disneyland As 2-Headed Child of TV & Hollywood Shoots for $18 Mil B.O.," *Variety*, 20 July 1955, 2. Chandler observes that the inauguration of Disneyland marked the "integration and interdependence of all phases of show biz."

51. Dean MacCannell, *The Tourist: A New Theory of the Leisure Class* (New York: Schocken Books, 1976), 159.

52. "How To Make a Buck," *Time*, 29 July 1957, 76.

53. Schickel, *The Disney Version*, 316.

FIVE

Popular Discrimination

John Fiske

Films such as *Ishtar* with major stars, huge budgets, and expensive marketing still fail at the box office. Four out of five new prime time TV shows,
carefully researched and expensively produced, will be axed before the end
of the season, despite their so-called captive audience. Eight or nine out
of ten new products, however heavily advertised, fail in the marketplace
in their first year, and twelve out of thirteen pop records fail to make a
profit. The ability of the people to discriminate between the products of
capitalism, particularly those of its culture industries, should never be
underestimated.

Yet academia has, until comparatively recently, consistently underestimated and ignored this complex process that plays so central a role in
our contemporary society and its culture. Indeed, implicitly if not directly,
popular culture has been denied discriminatory ability, for the concept of
critical discrimination has been applied exclusively to high culture in its
constant effort to establish its superiority over and difference from mass
or popular culture. In the line of thought that can be traced from Coleridge
through Matthew Arnold to T. S. Eliot, F. R. Leavis, and most recently
Alan Bloom, the ability to discriminate is the one quality that best distinguishes "the cultured" from the "uncultured"—whether these be, in
Arnold's terms, the Philistines (the new materialist middle class of trades-
people and industrialists) or the Barbarians (the decaying, degenerate aris-
tocracy) or the Populace—the new working class who had *no* culture and
were thus a potential source of anarchy and social disintegration. The concept of critical discrimination has always contained, however repressed, a
dimension of social discrimination.

What I wish to do in this essay is sketch in some of the criteria and
processes by which discrimination operates in popular culture. Popular
culture in our society is made by the various formations of the people at
the interface between the products of capitalism and everyday life. But the
products of capitalism always exceed the needs of the people, so popular
discrimination begins with the choice of which products to use in the production of popular culture and then passes on to the imaginative linking

of the meanings and pleasure produced from them with the conditions of everyday life. The two key characteristics of popular discrimination are, therefore, those of relevance and productivity and, even though we may separate them for analytical purposes, in practice they are almost indistinguishable.

Popular discrimination is thus quite different from the critical discrimination valued so highly by the educated bourgeoisie and institutionalized so effectively in the academic critical industry. The major difference is that between productivity and relevance on the one hand and quality and aesthetics on the other. Raymond Williams relates the increasing importance of aesthetics in the nineteenth century to the growth of industrialism with both its materialist values and its new, and potentially terrifying, urban working class.[1] Aestheticism, therefore, became a weapon in the class struggle, for it functioned to distinguish the cultured, fine sensibility from the rest. These cultured sensibilities were found almost exclusively among the educated fractions of the high bourgeoisie and the "culture" they enabled their owners to appreciate was that of their class and gender, particularly the Graeco-Roman and European "great tradition" in literature, music, and the visual arts. What aestheticism did was to universalize these social tastes into ahistorical, asocial values of beauty and harmony, and to construct from them an artificial set of universals that claimed to express the finest, best, and most moral elements of the human condition: the taste of the high bourgeois white male was universalized into the essence of humanity—a major ideological prize for any class to win! The function of critical discrimination, then, was to mask the social under the aesthetic, so that aesthetic "quality" became a hidden marker of the social quality of those who could appreciate it.

Popular discrimination's concern with relevance, then, separates it clearly from the universals of critical discrimination, for relevance is the interconnections between a text and the immediate social situation of its readers—it is therefore socially and historically specific and will change as a text moves through the social structure or through history. Ien Ang has shown for instance, how Dutch Marxists and feminists find in *Dallas* meanings and pleasures that are relevant to them: they can, and do, read its representations of the excesses of patriarchy and capitalism as critical of both.[2] So, too, Australian Aboriginals living a tribal life in the center of the continent made Rambo one of their most popular heroes, but read the major conflict in the movies not as that between the democratic, humanitarian West and the totalitarian, inhuman Communist bloc, but that between Rambo as a member of the racially subordinate and the white officer class—a set of meanings that were clearly relevant to their social situation of having to deal with a white bureaucracy whose paternalism they saw as hostile, not benevolent. George Lipsitz shows how New Orleans blacks in the audience of traveling Wild West shows at the end of the nineteenth century made the shows relevant to their situation by reading them not as accounts of the march of progress and civilization but as stories of genocide and racial imperialism.[3] They formed affective allegiances with the plight of the American Indians which eventually led to their forming the black Indian tribes that play such a highly visible role in the Mardi Gras festivities and a less public, but still important, role in New Orleans black culture in general. This finding is interestingly paralleled in a contemporary setting by Robert Hodge and David Tripp who found that young urban Aboriginals in Australia watching old westerns on Saturday morning television allied themselves imaginatively with the Indians against the whites as they perceived relevance between the Indians' social relationships to whites and to the land, and their own.[4]

A friend of mine returning from South America told me of the popularity of *Miami Vice* there because of the pleasures of its representations of Hispanics enjoying wealth and power in the United States. These pleasures far outweighed the narrative positioning of those Hispanics as villainous drug dealers who ultimately fall to the heroes Crockett and Tubbs. Indeed, it is quite possible that their status of villains enhanced their relevance, insofar as it could function as a concrete metaphor for Latin America's sense of how its nations are regarded by the United States. In popular culture, social relevance is far more powerful than textual structure.

This points to another difference between the aesthetic and the popular—the popular is functional. Aestheticism distances art from necessity in a way that parallels the freedom of the monied classes from economic necessity. The antimaterialism of aesthetics means that the artwork it appreciates is seen as self-contained. It is completed, finished, and contains within itself all that is necessary to appreciate it: the work of art awaits only the cultured sensibility that has the key to unlock its intricate secrets. So, as Pierre Bourdieu argues, to ask of an aesthetic object "What is it *for?*" or "What use is it?" amounts almost to sacrilege, for this suggests that it needs to be *used* in order to be completed.[5] But proletarian tastes are for artworks that are functional—they serve as reminders of holidays, or family histories, or they help one make sense of, and thus cope with, one's subordination in society. J. D'Acci's study of *Cagney and Lacey* fans revealed, for example, a common pattern: fans found (different) ways that the show helped them to understand their experiences as women in male-dominated institutions—particularly work places and schools—and for some this understanding led to more assertive ways of behaving within and against such subordination.[6] David Halle's study of the paintings hanging in the homes of different classes in and around New York gives us further examples of popular functionalism and bourgeois aesthetic distance.[7] In both upper-middle- and working-class (mainly Polish and Italian) homes, the most common genre was landscape. But the landscapes in the working-class homes were either painted by family members or friends, or were of the homeland—they were relevantly connected to people's lives and served as reminders of family membership and histories. The landscapes in the upper-middle-class homes, however, bore no relationship to family origin: they were, in order of frequency, of Japan, England, and Europe and were chosen by aesthetic criteria rather than those of relevance or function.

This functionalism of art, like its relevance, works to pluralize the meanings, pleasures, and uses of the text, for it must serve different functions for different socially situated readers. Indeed, functionalism and relevance are directly related—for an artwork can only be useful if it is relevant, and one of the criteria of its relevance is its potential function. Popular taste, then, is for polysemic texts that are open to a variety of readings. This polysemy is different from that of aestheticism, for it is not organized into a textured, multilayered organic unity of meaningfulness, but is rather a resource bank from which different, possibly widely divergent, readings can be made. This means that there can be no hierarchy of readings, for there is no universal set of criteria by which to judge that one reading is better (i.e., more insightful, richer, closer to the artist's intention, or ultimately more correct) than another. Thus in popular discrimination the critic cannot play his or her traditional role of guardian and revealer of the true meanings of the text, for, as the birth of the cinema caused Walter Benjamin to remark, in popular art everyone is his or her own expert.[8] So David Bordwell shows that film reviews in bourgeois publications are likely to include some interpretation of the film's meaning, but interpretation is shunned in reviews in the popular press, which concentrate rather on the pleasures and sensations the film may offer.[9]

The role of the academic critic of popular culture is social as much as, if not more than, textual. As well as tracing the play of meanings within the text, he or she also traces which meanings are generated and put into circulation in which social formation, and how this social play of meaning relates to the social structure at large, in particular its differential distribution of power.

Texts that meet the criteria of popular discrimination are cultural resources rather than art objects. Michel de Certeau uses the metaphor of the text as a supermarket from which readers select the items that they want, combine them with those already in their cultural "pantry" at home, and cook up new meals or new readings according to their own needs and creativities.[10] This sort of text is the product of a completely different reading practice. The reader of the aesthetic text attempts to read it on *its* terms, to subjugate him- or herself to its aesthetic discipline. The reader reveres the text. The popular reader, on the other hand, holds no such reverence for the text but views it as a resource to be used at will. Aesthetic appreciation of a text requires the understanding of how its elements relate and contribute to its overall unity, and an appreciation of this final, completed unity is its ultimate goal. Popular readers, on the other hand, are concerned less with the final unity of a text than with the pleasures and meanings that its elements can provoke. They are undisciplined, dipping into and out of a text at will. Television detective shows, for instance, can be watched quite differently, which means that different elements are selected as significant by different viewers. The urban working-class men of Italian origin studied by Herbert Gans, for example, first selected those shows in which the hero respected and worked with the urban working class, and then selected, within each show, the opening and closing sequences when masculine power and performance were best displayed.[11] Women viewers of *Charlie's Angels*, however, tended to ignore the closing sequence (some even left the room) when masculine control reasserted itself over the women detectives, and concentrated instead on the central section of the narrative as the women gradually ran the criminal to ground.[12]

Many soap opera viewers watch only those storylines that interest them, or are relevant to them, and ignore the rest. Children, too, "frequently" show no respect for any unity of the television text, but pay only sporadic attention to it, focusing often on moments of high spectacle or comedy rather than narrative sequence or unity.[13]

This disrespect for the integrity of the text frequently accompanies a disregard for the artist in popular culture that again differentiates it from the aesthetic. The working-class woman who, when asked who painted Van Gogh's sunflowers hanging on her wall, peered at the reproduction and read out, "Vincent" is typical,[14] for popular discrimination focuses on the conditions of consumption of art rather than those of its production. In aesthetics, however, the uniqueness of the text leaks into the uniqueness of the artistic imagination that produced it. The former is displaced onto the individuality of the artist and its highly prized emblem—the signature (whether literal or stylistic) that authentically ties the unique text to its unique producer. Of course, such authenticity is as highly valued financially as it is aesthetically, for in the world of bourgeois culture, the two value systems underwrite and guarantee each other so that the functions of the critic and the insurance assessor become almost indistinguishable.

The respect for uniqueness of the author/text surfaces in a number of ways. Halle's study found, for instance, that upper-middle-class people were not only far more likely than blue-collar workers to know the names of the artists of their pictures but also to know something about them.[15] So, too, when *The Shining* was released in Britain, the middle-class press identified it as a Stanley Kubrick film and looked for his stylistic signature in its long tracking shots, its control of pace, and so on. Its point of comparison was always other Kubrick films. The popular papers, however, identified it as a horror movie and focused on its sensational moments: for them, its point of comparison was with other horror movies; it was a genre film, not an auteur film.

This evacuation of the author from the popular text is also, of course, an evacuation of authority. Because the text or artwork is not seen as a uniquely crafted, completed object—Keats's Grecian urn that Cleanth Brooks turned into the apogee of the totally self-sufficient, totally completed aesthetic object—but as a cultural resource bank, there can be no discipline exerted on its readers to subject themselves to its meanings. Indeed, I have argued elsewhere that one of the defining characteristics of texts in the popular domain is that they should be treated as unfinished and inadequate in themselves: they are "completed" only by the productivity of popular readers and by their relevant insertion into readers' everyday lives.[16]

Popular films, novels, and TV narratives such as soap opera are frequently dismissed by highbrow critics for three main sets of reasons: One set clusters around their conventionality, their conforming to generic patterns and their conditions of mass production. Another set centers on criteria such as superficiality, sensationalism, obviousness, and predictability, while the third is concerned with their easiness, their failure to offer any challenge. Yet these qualities, which in aesthetic or critical discrimination are negative, are, in the realm of the popular, precisely those which enable the text to be taken up and used in the culture of the people.

Popular taste tends to ignore traces of authorial signature and focuses rather on generic convention, for genres are the result of a three-way contract between audience, producer, and text. A generic text meets not only the current tastes of its audiences but also the production needs of its producers. But this is a loose contract which leaves plenty of space for different readers to produce different forms of popular culture from it. *Dallas*, for example, whose audience readings have been widely studied, can offer pro- and anticapitalist meanings, pro- and antipatriarchal meanings, pro-family and antibusiness ones or vice versa, and so on.[17]

This necessary openness of the popular text is due not only to its conventionality, but also to its superficiality, its lack of depth. Its appeal is all on the surface, so the "meanings" of that surface have to be supplied by the reader. *Dallas*'s rich interior decorations and costumings are indicative of a generalized class and national life-style rather than of the individuality of their characters, which has to be supplied, if it is wanted, by a productive reading. So, too, the acting style does not project individually held feelings and reactions, but relies on the viewer to "read" a raised eyebrow or a downturn of the corner of the mouth. The camera, in *Dallas* as in soap opera in general, dwells on such conventional expressions and offers them up for viewer interpretation. And different readers read them differently. By contrast, a literary novel or Broadway play will attempt to express the inner feelings and thoughts of its characters as precisely and sensitively as possible and will thus require its readers to "decipher" its meanings rather than produce their meanings of and from it. Conventionality and superficiality not only keep production costs down, they also open the text up to productive reading strategies.

The conventionality of plot lines, too, enables readers to write ahead, to predict what will happen and then to find pleasure (or sometimes frustration) in comparing their own projected "scripts" with those actually broadcast. They frequently feel that their "scripts" are superior to the scriptwriters', that they "know" the characters better and are thus better able to say how they should behave or react. The "authored" text does not allow its readers such an empowered or productive reading position. Generic readers know the conventions and are thus situated in a far more democratic relationship with the text than are the readers of highbrow literature, with its authoritative authors.

Because authors and their texts are not seen as "superior" to their popular readers there is no requirement, in the popular domain, for a text to be difficult, challenging, or complex. In fact, just the reverse is the case. The popular text must align itself with the tastes and concerns of its readers, not its author, if the readers are to choose it from the wide repertoire of other texts available: it must offer inviting access to the pleasures and meanings it may provoke. But the accessibility of the text does not mean the passivity of the reader, for all the studies of popular reading show how active that process is, though the activity is not necessarily laborious. The "difficulty" of highbrow texts functions less to ensure or measure the "quality" of the text itself and more as a social turnstyle: it works to exclude those who have not the cultural competence (or the motivation) to decode it on its own terms. "Difficulty" is finally a measure of social exclusivity rather than of textual quality, and, of course, it is much prized by the criticism industry because it guarantees the role of the critic.

The idea that a text should be "challenging" is an important and paradoxical one to explore. Popular texts can be and are challenging; but they offer a different sort of challenge to that of highbrow texts, and the difference lies mainly in *who* is challenged, that is, in what social conflicts are activated. The challenge of the highbrow however, is aesthetic, and occurs in two main arenas—the individual and the social. The individualized challenge is that between the reader and the decoding of the text and involves the development of a finer hermeneutic sensibility that Leavis, for instance, believed would lead to a finer understanding of human life in general. These abilities would then produce a superior individual who would, in company with his [sic] fellows produce an elite who would ensure a high-quality society. What Leavis did not point out, of course, was that the individuals who were most likely to develop these fine sensibilities were already members of the dominant class, so that aesthetic discrimination worked socially as a self-confirming conservatism. Textual challenge still had social distinction built into it, but the distinction worked not only to maintain, but actually to increase, social difference and to defend current power relations. The social dimension is thus not challenging but confirming: the challenge occurs on the level of the individual's self-development through aesthetic discrimination.

The more socially inflected challenge of the aesthetic is that offered by the avant-garde to the more traditional art forms, but although the avant-garde may be radical aesthetically, Roland Barthes doubts if the challenge it offers can ever be social, for it is comfortably confined not only within the bourgeoisie, but within that fraction of the bourgeoisie which Arnold called the cultured (against the Philistines)[18] and which Bourdieu has characterized as possessing more cultural than economic capital (the Philistines, of course, possess more economic than cultural): Bourdieu calls them, in a provocative phrase, "the dominated dominant."[19]

The challenge of highbrow texts, then, is always offered primarily within the realm of the aesthetic and any social dimension never crosses class barriers and thus never challenges the economic base of society, nor its differential distribution of power. Recently, feminists have produced a wide variety of avant-garde art with a powerful social dimension that offers a direct challenge to patriarchal power. But this challenge still fails to cross class barriers and even to reach out to other fractions of the middle class, such as Arnold's Philistines.

The challenge of popular art, however, is not aesthetic but social. The various formations of the people who experience various forms of subordination are challenged constantly by the conditions of their social experience: they do not need challenge in their art as well. What they do need is that their art should be functional and thus should be of use in meeting the challenges of which their daily lives are comprised. The New Orleans Afro-Americans and the Australian Aboriginals who made antiwhite meanings out of westerns and Rambo did not find the texts aesthetically challenging, but used them in understanding the challenge of white domination, and possibly (we do not know for sure, but the potential exists) in enhancing the challenge they could offer in response. The schoolgirl fan of *Cagney and Lacey* whose fandom made her feel as good as boys at school almost certainly felt better able to challenge patriarchy as it operated in her daily life as a result of her textual experience.[20] The Korean soap opera fan offers the same sort of enhanced challenge to her husband's patriarchal power as do some of Ellen Seiter's working-class Oregon fans or Janice Radway's romance reader when she reports:

> We talked about the program till one o'clock in the morning. I did not understand why he sympathized with the husband [who had been divorced after an affair]—We then changed the topic and ended up with talking about my career

when we returned to Korea so I said to him "women too should have a career to avoid that problem." He said "no" and I said "yes"—we had a terrible fight that night.[21]

The meanings, complexities, and challenges of popular art are to be found in the ways in which its potential is mobilized socially, not in its texts alone. The reader who becomes intensely involved in popular culture will often become a fan, and when this occurs some interesting changes begin to take place. Fandom is poised between popular culture and high culture, so the fan works with features of both popular and aesthetic discrimination.

In its relations with popular culture, fandom is marked by excess: fans are frequently not content to produce their own readings from the texts of the culture industry, but turn these readings into full-blown fan texts which in many cases they will circulate among themselves through a distribution network that is almost as well organized as that of the industry. So "Trek-kies" (fans of *Star Trek*) not only write newsletters about the program, but some write novels, sometimes semipornographic, in which they fill in the gaps left in the original text—in this case the unwritten love life of Spock and his fellow space travellers.[22] This exceeds in degree, but does not differ in kind from, the writing in the gaps that Robert Allen and Charlotte Bruns-don, for example, find typical of soap opera fans: the difference is that most soap opera fan "writing" takes place in the imagination, or, if it is given expression, is confined to talk with other fans.[23]

C. Bacon-Smith, too, has found science fiction TV fans who make their own music videos by combining shots from their favorite episodes over the sound track of a popular song.[24] Both of these practices treat the original text with a degree of disrespect for its authenticity and aesthetic integrity that in no way affects the adoration that, paradoxically, they feel simulta-neously toward it. Indeed, the strength of their affection for the original text is what motivates them, not to appreciate and preserve it, but to par-ticipate in it and complete it by imbricating it into their everyday lives. So the Madonna fan who completes the textuality of Madonna by extending it onto her bedroom wall, her body, her hair, and her high school book bag adores Madonna (whom she knows only as a textual construct, a bun-dle of meanings and pleasures) and her adoration makes her want to col-lapse the distance between art object and reader (often called "critical distance") and instead participate in the reproduction and recirculation of the object of her fandom.

I have shown elsewhere how adolescent girls construct relevances be-tween Madonna's sexuality and their own conditions of existence.[25] Just as they begin to develop a sense of their own sexuality, patriarchy robs them of it and "gives" it to men: Madonna, on the other hand, shows them that female sexuality can be reclaimed for women, can be a source of strength and independence for them, and need not subordinate them to men's acceptance and approval. When Madonna and MTV invited fans to make a video for her song "True Blue" they were inundated with thousands of entries, and running through them were recurrent patterns of relevance and empowerment—Madonna was inserted into the fans' everyday lives, they impersonated her in their suburban homes, their cars, their bedrooms, and they incorporated her into their routines of household chores, school, and shopping. In their Madonna role they were empowered in this environment which normally disempowers them, so the mini-narratives of the videos show the fan controlling schoolteachers, boyfriends, and in one instance, the world as she became president of the United States and averted a world war!

Popular readership requires a well developed cultural competence that is specifically a generic competence, and it is this that enables readers to write in the gaps so effectively. It is, in fact, a competence shared with the industrial scriptwriters or video makers which involves not only a familiarity with generic conventions but also a sense of their productivity, of what can and cannot be done with conventions. This cultural competence results in the fan's often feeling able to produce better scripts than the professional—many fans think that their favorite character or star has been "let down" by scriptwriters, directors, or producers and that they could do better. It is this sense of equality with, if not superiority to, the producers of the industrial text that enables fans to treat it with disrespect, to rewrite and rework it, to raid it for what they want and ignore what they don't. The highbrow reverence for the author sets up quite different reading relations and therefore different reading practices.

It is also generic cultural competence that enables fans to effect a genre-shift in which, for instance, the science fiction *Star Trek* gets rewritten into a romance or into a music video. This genre-shift can also make the original more relevant; the most productive Trekkies, for instance, are women whose rewriting and genre-shifting makes the original less masculine, more feminine, and thus facilitates its relevant imbrication into their day-to-day lives.

If many of the practices of fandom are exaggerations of those of the more popular reader, there are others which align themselves with those of critical discrimination. Some fans, for example, become acute at recognizing an individual artist's stylistic signature—whether of a musician who may play or have played in a number of bands, or of a visual artist who illustrated particular issues of a comic. This fan knowledge or expertise, which may at times be both voluminous and esoteric, constitutes a fan cultural capital that is the equivalent of the official cultural capital of the educated bourgeoisie. It brings with it similar social benefits—prestige, the sense of belonging to an elite minority that is sharply distinguished from those who lack it, and a feeling of self-worth—but it also differs from official cultural capital in that it cannot be so readily converted into economic capital. Official cultural capital, produced and promoted by the educational system, can become economically profitable because of its convertibility, via "qualifications," into careers, salaries, and pensions. Fan cultural capital, however, is part of the world of popular discrimination and thus is excluded from the social (and therefore economic) rewards of critical or aesthetic discrimination.

But there is one area of fandom where its cultural capital is convertible into economic capital. Some fan memorabilia and industrial texts can become economically valuable according to criteria similar to those operating in high art. So first issues of comics or first releases of records are now economically valuable, as are first editions of books, and fans often speak of, and I suspect exaggerate, the economic value of their collections. The value attached to the "first" edition/issue/release is the equivalent, in the world of the mass reproduction of cultural objects, of the unique original artwork: a value that in the economic domain is a function of its scarcity, in the social of its distinctiveness, and in the cultural of its authenticity. The final step in this "gentrifying" of the popular artwork occurs when its value is enhanced still further if it is in "mint" condition—that is, if it is unread, unused—for this signals its final shift from a popular cultural resource to be used to an art object to be revered and preserved. So, too, autographed photographs, bats, balls, posters, etc. in fandom are of higher value than their otherwise identical counterparts because of their cultural authenticity, their social distinctiveness, and their material scarcity. The "signature" guarantees the convertibility of cultural into economic capital in the world of fandom just as much as in the Manhattan art gallery.

It must be said, too, that the (generally welcome) inclusion of popular culture into academia allows for its conversion into economic rewards and social status for academics, at least. My professional status and its rewards, to take a personal example, come at least as much from my enjoyment of television and popular culture, from my wholehearted participation in its pleasures, as from the official cultural capital I acquired through my education and my reproduction of much that it stands for in my teaching and writing. So too, other academics who are well endowed with official cultural capital are increasing their "investment" by bringing to it their popular cultural capital and its knowledge and competencies: they not only enjoy and experience rock music, soap opera, or sport in their alignment with "the popular," but also theorize, write, and teach about the objects of their enthusiasm in their alignment with institutional power. It requires a developed political sensitivity on the part of these academics to prevent their insertion of the popular into the academic canon from becoming an act of incorporation, for in some ways, the academic and the popular must remain in conflict.

"The people" is a remarkably difficult concept to define: it consists of a shifting set of allegiances that is mapped onto, but can cross, the structures of social power and subordination—class, gender, race, region, education, religion, and so on. But, as Stuart Hall argues, the people must always be conceived of as antagonistic in some way to the interests of the power-bloc.[26] I have situated the cultural arena for this struggle in the interface between the textual and the social. In the last instance it is not the text or art object itself which determines whether or not it is part of high or popular culture, but its social circulation within which criticism, academia, and other cultural institutions play such crucial roles. Lawrence Levine, for instance, has shown how Shakespeare was moved from popular to bourgeois culture in late-nineteenth- and early twentieth-century America.[27] When his plays were popular their texts were treated disrespectfully —they were cut, given new endings, interrupted with vaudeville acts, performed to rowdy, "participatory" audiences—and their gentrification entailed a return to their original authentic versions, a reverent distance from the audience, and so on. So, too, a Van Gogh reproduction (unrecognized though the artist may be) may hang in many a working-class home. It is the social use of texts rather than their essential qualities that determines their "brow" level.

Having said this, however, we must recognize that some texts are less likely to move between levels than others and that there are textual characteristics that facilitate such movement.[28] The presence of such characteristics, however, does not guarantee a text's social mobility, though their absence makes it less likely. It also appears that in twentieth-century capitalist societies, few texts or art objects appeal to different class tastes simultaneously—the social mobility of a text occurs only with historical change. This again supports the thesis that difference in cultural taste is a reenactment of social difference, and that cultural and social discrimination are part and parcel of the same process. Popular discrimination, then, is necessarily opposed to aesthetic or critical discrimination.

Academia is uneasily situated in this relationship: its institutionalization (which is now almost total; the independent scholar is practically extinct) necessarily aligns it with the power-bloc, yet within this alliance of interests it holds a somewhat privileged position, for it is expected to critically examine its own society, and, besides producing those who will conform to and further the interests of white patriarchal capitalism, it is also expected to produce a minority (albeit not too large and not too vocal) who will criticize that social system and its operation. There is little doubt that a study of the popular can enhance academia's ability to critically examine the society of which it is a part, but we must take pains to ensure that the benefits are not one-way, and the forces of the popular gain from our academic intrusion into them. We must do all that we can to ensure that our investigation and theorization of the popular eventually, by however dispersed means, feed back into it and enhance the challenge it offers to the power-bloc.

I have, therefore, structured this essay around an antagonism that, for rhetorical purposes (as well as for considerations of length) I have reduced to its skeleton. I am well aware that among the social practices of high or bourgeois art there are few which will conform to *all* the characteristics I have attributed to them, and many that will contradict and complicate them. But changes in flesh and muscle can only reshape a skeleton so far. Literature teachers, for example, often teach literature as *relevant*, as offering lessons for living, but in doing this will not necessarily give up the authority and integrity of the text, or allow their students to raid it as a resource bank, rejecting some of it and accepting the rest according to *their* needs. And it is a rare teacher indeed who does not have some sense of the "right" reading (which he or she "knows") and who will not give the highest grades to those students who most closely approximate it.

In the realm of theory, too, there have been welcome signs of rebellion against many of the taken-for-granted assumptions of the western humanistic tradition—deconstruction, feminism, reception theory, postmodernism all challenge some of the characteristics I have ascribed to bourgeois art, yet their challenge, like that of the avant-garde to the traditional, is largely confined within the educated fraction of the bourgeoisie: it is a struggle within academia and within the established art world.

The challenge offered by popular culture, however, comes from outside this social, cultural, and academic terrain: the structure of this essay around the antagonism between dominant and popular culture is intended to emphasize this challenge and to help resist its incorporation. If, as a result, I am charged with oversimplifying the dominant, then that is a price which my academic politics lead me to think is worth paying.

Notes

1. Raymond Williams, *Keywords* (London: Fontana, 1976).
2. Ien Ang, *Watching Dallas* (London: Methuen, 1985).
3. George Lipsitz, "Mardi Gras Indians: Carnival and Counter Narrative in Black New Orleans," *Cultural Critique* 10 (1988): 99–121.
4. Robert Hodge and David Tripp, *Children and Television* (Cambridge: Polity Press, 1986).
5. Pierre Bourdieu, *Distinction: A Social Critique of the Judgement of Taste* (Cambridge: Harvard University Press, 1984).
6. J. D'Acci, *Women, "Woman" and Television*. Ph.D. dissertation, University of Wisconsin-Madison, 1988.
7. David Halle, "Deconstructing Taste: Class and Culture in Modern America," presented at the American Sociological Association Conference, San Francisco, August 1989.
8. Walter Benjamin, *Illuminations*, trans. Harry Zohn (New York: Schocken, 1969).

9. David Bordwell, *Making Meaning: Inference and Rhetoric in the Interpretation of Cinema* (Cambridge: Harvard University Press, 1989).

10. Michel de Certeau, *The Practice of Everyday Life* (Berkeley: University of California Press, 1984).

11. Herbert Gans, *The Urban Villagers: Group and Class in the Life of Italian-Americans* (New York: Free Press, 1962).

12. John Fiske, *Television Culture* (London: Methuen, 1987).

13. Henry Jenkins, "Star Trek: Rerun, Reread, Rewritten: Fan Writing as Textual Poaching," *Critical Studies in Mass Communication* 5, no. 2 (1989): 85–107; Patricia Palmer, *The Lively Audience: A Study of Children around the TV Set* (Sydney: Allen and Unwin, 1986).

14. Halle, "Deconstructing Taste."

15. Ibid.

16. John Fiske, *Understanding Popular Culture* (Boston: Unwin Hyman, 1989).

17. Ang, *Watching Dallas.*

18. Roland Barthes, *Mythologies* (London: Cape, 1970).

19. Bourdieu, *Distinction.*

20. D'Acci, *Women, "Woman" and Television.*

21. Ellen Seiter et al., "Don't Treat Us like We're so Stupid and Naive: Towards an Ethnography of Soap Opera Viewers," in *Remote Control: Television and Its Audience,* ed. E. Seiter et al. (London: Routledge, 1989); Janice Radway, *Reading the Romance: Feminism and the Representation of Women in Popular Culture* (Chapel Hill: University of North Carolina Press, 1984); M. Lee and C. Cho, "Women Watching Together: An Ethnographic Study of Korean Soap Opera Fans in the U.S.," *Cultural Studies* 3:1, 30–44.

22. Jenkins, "Star Trek."

23. Robert Allen, *Speaking of Soap Operas* (Chapel Hill: University of North Carolina Press, 1985); Charlotte Brunsdon, "Writing about Soap Opera," in *Television Mythologies: Stars, Shows and Signs,* ed. L. Masterman (London: Comedia, MK Media Press, 1984).

24. C. Bacon-Smith, "Acquisition and Transformation of Popular Culture: International Video Circuit and Fanzine Community," paper presented at the International Communication Association Conference, New Orleans, May 1988.

25. John Fiske, *Reading the Popular* (Boston: Unwin Hyman, 1989).

26. Stuart Hall, "Notes on Deconstructing the Popular," in *People's History and Socialist Theory,* ed. Raphael Samuel (London: Routledge and Kegan Paul, 1981).

27. Lawrence Levine, *Highbrow/Lowbrow: The Emergence of Cultural Hierarchy in America* (Cambridge, MA: Harvard University Press, 1988).

28. Fiske, *Understanding Popular Culture.*

Digressions at the Cinema: Commodification and Reception in Mass Culture

Barbara Klinger

> . . . it has also to be seen that a film
> must never end . . . it must ex-
> ist . . . [even] before we enter the cin-
> ema—in a kind of englobingly
> extensive prolongation. The commerce
> of film depends on this too, recog-
> nized in a whole host of epiphenom-
> ena from trailers to remakes, from
> weekly reviews to star magazines,
> from publicity still to memento (rubber
> sharks, tee shirts). More crucially,
> since the individual film counts for lit-
> tle in its particularity as opposed to
> the general circulation which guaran-
> tees the survival of the industry and
> in which it is a unit . . . a film is a
> constant doing over again. . . . [1]

Most everyone who frequents movie theaters has experienced the phenomenon of the errant spectator who will sometimes respond audibly to
individual scenes in excess of their function within the narrative. Such
responses may include attempts at narrative decipherment (remarks about
plot changes and character motivations), but they also extend considerably
past alliance with the narrative proper. They range from a variety of reactions to stars (swooning, discussion of the actors' past roles and personal
lives), to anecdotes about the making of a film or the background of its
director, to passionate outbursts that can assume multifarious forms: the
man who sang out loud in accompaniment to every song in *Sweet Dreams*,
the teen who recited lines from *The Terminator* during *The Golden Child*.
    Such in-theater commentary is seldom assigned importance in the

analysis of text/spectator relations. At best, it seems a sociological phenomenon, indicating the degenerate viewing habits of the TV generation;
at worst, its transient and idiosyncratic appearance encourages a less systematic explanation, as a purely individual and contingent event.

The lack of critical relevance such responses seem to have rests particularly on their incommensurability with any notion of "ideal" spectatorship. That is, these reactions are incompatible with dominant theoretical
paradigms, which define spectatorship as a product of the operations of a
text. Despite substantial differences in perspectives, theorists often treat
the category of the spectator as synonymous with the narrative and visual
operations specific to a textual system.[2] As a result, the entire film/spectator
interaction is irredeemably fixed and isolated from the impact of social
contingencies. That which is variable and "textually divergent" is inad-
missible to this scheme, since such responses participate neither in the
establishment of a coherent textual system, nor a profile of the ideal spectator, the "spectator-in-the-text."[3]

While divergence is clearly irreconcilable with formalist or text-based
analysis, responses determined by factors other than The Text have been
particularly interesting to critics associated with cultural studies. Recent
cultural criticism regards differences in viewing not as insubstantial, but
as significant to an understanding of the social dynamics involved in reception. David Morley, for example, argues that multiple decodings of a
television text are produced from such social predispositions of the individual viewer as occupation, class, and race, while Tony Bennett and Janet
Woollacott emphasize the diversifying effect mass cultural discourses, such
as authorial interviews and advertisements, have on interpretation.[4] The
cultural studies critic, in addition, will often define different decodings as
oppositional to the intended ideological meaning of a text.

I propose similarly to treat cinematic detours or "digressions" as a significant social dynamic—one that helps us understand the "everyday" social spectator and the reception of mainstream texts. However, I believe
this dynamic, which seems to defy textual control, does not represent an
oppositional response. Rather, it demonstrates how diverse positions of
viewing are encouraged by social and intertextual agencies within mass
culture—agencies that seek to structure reception beyond textual boundaries, keeping it within the dominant ideology.

To approach the operations of these agencies, I will consider two quite
distinct theories which have addressed the phenomenon of digression as
a systematic feature within the text/viewer interaction: semiotics, particularly the work of Roland Barthes and Umberto Eco, and the mass culture
theory of the Frankfurt School. Both Barthes and Eco have treated digression as a part of the reading process that attests strongly to the profound
intertextual location of text and reader.[5] A relation between digression and
intertextuality is also evident in my opening examples. What each of these

types of cinematic digression has in common is the activity of intertextual forms: from generic or narrative intertexts, which school the spectator in dramatic conventions; to a host of promotional forms, such as media stories about the stars, the director, and the making of the film, which arm the spectator with background information; to other heterogeneous media forms, such as records (in the case of the Patsy Cline film, *Sweet Dreams*) or popular films (*The Terminator*), which fall into relation with moments of the film being screened. We can then initially consider digression not as an aberration, but as a *mark* of the complex intertextual situations governing the process of viewing.

Members of the Frankfurt School have invoked a related term, *distraction*, to identify a key dynamic of reception in mass culture. For Benjamin, Kracauer, Adorno, and Horkheimer, mechanical reproduction within a capitalist regime transforms reception from a state of absorption in the totality of the artwork to one of inattentiveness, resulting in the atomization of the work.[6] Adorno's perspective on the culture industry in particular links distraction to procedures of commodification which define a work for consumption in the "age of mechanical reproduction." As the epigraph taken from Stephen Heath's work indicates, an important part of a film's social circulation is defined by its promotional campaign, initiated by the film industry of which it is a part. Though such campaigns are often viewed as simply extraneous accompaniments to a film, Adorno's work encourages us to consider how commodification, as a systematic operation in mass culture, acts vitally on the social apprehension of texts.

Both semiotic and mass culture theories treat textual divergence as central to the reading/viewing experience, though they differ on the chief influence—the activities of intertextuality and commodification, respectively. While these formulations otherwise share little common ground, taken together they are very suggestive for analysis of one of the major social dimensions of reception: how certain types of textual response are motivated by forms directly associated with defining the text as a product—what Heath refers to as "epiphenomena." Epiphenomena currently include such exhibition materials as posters, ads, and trailers, as well as an extensive array of media coverage which features pieces on stars, directors, and the making of films, and the marketing of products such as toys and tee-shirts. Despite their helter-skelter appearance, such promotional forms, I will argue, exemplify a relation between intertextuality and aesthetic commodification; they operate as an intertextual network designed to identify a film for consumption. Films circulate as products, not in a semantic vacuum, but in a mass cultural environment teeming with related commercial significations. Epiphenomena constitute this adjacent territory; they create not only a commercial life-support system for a film, but also a socially meaningful network of relations around it which enter into reception. Promotion thus represents a sphere of intertextual discourse that can help explain the complex relation between commodity discourses and reception.

Digressions are a symptom of this relation. There are digressive responses specifically motivated by a signifying interchange between film and promotion. These responses, which occur both in audible and in silent, more meditative forms, can be defined as a reaction precipitated by an intertextual link between moments in the text and promotional epiphenomena. The spectator is momentarily diverted from the linear flow of filmic elements by this commodifying association.

But while we can initially define digressive impulses as activated by promotion, mass cultural intertexts are not generally recognized as authoritatively influential on reception. For example, though Adorno recognizes the impact of commodification on reception, he provides no sense of how forms associated with this process could establish meaningful relations between text and viewer. Thus, to examine the role that promotional texts play in reception, existing formulations must be reconsidered and revised, to better effect the marriage of semiotic and commodity theories.

Intertextuality and the "Closed" Text

Though Barthes and Eco differ substantially in their theoretical perspectives (Barthes's post-structuralism, Eco's neo-Peircean perspective), they both reject the idea of a self-regulating text by emphasizing the crucial role intertextual factors play in the semantic actualization of a text. As such, their notions of intertextuality and its manifestation in digressive modalities of reading offer a provocative means of opening the text to the signifying activity of heterogeneous forms.

Digression assumes a particularly central place in Barthes's *S/Z*; here, digression is that dynamic which realizes the post-structural concept of the text as a volatile productivity actualized only during the process of its reading. Barthes conceives the text as a "broken or obliterated network," whose units "are themselves ventures out of the text, the sign of a virtual digression toward the remainder of a catalogue . . . fragments of something . . . *already* said."[7] His analysis forcefully realizes this textual status, by breaking the text down into lexia and employing the divagation, the "exit" commentary, to materialize the intertextual conditions governing the reading process. Commentary separates "in the manner of a minor earthquake, the blocks of signification of which reading grasps only the smooth surface . . . [it] cannot therefore work with 'respect' to the text . . . the work of commentary . . . consists precisely in *manhandling* the text, *interrupting* it."[8] Hence, Barthes depicts a kind of *textus interruptus*, a narrative consistently subject to intertextual interferences, which result in meaningful excursions during the process of its reading.

Similarly, Eco develops a host of terms to describe the semantic presence and authority of intertextuality over reading, including "inferential walks," "unlimited semiosis," and "abduction," with its two movements of over-coding and under-coding. Each of these represents a process of semantic realization drawn from the contextual situation in which reading occurs. Inferential walks, for example, occur when the reader must identify intertextual frames necessary to decipher the narrative, and so has to " 'walk' . . . outside the text, in order to gain intertextual support."[9]

While both perspectives insist that intertextuality plays an important role in reception, each theorist places a limit on the extent of intertextuality, particularly in relation to classic narrative. Barthes materializes this limit in his aesthetic distinction between closed and open texts, which he differentiates on the basis of the intertextual potentials they display. While the open text is characterized by a high degree of intertextuality not ultimately subject to rules of linearity, coherence, and closure, the closed text is only "parsimoniously plural," since its rule-bound narrative submits to the procedures of closure demanded by western discourse. A hallmark characteristic of the classic text, then, is that it ultimately forecloses the possibility of an excessive play of signification, because of the actual underlying control its structure exerts over polysemanticity.[10]

Barthes's dichotomy between closed and open texts, employed influentially in film studies to distinguish Hollywood films and those of the avant-garde, represents one of the most predominant assumptions about classic practice and its relation to intertextuality: that the classic text is a poor relation to the modernist text, because its structure constrains the possibilities of plural meanings. This perspective tends to place a premature curfew on the intertextual play involved in reading classic forms. By regarding formal dispositions as ultimately determinate, it inhibits a fuller realization of how external conditions exert influence over the process of reading. It underestimates conditions arising from sociohistorical situations that cannot be grasped by textual analysis (such as those defining production and exhibition), and it explores only one aspect of the role intertextuality has in reception: how the text incorporates intertextual activity. As Tony Bennett and Janet Woollacott suggest, a social theory of reading must shift such an orientation to grasp forces which "excorporate" the text by activating and appropriating its elements. They coin the concept of "inter-textuality" to address this type of intertextuality: the term refers "to the social organisation of the relations between texts within specific conditions of reading," that is, to the institutions and discourses that superintend reception at certain historical moments.[11] Bennett/Woollacott's inflection of intertextuality recognizes the influence that transient forms like star interviews and advertisements have in the process of reading; these materials function as "hermeneutic activators," directing readings of aspects of the text (e.g., character or the representation of women). Such forms participate in reception, but cannot be uncovered by exploring how a text embodies external references. The text's situation in a social, inter-textual context "opens" it to signifying activities which exceed incorpo-ration.

Once such contextual forms of intertextuality are recognized, the profile of the classic text is transformed. As I have suggested, the economy of the classic form within its mass cultural situation obliges that it be extended beyond itself: the text is accompanied by a host of promotional and other popular materials that have a semantic agenda bent on elaborating its ele-ments. Part of the text's mass cultural status relies on this lack of self-containment—its social life depends on the extension of its elements, through the agency of certain contextual forms, into the everyday social sphere. Thus, significatory play—the polysemanticity of textual elements constructed through complex external referential systems—is no stranger to the classic text. But in contrast to Barthes's conception, polysemanticity does not necessarily indicate a revolutionary status. The polysemanticity created by social inter-texts is the cultural status quo for the so-called closed text.

Eco's treatment of the classic text would seem to address an insufficient account of its relation to intertextuality. He not only executes a twist on the common correlation of classic practices with closed and modernist with open, but situates reception firmly within a social setting. Eco argues that James Bond novels may aim "at arousing a precise response on the part of a more or less precise empirical reader," but they are, in fact, "open to any possible 'aberrant' decoding," due to the complexity of factors which enter into their reception within a social context.[12] Eco, unlike Barthes, desig-nates the closed text as "immoderately open," given the plurality of possible interpretations.[13]

But here, what transforms the closed into an open form is the lack of control internal structures have over the process of reception. Popular forms are by definition immersed in a social environment which subjects them to interference and dissociation from their original authorial intent. The open work is able to ward off these social intrusions because of its difficult form, and thus maintains a closer bond with the sender of the message. But despite this distinction, Eco ultimately maintains that the popular text is "a complete and *closed* form in its uniqueness as a balanced organic whole, while at the same time constituting an *open* product on account of its sus-ceptibility to countless interpretations which do not impinge on its una-dulterable specificity."[14] Eco admits social context into the analysis of reading by acknowledging that the text circulates as a product and not just as an aesthetic object; but he does so in a way that preserves the text as an integral unit, protected from extrinsic adulteration. That is, Eco's place-ment of variable interpretations staunchly at the pole of the reader deflects the implication that social forces exercise a definitive power of transfor-mation over textual elements to such an extent that the text cannot be thought apart from its extrinsic activations. While Eco recognizes the diversity of intertextual activity around popular forms, he ultimately attributes systematicity and legitimate semantic power only to those readings which properly reconstruct a text. Inferential walks, then, even as they seem to approximate a digressive reading dynamic, are not whimsical forays on the part of the reader, but are "elicited by discursive structures and foreseen by the whole textual strategy."[15]

Eco's position ultimately demonstrates the same textual focus which characterized Barthes's theory. Eco's work, however, isolates another central issue in assessing the role of intertextuality in reception: what types of intertextual material qualify as essential to the text/receiver interaction? Eco admits textually allied forms, such as those which define generic or narrative conventions, but questions the legitimacy of social forms that do not ultimately participate in the proper interpretation—that threaten, in fact, to pluralize meaning beyond the grasp of an authoritative textual structure. The promotional network surrounding a film therefore seems alien to an analysis of reception for several reasons: such forms are so transient and heterogeneous that they do not seem to cohere into the kind of system necessary to discuss intertextual relations, especially in comparison to more stable examples like prior generic conventions. In addition, since advertising forms fragment and extend a text for the purposes of consumption, associating its elements with a network of commercial concerns, analysis of these forms does not necessarily lead to a coherent reconstruction of the text.

What Eco's theory neglects is the possibility that social institutions operate systematically on reception: that though institutions may not create coherent readings, they may exert substantial influence on the text/viewer interaction. In the case of promotional discourses, the fugitive appearance of individual examples of promotion—an ad, a poster, an interview with a director—belies the fact of a historically insistent and influential industrial practice. As Janet Staiger has recently argued, the association between advertising and classic textual practice is characterized by a long-standing dimension of reciprocity which reaches back into the "primitive" era of Hollywood filmmaking.[16] Staiger traces the close association between advertising and production practices in the early 1900s, examining how advertising affected the development and consolidation of the classic Hollywood style. Certain advertising values, such as stars, spectacle, realism, and popular genres became a set of standards that production practices had to satisfy. The internal components of a film were, then, partially fashioned to meet the external objectives of conventions of promotion.

Staiger's research suggests that an activity appearing to be completely external to a film—promotion—penetrates the very formulation of content and style. In addition, despite the apparent impermanence and heterogeneity of promotional forms, they establish certain consistent values that govern textual production and exhibition. These values constitute the chief means by which producers seek to establish a material link with potential consumers of the film—their bid for an influence in consumption. Promotional practices not only have a hand in constructing the film itself, but also supervise how it will be introduced to the viewing public.

Institutional practices thus figure instrumentally in a film's appearance. The impact of these practices supercedes notions of ultimate inconsequentiality or simple "influence." To engage the full semantic activity of promotion in relation to the text, its inter-textual status has to be recognized. Promotion acts semantically on a film by providing some of its elements with an inter-textual destiny: a premeditated network of advertising texts develops specific components of the text to define it for consumption. When, for example, *The Today Show* ran a five-part series of interviews/stories on *Rain Man*, they were taking part in a ritual of promotion designed not only to "hype" the film, but to emphasize how it should be consumed: among other things, interviews focused on the performance of Dustin Hoffman, on the problems of the character he played, and on the phenomenon of autism, as a means of steering reception toward the star and the serious social content of the film. The sheer range of promotion in these cases sharpens the significance of this steering activity. The producing company's ties with mass culture exceed the advertisements they produce in the form of posters, trailers, and media spots; these companies establish a vast array of media contacts to editors and writers on television, radio, newspapers, and magazines of every conceivable circulation that serve to promote the film through stories on its production and interviews with its stars. Such an intricate relation between film and promotion has only been intensified historically: every new invention in the media—radio, television, cable television, video cassettes—has provided new forums for advertising, substantially advancing the social range of promotion and, by implication, the insistence of its values.

Industrial practices of promotion thus constitute a tenacious inter-textual network of relations that figure into a text's reception. As I mentioned, these practices may not create a coherent reading of the text. Social groups may produce their own meaning: Richard Dyer's work on Judy Garland, for example, examines how the construction of her image by gay audiences influenced by mass cultural discourses led to an entire rereading of her films.[17] Promotion can, of course, lead to a full-blown interpretation of a text. Advertisements and magazine articles describe *Fatal Attraction* as relevant to real-life scenarios of extramarital affairs which result in obsessive and destructive love, thus encouraging spectators to view the film as a moral fable.[18] But the industry which creates these commercial epiphenomena is not primarily concerned with producing coherent interpretations of a film. Rather, the goal of promotion is to produce multiple avenues of access to the text that will make the film resonate as extensively as possible in the social sphere, to maximize its audience. Promotional categories will then often tend to diversify the text by addressing several of its elements, including, as I will later discuss, subject matter, stars, and style. But this particular type of inter-textual zone cannot be located within the textual system; it "raids" the text for features which can be accentuated and extended.

This type of inter-textuality makes it necessary for us to revise prior semiotic theories, especially when they propose the limited polysemanticity of the classic text and the illegitimacy of certain mass cultural forms of intertextuality. We need to recognize the effect that the film industry has on viewing—how industrial practices constitute an inter-textual network which pluralizes the classic text during its circulation as a commodity. A recognition of this inter-textuality helps us to better understand the text/spectator interaction, and to approach certain economies of viewing that *fragment* rather than assemble the text, truly "manhandling" and "interrupting" it.

Commodification and Reception

The film industry's promotional practices are part of a general process of commodification within mass culture. According to Adorno, a study of this process is key to ascertaining how the social value of a text is constituted. He argues that the internal configuration of a text is pervasively regulated by the apparatus of mass reproduction, whose operations extend beyond the simple reproduction and distribution of the text; they are allied with procedures of commodification that arrange the text's consumable identity. Commodification in turn produces a distracted viewer, attuned to only those aspects of the text that the process has delegated as valuable.

Adorno uses Marx's concept of commodity fetishism to explain aesthetic production in mass culture. The commodity fetish, according to Marx, is one of the principles which defines production in a capitalist system. Its operation results in the keen veneration of the exchange-value of the produced object.[19] The fetish represents a value assigned to the object through the social processes which determine its significance within the marketplace. As Adorno writes, "No object has inherent value; it is valuable only to the extent that it can be exchanged. The use value of art, its mode of being is treated as a fetish and the fetish, the work's social rating . . . becomes its use value and the only quality which is enjoyed."[20]

In music, the fetish can assume the form of a reified structural element (e.g., an isolated melodic phrase), a star personality (the conductor or performer), or some other kind of "special attraction." The point is that fetishization, as it assigns an exchange-value to the text, acts constitutionally on the text to hypostasize or condense it into a series of foregrounded elements which meet the conventions of consumption.

The fetishistic reprogramming of the work solicits a certain kind of listening/reception as well: "The fetish-character of music produces its own camouflage through the identity of the listener with the fetish."[21] Commodification attains a force in reception insofar as the reified structure of the media form becomes the means by which text/receiver relations are established. The listener identifies with some aspect of the crystallized structure of the music, whether it be the repeated musical phrase or the star-persona. This is the psychological aspect of the commodity-fetish, what Baudrillard later refers to as "the mode of sanctification, fascination and psychological subjection by which individuals internalize the general system of exchange-value."[22] The commodity-fetish exceeds evaluation, then, as simply bearing on the economic aspects of textual production, by embodying a mode of social appropriation of texts which transforms their identity and their reception.

Adorno's account of the relations between mass culture, work, and receiver is ultimately limited by the generality his wholesale condemnation of the culture industry lends to these relations. His polemic against mass culture renders the relations of texts and receivers as completely undifferentiated, and hence lacks a sense of the social variability and specificity necessary to a social theory of reception. The value of this otherwise steamrolling conception of textuality and subjectivity within culture lies in its implications—in its proposal that commodification plays a significant ideological role in reception. Though such cultural theorists as Dick Hebdige and John Fiske have argued that commodities can attain an oppositional dimension through particular kinds of individual uses, commodification has other socially specifiable but less radical functions, which still remain relatively unexplored in reception theory.[23] Adorno introduces a sense of how this contextual factor operates on text and receiver to literally translate the materiality of the text into a series of heightened, specialized, "starred" elements. His work implies that the negotiations between text and receiver are not managed purely through the "native" language of the text, but also by social, metonymic transformations.

How does the initial process of fragmentation into a series of specialized or "starred" elements develop into a meaningful social dynamic? I would suggest a link between the fetishized details and the network of promotional inter-texts referred to earlier. The elements foregrounded through the process of commodification are given to frequent reworking through promotional materials devoted to extending a film into the social sphere. The fetish elements are connected to a network of cultural signification which elaborates and extends the text's "capitalizable" components. The circulation of film as a commodity, therefore, engenders its fetishization into a series of specialized features which will establish its exchange-value, but also guarantees its extension into the social sphere through the signifying activities of the promotional network attached to its commodification.

Though the specifics of this network may vary, depending on such factors as genre, technological development, or the social period in which a film is released, certain things are consistently subject to commodification: characters/stars; subject matter/genre; and style, including mise-en-scène (setting, costumes, etc.) and cinematography.[24] The promotion of these items is, in turn, frequently pervaded by considerations of spectacle and realism. Hence, the promotional values described by Staiger linger in more contemporary examples.

Directors and stars present one of the most visible examples of the relation between commodity-fetishism and promotion. When a director such as Steven Spielberg is used as a point of commodification, his films undergo reification; they become a series of scenic exemplifications of his talent or stylistic signature (the giant rolling rock scene at the beginning of *Raiders of the Lost Ark*, the shark/Orca chase scenes in *Jaws*)—a commodified version of auteurism. At the same time, background stories which are released by promotional agencies or produced by their media contacts provide detailed information about the director's professional and personal history, so that the reification is magnified and earns a "deeper" place in the social sphere. Similarly, a film can be apprehended as a star-vehicle, and thus be valued for the series of images it provides of the star in question, whether Sylvester Stallone or Marilyn Monroe. But again the fetishization of the film is bolstered by a host of background stories featured in all the media through interviews or cover stories—stories which not only relate details of the star's attitude toward making the picture, but also conjure up a whole history of the star's personal and professional life. Character in a particular film is tied to star discourse as a means of distinguishing the character/star unit as a consumer highlight and of endowing this unit with an instant inter-textual history to establish its social presence.[25]

Perhaps more subtly, subject matter and style also become specialized features of promotional inter-textuality. Advertising and promotion for Douglas Sirk's *Written on the Wind* (1956), for example, concentrated on scenes that would help portray the film as an "adult" feature—a popular genre of the time that promised the audience a combination of sensationalistic subject matter and socially relevant themes. For this reason, posters, trailers, lobby cards, and media coverage emphasized those moments which depicted such sensational "problems" as nymphomania, sterility, alcoholism, adultery, and murder. Elements which could represent an "adult" subject matter were extrapolated from the film to support a generic identity with established audience appeal.[26] Commodification, then, can operate to define films as exempla of a popular genre or subject matter.

This concentration on a subject matter that combines sensationalism and ostensibly relevant material continues to be important in designating more recent dramas such as *Fatal Attraction* and *The Accused*. One ramification of the promotion of a film's subject matter is that the audience is encouraged to locate the subject matter of the film (e.g., adultery or rape) in relation to their own lives. In the case of both of these recent films, the relevance of the subject matter is further developed through TV talk shows and magazine articles that feature stories on "real life fatal attractions" or on Kelly McGillis's experience with rape.[27] Once again an initial process of reification attains a broad social dimension. But clearly not all of the tactics of extrapolation and extension for films within other genres—the slasher film or comedy, for example—operate to these same ends. Dramas provide an example of one type of promotional strategy that develops subject matter/genre as socially important.

The promotional impulse behind style tends to present certain stylistic features of a film as testaments to the director's expertise, as in the case of Spielberg, and/or as literally "sights worth seeing," as authentic re-creations or sensational spectacles. Promotional discourse on mise-en-scène can focus on the construction of sets that simulate an original location (*All the President's Men*) or on the spectacular production design of certain fantastic worlds (*Alien* or *Batman*). Promotion of cinematography has recently focused on the polished "look" of a film (*The Untouchables*) or on special effects (space battles in *Star Wars*, the robot in *The Terminator*). The most significant aspect of stylistic discourse lies in its presentation of background stories on how a certain scene or effect was accomplished. Promotion provides background stories, as it did in the case of the star, with an emphasis on a behind-the-scenes view of the making of a film that testifies to authorial and technical achievements. This phenomenon, rampant also in video—e.g., "The Making of Michael Jackson's *Thriller*"—has a staunch place in film promotion with books and TV shows devoted to, for example, how *Jaws*, *The Terminator*, or *Gone with the Wind* were made.[28]

Thus, the process of commodification engenders both the reification of the text into an assortment of elements (characters/stars, subject matter/genre and style) and the treatment of those elements to further commentary through a promotional network of forms. Within this extra-textual network, foregrounded elements are given to rhapsodic extension in the service of promoting the work. This process then raises the intertextual stakes, since the pertinent network surrounding the film includes strongly associated, extra-textual practices that dislocate and further reify textual elements. The single element in a film—the character a star plays, a scene composed by special effects—is never just "itself," its function in the narrative, but the source of polysemic extension, grist for other kinds of signification. Such inter-textual forms do not exist in some agreeably neutered semantic space, but *signify* in relation to the film, staking out its elements for definition within a mass cultural context.

One of the chief activities of commodification then is top pry open the insularity of the text as object and to disperse it into an assortment of capitalizable elements. The consumable textual economy relies on this extension, this contextual life-support system; and it is this type of economy that primes the text for digression.

"Other" Narratives and Digression

The signifying relations between textual element and forms of promotional inter-textuality are largely secured by a process of "re-narrativizing"—that is, by placing specific textual elements within *other narratives*. The excerpts or fragments of a text are assimilated into inter-textual commentary that usually constructs a narrative around those excerpts—most notably in the form of a background story. A character has a narrative role in terms of the action and progress of the narrative in which he/she appears: Indiana Jones leaves on a mission to find the Lost Ark, etc. But this character is indissolubly attached to a star, becoming part of a character/star unit: Indiana Jones/Harrison Ford. Because this unit is a source of inter-textual background stories that provide information about the star, it surpasses its intrinsic narrative function; that is, the unit is re-narrativized, becomes a player in other narratives that endow it with extra signification. The character/star unit provides a site for a double process: the generation of further media narratives detailing the star's professional and personal life, the way he/she felt about making the film, etc.; and the relation these narratives have to the unit as they return to invest it with a surplus meaning. That is, by referring to an element in the original text, other narratives build correlations to it that return with additional semiotic baggage. Promotional texts ultimately result, through a sort of boomerang effect, in a potential extra-signification of the element in question—an additional discursive endowment which enters into the process of reception.

The correlation built by these other narratives between the textual element and its inter-textual accompaniment provokes the distraction inherent in the digressive response. Digression is prompted by the promotional bridge between the filmic element, whether star, subject matter, or style, and those inter-textual frames of reference that extend those elements into the social sphere. As promotion acts to extend elements of the film into the social sphere, it in turn acts on reception by galvanizing those filmic elements for momentary guided exits from the text. The star's presence on screen, for example, can cause the spectator to digress momentarily into the series of other narratives that the film's promotion has engendered. Hence, the spectator who watches Patrick Swayze in *Dirty Dancing* may digress from the progress of the narrative to meditate on how this actor has struggled to get where he is, on his dancing background, on his status as heterosexual heartthrob, or on any information provided by Swayze's interviews. Similarly, the spectator may digress into promotional inter-textual frames in those scenes from *The Terminator* that require special ef-fects: the Movie Channel provided a "Behind-the-Scenes" documentary on how the crew managed to shoot and manipulate the scenes featuring the robot-Terminator, while interviews with Arnold Schwarzenegger and coverage in science fiction fan magazines stressed the complex interaction between actors and the special effects employed in the film.

This type of response approximates Eco's inferential walks, where the reader digresses to gather the intertextual support necessary to decipher a moment within the narrative. In this case, however, the external field re-ferred to by the reader (background stories) does not assist in what Eco regards as the proper assembly of the text or perhaps in any sort of complete reading at all. Instead this field guides the spectator into inter-textual frames of reference that result in readings of textual fragments. The spectator, motivated by the activity of these referential frames, fragments the text by resorting to background stories that draw the text out and give it a social identity—an identity incommensurate with what Eco deems its "unadul-terable specificity." As Eco later reasons in his essay on *Casablanca* as a cult film, the reading of such popular cultural phenomena requires a compe-tence which is "not only inter-cinematic . . . [but] intermedia in the sense that the spectator must know not only other movies, but the whole mass media gossip about the movies."[29] If we extend this observation to the nature of reception in mass culture in general, the spectator who fragments the text according to his/her knowledge of "mass media gossip" is not incompetent for want of reproducing the proper reading of a text, but, on the contrary, highly competent in an inter-textual sense, the good viewer solicited by the commercial apparatus.

It is in this sense that the text is "open" during the process of its social apprehension: that its productivity is amplified; its individual elements are polysemic without submitting to the procedures of closure; that it is man-handled, subject to interruptions, and given to inferential walks that stray too far from the exact provinces of the text. It is open, not by virtue of every conceivable accident of reading, but through the agency of certain definitive cultural, contextual operations. The classic film, then, is not a self-enclosed entity, but a source for and a recipient of the activity of a constellation of other narratives: in my example, stories that background particular filmic elements for the purposes of promotion.

This type of re-narrativizing provides a single instance of how texts are continuously prone to being restructured from "the outside." In addition, promotional inter-textuality defines the film industry's attempts to produce meaning—through incessant procedures of backgrounding its own productions, by providing "behind-the-scenes" information about the making of a film or about its stars, or by drawing a relation between the film's subject matter and the spectator's own world. The film industry is more than willing to be self-reflexive; exposing the star behind the character, the mechanics behind a special-effects scene, or the intentions behind the choice of a certain subject only serves to provide yet other means for fetishizing the text in question. Hence, the spectator of science fiction films learns how certain special effects were accomplished, and relates to the film through a "how-this-was-done" mentality, testifying to the ability of the industry to create fascinated spectators—fans—on the basis of the exposé. Films act as frameworks for such expeditions—moments of digression set off by promotional narratives that address how a scene was done, the star's marital history or status as a romantic icon, what other films a director has made. The spectator subject to this type of "mass media gossip" reproduces these facts as if, sometimes, they established a history as substantial as that of national current events.

The text is thus primed for digressions through the inter-textual extension of its consumable components into other narratives. This activity produces the possibility of digression, as it acts to momentarily equip an element with its inter-textual range during the process of reception.

Mass culture of course abounds in intertextual possibilities. My inquiry has focused on a *particular region* of inter-textuality and type of digression associated with a film's circulation through culture as a commodity. This region, in remaining relatively close to the release and circulation of the film, does not exhaust the extent or range of the influence of inter-textuality on reception. Promotion is part of a chain of events that subjects the text to the influence of other discourses during the course of its social circulation; its specific discursive activity issues from an institutional practice that attempts to wed commerce with reception.

Similarly, the existence of a digressive dynamic in reception prompted by commodification does not rule out the presence of other modes of response occurring in mass culture, including "wilder" forms of digression or oppositional readings. This type of digression describes, rather, a single economy of viewing produced by a concerted effort on the part of the film industry to encourage certain diverse readings of a film. While commodification represents a significant component in the film/viewer interaction, reception in mass culture is influenced by such a diversity of factors that no single dynamic can be comprehensive.

At the same time, digression *does* present an example of a difference in viewing—that is, a type of viewing that does not reproduce the single intended structure and meaning of a text—which is not *therefore* oppositional or alternative. Digression designates a sphere of reactions available to the "everyday" social spectator that are influenced by social institutions seeking to multiply readings of a text within ideological parameters. The activity of commodification here attains a very personal dimension, as it extends aspects of the film into the spectator's experience and knowledge. This perspective provides a different dimension to the relation between commodification and reception than that represented, for instance, by John Fiske's work on Madonna; such perspectives tend to claim that *because* commodities become highly personalized, this signifies the complete autonomy of the user of the commodity and a transformation of the original ideological purposes of commodification.[30] My analysis of promotion suggests that the success of commodification relies on a personalization or privatization of what are originally public discourses; the further a text can be extended into the social and individual realm by promotional discourses, the better its commercial destiny. The process of commodification is socially meaningful, in that the mini-narratives it produces to background the production of a film *encourage* the spectator to internalize the phenomena of the film by becoming an expert in its behind-the-scenes history or by identifying the subject matter of a film with his or her own experience (i.e., relevant social problems). In such cases, the individual's manipulation of commodity discourses may not testify to his/her autonomy and ability to react to the system, but to the achieved strategies of these discourses.

The intense intertextual environment of mass culture, then, is not simply a context full of free-floating signifiers that can be operated by members of society as they will; mass culture also embodies a series of ideological procedures accompanying textual production that bear significantly on reception—procedures marked in this particular case by the digressing spectator.

Notes

1. Stephen Heath, "Screen Images, Film Memory," *Edinburgh Magazine*, no. 1 (1976): 33–42.

2. For example, a formalist approach in Ed Branigan, "Subjectivity under Siege . . . ," *Screen* 19, no. 1 (1978): 7–40; a psychoanalytic treatment in Raymond Bellour, "Hitchcock, the Enunciator," *Camera Obscura*, no. 2 (1977): 66–91; and, on the subject of suture, Daniel Dayan, "The Tutor Code of Classical Cinema," in *Movies and Methods*, ed. Bill Nichols (Berkeley: University of California Press, 1976), 438–51.

3. Divergent responses have not been, however, wholly overlooked in film theory. Christian Metz has distinguished spectatorial interventions as responses which are incited by the nature of the cinematic illusion itself, as it relies on a confusion of film and dream states. Interventions arise from momentary lapses in the spectator's awareness of the unreality of the cinematic illusion, when he/she

believes in the illusion and is moved toward excessive affective participation ("Film and Dream: The Knowledge of the Spectator," in *The Imaginary Signifier*, trans. Celia Britton et al. [Bloomington: Indiana University Press, 1977], 101–8). While Metz's formulation is valuable in defining the psycho-perceptual foundations for divergent responses, the question still remains as to the place such responses have in the text/viewer interaction beyond the generality of the effects of the cinematic illusion.

4. David Morley, *The "Nationwide" Audience* (London: British Film Institute, 1980); Tony Bennett and Janet Woollacott, *Bond and Beyond: The Political Career of a Popular Hero* (New York: Methuen, Inc., 1987).

5. Roland Barthes, *S/Z*, trans. Richard Miller (New York: Hill and Wang, 1974); Umberto Eco, *The Role of the Reader* (Bloomington: Indiana University Press, 1979).

6. These theorists do not agree, however, on the relative merits of such a development. See Walter Benjamin, "The Work of Art in the Age of Mechanical Reproduction," *Illumination*, trans. Harry Zohn (New York: Schocken Books), 1969, 217–52; Siegfried Kracauer, "The Mass Ornament," trans. Barbara Correll and Jack Zipes, *New German Critique* 5 (Spring 1975): 67–76; Max Horkheimer and Theodor Adorno, "The Culture Industry: Enlightenment as Mass Deception," in *Dialectic of Enlightenment*, trans. John Cumming (New York: Herder and Herder, 1977), 120–67; and Adorno, "On the Fetish Character in Music and the Regression of Listening," in *The Essential Frankfurt School Reader*, ed. Andrew Arato and Eike Gebhardt (New York: Urizen Books, 1978), 270–99.

7. Barthes, *S/Z*, 20.

8. Ibid., 13–15.

9. Eco, *The Role of the Reader*, 32.

10. Barthes, *S/Z*, 6.

11. Bennett and Woollacott, *Bond and Beyond*, 44–45.

12. Eco, *The Role of the Reader*, 10.

13. Ibid., 8.

14. Ibid., 49.

15. Ibid., 32.

16. David Bordwell, Janet Staiger, and Kristin Thompson, *The Classical Hollywood Cinema: Film Style Mode of Production to 1960* (New York: Columbia University Press, 1985), particularly 97–102.

17. *Heavenly Bodies: Film Stars and Society* (New York: St. Martin's Press, 1986).

18. The most recent ad for the film's cable release describes it as "designed to strike fear into the hearts of philanderers everywhere" (*TV Entertainment Weekly*, December 1988, 8).

19. *Capital: A Critique of the Political Economy I*, trans. Samuel Moore and Edward Aveling, ed. Frederick Engels (New York: International Publishers, 1974), 35–81.

20. Adorno, "The Fetish Character in Music," 158.

21. Ibid., 287.

22. Jean Baudrillard, *For a Critique of the Political Economy of the Sign*, trans. Charles Levin (St. Louis: Telos Press, 1981), 92.

23. Dick Hebdige, *Subculture: the Meaning of Style* (London and New York: Methuen, 1982); and John Fiske, "British Cultural Studies and Television," in *Channels of Discourse*, ed. Robert C. Allen (Chapel Hill and London: University of North Carolina Press, 1985), 254–90.

24. These observations are grounded in research I have done on Universal-International's advertising and promotion of *Written on the Wind* (1956). The studio selected these units for promotion, and through the exhibition cluster of materials— posters, lobby displays, and trailers—as well as inter-media ad spots, interviews

with and magazine coverage of the stars, attempted to establish the film's consumable identity. I am proposing that these elements have remained important ingredients for promotion.

25. There are of course both modifications and exceptions to this balance between star and character, where the history of the character shares or monopolizes the commercial spotlight—witness Dirty Harry, James Bond, or Freddy Krueger.

26. This information was gathered from the Doheny Library, The University of Southern California, Los Angeles.

27. Oprah Winfrey and Phil Donahue both ran shows about real fatal attractions, while *People* magazine ran a feature story on the same subject in an issue with the stars of *Fatal Attraction* on the cover, 28 December 1987, 92–101; *People* also ran a feature story on Kelly McGillis that related her experience with rape to *The Accused* entitled "Rape, Shame, Fear," 4 November 1988, 154–60.

28. For example, Edith Blake, *On Location on Martha's Vineyard: The Making of the Movie "JAWS"* (New York: Ballantine Books, 1975); and "The Making of *The Terminator*," which aired on the Movie Channel, Spring 1985; "The Making of a Legend," a documentary about special effects and other behind-the-scenes information on *Gone with the Wind* aired on TNT a few months before the release of its restored version in New York, Spring 1988. Each of these accounts ran in conjunction with or prior to the run of the film in question.

29. Umberto Eco,"*Casablanca*: Cult Movies and Intertextual Collage," *Substance* 47 (1985): 12.

30. Fiske, "British Cultural Studies and Television," especially 270–86.

SEVEN

Baudrillard's America (and Ours?): Image, Virus, Catastrophe

Stephen Watt

> *Images have become our true sex objects,*
> the object of our desire. . . . It is this
> promiscuity and the ubiquity of im-
> ages, this viral contamination of things
> by images which are the fatal charac-
> teristics of our culture.[1]
> —Jean Baudrillard

> It soon became apparent that the car
> not only would ease man's burden,
> but that it also would enable him to
> enjoy a fuller life. . . . With new lei-
> sure time people began to take motor
> trips. North America unfolded beyond
> the windshield . . . all became accessi-
> ble in a way that was not possible be-
> fore.[2]
> —Henry Ford II

Shortly before the last presidential election, C. Carr in *The Village Voice* proclaimed the imminent success of the "Bush/Flail" campaign a validation of "everything ever written by that poststructuralist webslinger, Jean Baudrillard." In what has become a common characterization of Baudrillard's writing, the *Voice* referred to his "apocalyptic vision" and underscored the importance of both commodification and simulation to his sociology. Both are important in American politics as well. The Republican party's impending victory was, in Carr's estimation, due to a successful advertising strategy in which George Bush and Dan Quayle were marketed "like a couple of Michelobs"; moreover, in merely *looking* like a "proper candidate," Quayle, in Carr's estimation the "ultimate in emptiness," amounted to a "Xerox of Bush, who's a Xerox of Reagan[,] who's a Xerox of fictional personalities."[3] In Baudrillard's America, political candidates are packaged as commodities, and thus located within a vast spiral of simulation effected by the media in which the real is effaced and replaced by the hyperreal or the neo-real: the "more real" produced by computer models, digital codes, and a vast network of cybernetic operations. The referent, the signified, difference—all are usurped by the image in its empty perfection. And with this usurpation comes the death of representation, as Baudrillard announces in *La Gauche divine* (1985), and a dispersion of political power that, as one effect, has led desperate politicians to actions which resemble "un calcul d'effects speciaux, d'ambiance et de performance" (p. 112). As if the decisive Bush-Quayle victory were not sufficient evidence of the accuracy of Baudrillard's portrayal of postmodern America, the cover of a recent *Time* magazine features a portrait of George Washington shedding an enormous tear accompanied by the query, "Is Government Dead?" Baudrillard's answer is a resounding "certainement": political power as we once knew it *is* dead, along with use value, the real, referentiality, representation, and, most crucially, difference.

A close relationship between simulation and commodification exists not only in the marketing of political candidates, but also in the formulation of Baudrillard's sociology, a relationship revealed in the image's pure iconicity. As Fredric Jameson explains, commodification involves a process that might be termed "imaging"—the emptying of an object's intrinsic value so as to reorganize it as one link in a chain of signifiers: "By its transformation into a commodity a thing, of whatever type, has been reduced to a means for its own consumption. It no longer has any qualitative value in itself, but only insofar as it can be "used": the various forms of activity lose their immanent intrinsic satisfactions as activity and become means to an end."[4] If, stripped of any "real" value, a commodity operates as a kind of image, the inverse is also true: an image stands as "the ultimate form of commodity reification in contemporary society." Acknowledging his indebtedness both to Baudrillard and Guy Debord, Jameson maintains that we consume less "the thing itself, than its abstract idea capable of the libidinal investments ingeniously arrayed for us by advertising."[5] Continually intrigued with our consumption of signifiers, Baudrillard, as Jennifer Wicke observes, almost always assesses simulations "at their point of reception, not at the point of production."[6] It is, therefore, in Baudrillard's foregrounding of the consumption of images that "viral contamination" takes place—and that the potential for change or mutation resides.

For Baudrillard the most fascinating, inexorable purveyor of images (commodities) is, of course, television, which "collaborated" with the automobile throughout the 1960s in "sustaining the dominant machinery of capitalist representation."[7] Both have collaborated as well in shaping Baudrillard's conception of America, a perversely paradisal site of hyperreal and obscene accessibility that counters Henry Ford II's exuberant letter to consumers that exalts the automobile's contribution to accessibility in my epigraph. Despite Jonathan Crary's claim that because of new technology like the VDT the "passive consumption of images that characterized the sixties['] spectator is over,"[8] students of mass culture like John Brenkman continue to argue persuasively that the "dominant cultural forms" of late capitalism strive "to sever social experience from the formation of counterideologies, to break collective experience into the monadic isolation of the private experience of individuals, and to pre-empt the effects of association by subsuming the discourses and images that regulate social life."[9] Similarly, while announcing the end of spectacle and thus the demise of the public/private opposition, Baudrillard evokes this sense of "monadic isolation" throughout his chronicle of travels across America. In *America* (1986; English translation, 1988), while contemplating the sky over New York City, Baudrillard implies that such a severing of the individual from the collective has already been accomplished: "Sexual solitude of clouds in the sky; solitude of men on the earth. The number of people here who think alone, sing alone, and eat and talk alone in the streets is mind-boggling" (p. 15). As pervasive as isolation, the acceleration of life in the fast lane of American highways finds its parallel in the simulations that circulate perpetually across our television sets: cars and images, speed and solitary spectation, mark our circulation between highway and family room awaiting the social apocalypse Baudrillard tells us is sure to come.

In my view, Baudrillard's consistently narrow focus on the consumption of images and his drawing of what Douglas Kellner deprecates as "especially exaggerated conclusions" from television's "alleged centrality" combine with his creation of analogies and seemingly apocalyptic metaphors drawn from contemporary scientific theory to produce both misreadings of and shortcomings in his conception of the roles and effects of simulation in postmodern culture.[10] Several of Baudrillard's most significant and problematic appropriations from scientific and mathematical discourse appear in the epigraph above, taken from *The Ecstasy of Communication* (1987): namely, that the "promiscuity and ubiquity of images," which Baudrillard insists are our "true sex objects," amount to a "viral contamination of things by images which are the fatal characteristics of our culture. And this knows no bounds." Insofar as an image might be replicated on a videotape or photograph, purchased, and thus possessed—Jameson invokes the paradigmatic instance of tourists' desire to hoard snapshots of monuments or expansive natural vistas like the Grand Canyon—it is not difficult to envision the image as a fetishized object. Hollywood studio moguls, advertisers, and the publishers of "men's magazines" discovered this phenomenon long ago. But how exactly does the image function as a virus, and how should we respond to Baudrillard's claim that such viruses amount to "the fatal characteristics of our culture"? What "culture" or host suffers this viral incursion, one identifiable by its excessiveness, and how are we to react to this "fatality"?

How, too, are we to react to Baudrillard himself, who has figured so prominently in, among other enterprises, the profoundly masochistic endeavor of theorizing the postmodern? As Kellner wryly comments, Baudrillard has indeed emerged as a "new guru of theoretical discourse" with "camp followers" eager "to announce the coming of the New Discourse and New Wave that go beyond modernity and philosophy, social theory and politics, as we have suffered them previously." Kellner is therefore justified in calling for less "idolatry of a new master thinker" and more "critical reception of Baudrillard's work."[11] Particularly since the translation and wide promotion of *America* in 1988, Baudrillard has provoked exactly this sort of reception, most conspicuously perhaps from Robert Hughes in a scathing review of *America* in *The New York Review of Books*. Hughes inveighs against what he regards as Baudrillard's "remarkable silliness," reiterating an all-too-familiar litany of complaints against any discourse with the faintest scintilla of au courant "theory": clotted prose style, "vogue words" and neologisms, "disdain for empirical sense," and so on. Hovering parodically over this indictment looms a caricature of Baudrillard, belching pearls of ill-wisdom that splash at his feet and thereby create the "marshy verge" at which, Hughes alleges, "bleating flocks of post-structuralists go each night to drink."[12] Of course, Kellner and Hughes are, in a broad sense, correct: who could fail to notice the rise of various post-structuralist "stars" in an academy that encourages some to behave like fan club members, disseminating through their scholarship homogenized "cover" versions of their star's big hits? (Clearly I shall "cover" Baudrillard in a similar manner in this essay.) But underlying Hughes's prickly response to Baudrillard's "absolutism" and "sophomoric nihilism"—somewhere beneath Hughes's deprecation of Baudrillard as a "patchy thinker" and "poor travel writer"—resides a more significant complaint. This, I think, concerns Baudrillard's disregard for idiosyncrasy or local difference, for writing particular sociologies, and his penchant, revealed in *America* perhaps more blatantly than in other texts, for totalizing pronouncements that masquerade as cultural analyses.

Like Hughes in his disparagement of the "deep vein of snobbery" Baudrillard excites in his "fans," Kellner also overstates the case by alleging that "almost every article on Baudrillard in English seems to presuppose that he is right . . . " (in fairness I should point out that this generalization came before the uneasy reception of *America* and at the same time that a number of writers were rising to meet Kellner's challenge).[13] On the contrary, Meaghan Morris and Richard Allen, to name but two, have offered effective critiques of Baudrillard, striking at his abolition of a naively conceived "real," then his reinstatement of the "more than real" as the "reality" of postmodern culture, and at his "magical" explanation of the mechanics of change or shift in cultural formation. Allen regards Baudrillard's social philosophy as "not only philosophically naive, but 'critically' bankrupt."[14] If the real has collapsed totally into the imaginary, Allen asks, from what point of solid ground can Baudrillard "purport to tell us what *really* is the case"?[15] And, as Morris notes, the polar or oppositional structuration Baudrillard typically refuses in a first instance in his discourse is "simply revived" in another, an instance marked by its excess and intensification of sameness: "Too much of something, for Baudrillard, is the same-but-worse as nothing at all."[16] Last, because Baudrillard fails to develop a clear plan of resistance, or because it is difficult to gauge the emancipatory potential of a counter-strategy defined by our conspicuous consumption of images, it is understandable how Carr and Wicke can agree about his "apocalyptic vision"—and how Jacques Delaruelle and John McDonald can refer to the "extreme pessimism, or more exactly the nihilism" of Baudrillard's considerations *and* to the "sense of exhilaration which accompany [*sic*] their expression."[17] How is such a paradox possible? Perhaps Lawrence Grossberg best sums up the theoretical limitations of Baudrillard's writing by insisting that "it is not the social that has imploded but a particular ideological structuration (private/public) which seems no longer effective."[18] For Grossberg, furthermore, Baudrillard is "less an analyst of our historical condition than another of its many billboards": "like the world he celebrates," Baudrillard "moves so quickly that nothing is allowed to impinge upon it, nothing can break its slippery surface."[19] Fast, slippery, and disturbingly celebratory of postmodern culture's annihilation—these are among the most unsettling characteristics of Baudrillard's writing.

While I in no way intend here to challenge Morris's and Allen's readings of Baudrillard's conceptualization of the real—nor can I dispute the wreckless speed of (dis)excursion in *America*—I shall elaborate several reasons for Allen's accusation of Baudrillard's "critical bankruptcy." Not surprisingly, these very reasons also account for Baudrillard's seemingly cheerful skepticism about formulating successful strategies of resistance. Such responses to Baudrillard are the product, it seems to me, of at least two (throughout I shall be suggesting more) factors: his ultimately idealistic conceptualization and deployment of such terms as "catastrophe"; and his aversion to but final backsliding toward a "radical" epistemology in which change is attained through oppositional or dialectical means. That is, when Allen declares Baudrillard's social theory " 'critically' bankrupt" and Kellner inveighs against Baudrillard's "semiotic determinism," they are in fact revealing their dismay at his dismissal of the possibility of a radical otherness or mechanism of resistance outside the imperial domain of postmodern simulation. As Kellner correctly explains, for Baudrillard "neither radical media theory nor politics make any sense, since the entire domain in his theory is a field of mystification, social control and manipulation"; further, Baudrillard's "posture . . . indicates a move into the Beyond, free from the ghosts and limitations of all the master thinkers of times past," especially Marxism, Freudianism, and structuralism.[20]

In fact, this "Beyond" is at least twice removed in Baudrillard's recent discourse from the master-texts of modernism (though it is inevitably related to his earlier revisions of Marx). Instead of engaging and revising these, as he did earlier in such works as *Le Système des objects* (1968) and *For a Critique of the Political Economy of the Sign* (1972), Baudrillard completely dismisses them, psychoanalysis in particular, as the detritus of an outmoded intellectual apparatus. He does so in part by appropriating from and subsequently battling with the very different master-texts of biological science and mathematical theory that contribute to the "postmodern condition," particularly Jacques Monod's *Hasard et la necessité* (1971) and elaborations of "catastrophe theory" like René Thom's *Stabilité structurelle et morphogenèse* (1972). Attacking Monod, especially insofar as he invokes chance or pure accident as a causal agent of change, Baudrillard returns again and again to biological science: to viruses, biological mechanisms, and, most importantly, to DNA and the genetic code. Against the unidirectional and putatively irreversible force of the genetic code, Baudrillard counterposes a "catastrophic order" of reversibility based loosely on Thom's mathematics (and that of his English-speaking followers such as E. C. Zeeman). Such explanations of nature and change would completely transform liberal-humanist and politically "radical" ideologies founded on dialectical or binary understandings of reality. In *The Ecstasy of Communication* Baudrillard refers to this shattering of oppositional tension as "seduction"— one of several such overdetermined terms in the Baudrillardian lexicon— and describes what would amount to a seductive theory of language:

> One could conceive of a theory dealing with signs, terms, and values . . . not in terms of their contrast or calculated opposition. . . .
> A theory in which there would be many instances of this seductive operation, of this lightning flash of seduction melting the polar opposites of meaning. . . .
> For what has happened to good and evil, to the true and the false, to all these great distinctions which we need to decipher and make sense of the world? All these terms, torn asunder at the cost of unbounded energy, are ready at any moment to extinguish one other, and collapse *to our greatest joy.* (pp. 58–59)

This is the sort of theory most of us find alien or even absurd—and certainly not empowering or indicative of agency—because it posits a singularity or unidirectionality that, after the tension between the Hegelian thesis and antithesis, the Freudian superego and id, the Saussurian signifier/signified, strips us of the security of our familiar master-thinkers. What is worse, Baudrillard apparently expects us to be accepting of, if not jovial about, the prospect of such an implosive end to the secure paradigms of modernism upon which we have for so long relied.

My project here is therefore a dual one: to explicate Baudrillard's employment of Monod and catastrophe theory, and to adumbrate the ways in which both *America* and his work on simulation in particular illuminate recent political and aesthetic practices in America. That is, for me one of the most intriguing things about Baudrillard, regardless of the difficulties in his theory and its myriad of unsettling implications, is the at times uncanny accuracy of his description of postmodern cultural practices. To demonstrate this, I shall not only return to the commercial packaging of the Reagan-Bush-Quayle troika, but also consider several examples from the contemporary American theatre, which in my view has been virtually ignored in most discussions of postmodernism. Indeed, although the past several years have witnessed numerous influential studies of postmodern fiction and poetry—Brian McHale's *Postmodernist Fiction*, Charles Newman's *The Postmodern Aura*, David Porush's *The Soft Machine*, Linda Hutcheon on historical meta-fiction, and Marjorie Perloff on poetry—with the exception of Herbert Blau's writing and various contributions to performance theory, little discussion of contemporary American drama has been much concerned with postmodernism. So, after an explication of Baudrillard's *America* and the master-texts that inform it, I shall turn to Baudrillard's (and our) Americas, assessing their Baudrillardian qualities and the at times troublesome ramifications of accepting his judgments.

Catastrophes and DNA, Reversibility and Irreversibility

"Nostalgia born of the immensity of the Texas hills and the Sierras of New Mexico: gliding down the freeway. . . . Snapshots aren't enough. We'd need the whole film of the trip in real time. . . . The unfolding of the desert is infinitely close to the timelessness of film." (*America*, p. 1)

"Astral America. The lyrical nature of pure circulation. . . . The direct star-blast from vectors and signals, from the vertical and the spatial. As against the fevered distance of the cultural gaze. Joy in the collapse of metaphor." (*America*, p. 27)

While Stanley Aronowitz seems accurate enough in asserting that "postmodernism" registers the arrival of a "shift in sensibility" predicted by Nietzsche—one "marked by the renunciation of foundational thought; of rules governing art; and of the ideological 'master discourses' liberalism and marxism"—Baudrillard asks us to make at least two such shifts.[21] One is identifiable by the irreversibility and mechanistic qualities of Monod's genetic code, qualities capable of inducing the nihilism so many readers find inherent in Baudrillard's writing; the other marks the potential for sudden change, a stemming of the seemingly ineluctable operation of a dynamic system described by catastrophe theorists. Of course, neither Monod's biology nor catastrophe theory is "news" these days to working scientists (as several of my colleagues in these fields have taken great delight in informing me). So much for au courant cultural theory, often notorious for its reinvention of the wheels of science and mathematics to help convey its own project. Baudrillard is so inclined, and the two excerpts above from *America* typify the persistent opposition in his work between an irreversible cultural mechanism driven by media technology and a symbolic reversal of this mechanism. No matter that power is dispersed, metaphor and opposition collapsed in Baudrillard's *theory*; they exist problematically in his *practice*. And they are the subject of what follows.

Simulation, construed by Baudrillard to be an irreducibly American phenomenon that is spreading worldwide, wherever people huddle to watch *Dallas* and *Falcon Crest*, is crucial to conceptions of postmodernism as a term of periodization, or to what Grossberg terms "pose-modernism" in the media's "performance of particular poses": "a set of discursive practices which is only visible in the complex articulations within and among the various cultural media," all of which "relate problematically to the real."[22] Here is where the cybernetic modelling that Baudrillard invests with a power of determination analogous to that of the genetic code comes into play. In Baudrillard's admittedly pessimistic chronicle—one vaguely reminiscent of Foucault's, which Baudrillard has advised us we are better off to forget[23]—we have passed through to a third order of simulacra: from the counterfeiting of an original in the Renaissance; to the conveyor-belt serialization of objects in nineteenth-century and modern industrial simulacrum; to a third order in which the model predominates and precedes a now superfluous original, one we would not recognize even if it did exist. Although Baudrillard characterizes this process in terms resonant of cybernetic metaphors, even these are finally subsumed under the biological figures in his discourse of viruses, mutations, and the all-powerful genetic code:

> Instead of a process which is finalized according to its ideal development, we generalize from a *model*. . . . From a capitalist-productivist society to a neo-capitalist cybernetic order that aims now at total control. This is the mutation for which the biological theorization of code prepares the ground. There is nothing of an accident in this mutation. It is the end of history in which, successively, God, man, Progress, and History die to profit the code. . . . (*Simulations* , p. 111)

All the explanatory metaphors of modernist thought—the vertical metaphor of conscious and unconscious, or surface and depth, in Freud; the dialectical tension between base and superstructure in Marx—are flattened by the code. All subjects are reduced to screens, all classes relegated to the silent majority, all of us turned into more or less equivalent consumers of signs (a most uncritical hypothesis that combines problematically, as Grossberg points out, with Baudrillard's failure to theorize both the specific apparatuses and the spectating conventions of various media). In this culture, the mirror of production is so shattered by the screens of perfect simulation that we grow incapable of ascertaining what original reality is being reproduced.

From his critique of Marxism in *Le Système des objets* and *For a Critique of the Political Economy of the Sign* to the more recent *America* and *The Ecstasy of Communications*, Baudrillard has inexhaustibly reiterated the terms of contemporary culture's erasure of the real, of the referent, of the signified. For Baudrillard, our belief in "a real subject, motivated by needs and confronted by real objects as sources of satisfaction" amounts to a "thoroughly vulgar metaphysic" (*Critique*, p. 63). The object and "need" in this transaction, according to Baudrillard, are as insubstantial as Cordelia's response to King Lear's foolish question in the opening act of Shakespeare's play: "Nothing." In the fetishist theory of consumption, Baudrillard explained nearly twenty years ago, "one forgets that what we are dealing with [in objects, in commodities] first is signs": a "generalized code of signs, a totally arbitrary code of differences, *and that it is on this basis, and not at all on account of their use values or their innate 'virtues,' that objects exercise their fascination*" (*Critique*, p. 91). In this model, the desire to consume is also systematically reproduced, as use-value—claims made of an object's vital or anthropological utility based on need—becomes merely a "satellite" or, more insidiously, an "alibi" for consumption. "Need" thus has an "ideological genesis," not a physical or biological one: it must be reproduced so as to maintain consumption, and this imperative is realized through the proliferation of signfiers.

From this characterization of the consumer society, it is merely one or two leaps and homologies to *Simulations*: signifier supersedes signified (referent); exchange value overwhelms use value, obliterating any claim to "real" need; simulation or model precedes and produces reality. From this premise Baudrillard inaugurates *Simulations* (1983), in which the code, best exemplified by the unopposed operations of DNA, rises to preeminence. In fact, Baudrillard's writing has been saturated with Monod's biology for nearly fifteen years, a biology he returns to over and over in his at times gloomy indictments of postmodern culture. Monod's mechanistic understanding of DNA and its implications in understanding human evolution in *Hasard et la necessité* drives both Baudrillard's theories of simulation and his reading of Foucault in *Oublier Foucault* (1977), an indebtedness made clear from the outset:

> For Foucault, power operates right away like Monod's genetic code, according to a diagram of dispersion and command (DNA), and according to a *teleonomical* order. . . . Teleonomy is the end of all final determination and of all dialectic: it is the kind of generative inscription of the code that one expects—an immanent, ineluctable, and always positive inscription that yields only to infinitesimal mutations. (p. 34)

Hence, Baudrillard announces with bemused irritation that "until further notice—and this could be the only one—the *true* molecule is not that of the revolutionaries; it is Monod's molecule of the genetic code and the 'complex spirals of DNA' " (*Forget Foucault*, p. 34). Inflected by Monod's description of the genetic code, "irreversible" becomes in Baudrillard's discourse an adjective for immanence and modelling capacity: we have made "an irreversible agency (*instance*) out of both sex and power"; these exert an "irreversible energy"; and, in an inference gleaned from our privileging of sex and power, "we give meaning . . . only to what is irreversible (*Forget Foucault*, p. 47).

Allusions to Monod remain central to most of Baudrillard's writing after *L'Échange symbolique et la mort* (1976), and thus are equally central to his description of a postmodern world of third-order simulation. For Monod, a molecular biologist who won a Nobel Prize for his work on messenger RNA, the chemical structure of DNA accounts for its capacity to replicate exact copies of nucleotide sequences, then through its complex code to translate the nucleotide sequence into an amino acid sequence in a protein. Throughout his description of the replication and translation processes, Monod invokes metaphors of machinery—in normal organisms this "microscopic precision machinery confers a remarkable accuracy upon the process of translation," for instance—and reaches a view of biology some of his colleagues have found distressing: "It [the DNA system] is not Hegelian [dialectical] at all, but thoroughly Cartesian: the cell is indeed a *machine*."[24] Rather paradoxically, this conservative system also contains both accidents (mutations) and thus slow but certain evolutionary potential. But the issue is even more complicated: because the chemistry of the genetic code is, in some senses, arbitrary, and because this arbitrary chemistry causes random mutations which aid evolution, then the following conclusion about evolution is inescapable:

> We call these events [RNA "mistranslations"] accidental; we say that they are random occurrences. And since they constitute the *only* possible source of modifications in the genetic text, itself the *sole* repository of the organism's hereditary structures, it necessarily follows that chance *alone* is at the source of every innovation, of all creation in the biosphere. Pure chance, absolutely free but blind, at the very root of the stupendous edifice of evolution. . . . It is today the *sole* conceivable hypothesis.[25]

It is, therefore, so much "noise" in the intracellular cybernetic network, so many "fortuitous perturbations" in the closed system of DNA operationality, that amounts to "the progenitor of evolution in the biosphere."[26] Chance and accident, common to both the world of DNA and the Beckettian wasteland of *Waiting for Godot*, explain change in the postmodern world.

What Aronowitz refers to as postmodernism's "renunciation" of both "foundational thought" and ideological "master discourses" like liberalism and Marxism becomes in *The Ecstasy of Communication* a much more starkly drawn portrait. As in *Oublier Foucault*, it is one whose perspective derives largely from the "master discourse" of Monod. Here is Baudrillard ruminating on the primacy of Monod's genetic code:

> The religious, metaphysical, or philosophical definition of being has given way to an operational definition in terms of the genetic code (DNA). . . . We are in a system where there is no more soul. . . .
> This having been established, there are no more individuals, but only potential biological mutants. From a biological, genetic and cybernetic viewpoint we are all mutants. (*Ecstasy*, pp. 50–51)

And we are all screens, aglow in the always already there "finality" that is clearly "inscribed in the code" (*Simulations*, p. 109). No more subjectivity, no more natural love-object or object of desire—only an image like Max Headroom flashing across the monitor. Baudrillard delineates this cyberneticized sexuality in more detail in *The Ecstasy of Communication*:

> *Images have become our true sex object*, the object of our desire. The obscenity of our culture resides in the confusion and its equivalent materialized in the image. . . . It is this promiscuity, the ubiquity of images, this viral contamination of things by images, which are the fatal characteristics of our culture. And this knows no bounds, because unlike sexed animal species protected by a kind of internal regulatory system, images cannot be prevented proliferating indefinitely. (pp. 35–36)

The result is a kind of *"social genetic code"* which "no longer leaves any room for planned reversal; and this is its true violence" (*Simulations*, p. 112). Digitality is "its metaphysical principle," DNA its "prophet" (*Simulations*, p. 103).

The implications of this pronouncement are staggering. There is, for example, a clear sense of the pornography of such a culture, one in which there is no more secret, but everything exposed (accessible) and mechanized like performers in the sleaziest of sexually explicit films and entertainments. The body *is*, in this sense as well as in Monod's more scientific one, a machine, but neither a perfect nor an empowered one with any potential for agency. More important, if difference itself is eroded, then what becomes of such discourses as feminism, which, especially in its reading of contemporary aesthetic practices, frequently assumes an intervenient posture between the representations of a dominant male culture and something else—truth, whatever variance or nuance it incorporates?[27] Most feminist projects have a vested interest in reality and representation, in difference, all of which Baudrillard's viral imaging destroys. Like the

HIV virus, which through the enzyme reverse transcriptase proliferates slyly by effecting reversals an organism is slow to recognize until finally the virus becomes a part of the host chromosome and its genetic information, the image in the third order of simulation is at work too, twenty-four hours a day and seven days a week, effecting changes which may be barely discernible as it sells itself and the ideology that manipulates it. Such a process, as Baudrillard reminds us, is especially evident in America:

> . . . the country indulges in a kind of promotional hype. America has a sort of mythical power throughout the world, a power based on the advertising image. . . . It is this way . . . that an entire society becomes stabilized beneath a perfusion of advertising.
> Yet it is a fragile meta-stability. . . . For in the last resort, it is due to the evaporation of any real alternative, to the disappearance of resistances and antibodies. (*America*, p. 116)

Biological metaphors emerge again when he depicts American cities and their inhabitants as "a loose network of individual, successive functions, a hypertrophied cell tissue proliferating in all directions" (*America*, p. 125). This is the subtle paradox of Monod's evolution: in an inherently conservative system like late capitalism, one which replicates sameness and creates desire in consumers to ingest its magical commodities with their implicit promise of gratification, small mutations are nonetheless effected in this proliferating cellular network. Most are "regular" or predictable; others are "catastrophic" or exceptional, hence as unpredictable as they are evolutionary. For Baudrillard, images, like viruses, effect these mutations, becoming in the process both host cell and parasite.

References to "catastrophe" in Baudrillard's writing might also assist Delaruelle and McDonald in their search for any formulation of effective strategies of resistance to the automatic spirals of simulation analogous in force to Monod's spirals of DNA. As Baudrillard repeatedly insists, a definition of such strategies is unthinkable in the oppositional terms in which resistance or radicalism is normally conceived. This is the case because in Baudrillard, Monod, and the "catastrophic theory" of mathematicians like Rene Thom, the analysis of change and even careful morphological inspection do not reveal a process of oppositional friction or predictable meiosis, but a systematized, albeit largely unpredictable, indeterminacy. Here is where Baudrillard, it seems to me, becomes especially problematic—and where his application of mathematical hypotheses is particularly tenuous. In *Forget Baudrillard*, he describes "catastrophe" in various ways, all of which reiterate its capacity to reverse the irreversible: catastrophe constitutes an "order of the fatal" in which is reposited a "dual reversibility, an agonistic challenge" (p. 84); it is not so much an accident, but a fated "necessity" in Monod's use of this term (p. 91); it denotes an order that counters rational or causal sequences and includes "seductive sequences" (p. 93). Catastrophe becomes in Baudrillard a designation for something "beyond" politics in which cultural forms are transposed in potentially terrifying ways: "It's the other form of the ecstatic, its catastrophic form, in the almost neutral sense of the term, in its mathematical extension. It is a completely alien response of the object world to the subject world . . . which occurs with an absolute surprise and whose symbolic wave strikes the human world" (p. 99). Hence, the double spiral of ecstasy and catastrophe that, in a moment of self-reflexivity, Baudrillard sees as underlying his theorizing from *Le Système des objets* through *Fatal Strategies*: "On the one hand: political economy, production, the code, the system, simulation. On the other hand: potlach, expenditure, sacrifice, death, the feminine, seduction, and in the end, the fatal" (*Ecstasy*, p. 79). So what is the status of "catastrophe" in Baudrillard? In one sense, it forms part of a structural binarism to which, as Morris has indicated, he is inevitably drawn. In the binarism's internal tension, one side will overwhelm the other with the speed of a lightning flash—and in this way polarity itself is destroyed by the catastrophe.

Catastrophe, then, is the magical, excessive counter to the ecstasy that characterizes the code and postmodern culture. Because the ecstasy of communication in postmodern America, like the hypertrophic proliferation of its cities, itself tends to extremes—the "truer than the truth" or in fashion "what's more beautiful than beautiful" (*Forget Baudrillard*, p. 99)—in a fatal strategy, part of the catastrophic order, we do not oppose "the beautiful and the ugly; we will seek what is more ugly than ugly: the monstrous. We will not oppose the visible to the hidden; we will seek what is more hidden than hidden: the secret" (*Selected Writings*, p. 185). We might say that ecstasy resides in close proximity to hype which, according to Morris, might be defined as

> the strategy of invoking that which is most, the spiral of moster and moster; . . . the same but more so; the frenzy of attributes outbidding each other in an ecstasy of one-upping.
>
> Hype is always and blatantly false than false. . . . Hype is never realistic, credible; rather, in the best of hype credibility is displayed as a super special effect. Hype is pure promotion promoting itself: the object (brand X) is only ever a pretext, a decoy, a ceremonial trigger; we are summoned not to differentiate objects, but to discriminate, in fascination, between competing brands of hype.[28]

Anyone who has watched even fifteen minutes of televised professional wrestling will appreciate Morris's definition, since most broadcasts conventionally spend as much time promoting future "conflicts" between major stars as they do showing athletic "competition." Hype is what affords stars like Hulk Hogan an income in excess of two million dollars per year (according to *Sport* magazine), and his animosity toward perennial rivals like Andre the Giant and, more recently, the Big Boss Man, must be false (the more extravagantly and blatantly so, the better) if these performers are to remain healthy enough to perform weekly as the valuable attractions they have become. The operation of "one upping" or "moster and moster," the chain of "super special effects," sells out arenas throughout the country. So, hype means the more false and outrageous, the better—an unfolding of unidirectional excess.

If hype and ecstasy are so closely related—or, using Baudrillard's own construction, if hype is the "side" of ecstasy to be displaced or terminated by a catastrophic order—what characterizes catastrophe or any of its kindred spirits such as seduction and fatal strategy? "Fatal strategy," as Mark Poster defines it, has as its primary denotation the senses of "fateful" or "fated" and only secondarily connotes "destruction" or "disaster" (*Selected Writings*, p. 206); and while Poster deemphasizes this second, perhaps more common connotation of "fatal" (and of "catastrophe" as well), Baudrillard at times does not, a lexical indiscrimination which further muddles the concept in his writing. Thus, in *America* he notes that "everywhere survival has become a burning issue, perhaps by some obscure weariness of life, or a collective desire for catastrophe (though we should not take all this too seriously; it is also a playing at catastrophe)" (p. 42). In this at times indiscriminate use of apocalyptic figures of speech to articulate theories that challenge orthodox or positivistic explanations of evolution, Baudrillard follows biologists and mathematicians of the 1970s and early '80s who have exerted the most pronounced influence on him. Certainly, when adumbrating their "theories of catastrophe"—which a few years ago sparked in departments of mathematics controversy similar to that occasioned by Derridean deconstruction in the humanities—René Thom and other mathematicians in no way invoke a sense of disaster; rather, as Thom explains, "In the theory of catastrophes . . . one attempts to describe discontinuities that may occur in the evolution of a system."[29] Thom continues by invoking a model of the internal mechanisms of a closed system of inputs and outputs, explaining that his theory of catastrophes attempts to reveal outputs which assume a "very unique form, one very different from the usual form."[30] "Catastrophe," then, connotes an overturning or change, an irregular, indeterminate, or unpredictable behavior or trajectory—not necessarily disastrous change, and certainly not change brought about by polarity or opposition.

Not surprisingly, catastrophe theory itself, a widely publicized, indeed popularized "revolution" in mathematics during the 1970s, has met with significant opposition. Speaking of it in the past tense (catastrophe is dead?) Ivar Ekeland, for instance, emphasizes that "the word 'catastrophe' conveys more than it means, and led people to expect from catastrophe theory much more than it can actually deliver—which never was very much."[31] Catastrophe theory, Ekeland stresses, does not lead to "precise, quantitative predictions." Neither can it "be proved or disproved by an experiment, and so the question arises whether it is a scientific theory at all."[32] What catastrophe theory *can* do, Ekeland believes, and what it depends upon, is fairly clear:

> It is essential for catastrophe theory that a small number of external variables be chosen [external to a dynamic system] . . . which will be the only ones to vary, all other parameters being fixed. . . . The system then jumps to another stable equilibrium: that is, we get a discontinuous change to a continuous change in the external variables. The set of parameter values where this happens is called the catastrophe set. . . . This change of equilibrium will be perceived by the observer as a sudden and substantial change in the properties of the system—a phase transition, for instance, like water solidifying into ice.[33]

Catastrophes then require both agency and manipulation from the outside, the variation of external factors, before "jump phenomena" are observed. Also, depending on the system being examined, the transition may be reversible and may not be. As Ekeland mentions, catastrophe theory amounts to a "mathematical code" to help us "make some sense out of the hopeless tangle of natural phenomena."[34]

For Baudrillard, conversely, catastrophe theory seems to offer a code that will help us overturn the *un*natural phenomena of postmodern life— and cause evolutionary "jumps" and transition from one "equilibrium point" to another. But whether the second of these equilibria is stable or not and whether the shift minimizes or maximizes the potential of a system remain unanswerable questions. Never mind that one needs to get outside the simulations that in Baudrillard can never be transcended or that such shifts can never be predicted. In short, if for mathematicians catastrophe theory augurs the problematic "comeback" of geometry, it is even more problematic in Baudrillard's sociology. It constitutes an unpredictable, almost magical reversal of the irreversibilities of postmodern simulation and excess, fighting hype with hype, image with image so the water might suddenly turn to ice, the ice to water.

Simulation, Image, Hype

> The appeal of simulated imagery lies in its promise to improve upon the original, to offer an image of the world which is larger than life, to create a degree of resolution that is beyond human perception—a hyperrealism.
>
> The oppositions that traditionally organized both social life and social critique— oppositions between surface and depth, the authentic and the inauthentic, the imaginary and the real, signifier and signified seem to have broken down.

The first passage is from Lili Berko's recent positioning of Max Headroom, the techno-culture's answer to Johnny Carson, within a simulacrum that "deconstructs the real," finally installing "digitality as its generalizing formula (and one which circumscribes all others)."[35] The second quotation, taken from Michael Paul Rogin's *Ronald Reagan, The Movie*, continues as follows: "From this point of view, Reagan's easy slippage between movies and reality is synecdochic for a political culture increasingly impervious to distortions between fiction and history."[36] Max Headroom and Ronald Reagan: stranger bedfellows, perhaps, than a future president and a chimpanzee, yet more related as well. For example: "Simulated objects and persons, in contrast to conventional mass media representations, do not stand in direct relationship to objects outside of their technological space."[37] Of course, this is Berko speaking of Max Headroom, but if we have ever wondered where the real president is amidst the staged shots and canned press conference responses, then we are asking, in effect, whether what we are viewing is a representation of some concrete reality or a simulation like Max. Berko explains the implications of this erasure of the real effected by images which, at one and the same time, are also commodities: "Through our acceptance of computerized video graphic images, simulation and its attendant codes have infiltrated our perception of the commonplace, the everyday, the real. These images . . . are the high concepts of the hyperreal."[38] Berko's observations are seminal Baudrillard: Max Headroom and Ronald Reagan as images—which means, given the metaphors developed above, that they are not only also commodities, but also viruses, potential agents for change, and possible "catastrophes."

Baudrillard's postmodernism of hype and simulation, as *The Village Voice* proclaimed shortly before the Bush-Quayle victory, has been confirmed by the primacy of the image in the Republican party's national campaign and the silent majority's clear preference for spectacle and disdain for meaning. This is not the occasion for me to scrutinize Baudrillard's insistence that such consumption constitutes a viable "defiance of the political" or to interrogate his statement that the "masses are a stronger medium than all the media," being as they are a diffuse and decentered reality which forces would-be patterns of manipulation to hover in endless circles over the nation's television sets (*Silent Majority*, p. 44). But whatever their problems, Baudrillard's views of simulation are uncannily descriptive of various aesthetic and political practices within American culture today.

How else can one explain George Bush playing Dirty Harry in thirty-second television spots—speed being a significant component of imaging—except perhaps as a replication of the same strategy the Republicans have been cultivating for at least twenty years? At the Republican party convention in Miami in 1968, one of the most effective speakers was John Wayne, reading a speech entitled "Why I Am Proud to Be an American," and one can almost envision Reagan aides—in the backseat priming their candidate while Richard Nixon took over the driving—taking notes for future use. During his administration, Reagan found the time to play this macho western role ("Dutch" as "Duke"?), substituting Clint Eastwood for Wayne, when he told Congress, "Go ahead. Make my day," vowing to use his power of veto to block any tax increases.[39] Predictably enough, immediately after his victory was imminent in November 1988, Bush's running mate followed *his* gurus' ploy of invoking filmic images: not the image of the rugged individualist with six-shooter or .44 magnum blazing, but of the all-American boy and team player by announcing exuberantly, "We won one for the Gipper." The "Gipper" is, of course, Reagan in his favorite role as the Notre Dame football player who dies of viral pneumonia in *Knute Rockne—All American* (1940). We recognize in the vice-president-elect's sentence both a dissimulation and several layers of simulation: he deflects or dissimulates by hiding the fact that he was clearly a drag on the presidential ticket, not an asset; he simulates by placing politics within the spiral of sports and the movies, with himself and Bush in the roles of football heroes and Reagan, this time, in another favorite role as martyr in the holy wars of intercollegiate athletics.

A similar repertory of images was invoked during the Iran-Contra hearings by Oliver North, who, at various times, assumed personas similar to those manipulated so deftly by Reagan: macho soldier who, at one moment during the proceedings, said he would meet Daniel Ortega face to face anywhere in the world; and victim or would-be martyr, facing an overwhelming barrage of questions and an army of powerful inquisitors. Here, North appropriates two powerful images developed during the Reagan years—the western hero with a chestful of commendations, and the patriotic scapegoat who will suffer any indignity to keep the Nicaraguans and Cubans from marching through Mexico to Texas and capturing the Alamo.

But, even without casting Baudrillard in the role of "tragic" prophet (a role for which in *Forget Baudrillard* he clearly expresses disdain), his vision of contemporary culture is approximated or even replicated in scores of contemporary American texts. Take, for example, Sam Shepard's *Motel Chronicles*, where he bemoans the primacy of the image and its effects on selfhood: "Men turning themselves into advertisements of Men. . . . Women turning themselves into advertisements of Women."[40] Or consider the nostalgia that permeates his plays and prose: a nostalgia for old movies, old actors, and '57 Chevies. Not so pessimistic as Baudrillard, Shepard still believes that Nature, the real, and sexual desire exist—or so his brief song to the "natural woman" would seem to attest:

> I've about seen
> all the nose jobs

     capped teeth
     and silly-cone tits
     I can handle

     I'm heading back
     to my natural woman.[41]

Regrettably, to recuperate the real in Shepard, David Rabe, and David Mamet—to name but three theatrical and filmic chroniclers of postmodern American culture—one also frequently confronts the power of the phallus and the "reality" of violence against or the marginalization of women. Extravagant displays of cruelty in their work perhaps comprise a reaction to what Baudrillard in *America* sees as the collapse of the male/female polarization and the rise to prominence of "gender-benders" like Michael Jackson, Boy George, and David Bowie. Among the other confusions of life in postmodern America, Baudrillard reports, sexual identity has been rendered problematic; the copious lovemaking and production of children in America are, admittedly, proof for him that *"difference still exists*. But not for long": "Already, the 'muscle-woman,' who, simply by using her vaginal muscles, manages to reproduce the effect of male penetration exactly, is a good example of self-referentiality and of getting along without difference—she at least has found her label" (*America*, p. 47).

 This destabilization of sexual identity, both in Baudrillard and in playwrights like David Rabe, is often linked to the power of the mass media. So, in Rabe's *Hurlyburly* (1985), set in the present-day Hollywood of struggling actors, cocaine abuse, and rampant sexism, the final contact with the real for some characters is sexual intercourse with a young runaway. And, besides cocaine and alcohol, the virus of television is in large measure responsible for this condition. Eddie, Rabe's central character, reminds his friends that "This is America. This is TV," a comment he explains more fully later in the play: "You know, we're all just background in one another's life. Cardboard cutouts bumping around in this vague, you know, hurlyburly, this spin-off of what was once prime-time life."[42] In an earlier moment Mickey and Eddie recall an actor-friend's prior sexual escapade with Bonnie, a disturbed, indiscreet woman whose small child witnessed the event from the front seat of Eddie's car. In Eddie's analysis, television is responsible for the spectacle: "She couldn't help herself. . . . I mean, what does she watch? About a million hours of TV a week, so the airwaves are all mixed with TV waves and then the whole thing is scrambled in her brainwaves so, you know, her head is just full of this static, this fog of TV thoughts."[43] Certainly this is a cop-out, a rationalization that cannot stand as a subsumptive explanation of human behavior. But, in the most frightening scenes of *Hurlyburly*, as in his recent film collaboration with Brian DePalma in *Casualties of War* (1989), Rabe presents us with characters who are frequently incapable of seeing others as anything but images. Thus,

Phil blames Donna, the young runaway, for invading his thoughts in a manner analogous to the viral invasion and fog of TV images Eddie deplores: " . . . I'm thinking about football, and you gotta be here . . . so that's all I'm thinkin' about from the minute I see you is tits and ass. . . . I don't have a prayer to have my own thoughts. . . . My privacy has been demolished."[44] Somewhat similarly, especially in its brutality and evocation of the woman as image, in *Casualties of War* after Sergeant Tony Meserve (Sean Penn) rapes a young Vietnamese woman he and his battalion have kidnapped, he is asked by a particularly dull soldier, "Hey Sarge, how long has it been since you had a *real* woman?" Meserve's answer, "She was real—I think she was real," contains a double charge of horror, as he appears both to relish his violation and to be confused about the ontological status of his victim.[45] "I *think* she was real"—the pause implies that he might have been able to conceptualize the woman as unreal, as image, hence a commodity to consume as he wishes. This reading is reinforced by one voyeuristic soldier's repeated comment during the rape about how well a "cold beer" would go with the "event," as if it were a sporting event or film to be viewed—a simulation.

The Hollywood of *Hurlyburly* is also the scene of David Mamet's recent Broadway success *Speed-the-Plow* (1987) and Arthur Kopit's *Bone-the-Fish* (1989), in part a parody of Mamet. Both plays, representing the Hollywood mass culture industry at its most unctuously commercial, follow in a long line of theatrical dissections of the movie business that includes Clifford Odets's *The Big Knife* (1949), Shepard's *True West* (1980), and Christopher Hampton's *Tales from Hollywood* (1983). Kopit's often vulgar and scatological play is Baudrillardian both in its excess and in its treatment of the image as sexual object. Al Sereno, a sleazy, drug-dealing producer, and his girlfriend Lou have secured an option on a blockbuster filmscript: the biography of the reigning pop superstar, Zalinka, called *Moby Dick*, with Zalinka playing Ahab and Melville's whale transformed into a phallus. All Al and Lou need is the technical expertise of Al's former partner Jerry, who has left Hollywood and embarked upon the less lucrative career of making educational films. Al and Lou have to be certain about Jerry's commitment to this project and therefore demand of him increasingly severe rituals that test his commitment. These include first making a small incision in his wrists, as both Al and Lou have previously done—shedding some blood for the partnership. Act One ends with an absurd extension of Al's predictions of the lengths other producers would go to make this film. A waiter enters and places a covered serving dish in front of Jerry that, after uncovered, is seen to contain excrement. Jerry exclaims, "Holy Shit!" to which Al responds, "It's as close as we could get"—"pure nun shit" obtained from a nearby convent: symbolic material which, as Al emphasizes, cannot be bought. The Act One lights come down with Jerry, spoon in hand, contemplating his dilemma to Al and Lou's chorus, "One spoon for the Kingdom! One spoon or you're out."

Al and Lou take Jerry to Zalinka's mansion in Act Two and, after an appropriately dramatic delay, she is introduced by an announcer and enters to the music of one of her hits blaring out of a public address system. The refrain of her song, "Who I Am," seems particularly important to Kopit's (and Baudrillard's) conception of the image as sex-object: "This is it! / Who I am / I am everything you want me to be / This is it! Who I am / Come inside of me." Zalinka dons a variety of disguises throughout the scene, ones that conceal her face especially, the only part of her body that is private: in performance, her "public" made-up face and the rest of her body— especially her tatooed breasts—belong to the public. Al's hyping of the project and the rituals assuring Jerry's commitment continue full force in the second act of Bone-the-Fish, culminating in Jerry's once again being asked, this time by Zalinka, to make a symbolic gesture of his resolve. After inspecting his "private parts," Zalinka, who has a surgeon on her house staff and an operating room under her mansion, demands that Jerry surrender a testicle to her as a sign of his loyalty. Appalled, Jerry runs to Al exclaiming, "She wants my balls," a price that even Al considers to be too dear. After calming himself, Jerry explains Zalinka's demand for only one testicle, to which Al, who misunderstood the extent of the sacrifice as Jerry first reported it, responds, "So, you mean she'll let you keep a ball?" The loss of both testicles is too much even for Al, who has already made a similar gesture of commitment, but as he explains, "for this deal a one-ball give-back isn't bad." The play ends with Jerry entering the operating room, screaming in the distance, and Al predicting that someday, after making this film, tourists will pass by his house in wonder, pointing and saying, "That's where Al and Lou Sereno live!"[46]

These texts are all part of Baudrillard's America. Amidst the collapse of once stable binarisms (clearly both image/reality and male/female are collapsed in Kopit's play), in the fog of Rabe's "TV thoughts," and in the imperialism of excess and hype, image-viruses are at work effecting slight but certain mutations in our culture. Some of these may even prove to be more than slight; they might be fatal or catastrophic, though it's impossible to predict these things. In Baudrillard's brand of nihilism, the apocalypse will come. Have a little faith—and until then expect to be further awash in the realer than real while circulating at an ever-accelerating pace on the highways surrounding our cities, or moving unidirectionally across the desert of postmodern culture.

Notes

1. In most instances, I have relied upon English translations of Baudrillard's texts and of Monod's Hasard et la necessité. However, in cases where translations

are either unavailable or incomplete—for *La Gauche divine* and René Thom's *Paraboles et catastrophes*—I have translated myself from the originals. Page numbers and, where necessary, shortened titles will follow quotations in the text from the following works by Baudrillard (whose dates of publication, save in the case of *La Gauche divine*, refer to English translations): *America*, trans. Chris Turner (London: Verso, 1988); *The Ecstasy of Communication*, trans. Bernard and Caroline Schutze, ed. Slyvere Lotringer (New York: Semiotext(e), 1987); *For a Critique of the Political Economy of the Sign*, trans. Charles Levin (St. Louis: Telos Press, 1981); *Forget Foucault* and (with Slyvere Lotringer) *Forget Baudrillard* (New York: Semiotext(e), 1987); *In the Shadow of the Silent Majority*, trans. Paul Foss, Paul Patton, and John Johnston (New York: Semiotext(e), 1983); *La Gauche divine* (Paris: Bernard Grasset, 1985); *Selected Writings*, ed. Mark Poster (Stanford: Stanford UP, 1988); *Simulations*, trans. Paul Foss, Paul Patton, and Philip Beitchman (New York: Semiotext(e), 1983). I wish here to express my gratitude to Margaret Gray-McDonald for her helpful suggestions on an earlier draft of this essay.

2. Henry Ford II, "We Begin Our 75th Year," *1978 Ford Service Policy Book* (Dearborn, Michigan: Ford Training and Publishing Department, 1978), p. 1.

3. C. Carr, "Are You Now or Have You Ever Been?" *The Village Voice*, 1 November 1988, p. 38.

4. Fredric Jameson, "Reification and Utopia in Mass Culture," *Social Text* 1 (Winter 1979): 131.

5. Jameson, p. 132.

6. Jennifer Wicke, "Postmodernism: The Perfume of Imitation," *Yale Journal of Criticism* 1 (Spring 1988): 154.

7. Jonathan Crary, "Eclipse of the Spectacle," in *Art After Modernism: Rethinking Representation*, ed. Brian Wallis (New York: The New Museum of Contemporary Art in association with David R. Godine, 1984), p. 289.

8. Crary, p. 293.

9. John Brenkman, "Mass Media: From Collective Experience to the Culture of Privatization," *Social Text* 1 (Winter 1979): 98. Brenkman, after the Frankfurt School, emphasizes that the means of production reduced "bodies to tools whose productive capacity could be bought and sold in the marketplace." Mass culture sets against this instrumentalized body the "subject's relation to the erotogenic body with its complex networks of ties to the symbolic formations and affective experiences that comprise the whole of social experience" (95).

10. Douglas Kellner, "Baudrillard, Semiurgy, and Death," *Theory, Culture & Society* 4 (1987): 132. In "Room 101 or A Few Worst Things in the World," in *Seduced and Abandoned: The Baudrillard Scene*, ed. André Frankovits (Glebe, Australia/New York: Stonemoss/Semiotext(e), 1984), Meaghan Morris aptly observes that for Baudrillard description itself is "apocalyptic: our impasse of death today is that the real ('stockage of dead matter, dead bodies, dead language') is a descriptive disaster" (p. 96).

11. Kellner, p. 126.

12. Robert Hughes, "The Patron Saint of Neo-Pop," *New York Review of Books*, 1 June 1989, pp. 29–30.

13. Kellner, p. 131. I should note here that this essay was drafted before the publication of Kellner's recent book on Baudrillard by Stanford University Press which I therefore could not consider. On the issue of Baudrillard and the media, see also Kuan-Hsing Chen, "The Masses and the Media: Baudrillard's Implosive Postmodernism," *Theory, Culture & Society* 4 (1987): 71–88.

14. Richard Allen, "Critical Theory and the Paradox of Modernist Discourse," *Screen* 28 (Spring 1987): 82. See also Morris, "Room 101 or A Few Worst Things In The World," in *Seduced and Abandoned: The Baudrillard Scene*, pp. 91–117.

15. Allen, p. 80.

16. Morris, pp. 92, 98.

17. Jacques Delaruelle and John McDonald, "Resistance and Submission," in *Seduced and Abandoned: The Baudrillard Scene*, p. 18.

18. Lawrence Grossberg, "The In-Difference of Television," *Screen* 28 (Spring 1987): 43.

19. Grossberg, p. 43.

20. Kellner, pp. 137, 130.

21. Stanley Aronowitz, "Postmodernism and Politics," *Social Text* 18 (Winter 1987/88): 99.

22. Grossberg, p. 39.

23. For a brief exchange concerning Foucault's "archaeology of things" and Baudrillard's "L'Ordre des Simulacres," see *Forget Foucault/Forget Baudrillard*, pp. 73–74.

24. Jacques Monod, *Chance and Necessity: An Essay on the Natural Philosophy of Modern Biology*, trans. Austryn Wainhouse (New York: Knopf, 1971), pp. 109, 110–11. Monod's text provoked a number of strong responses in addition to Baudrillard's, such as *Beyond Chance and Necessity*, ed. John Lewis (London: Garnstone Press, 1974). Lewis asserts, for example, that "criticism must not be silent when Professor Monod follows his scientific statements with metaphysical speculations," ones which "cannot but induce despair for the future of mankind." Baudrillard, who considers himself "if anything, a 'metaphysician' " (*Forget Baudrillard*, p. 84), might also be regarded as a writer building metaphysical speculation upon scientific statement. Lewis particularly objects to Monod's metaphors of man as machine, maintaining that "anything can be reduced to simple, obvious, mechanical interactions. The cell is a machine; the animal is a machine; man is a machine" (p. ix).

25. Monod, pp. 112–13.

26. Monod, p. 116.

27. Elin Diamond makes this point in "Mimesis, Mimicry, and the 'True-Real,' " *Modern Drama* 32 (March 1989): 58–72. In the same issue, a special number on women in the theatre, Janelle Reinelt discusses the problematic status of representation and performance in feminist writing on the theatre. See her "Feminist Theory and the Problem of Performance," pp. 48–57.

28. Morris, p. 113.

29. René Thom, *Paraboles et catastrophes* (Paris: Flammarion, 1983), p. 60.

30. Thom, p. 61.

31. Ivar Ekeland, *Mathematics and the Unexpected* (Chicago: University of Chicago Press, 1988), p. 102.

32. Ekeland, p. 76.

33. Ekeland, p. 91.

34. Ekeland, p. 77.

35. Lili Berko, "Simulation and High Concept Imagery: The Case of Max Headroom," *Wide Angle* 10 (1988): 51.

36. Michael Paul Rogin, *Ronald Reagan, The Movie and Other Episodes in Political Demonology* (Berkeley: University of California Press, 1988), p. 9.

37. Berko, p. 51.

38. Berko, p. 56.

39. Rogin, p. 7.

40. Sam Shepard, *Motel Chronicles* (San Francisco: City Lights Books, 1982), p. 81.

41. Shepard, p. 102.

42. David Rabe, *Hurlyburly* (New York: Grove Press, 1985), pp. 19, 115.

43. Rabe, p. 93.

44. Rabe, p. 58.

45. Brian DePalma, director, and David Rabe, screenwriter, *Casualties of War*. Columbia Pictures, 1989.

46. Arthur Kopit, *Bone-the-Fish*. Author's typescript for premiere at the Actors Theatre of Louisville, March 1989. My thanks to Arthur Kopit for so generously allowing me access to this script.

EIGHT

Undoing Feminism in Anne Rice's Vampire Chronicles

Devon Hodges and Janice L. Doane

How do we represent the mother? As constructed in traditional accounts, she is lacking in full subjectivity, silent, excluded, or at best marginal, her sexuality limited and constrained to her reproductive function. In recent years, the energy of a great many feminists has gone into reinterpreting the domain of the mother. Acknowledging that the mother's degraded status is intimately connected to the child's accession to the Law of the Father in the oedipal moment, recent psychoanalytic feminism has focused upon the shadowy preoedipal period, that stage of development linked to the mother and often to feminine development and desire. Yet this interpretive project dedicated to elevating the importance of the mother is frequently lured into the trap of positing an originary moment, more primal and real than the oedipal stage, that seems to promise a solution to oppressive constructions of sexual difference. Anne Rice's massively popular vampire books—*Interview with the Vampire, The Vampire Lestat,* and most recently, *The Queen of the Damned* —provide a useful way of beginning to explore the difficulties of the feminist attempt to speak the mother through the language of the preoedipal. Rice's books demonstrate the conservative influence this form of feminism has had on narratives of mass culture. Easily assimilating feminist readings of the originary power of the mother, Rice's novels have an almost vampiric relation to feminism. Furthermore, their huge success raises questions about why this psychoanalytic account has been so greedily ingested by American readers. It is time to investigate the relation between the feminist project to develop an emancipatory maternal rhetoric and conservative, postfeminist narratives of mass culture.[1] Rice's *The Vampire Lestat* and *The Queen of the Damned* are postfeminist novels that have been authorized by this recent trend in psychoanalytic feminism.

Examples of this trend abound. In *The (M)other Tongue,* for instance, Claire Kahane argues that traditional oedipal interpretations of that literature of fear known as the gothic have, in emphasizing the son's relationship to the father, worked to exclude the subplot of a female bildungsroman in texts authored by women. A focus on the preoedipal, she hopes, will allow the female reader to confront the pleasures and terrors of female identity and its dependence on a relation to the mother. Characters in the Gothic, she writes, are "face to face with the danger inherent in female identity—face to face, that is, with mothers."[2] Accepting this line of reasoning, William Veeder begins his discussion of Bram Stoker's *Dracula*, the popular Victorian antecedent to Rice's books, with a complaint about oedipal readings of the story. Veeder insists that Stoker, like Freud, tells a tale about male conflict to screen a more threatening preoedipal drama in which the mother is all too powerful. In his analysis of *Dracula*, the "terrible mother" is found to be everywhere present in the novel, disrupting the "myth of the benign mother" Victorians found so consoling, and threatening the sons with anxieties about paternal lack and castration.[3] Though of course they are focusing on the affect of fear, for Kahane and Veeder the promise of a psychoanalytic reading privileging the preoedipal is that it tells a different story, one that oedipal interpretations apparently occlude, a story that threatens, perhaps disrupts patriarchy because it insists on an alliance of mother and child that is originary, more important than the child's relation with the father.

Influenced by this feminist insistence upon the preoedipal, Anne Rice seems to be on the same path. Her first vampire novel depends on an oedipal paradigm, the later books on the preoedipal. In *Interview with the Vampire*, a popular seventies book, a decidedly angry woman does battle with men in her hopes to rewrite the script for femininity. She fails, though the precariousness of male bonds at the end of the novel suggests that patriarchy has been nonetheless weakened. Rice's next book, *The Vampire Lestat*, a product of the eighties, culminates in the discovery and valorization of an archaic mother, and with this new focus upon the mother (found also in *The Queen of the Damned*) comes an increased emphasis on the vampire's attachment to preoedipal pleasures of sucking, biting, and symbiosis. The general thematic movement from *Interview* to *Lestat* is regressive, from oedipal to preoedipal, tending toward a discovery of ever more archaic "origins" centering on the figure of the mother.

In *Interview with the Vampire*, a woman author explores primarily oedipal issues, and given the conditions of patriarchy, the oedipal reading may not simply be a screen for deeper anxieties: this oedipal story seems horrifying enough. There is no spectral presence of a dead-undead mother haunting us here, but rather sympathy for a "daughter" locked into the oedipal moment and a protest against the kind of femininity offered to women in a patriarchal culture. As does the classic monster narrative, *Interview* has a tripartite structure: the monster is first invited in, then entertained, and finally expelled.[4] Rice's novel begins as a vampire named Louis tells his story to a young male interviewer, and it is the vampire's story that admits the monster—a girl vampire named Claudia—whose death leads to the reestablishment of homosocial bonds between men. No longer is it the woman who must be protected from the monster—she is the monster. In place of the monstrous sexual appetites of Stoker's somewhat marginalized vampire women is the rage of a monstrous girl vampire against her infantilization and dependency in a world defined by the fathers. Written in the aftermath of feminism's "second wave," Rice's novel self-consciously insists on the affinity between women and monsters that Linda Williams has noted in the horror film. The girl vampire comes to understand how she has been entrapped, not in this case by the system of the look that Williams analyzes, but by what it represents: the oedipal configuration of a patriarchal culture that structures the feminine as both object of desire and object of horror.

The oedipal story is a narrative that encourages fantasies of male monogenesis because fathers, aligned as they are with the symbolic, produce subjects, if not babies. Indeed, this vampire story could be subtitled: "Two Men and a Baby." When the male vampire couple, Lestat and Louis, "create" Claudia she is five years old and presumably just ready for female subjectivity, to turn away from the mother toward the father who becomes all things, father and mother. Claudia, newly made a vampire, protests to the men, "I'm not your daughter . . . I'm my mamma's daughter"; then she is told, "No, dear, not anymore." The passage continues: "[Lestat] glanced at the window, and then he shut the bedroom door behind us and turned the key in the lock. 'You're our daughter, Louis's daughter and my daughter, do you see? Now, whom should you sleep with? Louis or me?'"[5] This perfect staging of the oedipal moment uncovers not the girl's desire for the father so much as the father's desire for the girl child, the infantilized woman who is a perfectly obedient and dependent object of desire. But though Claudia is a male creation and so apparently controllable—this vampire little girl will never grow up—she is nevertheless the source of monstrous disturbance. Claudia's vampire fathers can't figure out what goes wrong: "She grew cold to Lestat. She fell to staring at him for hours. When he spoke, often she didn't answer him, and one could hardly tell if it was contempt or that she didn't hear. And our fragile domestic tranquility erupted with his outrage. . . . I found myself in the wretched position of fighting him as I'd done years before she'd come to us. 'She's not a child any longer,' I whispered to him. 'I don't know what it is. She's a woman.' "[6]

What seems to mark "womanhood" is an apparently inexplicable hatred of the father. In Claudia's case, becoming a woman does not entail physical development. (Lestat teases her about her "lack of endowment," and she will never be able to reproduce.) Instead, the male vampires get to be mothers. Not only do they create and nurture the child but Louis constantly refers to Claudia as his "doll," which Freud claims is the psychological equivalent of a "baby from the father."[7] Yet unlike the film *Three Men and a Baby* , in which the substitution of an eroticized infant girl for a mature woman seems a pleasant release for the male characters, Rice's novel protests this cozy arrangement.[8] Freud depicts oedipal development in the girl as leading to a rejection of the mother and embrace of the father; Rice sees the oedipal moment as beginning with the father's embrace of the girl child in a patriarchal order that so restricts her possibilities for development—Claudia is called "Doll," "My Bride," "Lover," "Infant Death," "Daughter"—that she develops murderous rages against the father. Though Freud calls the oedipal stage a "haven, a refuge" for the girl, Rice shows it to be a coffin.[9] Furious for decades, Claudia finally tries to kill Lestat. She provides him with two beautiful little boys that she has poisoned with laudanum and absinthe. After Lestat has drunk from them she stabs him with a kitchen knife. This erotic scene of violence depicts male homoerotic desire as both an obstacle to women's desire for power—the homoerotic relation between men supports homosocial bonds that make women into objects of exchange—and as a vulnerability. Men's taste for boys leaves them too preoccupied to keep track of the machinations of women, with whom they are not comfortable or familiar anyway. Claudia's killing of Lestat seems at first to free her and Louis—the male vampire who is most maternal—but they have only an illusory freedom from the father. After Lestat's apparent death, Claudia and Louis travel to Europe searching for their origins. Louis looks for a homosocial origin in older male vampires; Claudia for a surrogate mother. The mother she finds is herself a dollmaker and mad from the loss of her girl child. The mother, Madeleine, is no less defined by male society than Claudia has been, though the attachment between the women reveals a shared desire to repudiate paternal control.[10] In *Interview with the Vampire*, then, Rice insists that cultural structures are extremely oppressive to women and the world of mothers and daughters is no safe haven.

One of the lessons of the vampire novel, and one made by Lacanian psychoanalysis, is that it is impossible to kill the father because the law of the symbolic is the law of a dead, not living father.[11] Lestat, like all vampire fathers, is already dead; death does not compromise his power to kill the women and restore what was never really lost, a patriarchal order. Yet this order is strangely hollow. Near the end of the novel Louis intones, "I tell you nothing really happened. Nothing that wasn't merely inevitable . . . I was dead. I was changeless"[12]. These words do not record a victory. Louis was never much happier than Claudia about the imperatives of the Oedipus complex. Explicitly identified with the maternal, Louis *desires* the father; he does not want to *become* the father. Male vampires act out their unwillingness to work through the oedipal complex in their sadomasochistic relations to each other, alternating the roles of hunter and prey that Melanie Klein finds originating in the oral stage and the aggressive desire to suck the breast that engenders both a feared and desired punishment.[13] Fear of persecution for sadistic impulses takes the form of castration anxiety, while persecution by imagined enemies also satisfies the excessive demands of the superego for punishing destructive impulses. For Klein, then, sado-masochism takes place where the oral and oedipal stages merge.[14]

In "Master and Slave: The Fantasy of Erotic Domination," Jessica Benjamin tells a somewhat different story, one that vacillates in its way of positioning the preoedipal stage in relation to the oedipal.[15] Benjamin argues that the sadomasochistic fantasies which permeate sexual imagery in our culture reflect conflicts between the desire for individuation and for merging: dominance, she says, is a desire for autonomous mastery and submission is the desire to efface the self. These roles, almost universalized in this account, are also gendered: the male occupies the active role of the sadist and the woman the passive role of masochistic victim. In Rice's novel, things are not quite so simple. The most graphic presentation of erotic violence is literally staged in a "Theater of the Vampires." In the scene a voluptuous young blonde (who is also described as "like a child") is stripped of her clothes in front of the audience, while she murmurs "No pain" to the terrifying but seductive male vampire. This vignette seems to encourage identification with both the woman and the man. On the one hand it warns the girl vampire, Claudia, of the dangers of growing up female. Yet an identification between Claudia and the female victim cannot perhaps be called masochistic since what she is shown is not a woman achieving a desired and perverse pleasure but a woman suffering the imposition of male power. As Kaja Silverman remarks, female maso-chism does not usually threaten anything but "its victim's capacities and health."[16] In this instance, the woman is murdered, as Claudia will be later. In Louis, the male vampire, the scene creates intense pleasurable feelings that involve both the promise of sadistic power and the abandon linked with passive victimization. Indeed, Louis's identification with the victim-izer, Armand, impels Louis toward a homoerotic relationship with him. In Rice's novel, the woman who resists her position as an infantilized object of desire is eventually contained by being redefined as an object of exchange between men, in this case predatory men who also willingly adopt a femi-nized passivity, another way of absorbing and containing femininity. Rice's resolution of the tension between women's desire for power and a system of male bonding linked to the devaluation of women (a tension articulated but not developed by Eve Sedgwick because she does not discuss women as agents as well as objects) is provided in the sequels to *Interview with the Vampire*.[17] In these books, homosexuality and sadomasochism are more explicitly linked with a preoedipal realm. In this realm, sexual difference apparently can be both affirmed and redeemed.

Jessica Benjamin reads sadomasochistic fantasies as rooted in our cul-ture's insistence that the boy child repudiate his early identification with the mother to assume the father's mastery and the insistence on the girl child's over-identification with a mother whose position is devalued in patriarchy. Obviously, this interpretation is greatly influenced by Nancy Chodorow's use of object relations theory to account for gender differences as originating in preoedipal identifications—though in both Chodorow and Benjamin this preoedipal moment is at once an origin and an effect of inequalities of power. Such feminist psychoanalytic work insists that we need to look closely at early childhood experiences to understand sexual difference. Women's mothering is seen as the key to women's special nurturing and affiliating capacities (capacities men need to adopt by becoming nurturers and so helping to rectify both their son's desires for dominance and their daughter's problems with differentiation). In other words, these theorists construct the mother-child dyad (or, presumably better, the father-mother-child triad) as an origin even as they admit that this origin is already structured by the oedipal configurations of a culture that devalues women.[18] Rice's books show the dangers of a theory of the maternal that encourages, even halfheartedly, a separation to take place between the preoedipal and oedipal as if one were causal and internal, the other secondary and external, especially since the new primacy of the preoedipal has been often used either to fix and valorize sexual difference (women's selves are essentially more fluid and nurturing than men's) or to provide the occasion for a premature celebration of gender subversion (by refusing the Oedipus complex, men and women apparently are freed to enjoy a polymorphous sexuality).

These dangers become more obvious in Rice's first sequel to *Interview with the Vampire, The Vampire Lestat.* In *Interview with the Vampire* , Claudia does not find the mother she seeks, only women who are mad and punished for their independence. The *Vampire Lestat* revaluates the mother, putting her in a more privileged position. This is the book feminists might applaud. When the vampire Lestat awakens after a hundred-year sleep he discovers that in this brave new world of the twentieth century, musicians are "beguilingly androgynous" and women "for the first time in history, perhaps, . . . were as strong and interesting as men."[19] Moreover, "fascinating new phrases like 'it's so Freudian' . . . are on everyone's lips"[20] and indeed, Lestat's life story, beginning with "his great and unshakeable love" for his mother, Gabrielle, is so "Freudian" that one hardly needs to tease out the repressed content.[21]

Rice self-consciously makes use of a psychoanalytic account of human development from the infant's perspective as she recounts Lestat's story. Lestat is born into a feudal family where the father's power is diminishing—he is weak, poor, and blind. The father nonetheless exercises a tyrannical control over his children and wife. Lestat is placed in an effeminate position in relation to his father and brothers. As the youngest son, he is left no place for effective action, is impoverished and dependent. Because of his position he is filled with rage—his most salient characteristic—and he identifies with his mother, who is also filled with rage. Lestat is her favorite, and she is the one responsible for providing him with ways to prove his masculinity. By giving him dogs and a gun, she turns him into a hunter "who provides food" for the family and he becomes a killer of wolves, the hero of the village. Significantly, she compares this heroic accomplishment to her experience of childbirth. Lestat and she meet often, intimately, in either his bedroom or hers. Rice makes it explicit that she knows what is going on here. Gabrielle has penis envy and is living her life through her favorite son: "She spoke in an eerie way of my being a secret part of her anatomy, of my being the organ for her which women do not really have."[22] During these meetings, Lestat vacillates between an incestuous love for his mother and an identification with her rage against the father. They admit in one scene their mutual desire to kill the father and brothers, and after a good laugh at this wonderful possibility, Gabrielle qualifies it. Acknowledging that she would love to indulge in a promiscuity that would carry her beyond the law of the father and family, she says that what is important to achieve is not so much "the murdering of them as an abandon which disregards them completely."[23] To effect this abandonment, or at least to enable her substitute, Lestat, to effect it, she constantly attempts to help Lestat escape his father's house, and she finally succeeds in sending him to Paris. From Paris, Lestat continues to write home to her, though he finds a concrete replacement of her in his affair with Nicholas, who, it is suggested, is intimately connected to the mother—it is she who initiates and encourages their friendship: both she and Nicholas appreciate music, and later she shows an intuitive understanding of Nicholas's needs. Both Rice and Freud suggest that homosexuality arises from an overidentification with the mother. This thesis defines homosexuality as regressive, involved in what is for Rice a privileged return to origins and to a titillating erotic domain.

For Rice, the son's overidentification with the mother is a source of empowerment. Lestat's human story of his relationship with his mother—the story of mom and her son enjoying intimate moments—is essentially the kernel of the novel, repeated again and again on an increasingly intensified level in the story of the vampires. To be turned into a vampire is to return to the mother. The vampire, the monstrous, is ultimately maternal and the experience of initiation a preoedipal one. Here, for instance, is Lestat's description of his initiation. Though his initiation is seemingly at the hands of a powerful father figure, Magnus, the description makes it clear that Lestat is returned to a babe in mother's arms. Father is really mother: "I knew that I was being held in the thing's arms . . . Rapture . . . I was no longer breathing. Yet something was making me breathe. It was breathing for me and the breaths came with the rhythm of the gong, which was nothing to do with my body, and I loved it, the rhythm, the way that it went on and on, and I no longer had to breathe or speak or know anything. My mother smiled at me. And I said, "I love you. . . . "[24] When he awakens, Lestat drinks from a bottle—of wine—and experiences all of his senses as if for the first time. He even goes through the mirror stage, alienated by the new identity he discovers: "I looked into it [a pearl-handled mirror] almost unconsciously as one often glances in mirrors. And there I saw myself as a man might expect, except that my skin was very white. . . . In fact, this was not Lestat in the mirror at all, but some replica of him made of other substances!"[25] But Lestat's story as a vampire does not "progress" from this stage; he does not become ever the more manly vampire. Rather we are carried back once again to mother.

In a bizarre scene that revels in preoedipal and incestuous pleasures, Lestat converts his mother into a vampire:

> All the memories of my life with her surrounded us; they wove their shroud around us and closed us off from the world, the soft poems and songs of childhood, and the sense of her before words when there had only been the flicker of the light on the ceiling above her pillows and the smell of her all around me and her voice silencing my crying, and then the hatred of her and the need of her and the losing of her behind a thousand closed doors, and cruel answers, and the terror of her and her complexity and her indifference and her indefinable strength.
>
> And jetting up into the current came the thirst, not obliterating but heating up every concept of her, until she was flesh and blood and mother and lover and all things beneath the cruel pressure of my fingers and my lips, everything I had ever desired. I drove my teeth into her, feeling her stiffen and gasp, and I felt my mouth grow wide to catch the hot flood when it came.[26]

Rice provides us here with a version of the whole process of childhood from the child's dyadic union with the mother to the achievement of heterosexuality when the mother becomes a lover. The sense of well-being provided by the fantasy of reunion is marred by an adult sense of loss. The scene being described by Lestat is, after all, already a memory that weaves a shroud around the mother and child. The passage also acknowledges the child's ambivalence: the mother is loved and hated, present and absent, strong and weak. Lestat wants the mother as lover and he wants to destroy her, to devour her. Though the memory is framed by an incestuous oedipal desire for the mother, the emphasis is upon the oral and upon preoedipal hungers.

It is within this realm of preoedipal hunger that we are locked for the rest of the novel. The tale is told from the point of view of the vampire, and the vampire's pleasures are by definition oral. In the many scenes where the vampires feed, Rice provides ornate, sensual descriptions of the pleasures of sucking and biting, which awaken the senses of the vampire as if for the first time. In what seems a parody of the "semiotic" stage of human development, as some psychoanalytic feminist critics might describe it, there is in this fluid space a fusion and blurring of identities—

child becomes mother, mother becomes child—and the emphasis is not only upon the oral, the mouth, but also upon aural pleasures, pleasures of a preverbal sort, always initiated by and associated with the mother's heartbeat—rhythmic noises, especially music, a music that disturbs and disrupts. At a rock concert depicted in the final scene of the novel, this music brings the audience close to mass hysteria.

These preoedipal pleasures are shrouded, as in the scene between Lestat and his mother, with a sense of yearning for that which cannot be recuperated. As Lestat searches the world, traveling widely to discover his origins, he meets new vampires whose tales of initiation only and inevitably bring us back, via tales within tales within tales, to a dyadic union with the mother—a symbiotic union and reunion that never satisfies, that is predictably broken into by a father figure, and that is always experienced as lost because the relationship with mother can never be retrieved. So we get an obsessive repetitive tale that never progresses, despite its hermeneutic, narrative promise of a "mystery" at the center, the mystery of origins. This mystery, this origin, is discovered to be a set of primal parents, Enkil and Akasha, but it is Akasha, the matriarch, who is important. Vampires are discovered to have originally been those who "serve the Holy Mother." Perhaps because she is so "primal" Lestat's feeding upon her, and in a crazy circuit, her feeding upon him and his feeding upon her et cetera, intensifies the description of previous "initiation" scenes to the point of near hysteria: "It was perfect, my mother, my lover, my powerful one, and the blood was penetrating every pulsing particle of me. . . . Out of every zinging vessel my blood was suddenly drawn into her, even as hers was being drawn into me. I saw it, the shimmering circuit, and more divinely I felt it because nothing else existed but our mouths locked to each other's throats and the relentless pounding path of the blood."[27] It is no surprise that this intimate union with Akasha provokes Enkil's rage. At this point in the story the reader can only be bored by the discovery, the hermeneutic solution of the mystery, for this is the oedipal story that culture tells us over and over again and that provides the repetitive structure of Rice's own novel. No wonder Lestat says so mournfully at the end of the book: "And weary finally of this complexity we dream of that long-ago time when we sat upon our mother's knee and each kiss was the perfect consummation of desire. What can we do but reach for the embrace that must now contain both heaven and hell: our doom again and again and again."[28]

Heaven and hell: preoedipal and oedipal? While Rice's novels demonstrate the implication of the preoedipal within the oedipal, her textual strategy seems to yearn for a utopian separation of the two. Rice's dramatic and thematic emphasis upon the mother is not so much empowering as obsessive, and it is certainly conservative. Not only does it lock us within the repetitions of near hysterically intense symbiotic union, not only is the "mother of us all," Akasha, the very embodiment of the maternal in patriarchal culture—aligned with nature, the moon, silence, and paralysis (she is literally a mummy)—but Rice's story itself is framed within the conservative oedipally based narrative that holds out the promise of progress and discovery only to be obsessed with repetition and return. Along with her nostalgia for the preoedipal as an originating moment, Rice yearns for the lost pleasures of realism. As in the relationship with the mother she so obsessively seeks, Rice searches for an art more direct, more immediate, more concretely there. Within a story that emphasizes oral pleasures, her novels are set up to be talked. Speech is privileged over writing. *The Vampire Lestat*, for example, is set both before and after his autobiography is actually written. The rock concert promises the immediacy of a *real* event—one with real vampires in attendance—"and yet everywhere," as Lestat exclaims, "the unfathomable trust that it was art, nothing but art!"[29] Not for Rice an avant-garde modernism that would play on the undecidability of representation. Rice would like to eliminate representation itself. Indeed, she depends upon the opposition between truth and lies to encourage the reader's desire for her sequels. *Interview with the Vampire*, too successful to be an end point, a truth itself, is turned into a fiction by *The Vampire Lestat*, in which Lestat tells us that Louis is a liar, and that he will tell us the true story.

Rice's next book, *The Queen of the Damned*, opens with self-conscious reminders that the reader will not know whether it is Louis or Lestat who is telling the truth until this new book, with its deeper truths, has been read. These truths bring the reader ever closer to the woman, Akasha, who is also called "The Mother." Since Rice has decided that this book, which was to have been the end of her "chronicles," is going to have a sequel, it is not surprising that "The Mother" turns out to be the "Queen of Lies." Again, this novel is "talked" by various characters, and this time the speaker who tells us the truth is one of Akasha's "daughters," Maharet. Maharet and her twin sister, Mekare, have been turned into vampires by the wicked queen because they dare to expose Akasha as a woman more interested in abstract systems than in what really matters: the natural family (or what is known in the novel as the dazzling "Great Family"). Indeed the unnatural Akasha is now identified with the symbolic, with the introduction of writing, with imperialism and patriarchal religion (she models herself after the "Queen of Heaven"), against which an even more archaic maternal must inevitably be posed. The battle is not between women and men as much as it is between women, or between versions of the maternal. On the one side is Akasha, whose feminine identity is too rigidly demarcated; she defines herself against all men except her son/prince, Lestat, and she shows no real ability to respond to other people. On the other side are Maharet and Mekare. These women have been maimed at Akasha's command: Maharet's eyes are plucked out; Mekare loses her tongue to demonstrate the price women pay to enter the symbolic, now an oppressive domain ruled by a dead, not living, mother. They speak—if with difficulty—for a real, deeper female identity that manages to be matriarchal without becoming hostile to men. Their femaleness, unlike Akasha's, is linked to heightened capacities for identification and affiliation. These sisters, in their relation to each other, to their biological mother, to nature itself, show a fluid sense of self, the sort of self often privileged in feminist accounts of the relations between daughters and mothers. Rice associates this selfhood that denies rigid boundaries with the ancient practice of eating dead loved ones, a rite Akasha has outlawed in the name of civilization. In this cannibalistic rite, feminists may find a disconcerting effort by a woman writer to stage the "feminist dream-wish" that a daughter establish a redemptive relation to the maternal body, in this novel a relation made possible by a holy process of incorporation that heals the rift between two generations of women.[30]

As a matriarch finally identified with the symbolic, Akasha turns out to be, what else?, a feminist monster, a woman more interested in maternal theories than in real people. Savage and power-hungry, she explains her reductive scheme to return the world to Edenic bliss this way: "You know, as I know, that there will be universal peace if the male population is limited to one per one hundred women. All forms of random violence will very simply come to an end."[31] Though Rice has capitalized on recent trends in feminism—its utopian hopes, its hope for liberation in mother goddesses and in returns to the preoedipal—she now shows herself to be seemingly more progressive than these feminisms. She sees beyond such "reductive" exaltations of women's difference to a new age in which androgynous beings coexist harmoniously. In this postfeminist world, imbalances of power are effaced. As one of her vampires explains about humans: "in the last hundred years their progress has been miraculous, they have righted wrongs that mankind thought were inevitable; they have for the first time developed a true family of man [sic]."[32] Presumably this true family lives in a kinder and gentler nation, a depiction of cultural reality that is in tension with Rice's simultaneous insistence that this nation is host and spawn of a parasitic vampire elite. Rice leaves behind this dark view of symbiosis through a relation to the good mother, a mother good for eliminating disturbing differences.[33]

The return to the mother that seems to disrupt gender boundaries by feminizing the son who embraces the maternal, and by lending to the mother the son's phallic power, is also a path to postfeminism. Ironically, the return to the mother is what allows Rice to kill her off and transcend feminist politics. No wonder, then, that in Rice's books the vampire, with its polymorphous sexuality, is no longer an object of fear. Congratulations to all: sexual difference is a dead issue. Indeed, at the end of *The Queen of the Damned*, "The Mother" is literally a dead matter, killed by Mekare, a woman more primal and real than she. (Mekare literally rises from the deeps of the ocean, earth, and jungles in order to avenge herself against the surrogate matriarch.[34]) At the novel's close, the mother's body is cannibalized in a sacred rite so that she can be effectively internalized and transcended. This ritual, however, is also but a temporary stopping point in what we have seen to be a repetitious, sadomasochistic circuit of consumption and punishment, pleasure and pain.

In a curious way, recent discussions of mass culture have worked the same way, invoking a maternal metaphorics in order to move beyond it, yet still implicated in the pleasurable pain of a relation to the maternal. Andreas Huyssen has remarked that mass culture traditionally "appears as monolithic, engulfing, totalitarian, and on the side of regression and the feminine."[35] He adds, however, that this "notion belongs to another age" (Minoan/Mycenean perhaps?) because the emergence of women artists in elite and mass culture has "rendered the old gendering device obsolete."[36] Yet figurations of the mass media as maternal continue to proliferate, often introduced, as by Huyssen, even if only to be left behind. Fredric Jameson, for example, in an article on pleasure, recalls the collective fantasy of the fifties as the "psychoanalytic terror of a consuming Mom, who not only presided over all new post-war products but also threatened to eat you up as well: a consumption fantasy with teeth in it."[37] From this supposedly outdated fantasy, Jameson, appropriating Lyotard's terms for the postmodern, moves to a reconceptualization of pleasure in terms of the sublime, of the ambivalent pleasures accompanying the reception of globalizing, terrifying forces, forces that may not be so far from the horrors of the mother after all if we recall Huyssen's description of feminized mass culture as "engulfing and totalitarian." Ariel Dorfman, discussing the infantilizing of culture in America that has nearly, though not entirely, turned audiences into "lost souls cannibalized, eaten up, devoured by the fictions they enjoy,"[38] inevitably comes to give labels to the dominant media that are maternal. He calls the mass media first "The Medusa" and then "The Hydra,"[39] both monstrous mother figures who are defeated at the hands of heroic men. W. F. Haug uses the same language to describe the dangerously sensuous power of commodity aesthetics: "Now this insatiable hunger, and the reproductive drive of this 'Hydra-headed monster,' whose every mouth snatches as much as possible from the next, is taking up a position behind the sensual world, and its corresponding system of subjective sensuality."[40] If, as Tania Modleski has noted, "woman is frequently associated with the monster mass culture," it is woman as a mother with voracious appetites and uncontrollable reproductive powers.[41]

The problematic way in which mass culture is linked with the mother cannot be avoided by simply trying to keep distinct the realms of fantasy and history as Franco Moretti does in his analysis of Stoker's *Dracula*. Moretti insists that the vampire metaphor provides a screen for two separate signifieds, monopoly capital and the fear of the mother. He writes, "they are, clearly, different signifieds, and it is hard to unite them harmoniously. I do not propose here to reconstruct the many missing links that might connect socio-economic structures and sexual psychological structures in a single conceptual chain."[42] All that links them, apparently, is the metaphor of "the vampire" that evokes and also hides these referents. Indeed, for Moretti, their hiddenness is the key to their power. *Dracula* hides monopoly capital under the cloak of a feudal past and the terror of the mother in the form of a male figure. In this way, Moretti argues, bedrock truths, so nearly communicated in all their frightening power, are distorted and contained. This argument not only keeps the social sphere separate from the sphere of fantasy, a classic separation of the public and private, but it also preserves the referent, the repressed, as objects of Moretti's privileged understanding. He places himself in a neutral interpretive space located safely outside fantasized history. Of course, this place of pure lucidity long associated with masculinity is recognized by psychoanalysis as offering a fantasy of control that screens anxieties about mom and money, seductive figures offering terrifying pleasures of consumption that threaten autonomous subjectivity.

Moretti's way of opposing "metaphor" to signified, and history to subjective fantasy, allows him to fix the turbulent meanings of a text, but only because he refuses to articulate the complex play between subject and object crucial to understanding mass culture and the position of women. Rice's books, for example, excite an appetite to consume them that is mirrored and elicited by her vampires, themselves in love with consumption as a way of achieving a radical self-sufficiency, an end of otherness, promised in the infantile relation to the mother. This hunger for an essence—the true self, ultimate passion, revealed knowledge—is a form of hunger for the kind of reality Moretti seems to offer, bedrock truths. The return to origins—in Rice's books figured as a mother who herself is found in the mythic dawn of history—promises omnipotent power: the reader, like the vampire, has godlike powers to surrender safely. No virus contaminates the exchanges of blood in these vampire stories, nor the exchanges of pleasure between text and the reader. But the story at the same time encourages anxieties about being eaten up: the end of otherness is also the end of the autonomous self. The pleasures of Rice's text are thus sadomasochistic pleasures, fantasies of power and surrender, that are linked as we have seen, to the desires and fears of infantile dependency. Of such pleasures, no one can seemingly get enough. Rice's books are not simply enjoyed by women readers hungering for female nurturance, men hunger for the mother too. (One recalls Bernardo Bertolucci's remarks on receiving an Oscar, on being embraced by the seemingly remote Academy: "Tonight, to me, Hollywood must be the Big Nipple.")

Who is to blame for our unsatisfied hungers? Whom do we thank for our sense of fullness? Mom, who in the late eighties has been valorized on the right and on the left as the nurturer of children and who is linked both to the idealized values associated with the private realm and to the denigrated desires to consume also associated with the home. The return to the mother as the true origin, a return that makes a novel seem progressive in direct proportion to its validation of preoedipal pleasures, is of course also the same old thing. A maternal metaphorics linked to a valorized preoedipal realm encourages a fantasy of the real, a domain removed from the unconscious by its very pretense to speak the repressed in all its truth across divisions of sex. That this effort to neutralize sexual difference is part of a larger effort to produce a falsely homogeneous social order as a cultural truth is shown also by Rice's ways of constituting class and race so that they do not exist. Vampires are effortlessly rich and Rice's hero Lestat is a blonde, blue-eyed Aryan who participates with other vampires in selective breeding and in eliminating undesirables. These vampires are completely at home in late-twentieth-century America as she constructs it. This America is a world of leisure, of inhabitants devoted to consumption, a picture of America that reproduces familiar notions of the private sphere as an idealized haven, now a nationalized one. When Lestat wakes into the America of the eighties, he finds himself in a utopia: "In fact, the poverty and filth that had been common in the big cities of the earth since time immemorial had been washed away. You just didn't see immigrants dropping dead of starvation in the alleyways. There weren't slums where people slept eight and ten to a room. Nobody threw the slops in the gutters. The beggars, the cripples, the orphans, the hopelessly diseased were so diminished as to constitute no presence in the immaculate streets at all."[43] Such euphoric rhetoric goes on for pages, encouraged by the invocation of utopian possibilities basic to a maternal metaphorics that can seemingly transcend the boundaries between the sexes. One thinks again of Miranda's words in *The Tempest*: "O brave new world that has such people in't!"[44]

But attacks on this maternal discourse, despite its resonance with an aggressively apolitical realism, are not necessarily progressive because women cannot escape their fantasized and historical identification with the maternal. Julia Kristeva is particularly acute in her analysis of this problem. Her article, "Stabat Mater," an analysis of the decline of our paradigmatic discourse for maternity, the discourse on the Virgin Mary, seems particularly relevant to an analysis of a trilogy which culminates—at least momentarily—in a novel entitled *The Queen of the Damned*. Kristeva writes that motherhood as it is represented in Western culture "is a *fantasy* that is nurtured by the adult, man or woman, of a lost territory [that] involves less an idealized archaic mother than the idealization of the *relationship* that binds us to her."[45] Here, in her emphasis upon this relationship as fantasy, Kristeva resolutely avoids the essentialism that Rice falls prey to by idealizing the preoedipal, an essentialism that simply encourages reversals: evil is good, degraded mother becomes privileged mother and origin. Yet in rejecting this "misconception" of the mother, the fantasies of her, feminists must be careful, Kristeva warns, not to reject motherhood altogether or to circumvent "the real experience that fantasy overshadows."[46]

The question, though, is how to refuse the gesture of overthrowing the mother, the Medusa, the Hydra, without simply engaging in a reactive discourse idealizing the mother and the preoedipal as origins. In addition to writing a critique, Kristeva's "solution" is to write as a mother using a fluid, personal language. This language, unfortunately, is easily appropriated and depoliticized: late capitalist culture is all too happy to provide novel, though seemingly natural and familial spheres of representation. Rice's vampire novels, for example, successfully colonize the preoedipal as the site of powerful consumption fantasies. Yet neither growing up female nor growing up feminist can mean leaving the mother behind, especially since a rejection of the maternal seems to require an embrace of the new, nurturing man who would just as soon do without woman by replacing her or becoming her as do Rice's male heroes, the real immortals. This new man, incarnated in the state, becomes the new paternalism. The state as feminized father is said to behave like a mother by perpetuating the dependency of its populace, as does the feminized mass media. The idea of the maternal seems to burden whatever or whoever must stand for it: the state, mass culture, and always women themselves. Anne Rice may herself have best articulated the nature of our struggle neither to celebrate our maternal difference nor to triumph over it. At the end of her vampire books, a space is always reserved for the words, "To be continued." For feminists the writing tasks "to be continued" must reach beyond the impasse of a maternal discourse that has given up its historical context—the specific and various social and psychic experiences of women—to find relief from the pain of sexual difference in the timeless havens of the preoedipal and post-feminism. Touted as spaces of liberation, these havens prematurely enclose or elide the feminine, providing fictions of difference and equality easily appropriated for depictions of America as a land in which the dreams of the oppressed are magically, if disturbingly, fulfilled.

Notes

1. The discussion of the maternal in academic feminism has become increasingly self-referential. In 1985, *The (M)other Tongue: Essays in Feminist Psychoanalytic Interpretation* (Ithaca: Cornell University Press), an anthology of psychoanalytic feminist essays edited by Shirley Nelson Garner, Claire Kahane, and Madelon Springnether, was published to provide an introduction to feminist psychoanalytic discourse about the mother. This anthology included, as its first essay, an excerpt from Jane Gallop's

fine book, *The Daughter's Seduction: Feminism and Psychoanalysis* (Ithaca: Cornell University Press, 1982). In 1987, Gallop published a critique of *The (M)other Tongue*, in which she argues that the figure of the mother is often used "to cover over differences between feminists"("Reading the Mother Tongue: Psychoanalytic Feminist Criticism," *Critical Inquiry* 13, no. 2 [1987]: 318). In 1989, Claire Kahane, an editor of *The (M)other Tongue* and the author of an essay included within it, published a response to Gallop which recapitulates arguments about the dangers and possibilities of theories based on the idea of the maternal voice ("Questioning the Maternal Voice," *Genders* 3 [1988]: 82–91). While our essay hardly exists outside this self-referential circuit of psychoanalytic feminism—we are citing Kahane and Gallop in our first footnote and this will not be the last citation—we do hope to show that the valorization of the preoedipal is taking place in other discursive networks than simply the academic, that is, popular culture has picked up on this trend in feminism.

2. Claire Kahane, "The Gothic Mirror," in *The (M)other Tongue*, 347.

3. Though William Veeder begins his essay, "Tales That Culture Tells Itself: *Dracula* and the Mothers" (unpublished paper delivered at the MLA Convention, 1986), with an approving account of recent efforts by psychoanalytic critics to excavate the mother (as Anne Rice may have noticed, a certain necrophilia infects the metaphors associated with the effort to retrieve the preoedipal mother because she is positioned as if in an occluded, enclosed place), he changes his tack after thirty-eight pages when he disassociates himself from Kahane and others to argue that the "reality" of the mother is itself built on an exchange of representations. How this exchange exists within a social field in which gender representations are being contested, the field he evokes so promisingly in his title, is not developed in the remaining pages of his essay.

4. Christopher Craft's discussion of this model, in his "Kiss Me with Those Red Lips: Gender and Inversion in Bram Stoker's *Dracula*" (*Representations* 8 [1984]: 107–33), shows how this narrative rhythm both manages and enacts anxiety. Rice's books become less and less anxious as they work to solve the problem of both sexual difference and its erasure with the help of a maternal metaphorics linked to an idealized preoedipal realm.

5. Anne Rice, *Interview with the Vampire* (New York: Ballantine Books, 1976), 95.

6. Ibid., 106.

7. Ibid., 128.

8. Tania Modleski, in her "Three Men and Baby M" (*Camera Obscura* 17 [1988]: 69–81) provides a powerful analysis of the way that the mass media fascination with the father-daughter romance works as a strategy of postfeminism. The film suggests that men have taken feminists' demands to heart—they now want to be involved in nurturing—while also constructing a world in which women are more marginal than ever.

9. Rice, *Interview with the Vampire*, 129.

10. Claudia is also a double for Babette, an earlier love of Louis's. Claudia is created immediately after Babette dies (Babette's name also marks her as a doll/baby) and Claudia looks like Babette: "Her eyes were as wide and clear as Babette's." And, like Madeleine, Babette becomes mad. What distinguishes the relation between Claudia and Madeleine is that the attachment between them is erotic as well as familial. In Rice's vampire books, lesbian relationships are marginalized while male homosexual relations are emphasized. An explanation for this emphasis is given in the sequels to *Interview with the Vampire*, in which male homosexuality is defined as based on a relation to the mother which involves not only a feminizing identification but also an incestuous desire. In Rice's books, male homosexuality

is thus conveniently recuperated by the heterosexual while still used to offer the promise of a taboo, possibly liberatory pleasure.

11. Jane Gallop, in *The Daughter's Seduction*, risks articulating the implications for feminism of the notion that patriarchal culture is "the law of the symbolic, the dead Father": "It is not patriarchal culture, but the biologistic reduction of the Law of the Dead Father to the rule of the actual, living male that must be struggled against" (14).

12. Rice, *Interview with the Vampire*, 324.

13. Anne Rice has written explicitly sadomasochistic novels—described on their jackets as "S/M books for the eighties"—under the pseudonym "A. N. Roquelaure." The novels are set in a fairytale past and feature the pleasurable trials and tribulations of one "Sleeping Beauty," who wakes up to find herself the prince's love slave. Rice shows her eighties sensibility by seeing to it that both men and women become masters and slaves, though not surprisingly "Beauty" prefers masochistic pleasures. The "freedom" to choose either the pleasures associated with domination or submission is the only kind of liberation possible in these repetitious, claustrophobic books that suggest there is no alternative to sadomasochism as a social and psychic organizing principle.

14. Klein does not discuss the preoedipal. Her interest is in what she calls the early oedipal position. Infantile sadism is a recurrent subject of her writing: see, for example, the essays in *The Selected Melanie Klein*, ed. Juliet Mitchell (Harmondsworth, Middlesex: Penguin Books, 1986).

15. Jessica Benjamin, "Master and Slave: The Fantasy of Erotic Domination," in *Powers of Desire: The Politics of Sexuality*, ed. Ann Snitow et al. (New York: Monthly Review Press, 1983), 280–99.

16. Kaja Silverman, "Male Masochism," *Camera Obscura* 17 (1988): 59.

17. Eve Kosofsky Sedgwick's compelling book *Between Men: English Literature and Male Homosocial Desire* (New York: Columbia University Press, 1985) has received an ambivalent reception from feminists because its anthropological model—women are objects of exchange between men—universalizes women's oppression while trying to historicize it.

18. See our *Nostalgia and Sexual Difference: The Resistance to Contemporary Feminism* (New York and London: Methuen, 1987) for a discussion of neoconservative efforts to create the triad, father-mother-child, as a stable referent.

19. Anne Rice, *The Vampire Lestat* (New York: Ballantine Books, 1985), 7.

20. Ibid., 8.

21. Ibid., 30.

22. Ibid., 62.

23. Ibid., 39.

24. Ibid., 81–82.

25. Ibid., 103.

26. Ibid., 157.

27. Ibid., 486.

28. Ibid., 494.

29. Ibid., 538.

30. This is one of the recuperative projects that Claire Kahane describes in "Questioning the Maternal Voice," an essay that provides an overview of feminist dreams and concerns about the maternal voice. Kahane's essay is a curious effort to articulate arguments about idealizing the maternal voice in such a way as to defend a continuing feminist practice of idealization, a sort of idealization with provisos. For a more carefully positioned discussion of the maternal voice, one that insists on

placing the maternal voice within the symbolic, see Kaja Silverman's excellent *The Acoustic Mirror* (Bloomington: Indiana University Press, 1988).

31. Anne Rice, *The Queen of the Damned* (New York: Alfred A. Knopf, 1988), 400.

32. Ibid., 404.

33. Jane Gallop discovers in feminist glorifications of the mother the same effort to eliminate disturbing differences. "In the mother," she writes, "we [feminists] are not divided" ("Reading the Mother Tongue," 318).

34. Anne Rice's narrative anticipates the preoccupation with distinguishing real from surrogate mothers that characterized the Baby M case. See our "Risky Business: Familial Ideology and the Case of Baby M," *Differences* (1989): 67–81.

35. Andreas Huyssen, *After the Great Divide: Modernism, Mass Culture, Postmodernism* (Bloomington: Indiana University Press, 1986), 58.

36. Ibid., 62.

37. Fredric Jameson, "Pleasure: A Personal Issue," in *Formations of Pleasure* (Boston: Routledge and Kegan Paul, 1983), 4.

38. Ariel Dorfman, "The Infantalizing of Culture," in *American Media and Mass Culture: Left Perspectives*, ed. Donald Lazere (Berkeley: University of California Press, 1987), 150.

39. Ibid., 152.

40. W. F. Haug, *Critique of Commodity Aesthetics: Appearance, Sexuality, and Advertising in Capitalist Society*, trans. Robert Bock (Minneapolis: University of Minnesota Press, 1986), 99–100.

41. Tania Modleski, "The Terror of Pleasure: The Contemporary Horror Film and Postmodern Theory," in *Studies in Entertainment: Critical Approaches to Mass Culture*, ed. Tania Modleski (Bloomington: Indiana University Press, 1986), 163.

42. Franco Moretti, *Signs Taken for Wonders*, trans. Susan Fischer et al. (London: Verso, 1983), 104.

43. Rice, *The Vampire Lestat*, 8.

44. V.i.184–85.

45. Julia Kristeva, "Stabat Mater," in *The Kristeva Reader*, ed. Toril Moi (New York: Columbia University Press, 1986), 161.

46. Ibid., 161.

NINE

███

Tube Tied: Reproductive Politics and *Moonlighting*

Lynne Joyrich

I. TV's Family Affair: The Union of Technical and Sexual Reproduction

In 1979, Roland Barthes observed that "television condemns us to the Family, whose household utensil it has become"; in 1989, this observation still seems to ring true.[1] However, just what the family is or should be, how it is to be constituted, and who has the power to determine this are matters of heated debate within contemporary American culture. The resurgence of legislative battles around the issue of abortion, the development of controversial forms of birth control, and the rise of new reproductive technologies—not to mention such social factors as divorce rates, alternative living arrangements, and the growth of single-parent households—have led to a general state of confusion about the family and its regeneration in the late 1980s. As reproduction becomes increasingly divorced from sexuality, sexuality detaches itself from the nuclear family, and both appear to disclaim "biological destiny," a certain amount of discomfort and ambivalence over these changes is expressed on the part of men and women alike—a situation that is perhaps most apparent in the debates revolving around reproductive technologies. On the one hand (and despite previous feminist goals), many women fear that the disruption of "natural" processes of reproduction will accelerate women's expendability under patriarchy, producing new forms of medicalization and domination with which to contain and control the female body.[2] On the other (and responding to a contradictory fantasy), men may fear the ways in which these same changes seem to enlarge the scope of the maternal generative sphere while further removing husbands and/or fathers from the seat of reproductive control.

Although, apart from some notable exceptions such as news shows and a few made-for-TV movies, television has rarely entered into the controversies surrounding sexual, reproductive, or family politics in any sustained or explicit way, it is necessarily enmeshed within the terms of these debates. Truly "a family affair," television is a medium in which the familial is both the dominant theme and the typical mode of address, and thus, television's construction of family dynamics as well as its place within them is significant for any analysis of our society's "domestic policies." Within our culture, not only is television often figured as a part of the family, but it is used to define notions of both familial harmony and household authority: bringing its families into our living rooms and us into theirs, it asserts a national family unity even as its patterns of use in the home articulate relations of power, positioning family members hierarchically within a larger social field.[3] It should then come as no surprise that the operations of electronic reproduction, the relations that define television's existence, intersect with those of sexual reproduction, relations that define the family's (and our own) existence, in a multitude of ways.

The discursive network by which the family and its modes of electronic and sexual reproduction are constructed necessarily establishes a relationship between television and sexual difference. Yet here again there is a complex dynamic between television's own cultural position and those constructions of gender by which television is articulated and which it, in turn, articulates. As I and others have argued, television tends to be figured in both critical and popular discourses alike as a "feminized" medium— as a textual form which, unlike the cinema, is unable to maintain the narrative focus, linear development, or concentrated, voyeuristic gaze that together constitute a masterful and masculine spectator.[4] Multiple and fragmented, television's look is a domestic and distracted one, a powerless look which requires the viewer to delegate his/her "eye" (as well as "I") to TV itself (as the viewer shares in television's familiar community of address— its regime of the fictive "we"). Or, as some might claim, a "feminine" look which accords with the domestic conditions of viewing by keeping the viewer caught up in an endless dispersal of consumer desire while "safely" tucked away within the confines of family life.[5]

Yet despite such apparent alignments between television and social constructions of domesticated femininity, television's gender inscriptions are more complex than they first appear to be, and the positions that television casts for its viewers involve displacements and multiple points of identification that resist attempts to sum them up under any one label. Within several TV programs and genres, for example, the desire to reassert male control is readily revealed. However, the strategies used to achieve this end are themselves often riddled with contradictions and disruptions. As I've elaborated elsewhere, in attempting to reverse its usual connotations by aligning itself with masculinity rather than femininity, television does not so much repudiate the feminine (although this, of course, also happens) as appropriate, and thereby reroute, these same clusters of meaning. Rather than preventing male viewers from assuming any kind of dominant position, TV thus assures them that the prerogatives of masculinity continue to exist even within the pacified family that television constructs (both within its fictions and among its "family" of viewers). In other words, while television may be figured as feminine or its viewers as feminized, it also attempts to restore a threatened masculinity, to reclaim any "feminization" in the name of a more encompassing vision of masculine self-sufficiency and plenitude.

In this context, it is interesting to investigate some trends in recent television history, particularly those pertaining to representations of the family—or as I will ultimately emphasize, representations of the search for an "acceptable" family. Employing a somewhat broad definition of the term, one can trace the ways in which women have become increasingly excluded from TV's "familial space."[6] With the goal of exploring this exclusion in mind, I will first briefly turn to some genres that effect an erasure of the woman by defining the world as one big masculine home: the cop/detective show in which men within the police or investigative "family" usurp the traits of femininity, often dispensing with women altogether since the men themselves can play the "female roles," and recent incarnations of the family situation comedy in which an appropriation of femininity/maternity allows men to move into the position of both mother and father. Although the strategies of exclusion upon which these texts rely may seem to be opposed (in that the aggression of the cop show seems to stand in marked contrast to the warmth and humor of the situation comedies discussed), in many ways, their results are quite similar indeed.

However, it is an episode of the romantic comedy *Moonlighting* which will be my primary focus. Going beyond the genres named above, this text brings violence and sentimentality together in a particularly striking way so as to forcibly expel women from the family—an expulsion that is only strengthened (rather than mediated) by the self-reflexivity associated with this series. By offering an in-depth analysis of the premiere episode of what, in fact, turned out to be *Moonlighting*'s last season—the show in which Maddie Hayes loses the baby which is the visible result of the previous season's (and specifically Maddie's) "sexual excess"—I hope both to expose the extent of television's engagement in sexual, reproductive, and domestic politics and to reveal how this program attempts to establish the prerogatives of masculinity within all of these domains. Reasserting the primacy of the patriarchal family by literally redefining this unit as a "family of man," *Moonlighting* performs a chilling excision of the maternal sphere. Yet in disrupting the "natural" course of both familial and narrative progression, the program disturbs the very ground of representation upon which television's construction of the family is based, unleashing a threat which it can only manage to recontain by turning in on itself in a particular way. In my discussion of *Moonlighting*'s "family practice," I thus plan to show not only how the text commits an assault upon the woman, but also how this series's noted strategies of self-reflexivity, far from being radical gestures, contribute to a containment of femininity so as to allow the fathered-family to appear.

II. Paternal Precedents

While, at first glance, it may seem odd to refer to such stereotypically "male" genres as the cop or detective show in a discussion of television's construction of the family, further "investigation" reveals that such a connection is not so farfetched. Although the crime drama is usually classified in terms of action and adventure, far removed from the realm of the melodrama in which a focus on the family is the norm, the particular conditions of television have driven these two genres closer and closer together. Because of the small size of the TV screen, its location in the home, and the low budget of its productions (as compared to cinematic ones), television in all of its forms turns, to some degree, to the strategies that we usually associate with the melodrama and its intimate presentation of domestic life (its use of the close-up, interior shots, background music to capture the attention of a distracted viewer, and so on). Furthermore, like the melodrama, television's cop/detective shows negotiate their social issues in primarily personal terms. Given the economic and institutional demands of the medium (in which the leading characters must continue to appear and in which no resolution can ever be final), the heroes of television's crime dramas are trapped within a confined realm of perpetual victimization and emotional pressure, forced to repeat their actions week after week as the restricted parameters that define a privatized melodramatic sphere limit the world of the cop show as well. It is thus no surprise that the emphasis of many cop and detective programs—the affective center that sustains viewer interest—revolves around the tensions and strains that exist between members of the investigative unit or police "family" itself.[7]

Within this unit, the same "myth of complementarity" that supposedly holds the heterosexual couple and the nuclear family together binds the members of the hero pair or team into a functional whole—the members take up separate and hierarchized roles, each supplying what the others lack.[8] These differences are often visually (and ideologically) expressed through racial or class distinctions, and by "wedding" cultural oppositions in this way, the crime show can insert a husband/wife or parent/child dynamic into the heart of its (usually) all-male detective pairs or teams while fully maintaining dominant norms. Yet as the familial and the "feminine" become subsumed within this masculine sphere, actual women often find themselves with no role to play. This can be seen in the distribution of positions along the axes of subject/object and pursuer/pursued as well as in the formation of a leader/helper dichotomy (the husband/wife or adult/child dynamic mentioned above). Within the cop or detective show, women may be visible as background scenery or decor, but in a world in which male criminals are the primary enigmas and objects of voyeurism, the woman is divested of all potency. Here, even the power of spectacle and masquerade, the ability to manipulate the image, belongs to the cop who must masquerade in order to lure his prey into captivity.[9]

The ways in which cop/detective shows like *Magnum, p.i.*, *Miami Vice*, or, more recently, *Wiseguy* have aligned their male characters with spectacle and the pleasures of the look have been critically as well as popularly applauded. According to some critics, not only does the genre's appropriation of a "feminine" concern with masquerade, image, and the display of surface style modify traditional representations of masculinity, but it signals the end of stable sexual identity itself.[10] But rather than prematurely celebrating the death of gender in the postmodern age, it seems more important to analyze the ways in which statements of this death actually work to increase the scope of sanctioned male play. While both the effort to bring a "human" (read "family") focus into the precinct and the alliance of masculinity with the surface gloss of style may at first seem surprising or even subversive, the hegemony of male power is, in last instance, still assured. By granting their heroes the best of both worlds, these texts extend the range of male dominance so that it might cover every narrative sphere. Furthermore, the alliance of masculinity with familial emotion or the image tends to result in the exclusion, rather than acceptance, of women—in appropriating the position traditionally reserved for femininity (as men take up both sides of the heterosexual coin, becoming, in turn, either husband and wife or subject and object of the investigatory gaze), masculinity gains a self-sufficiency that tends to leave no space for women in the narrative at all.

While the cop/detective show thus erases women from the screen, allowing men to usurp even "feminine" traits, this vision of the world as one large masculine clan is enacted even more explicitly within other television forms. In particular, recent incarnations of the family situation comedy promote male homosociality as their ultimate goal and reveal a disturbing desire on the part of men to appropriate women's reproductive and maternal roles. In fact, in television's 1987–88 season lineup, not a single new family oriented (as opposed to "work family") sitcom featured an actual mother—instead we were offered *My Two Dads* (in which a woman has died and left her "estate," a twelve year old daughter, to two of her ex-lovers—both of whom may be the father—who raise her together); *Full House* (in which a woman has died and left her husband with three daughters to bring up with the help of his brother-in-law and best male buddy); and *I Married Dora* (in which a woman has symbolically died by abandoning her family, leaving her husband to raise his two children with the help of his "alien" housekeeper—a woman he must now legalize and lovelessly marry so as to prevent her deportation). While, of the three programs, *I*

Married Dora at least involved an adult female character, not only was this show the most blatant in its attack on "real" mothers (in its presentation of the mother as villain and father as savior, not to mention its racist portrayal of the woman who steps into the maternal role as somehow "alien"), but it was also the only one that missed with the public, failing to achieve high enough ratings for renewal.[11]

Given the social and political realities of contemporary American culture, in which women are the primary caretakers of children, men notoriously neglect both financial and emotional parental responsibility, and almost all single-parent households are headed by women, TV's announcement through these texts of the strength of male "paternal instinct" appears quite curious, indeed. Commenting on this phenomena in an analysis of a similar text, the film *Three Men and a Baby* (a remake of the French film *Three Men and a Cradle*, and one inspiration for TV's own paternal themes), Tania Modleski discusses how anxieties revolving around paternal position and the threat of patriarchy's decline—fears provoked by new reproductive technologies as well as by changing social norms—are both manifested and allayed within such fantasies of the purely fathered child.[12] Not only are women now synonymous, at least in the media's eyes, with the "sexual revolution," but, as previously mentioned, the recent attention given to artificial insemination, in vitro fertilization, embryo transfer, and other techniques have raised male concerns over the rights of the father—especially as these technologies seem to increasingly minimize male participation in the process of conception. Giving voice to the contravening, almost contraceptive, fantasy of a male "virgin birth," these texts thus attempt to dispense with women altogether, conveniently ridding themselves of the mother so that male homosocial bonding can occur, not, as is typically the case, by exchanging women (although this is also implicit in the brother-in-law relationship on *Full House* and in the competition for/sharing of the woman that served as the premise to *My Two Dads*), but rather through the intervention of the young (and, most often, female) child.[13]

Providing the characters with both progeny and the pleasure of usurping feminine roles, these texts articulate a narcissistic fantasy in which men can have it all.[14] Assuming every family role (and thus literally embodying the feminization and infantilization often associated with television), these regressive "male moms" are not only the perfect companions to their young, but by drawing the viewer into a world of endless and childish play, they also help "reproduce" the power of television itself. In other words, they attract many viewers precisely because they present their visions of the purely fathered family as simply the source of innocent fun. The humor involved in these texts—a humor that depends upon the absence of the woman—can then mobilize/authorize what would otherwise stand out as a much more disturbing trend. Nonetheless, as in television's crime dramas, the feminization that plagues such male characters is not accepted without some form of appropriation or defense. While on the surface, this vision of nurturant and caring fathers may seem diametrically opposed to the violent behavior engaged in by TV's detectives and cops, we should be wary of valorizing it as a more humane, even feminist, image. Not only does the role of "mother" and the accompanying fear of being "unmanned" often give rise to the heroes' displays of masculine prowess and strength, but, in allowing their heroes to play all the parts, the programs implicitly suggest women's expendability and marginality in the family.[15]

As Modleski points out, although the desire to find alternatives to masculine aggression and to further involve men in the responsibilities of child care may speak to justifiable and important female needs, we must be careful not to unwittingly legitimize an aggressive male appropriation of the maternal realm, thereby authorizing our own expulsion from familial space.[16] Similarly, the fact that these sitcoms employ the form of comedy, constructing their role reversals as the source of "harmless" humor and "mere" entertainment, should not exempt them from critical scrutiny. If anything, the pleasure that they provide helps to mask the more sinister fantasies to which they give voice. While their humor may make these texts palatable and even appealing, it is precisely women's exclusion from the domestic sphere that engenders viewer laughter, allowing the negation of the feminine to become the cause for both enjoyment and applause.

III. Violation and the Law: Breaking into the Female Body

While, given the obvious correlations between the television shows mentioned above and *Three Men and a Baby*, Modleski's analysis of paternal desire within this film is important to my own argument, I would like to expand my discussion to incorporate some other trends within television's representation of the family (or the desire for family). More recently, television has not simply promoted male homosociality at the expense of women who are deemed expendable, but it has actually enacted a certain violence on the body of the would-be mother—a violence which, in *Moonlighting's* case, extends to the very rhetoric of representation itself. Specifically, I want to discuss how the aggressive expulsion of women from familial space (now redefined as a purely paternal domain) as evidenced in the 1987–88 television season was further exacerbated in the 1988–89 season which, instead of portraying an "unnatural" but desired male appropriation of feminine reproductive/nurturant capacities, chose to penalize a threatening female generative potency by stripping the woman of her "natural" role. Punishing the sexual woman who dares to claim her offspring as her own, or to put it another way, "castrating" the mother who wants both power and a child, three television programs (*Hooperman*, *thirtysomething*, and *Moonlighting*, all on ABC) presented miscarriage stories in their 1988 season premieres—a surprising plot device under any circumstances, but absolutely extraordinary considering the goal of building audience sympathy and loyalty that all premiere episodes share.

Because of the multiple and/or continuing plotlines that both texts involve, *Hooperman's* and *thirtysomething's* decision to use this device may not seem so farfetched—the miscarriages in these shows intersected with plots regarding women's struggles over relationships versus personal autonomy or family versus career decisions, and given the soap opera-influenced structure of both programs, a concern with romantic and family crisis is not totally out of place.[17] *Moonlighting*, on the other hand, had always revolved around the sexual tension, witty repartee, and unfulfilled passion between its two leads—Maddie Hayes (played by Cybill Shepherd) and David Addison (played by Bruce Willis). Maddie's pregnancy, carried over from the previous season and introduced when actress Cybill Shepherd was herself pregnant, thus raised the thorny issues of not only how to make a pregnant woman seem "sexy," but how to maintain the traditional focus of the show. In other words, due to its emphasis on a sole couple (until Shepherd's pregnancy largely prevented her from appearing in the episodes) and a narrative premise that rested on the now obviously redundant question of "will they or won't they?" both the pregnancy and *Moonlighting's* miscarriage plot stood out as much more disruptive textual breaks.

In an attempt to extricate themselves from this dilemma, the producers of *Moonlighting* ended Maddie's troublesome pregnancy in an astonishing way. While it incorporated shots of the actors preparing for work, clips from past seasons' programs, and brief scenes of Maddie and David at their detective agency and then at a baby shower, most of the action took place within Maddie's womb—in fact, the show was entitled "A Womb with a View." Thus enabled to reveal all that (its producers presume) we ever wanted to know, the episode served as an antidote to the paternal confusion informing texts like *My Two Dads*: while the previous season showed Maddie's sexual involvement with two suitors (hero David and rival Sam) and ultimate marriage to still a third man, this episode cleared up once and for all any doubts about the paternity of the child while still preventing Maddie from carrying to term.

Yet perhaps even more peculiar than either the choices of subject matter or mise-en-scène was the vehicle selected to frame what one might expect would be a rather sad tale. Instead of portraying the loss of a child as a "weepie" and employing the more predictable melodramatic mode, "A Womb with a View" was in fact presented as a classical Hollywood musical—a genre that is not only considered synonymous with Hollywood entertainment, but one that is associated with utopian fantasy as well. In utilizing this form, *Moonlighting* capitalized on a nostalgia not simply for a pre-television and pre–rock 'n' roll era (good naturedly critiquing its own associations with youth and media culture), but also for both the mythical days of stable paternity (when women knew their place) and the program's own successful past. Before the actual glimpse into the womb, the episode begins as the characters openly express their desire to regain their former popularity and the show's previously high ratings (before last season's fall from grace provoked, in part, by Maddie's/Cybill's pregnancy and the chaos that it brought both to the show's production schedule and to its premise of unfulfilled love), directly addressing the audience in the attempt to create a sense of intimacy, familiarity, and community.

This strategy is a common one in the Hollywood musical as well as in *Moonlighting*'s own formula—through the abolition of proscenium space, techniques of viewer recognition, and the use of "I"/"you" pronouns that disguise the *histoire* of recorded media as the *discours* of interpersonal interaction, both the musical and many forms of television present themselves as live, spontaneous, and communal endeavors, the better to mask their mediations and interpellate the viewer into their ideological orders.[18] Keeping with both of these traditions, *Moonlighting*'s "A Womb with a View" paradoxically denied any technical intervention even as it called attention to the medium of television. At the beginning of the episode, for example, the actors speak through the camera to individual and "familiar" viewers by name (creating an interesting reversal as the viewers are brought into the text while the characters themselves are allowed to move outside of it at will) and later push a "Please Stand By" title that interrupts a song-and-dance number out of their way as if it were merely a part of the set that they are constructing rather than the evidence of electronic mediation. It is precisely through such self-reflexive strategies that *Moonlighting* had always been able to set itself apart from other programs and achieve its status as quality television.[19] Building on this reputation, the use of this technique has a dual function here: not only does it underscore the innovative value of the show, but by drawing the production processes of the media into the fictional world of the program itself, *Moonlighting* manages to turn its extra-textual problems (including bad publicity and ratings) into the textual trouble that it sets out to resolve. Recognizing themselves as fictional constructs in search of our much needed approval, the characters nonetheless seem to inhabit our own world, and the sense of intimate connection with the audience that is thereby established is exactly what is needed to get the program back on track.

Yet if *Moonlighting*'s loss of ratings is the problem that these performers face, then, as in any good musical, the solution can be reached just by putting on a show. The episode thus goes into a typical backstage production number as the characters/actors express their wishes to reconstitute a new community of performers and viewers united within a utopian space—here to be literally figured by life in the womb. Despite this representation of a universal Eden, the utopian sensibility of the musical responds to specific historical tensions in conventionalized ways. Playing almost a mythical or ritualistic role, the musical allows the spectator to heal oppositions and resolve current social problems—in this case, the tensions surrounding sexual and reproductive politics—by apparently offering timeless solutions that facilitate our rededication to traditional goals.[20] As a general rule, in its final "wedding" of cultural polarities, the musical asserts the triumph of communal harmony over personal, social, or sexual conflicts, and not surprisingly, this social integration (or the integration of the individual into a warm, loving community) most often occurs through marriage and the consolidation of the heterosexual couple.[21]

In "A Womb with a View," however, rather than ultimately securing the Law through a contract of marriage, the desire for this Law (and the Name of the Father that stands as its sign) is directly expressed.[22] While there are a few jokes concerning "Baby Hayes's" prenatal interest in the opposite sex (particularly in relation to his mother), he reserves most of his awe for the sight of his dad. Although Maddie's "promiscuous" behavior has precluded certain knowledge of paternity for those existing within the social world, there is no such confusion for those in the womb—not only is Baby Hayes played by Bruce Willis (the same actor who plays David Addison, but here, as an infant, dressed in diapers, blue pajamas, and a little blue bow), but the "angel" who visits him in preparation for birth (Jerome, the "emissary of the Creator") summons a magical, giant family album in which the new member is already inscribed. In other words, the fact that Baby Hayes is truly Baby Addison—that, as a miniature but complete human being, he already carries the paternal legacy, that he is properly assigned as male through his little blue outfit, and that he is indeed his father's rather than his mother's child—is visibly confirmed.[23]

Nonetheless, Baby Hayes officially lacks his father's name—a gap that the narrative must eventually fill. When he is thus confronted with the picture of his mother, Baby Hayes predictably responds with a thrilled "Hubba Hubba," but he only attempts to attain recognition from the father he requires (calling out to him as "Dad!"). Therefore, if, as several critics have claimed, the musical number often functions as a means of "surrogate sex," there is here a crucial shift in both the surrogacy required and the value placed on sex. Instead of celebrating heterosexual love, this episode ultimately punishes Maddie for her interest in this "vice" and reveals a vengeful urge to make the woman merely the means of conception, to relegate her, in other words, to the position of "surrogate mother"—the term now used to discredit biological mothers so as to assert the overriding reality and rights of the father.[24]

IV. Television Dystopia and the Maternal Scene

In the previous season, Maddie's maternal potential had already been somewhat disparaged and condemned. Indeed, her ability to maintain any kind of feminine "propriety" was repeatedly called into question not only by the text itself, but by the secondary discourses that circulated around it—discourses which attacked Cybill Shepherd in many of the same terms that the show used in attacking Maddie Hayes. Detailing the path of a former model who attempts to orchestrate a new career, *Moonlighting's* premise both mirrored and relied upon the image of its star, and by blurring the distinction between fiction and "real life," Maddie's character elicited viewer fascination while at the same time provoking the hostility so often directed at women who attempt to take their lives into their own hands. Always figured as a shrew and a castrating terror (a position made explicit not only in the popular press's depiction of the battle of the sexes on the sets, but also in another of *Moonlighting's* tributes to the past, its re-presentation of *The Taming of the Shrew*), Maddie was made to seem positively grotesque in some of 1987–88's final episodes.[25]

For example, in the episode in which the pregnant Maddie marries Walter Bishop (the only one of her three "suitors" who is not a biological candidate for fatherhood but who, temporarily, seems to be the legally approved choice), Maddie's position within the constellation of characters makes her monstrous status perfectly clear. Displacing viewer judgment away from the triangle of men vying for Maddie's affection and onto a competing triangular configuration, this episode sets Maddie up against another pregnant woman—a friend of David's whom he has been assisting in Lamaze classes—and stands as the logical precursor to the miscarriage story in "A Womb with a View." Within this first show, after chasing David out of the church and into the hospital where his friend is about to give birth, Maddie bursts into the delivery room and interrupts the course of its "natural" proceedings. Exaggerating the effect of this narrative disturbance through its construction of mise-en-scène (Cybill Shepherd, already an imposing woman, is here not only shown to be obviously pregnant while wearing a virginal, white wedding gown, but she is also inserted into a tiny, crowded room—a setting that makes her appear almost hideous because she is so out of place), *Moonlighting* produces Maddie as the monstrous shrew precisely by locating her in opposition to the good mother whose delivery she disrupts. Acting almost as a "prequel" to next season's miscarriage show, this incident establishes the parental prospects of the characters quite well—not only are David's capabilities proven, but Maddie's are denounced. Unlike the "good" woman who has taken care of herself and her baby throughout her pregnancy (even, or especially, to the point of finding a good man to assist her), Maddie has unleashed terror and disorder for all of those around her—for the guests at the wedding, for the people in the delivery room, and even for the *Moonlighting* viewers themselves.

Given our culture's codes of representation and gender, such figurations of terrifying maternity, existing both in relation and in opposition to the sentimentality also attached to notions of motherhood, are not at all rare.

The (supposedly) dreadful nature of pregnancy is simply a variation on the alliance between the monstrous and the feminine commonly found within the genre of horror, and while presented as a musical-comedy, "A Womb with a View" has a horrific edge.[26] Blatantly dealing with issues that are typically idealized, repressed, or banished from the scene (sex, reproduction, birth and death, etc.), the episode's vision of miscarriage is shocking at best. In fact, its very exposure of the deeply ambivalent fantasies at the heart of the nostalgia that it exhibits toward both motherhood and the musical form makes "A Womb with a View" more a dystopian than utopian dream. Referring to the Hollywood musical's self-fulfilling "utopian" promise in terms which are remarkably literalized in *Moonlighting*'s spectacle of prenatal life (and its termination), Dennis Giles writes, "The show bears a resemblance to the state before birth, echoing its timelessness, its ultimate unity of lover and beloved. But it is also a preview of the death state, transforming all the terrors, all the flux of life into a state of permanent being."[27] Revealing the drive for death that's intimately intertwined with our regressive fantasies of utopian rebirth, *Moonlighting*'s musical-horror show raises the terrifying spectre of the ultimate abject.

According to Julia Kristeva, the abject—that "pseudo-something" which is neither subject nor object, a "pre-object" which cannot yet be recognized as an "other" for a "me"—disrupts all borders and rules, disturbs any identity or location, and both terrifies and fascinates as it collapses the distinctions between inside and out, sacred and defiled, life and death.[28] Existing on the vacillating frontier of signification and subjectivity, the abject both engrosses and divides, attracts us but repels, seduces us with the desire for meaning but sickens us as it draws us to a place where meaning falls apart. While the horror of abjection is related to the fear of femininity (and its supposedly permeable boundaries), Kristeva particularly associates it with the maternal body and the threat that it poses to the very existence of subjectivity for the child: "that of being swamped by the dual relationship, thereby risking the loss not of a part (castration) but of the totality of his living being."[29] In order for the subject to be born onto himself (as subject), the not-yet-"it" of the abject must therefore be excluded even at the price of one's "own" death—an exclusion that not only revolves around separation from the maternal entity "even before ex-isting outside of her," but one which uncannily resembles the trajectory of *Moonlighting*'s own miscarriage plot. Dissolving the bounds of the subject through a glorious expansion of its anarchic drives, maternal abjection must somehow be hemmed in so that the Law can take its place. In other words, while the abject may offer a kind of sublime rapture as it carries us away, there must be some release from the stifling power that it holds. It is therefore the function of symbolic systems, rituals, and myths—secular as well as religious—to "ward off the subject's fear of his very own identity sinking irretrievably into the mother."[30]

Frequently defined as a mythic or ritualistic form, the musical may seem to be a genre well-equipped to enact just such a defense—dazzling us with its vista of boundless delights yet harnessing this in the name of the Law, the musical sweeps us off of our feet only to firmly implant us once again on Symbolic ground. Yet a musical that is, for the most part, located precisely within "the desirable and terrifying, nourishing and murderous, fascinating and abject inside of the maternal body," as is "A Womb with a View," seems to raise more tensions than it is able to resolve.[31] While, traditionally, the musical's construction of the woman as image and object provokes viewer interest while still containing any threat that might be posed by the female form, in this episode, such allurement and mystique arises only in conjunction with the horror of the show (although the specularization that typically defines the female star in both the musical and in *Moonlighting* continues to operate even within this unusual text, albeit in a very literal way). Employing a notion taken directly out of the scientific debates on reproductive technologies (that of a "maternal environment"), in this episode, the mother no longer simply poses a possible threat of engulfment but is constructed as the realm that actually envelopes the text. The female body literally becomes a site for conflicts that cannot be directly represented in narrative terms.

Speaking of another text that crosses genre lines (in this case, those between science fiction and horror), Mary Ann Doane notes that within the film *Alien* (and its sequel *Aliens*), the woman similarly "merges with the environment and the mother-machine becomes mise-en-scène—the space within which the story plays itself out. . . . The maternal is not only the subject of the representation here but its ground."[32] In fact, the maternal body (and the abjection it involves) *cannot* be the subject of representation within either of these texts in any coherent or conventional way. Dissolving oppositions, the abject threatens to disrupt the possibility of representation/signification itself (necessarily based on the paternal law of differentiation), thereby undoing the very systems upon which narrative, history, subjectivity, and knowledge are based. Relating *Alien*'s preoccupation with this threat of dissolution to the same crisis in the reproductive sphere that Modleski notes, Doane explains that the issue is "no longer one of transgression and conflict with the father but of the struggle with and against what seems to become an overwhelming extension of the category of the maternal—it assumes monstrous proportions."[33]

While, of course, *Alien/Aliens* struggles with this horrifying expansion in terms which differ from those of "A Womb with a View" (*Alien* and *Aliens* focus on the vacillating border between human, inhuman, and technological reproduction while *Moonlighting* is concerned with erecting a boundary between socially sanctioned and illegimate procreation—in other words, between the sacred and profane, the pure and the impure), the threat of an ever-enlarging maternal domain, no longer as limited by biological or social constraints, hovers over both texts. The anxiety provoked by this vision is strikingly figured in *Moonlighting*'s show as it transforms the pregnant body into a space of both dread and utopian song/dance. While the musical numbers, in part, serve as terror's mask, they actually increase the violence of the scenes, producing, through the lethal combination of horror and escape, a textual dissection of the glamorous female star. It is thus no wonder that the text insistently calls for paternal relief. Enacting Kristeva's observation that, "fear of the archaic mother turns out to be essentially fear of her generative power . . . a dreaded [power] that patrilineal filiation has the burden of subduing," *Moonlighting*'s baby can only be "delivered" to the Father and the Law.[34]

Courting precisely the kinds of fears that Kristeva here describes, a minor subplot within "A Womb with a View" (involving two characters who often function as less "desirable" versions of David and Maddie) actually details the terms of such a struggle for parental control, foregrounding both the anxieties and antagonisms that inform current reproductive politics as well. Arguing about Maddie's upcoming baby shower, Herbert Viola tells Agnes di Pesto that pregnancy makes him uncomfortable—an admission that triggers all the aggression he can muster. Finally revealing his feelings of inadequacy when it comes to fatherhood, he states that he wouldn't want to pass his genetic weaknesses on to a child. Defending the "rights" of a mother against male assumption of sole parentage, Agnes retorts, "It wouldn't be just your gene pool; who's to say that your oddball genes would be the ones to carry the day?" Going on to assure him that he'd be a wonderful dad, she exclaims, "I could really get into your genes," clearly punning on "jeans" as they go into a love scene on the couch (with Agnes as the dominant partner). Yet as she walks out of the door after having assuaged him of his fear, she makes a face and calls him a jerk, indicating to the viewer that all she really wants from Herbert (and, by implication, what all women really want) is simply a willing donor to supply her with a child. Both denying and "exposing" the way in which women today supposedly use men as impregnation machines (rather than the ways in which women have been used as incubators by men concerned with passing on their lines), this exchange reveals the threat posed by the devouring woman/mother to men's control over reproduction—a threat that the episode as a whole seeks to contain.

V. All in the TV Family of Man

In order to effect such a containment and closure, Maddie must lose her child so that he can be born instead into the midst of the paternal domain. Near the end of the episode and moments before the birth should take place, the messenger who visits Baby Hayes within the womb receives a telephone call on his portable phone (a call presumably made by God himself) informing him of a major change of plans—a "last minute shuffle" which provokes a violent disruption within Maddie's life, but one which offers a solution to the problems in the text (not to mention a conclusion which upholds a patriarchal ideology at risk). Cutting between Jerome (the "emissary") reassuring a frightened Baby Hayes with shots of Maddie collapsing as she's attacked from within, the text manages to both reap vengeance on the body of the mother without having to damage the prospects of the child. While thus adhering to some degree to the conventions of horror (which often gleefully exhibits the destruction of the family), "A Womb with a View" nonetheless offers a more "hopeful" view: it celebrates the destruction that it reaps merely to reconstitute the family in a more "appropriate" form—namely, by assigning Baby Hayes to a couple that can offer him a "proper" (father's) name. Furthermore, rather than making television or technology into an agent of horror and feminization (as occurs in several films, *Videodrome* providing the exemplary case), television is here what saves Baby Hayes—it offers its own favorite dad to counter the (literally) maternal medium of "A Womb with a View" while still keeping the birth "all in the [television] family."

After hearing of the change in plans for the child, Jerome informs Baby Hayes that rather than having David and Maddie for parents, he will become instead either Kirk Cameron's little brother (a plug for ABC's own *Growing Pains*) or Bill Cosby's grandchild. Ultimately, of course, the choice comes down on the side of TV's truly "big name"—Baby Hayes is magically zapped out of the womb, and as the baby and "angel" dance up a stairway to heaven while doing the episode's final musical number ("On the Sunny Side of the Street"), birth into *The Cosby Show* is finally assured. Within today's television world, this is truly utopia: a domestic heaven where all racial, gender, and intergenerational conflicts are erased (at the price of naturalizing the class biases of the program), where one can have it all in an updated version of *Father Knows Best*.

The fact that this involves a reassignment of racial identity is never posed as a problem in the text—in fact, if anything, such a prenatal transfer helps to solidify the familial project of television. Rather than acknowledging the possibility of cultural difference, *Moonlighting* implies that, when it comes to the family, only one acceptable form exists. (Interestingly, the reason why Maddie and David fail to meet this requirement is because her independence prevents him from assuming adult responsibility—a charge most often leveled by dominant culture at "minority" couples, and one which thus assumes that any problem in the family, regardless of race, ethnicity, or historical construction, is based on the failure of women to stay in their place.) Foreclosing any recognition of either cultural construction or cultural diversity, the only choice that is offered by the logic of the text—the choice between lawful (paternal) placement or the lure of the (maternal) abyss—is portrayed as one that has already been made, as the decision that has been ordained by the "Creator" himself. The Name of the Father is the key to the gates of heaven approached by the child, and as the musical number announces, the road to this fulfillment has but one sunny side. Thus, while this mention of *The Cosby Show* might seem at first glance to promote another network at ABC's expense, it is only through such a reference that *Moonlighting*'s own vision of the ideal family can prevail. Not only does the power of this modern-day patriarch's name allow him to claim his own show (even though the character he plays is not called Cosby), but within the *Moonlighting* episode, no mother (nor an actual father) need even be mentioned—the grandfather's (or Symbolic Father's) name is all that really counts.[35]

Of course, there is a self-reflexive television joke at work here that, in some ways, reveals the identity of the mother. Telling the baby to "keep the Cosby thing under your hat; they're pretty self-conscious over there about the whole pregnancy business," the angel makes reference to *The Cosby Show* (and its spin-off, *A Different World*) actress Lisa Bonet's real-life pregnancy, which NBC chose to mask by erasing Bonet from the screen (much as *Moonlighting* itself often did when Cybill Shepherd was expecting). As previously noted, *Moonlighting* is known for just these sorts of referential jokes—underscoring its own textuality, the program's knowing allusions have largely contributed to its critical and popular success. Addressing itself to an extremely media-conscious audience, *Moonlighting* comments on its production constraints, television conventions, and numerous aspects of American popular culture, and by playing with the boundary between the fictional and the real, the program has attained a kind of critical acclaim. Though it's not the first program to call attention to the structures of TV, in foregrounding the discursive practices of television, *Moonlighting* has achieved its status as an innovative show.[36]

Yet there is a danger in valorizing the use of such techniques, of confusing textual strategy with political commitment. The problem of lauding *Moonlighting* as a radical or subversive text becomes apparent when one considers the ways in which self-reflexive devices generally function in television and, especially, how they operate in this particular case. As Mimi White has argued in a perceptive analysis of television's strategies of self- and inter-program referentiality, rather than undercutting the illusions at the basis of the media's appeal, television's imbrication of the fictional and real asserts a unity across temporal, spatial, and narrative diversity, a continuity that goes beyond the diegetic space of any individual show.[37] As the world on TV becomes increasingly equated with the world of TV, an imaginary coherency binds it together as a whole; securing the viewer across a variety of texts, television constitutes itself as a self-enclosed and self-perpetuating field. *Moonlighting*'s comical references to the world of broadcasting and to other programs then stand not as critiques of the medium, but simply as incitements for the consumption of more television—they both encourage further viewing in order to get all the jokes and make *Moonlighting* itself appear more "honest" and "live" through its exposure of television's usual artificiality. Portraying the world through media clichés (as Jerome describes life to Baby Hayes through recycled film/television images, introduces his parents and explains history through clips from past *Moonlighting* episodes, and reassures him of his birth through references to other TV families), "A Womb with a View" works to maintain television's dominance, remaining within this protective enclave so as to contain its own contradictions.

In addition to promoting television in this way, the intertextual joke of "A Womb with a View" provides the outlet that is needed to authorize the violence of this text. By assuring us that nothing bad is really going to happen to adorable Baby Hayes, *Moonlighting* can dispose of its "problem" in a most efficient way. The fact that "A Womb with a View" is presented as a musical pacifies the viewer all the more. Not only is our horror bought off by the relief of song and dance, but the text need only fall back upon itself in order to achieve its own alibi. In other words, by turning the womb into a theatrical arena, *Moonlighting* manages to stage TV itself as the answer to the loss that it presents: its characters simply assign themselves new roles in order to renew their hold on life. Jane Feuer argues that within the genre of the musical—where self-referentiality is also the norm—such reflexive strategies function in a conservative and self-justifying way:

> Musicals are unparalleled in presenting a vision of human liberation which is profoundly aesthetic. . . . [T]hey give us a glimpse of what it would be like to be free. . . . But the musical presents its vision of the unfettered human spirit in a way that forecloses a desire to translate that vision into reality. The Hollywood version of utopia is entirely solipsistic. In its endless reflexivity the musical can offer only itself, only entertainment, as its picture of utopia.[38]

Like television, the musical exists within a self-enclosed world in which its own productions are the objects of its dreams—or in this case, where the celebratory numbers offer an escape from the nightmare it describes.

While some critics suggest that the musical's utopian moments cannot be fully recuperated by the closure of the plot, this strategy of removing the show in time and place and situating it within its own self-contained space limits the critical potential that the form might otherwise provide. By presenting its own protected sphere as already fully whole, the text is unable to comment on the confines of the status quo. As Richard Dyer has explained in regard to the class of Hollywood musicals that create this kind of world, the contradictions developed in these films "are overridingly bought off by the nostalgia or primitivism which provides them with the point of departure."[39] Pointing backward toward a golden age instead of forward to the future, they actually reverse a utopianism that might allow their viewers to envision a process of social change. The fact that "A Womb with a View" engages in this type of regressive nostalgia seems plain enough. Yet the text reveals not only a sentimental nostalgia for life in the womb (or even for life in the tube); it also expresses a historical nostalgia for the (imaginary) days of unchallenged male rule—a fantasy that too requires *Moonlighting*'s construction of a self-enclosed space.

In a perceptive analysis of the relationship between character and environment unique to the genre, Martin Sutton notes that "space in the musical is the most expressive of media."[40] Often located within areas that provide the excuse for both movement and play (theatres, parks, gymnasiums, carnivals, and in *Moonlighting*, the womb figured as an inflatable bubble with a trampoline floor), the musical's space awaits activation by "an interpreter, an explorer" who claims it as his. Charged with meaning only by the dancer's performance, this site is encompassed by the figure who invades it, transforming it into a world of his own. Sutton argues that it is this imaginative use of space that makes the musical a utopian form, contrasting it to the horror film, in which the situation is reversed (since in horror, the characters fear, rather than revel in, a space whose darkness and shadows menace instead of please). Yet "A Womb with a View" combines music with dread—the abject space of the maternal always threatens to engulf the subject rather than the other way around. The conventions of the musical genre can thus offer a release. In allowing the little male hero to conquer the horror of feminine space, "A Womb with a View" makes the mother's body into a mere medium for man. In other words, within the most feminine sphere (in this case, triply feminized—located within the female body; within a genre that, like the melodrama, is often considered a "feminine" form; and within the "feminized" world of television), we discover a desire for the Law and the patriarchal Name.[41]

Moonlighting's spectacle that reformulates birth, like the preceding season's stories that had reconstituted the family as a purely fathered realm, may seem far removed from the blatant display of masculine power found within the cop/detective genre previously discussed. Yet all of these programs share a common desire to assert masculine dominance within the medium considered the most "feminine" of all. Revealing the concern for masculinity that underlies much of television's "feminine" world, television's exhibitions of male performance—whether through spectacles of strength or spectacles of song, camaraderie at work or fun and games at home, the stylized "dance" of slow-motion violence or an actual musical show—are efforts to achieve and flaunt a virility that is in danger of being aborted itself. Yet television's attempts to prove masculine potency are riddled with contradictions, and the tensions this involves are never finally repressed—both the exaggeration of maleness through a hypermasculine defense and the appropriation of femininity for the benefits of man produce ruptures that these texts can hardly contain. Able to succeed only by taking on the roles of the women they replace, only finding their identities through some form of masquerade (by way of virile poses or the staging of "paternal delights"), TV's male heroes are trapped within a circuit without end. More and more spectacle is always required, and this results in a curious situation in which television cannot help but disrupt the very divisions of gender that it strives to reinforce. Revealing the discord involved in attempts to manage the figurations of gender that TV itself helps to promote, these texts create their own "monstrous" excess.

VI. Epilogue: Resurrecting the Voice, or "Look Who's Talking" Now

Because *Moonlighting*'s family practice was prevented from ever reaching resolution within the confines of television, it may come as no surprise that Baby Hayes (or, more accurately, Baby Willis) could only find his home within another media form. While the *Moonlighting* series suffered its own "miscarriage" when it was cancelled at the end of the 1988–89 season, the narrative of "A Womb with a View" has almost had a rebirth that miraculously managed to resurrect its "blessed child." In the 1989 hit film *Look Who's Talking*, not only does actor Bruce Willis replay his role as a fetus in the womb (providing the running commentary for the pre- and postnatal infant Mikey), but he is able to project this role both forward and backward in time in order to ensure the security, legality, and ultimate dominance of the paternal function throughout every stage of reproductive and family life.[42] From the film's first images of sperm attempting to penetrate an egg until its final moments when the family is complete, the male reproductive cell/embryo/fetus/infant has a mind and a voice of his own (in fact, the only time that Mikey doesn't speak is when he is but a gleam in his father's leering eye).

In continuing the project of "A Womb with a View," the idea that reproduction is nothing if not a father's own affair is thus once again made absolutely clear. Within *Look Who's Talking*'s world, not only does human subjectivity lie in the sperm alone (the egg just passively and silently awaits the orgasmic pleasure that "he" provides her), but almost all that Mikey can "talk" about is his desire for a dad—a wish that's granted at the end of the film when Mikey (without Bruce Willis's voice-over) finally pronounces his first word for himself: "Dada" (of course). While the "dada" that he gets is not his biological dad, the film naturalizes this transfer by reproducing the conditions of his birth (just as *Moonlighting* naturalized its reassignment through the miraculous restagings of its self-reflexive joke): Mikey's mother goes into labor in the midst of a perilous cab ride, and later, our cab-driver hero repeats this same route in order to save Mikey's life, deliver him into the arms of his mom, and establish himself as the legitimate protector/possessor of his fated heir.[43] The similarity between this film and the *Moonlighting* episode is startling, and the characterizations of women in the two texts are basically the same—although both Maddie and Molly (the heroine of *Look Who's Talking*) are tough, independent women, neither of them are able to maintain a family on their own and they even lack the sense to (formally) bring in the proper man. It is up to the small male child to demand the family that he needs which, in both cases, involves actualizing a paternal heritage that is already inscribed within the structure of the text (Baby Hayes's desire for Cosby, and Mikey's desire to be granted legal access to the nurturant man and grandfather with whom he is already spending time).[44]

However, the difficulties that both "A Womb with a View" and *Look Who's Talking* have in bringing to fruition a family structure that they pose as preordained is telling in the light of the upheavals that have plagued a traditional vision of the familial American dream. Though striving to establish an immediate connection between sexuality, reproduction, and the patriarchal family, these texts cannot help but expose the gaps that lie between these terms. In figuring the fathered family as both natural and yet as a choice that must be made, these texts destabilize the very ground that they are attempting to secure. The labor of technological reproduction thus intersects with the labor of sexual reproduction in a very complex way—while the media work to bind our multiple desires into one overruling oedipal construction, they also reveal the contradictions within it, and it is precisely in the space that is thereby opened up that we must begin to formulate our interrogation of familial ideology. In fact, in the final moments of *Look Who's Talking*, the possibility of such a critical space is disclosed. After the hero and heroine have finally gotten together and solidified the family through the birth of a new child, the nuclear family seems to have reached its ideal form—mother, father, first-born son, and now a little girl. However, the sister's position within this family portrait threatens to unravel the narrative logic upon which the construction of the paternal order is based. Unable to be figured as a full-blown subject from the moment of attempted conception as was the little boy (for how can a little girl be figured as a talking sperm?), she nonetheless begins to "speak" (through Joan Rivers) once she emerges into the social sphere. Her first words, "Can we talk?" raise an important question for women in the text and in the audience alike—amidst the discourses that structure both sexual and technological reproduction today, how can the female subject gain access to a voice?

Notes

I wish to thank Robert Bechtel, Jamie Owen Daniel, Sandy Flitterman-Lewis, and Gloria Jean Masciarotte for their generous suggestions and helpful criticism.

1. Roland Barthes, "Upon Leaving the Movie Theatre," *Apparatus*, ed. Theresa Hak Kyung Cha (New York: Tanam Press, 1981), p. 2.

2. For a feminist critique of new reproductive technologies, see, for example, Gena Corea, *The Mother Machine: Reproductive Technologies from Artificial Insemination to Artificial Wombs* (New York: Harper and Row, 1985) and Gena Corea et al., *Man-Made Women: How New Reproductive Technologies Affect Women* (Bloomington: Indiana University Press, 1987). The primary feminist text which had earlier advocated the separation of sexuality and the family through the technological development of "artificial reproduction" is Shulamith Firestone's *The Dialectic of Sex: The Case for Feminist Revolution* (New York: William Morrow and Company, 1970). For an interesting analysis of the general shifts in feminist sexual politics and, specifically, of the way in which some branches of feminism seem to have moved from a critique of biological and "natural" explanations of gender, sexuality, and reproduction to an embracement of the "natural," see Alice Echols, "The Taming of the Id: Feminist Sexual Politics, 1968–1983," *Pleasure and Danger: Exploring Female Sexuality*, ed. Carole Vance (Boston: Routledge and Kegan Paul, 1984), pp. 50–72.

3. For further elaboration of these issues, see, for example, Jane Feuer, "The Concept of Live Television: Ontology as Ideology," *Regarding Television: Critical Approaches—An Anthology*, ed. E. Ann Kaplan (Frederick, MD: University Publications of America in association with the American Film Institute, 1983), pp. 12–22; David Morley, *Family Television: Cultural Power and Domestic Leisure* (London: Comedia Publishing Group, 1986); and Lynn Spigel, "Installing the Television Set: Popular Discourses on Television and Domestic Space, 1945–1955," *Camera Obscura*, no. 16 (January 1988), pp. 11–46.

4. I discuss television's figuration as a feminine medium in "Critical and Textual Hypermasculinity," *Logics of Television*, ed. Patricia Mellencamp (Bloomington: Indiana University Press, 1990). For related analyses of the "gendering" of TV or mass culture as a whole, see Patrice Petro, "Mass Culture and the Feminine: The 'Place' of Television in Film Studies," *Cinema Journal* 25, no. 3 (Spring 1986), pp. 5–21; Tania Modleski, "Femininity as Mas(s)querade: A Feminist Approach to Mass Culture," *High Theory/Low Culture: Analyzing Popular Television and Film*, ed. Colin MacCabe (New York: St. Martin's Press, 1986), pp. 37–52; and Andreas Huyssen, "Mass Culture as Woman: Modernism's Other," *After the Great Divide: Modernism, Mass Culture, Postmodernism* (Bloomington: Indiana University Press, 1986), pp. 44–62.

5. On these points, see John Ellis, *Visible Fictions: Cinema, Television, Video* (London: Routledge and Kegan Paul, 1982); Tania Modleski, "The Rhythms of Reception: Daytime Television and Women's Work," *Regarding Television*, pp. 67–74; and Sandy Flitterman, "The Real Soap Operas: TV Commercials," *Regarding Television*, pp. 84–96.

6. Although my discussion of the exclusion of women within television's familial space focuses on recent trends within television history, for an analysis that reveals the ways in which the mother was similarly marginalized in the domestic comedies of the 1950s, see Nina C. Leibman, "Leave Mother Out: The Fifties Family in American Film and Television," *Wide Angle* 10, no. 4 (1988), pp. 24–41.

7. I deal with these issues in greater detail in "All That Television Allows: TV Melodrama, Postmodernism, and Consumer Culture," *Camera Obscura*, no. 16 (January 1988), pp. 129–53. Also see David Thorburn, "Television Melodrama," *Television: The Critical View*, ed. Horace Newcomb, 4th ed. (New York: Oxford University Press, 1987), pp. 628–44.

8. This point comes from Andrew Ross's analysis of *Miami Vice*, in which he explains that the bond between the heroes Sonny Crockett and Ricardo Tubbs expresses the myth of complementarity that governs compulsory heterosexuality in our culture because the two men are "heteros" to one another, each "naturally"

supplying what the other lacks. See Ross, "Masculinity and *Miami Vice*: Selling In," *Oxford Literary Review* 8, no. 1–2 (1986), p. 153. Making a related point (but discussing the construction of a family unit rather than a "couple"), John Fiske explains how the distribution of social roles among members of the group in the TV show *The A-Team* falls along an adult/child (or parent/offspring) axis; John Fiske, *Television Culture* (New York: Methuen, 1987), p. 198–202.

9. For an elaboration of these issues in regard to *Miami Vice*, see Jeremy Butler, "*Miami Vice*: The Legacy of Film Noir," *Journal of Popular Film and Television* 13, no. 3 (Fall 1985), pp. 127–38, and my essay, "Critical and Textual Hypermasculinity."

10. See, for example, John Fiske's valorization of *Miami Vice*, masculine display, and the pleasures of postmodern style in *Television Culture*, pp. 221–22, 255–62. See especially p. 259 where, in a discussion of our commodified "culture of the spectacle" as evidenced in *Miami Vice*, Fiske announces the "death of gender" and writes: "in this spectacle, the gaze is neither masculine nor feminine, for it is not the gaze of a stable subject upon a stable object: both subject and object construct themselves out of the traditional signs and positions of either gender. This culture signals the death of authenticity, of any underlying 'true' meaning of gender or of anything else." For a competing analysis of male spectacle in the cop/detective genre (one that demonstrates how such display contributes to ideological notions about gender), see Sandy Flitterman, "Thighs and Whiskers—the Fascination of *Magnum, P. I.*," *Screen* 26, no. 2 (March–April 1985), pp. 42–58.

11. However, whether the failure of *I Married Dora* was due to its representation of gender and ethnicity, its flirtation with a racially/ethnically mixed romantic pair, or merely the poor quality of the show is beyond the scope of this argument.

12. Tania Modleski, "Three Men and Baby M," *Camera Obscura*, no. 17 (May 1988), pp. 69–81.

13. The notion of a male "virgin birth" comes from Modleski, p. 71. She discusses *Three Men and a Baby*'s construction of homosocial bonding (which occurs through the agency of the female infant rather than through the exchange of women) on p. 74.

14. See Modleski's discussion of the regressive nature of these fantasies and the "infantilizing of culture," pp. 74–75.

15. Modleski, pp. 72, 76. On p. 69, she also makes the important point that the patriarchal sphere has historically been limited by the assumption of mothers' custodial rights only within our own century, and it is in this context that we must read these shows.

16. See Modleski, pp. 79–80.

17. *Hooperman*'s second-season opener (November 30, 1988) dealt, in part, with the miscarriage suffered by Harry Hooperman's "girlfriend," Susan Smith, a woman Hooperman met (assuming that she was a man) while hiring a maintenance person for his building. Throughout the first season, Smith had rejected his offers for a serious relationship—a situation altered by the second season's miscarriage story (which carried over into the second episode). However, after deciding to try again for a child, she took a break to recover from her loss and then disappeared from the show.

Thirtysomething's premiere (December 6, 1988) focused on Hope's ambivalence about having a second child (which her husband is urging her to do) after going back to work and having been offered a chance at a writing career. She finds the mementos of a soldier's wife who once lived in their house and becomes drawn into her story of a miscarriage and the decision to have another baby. Having learned from this woman's tale that there is never a perfect time to try to have a baby, Hope is persuaded to attempt to conceive another child herself. Interestingly, the story of the soldier's wife almost functions as a premonition for the future of the series: later in the season, Hope has a miscarriage as well.

As stated in the text above, both of these stories involve women's choices in regard to family, relationship, and career decisions, and thus they narrate the conflicts related to contemporary sexual politics. In my analysis of *Moonlighting*'s miscarriage episode, I hope to demonstrate not so much how the text *narrates* such conflicts, but how the power struggles at the root of sexual and reproductive politics are actually *embodied* within the program's mise-en-scène and the terms of representation itself. This episode aired on December 6, 1988; Jay Daniel, executive producer. The series itself is produced by Picturemaker Productions in association with ABC Circle Films and was created by Glenn Gordon Caron.

18. The distinction between *"histoire"* or "story" (in which all marks of enunciation are suppressed in the assumption of third-person narration) and *"discours"*/ discourse (in which the positions of speaker and listener are acknowledged and revealed) comes from the linguist Emile Benveniste, *Problems in General Linguistics*, trans. Mary Elizabeth Meek (Coral Gables: University of Miami Press, 1972). In applying this distinction to film studies, Christian Metz has argued that the classical film disguises its discourse as story by effacing the signs of its own production and by disavowing the presence of the viewer. See Metz, "History/Discourse: Note on Two Voyeurisms," and Geoffrey Nowell-Smith, "A Note on History/Discourse," *Edinburgh Magazine*, no. 1 (1976), pp. 21–25 and pp. 25–32, respectively.

While Metz's analysis applies to most forms of classical cinema, it does not account for the ways in which the Hollywood musical and many forms of television acknowledge the viewer or insist on revealing the marks of enunciation so as to create the illusion of a live or shared work in the very process of construction. Discussing this issue in regard to the musical is Jane Feuer, *The Hollywood Musical* (London: BFI Publishing, 1982); and Jim Collins, "Toward Defining a Matrix of the Musical Comedy: The Place of the Spectator within the Textual Mechanisms," *Genre: The Musical*, ed. Rick Altman (London: BFI/Routledge and Kegan Paul, 1981), pp. 134–45. In relationship to television's illusion of liveness and discourse, see Jane Feuer, "The Concept of Live Television," and Margaret Morse, "The Television News Personality and Credibility: Reflections on the News in Transition," *Studies in Entertainment*, pp. 55–79.

19. For an analysis of the ways in which *Moonlighting* creates its own mystique precisely by demystifying the myth it is creating (in other words, how it manages to announce itself as a unique and "quality" show by exposing the production processes of television), see J. P. Williams, "The Mystique of Moonlighting: 'When You Care Enough to Watch the Very Best,' " *Journal of Popular Film and Television* 16, no. 3 (Fall 1988), pp. 90–99. On the notion of "quality television" and its relationship to self-reflexivity, see Jane Feuer, "The MTM Style," *MTM: "Quality Television,"* ed. by Jane Feuer, Paul Kerr, and Tise Vahimagi (London: BFI Publishing 1984), pp. 32–60.

20. On the historical impulses behind the musical's "escapist" fantasies, see Richard Dyer, "Entertainment and Utopia," *Genre: The Musical*, pp. 175–89, and Mark Roth, "Some Warners Musicals and the Spirit of the New Deal," *Genre: The Musical*, pp. 41–56.

21. On this point, see, for example, Martin Sutton, "Patterns of Meaning in the Musical," *Genre: The Musical*, pp. 194–95.

22. In a perceptive analysis of the musical comedy which outlines the specificity of the genre and the ways in which musical spectacles may rupture and/or mirror the narratives in which they are placed, Patricia Mellencamp writes: "musicals depict a literal version of 'family romance,' a thematic often embedded within another

'story' in other genres. Musicals virtually re-enact the ritual of re-creation/pro-creation of the privileged heterosexual couple, the nucleus of patriarchal society. As in classical narrative, the work of musicals is the containment of potentially disruptive sexuality, a threat to the sanctity of marriage and the family." As I attempt to show throughout this essay, the literalization of family romance and the containment of a disruptive (female) sexuality is nowhere more apparent than in "A Womb with a View." However, because its "ritual of pro-creation" is enacted through a desire for the paternal Law which is directly expressed (rather than mediated through the conventions of romance), the subversive power of spectacle is negated. Underscoring the patriarchal contract upon which the musical's fantasies are based, the spectacle of Baby Hayes's desire for a dad can only reduplicate and mirror the repression inherent in the narrative itself. See Patricia Mellencamp, "Spectacle and Spectator: Looking through the American Musical Comedy," *Ciné-tracts* 1, no. 2 (Summer 1977), p. 29; see also pp. 34–35.

23. Commenting on the debates regarding abortion and reproductive technologies in Great Britain, Jalna Hanmer writes: "That men identify with embryos and foetuses, and not mothers, is clear from the debates on abortion rights and, more recently, the Warnock recommendations and parliamentary response to limiting experimentation on human embryos. . . . Women are rarely mentioned in the Warnock Report as they are subsumed within men's identification as embryos, foetuses, children and men within the family." Her observation on the public discourse of reproductive politics resonates remarkably well with the terms of the television texts discussed above, and the relevancy of this *Moonlighting* episode to current debates within the United States should be obvious. By figuring the fetus in the womb as both a full subject (complete with language and already installed within the Symbolic Order) and as a familiar presence (since he is played by Bruce Willis—the "fun" member of the *Moonlighting* pair), there is no question not only as to when life begins, but even as to whose life has priority here. See Jalna Hanmer, "Transforming Consciousness: Women and the New Reproductive Technologies," *Man-Made Women*, p. 95.

24. On the function of the musical's dance numbers as a form of "surrogate sex," see, for example, Dennis Giles, "Show-making," *Genre: The Musical*, pp. 85–101; Jim Collins's essay in the same volume; and editor Rick Altman's introductory comments for both articles. In her discussion of *Three Men and a Baby*, Tania Modleski also refers to the way in which the term "surrogate mother" de-realizes motherhood, minimizing the woman's role in order to present the father as the "real thing" and thus justify his role as surrogate mother in the old sense of the term (Modleski, pp. 69, 80).

In critiquing the use of the term "surrogate mother," however, I am not trying to construct a general argument against the use of surrogacy (or any reproductive technology) as an alternative to "natural" forms of procreation. To do so, I believe, would oversimplify an issue which is too complex to elaborate here. While opponents of reproductive technologies often attack the ways in which these technologies deny or disrupt natural human processes, to accept this argument uncritically is not only to maintain an essentialist view which equates femininity with biological maternity, it is also to find ourselves within a web of contradictions. In other words, in order to both avoid the claim that women can only legitimately assume a maternal position if they are biologically ordained as mothers and to evade the confusion involved in attempting to legislate against reproductive technologies without having to also embrace laws that regulate women's reproductive freedoms (our access to birth control and abortion), feminists must reject any argument which rests on "natural" grounds. On the other hand, the attempt to avoid this essentialism by supporting current work in reproductive technologies may also paradoxically result in feminists' aligning themselves with those who demand respect for men's "instinctual needs" to father. The opposition between essentialism and anti-essentialism thus fails to clarify all the problems at hand. A similar case can be made for the ways in which arguments posed in terms of rights (parental rights, children's rights, the right to control one's own body, the right to enter into contracts, etc.) also fail to untangle the web of contradictions ensuing from the challenges now posed to both the family and ideologies of familialism. For an analysis of these issues, see Janice Doane and Devon Hodges, "Risky Business: Familial Ideology and the Case of Baby M," *Differences* 1, no. 1 (Winter 1989), pp. 67–81.

25. In noting the secondary discourses that circulated around the show and figured Cybill Shepherd as a "shrew," I am referring primarily to the tabloids' representations of the battles on the *Moonlighting* set, not to the articles that appeared in women's magazines which featured Shepherd with her twin children or emphasized her ability to combine motherhood with a career. For an analysis that investigates these other discourses (and the question of female narcissism) in order to reveal the complexity of Shepherd's position in women's magazines and in *Moonlighting*'s re-presentation of *The Taming of the Shrew*, see Hilary Radner, "Feminine Enunciation and U.S. Prime Time Television," paper presented at the International Television Studies Conference, London, July 1988 (forthcoming in *Genders*). Williams also discusses viewers' responses to Cybill/Maddie (and to the blurring of the boundary between character and actress) in "The Mystique of *Moonlighting*," pp. 93–94.

26. On the relationship between femininity/maternity and the monstrous within the genre of horror, see Linda Williams, "When the Woman Looks," *Re-vision: Essays in Feminist Film Criticism*, ed. Mary Ann Doane, Patricia Mellencamp, and Linda Williams (Frederick, MD: University Publications of America in association with the American Film Institute, 1984), pp. 83–99; and Barbara Creed, "Horror and the Monstrous-Feminine: An Imaginary Abjection," *Screen* 27, no. 1 (January–February 1986), pp. 44–71.

27. Giles, p. 87.

28. Julia Kristeva, *Powers of Horror: An Essay on Abjection* (New York: Columbia University Press, 1982). See particularly pp. 2–17.

29. Kristeva, p. 64. See also pp. 70–72, 83–85.

30. Kristeva, pp. 3, 13, 64.

31. Kristeva, p. 54. For a discussion of how the musical typically manages the tensions inherent in its form by containing the "momentarily subversive fantasy breaks" of spectacle within a suppresive process of narrativization, see Patricia Mellencamp, "Spectacle and Spectator," pp. 34–35.

32. Mary Ann Doane, "Technophobia: Technology, Representation and the Feminine," paper presented at the University of Wisconsin-Milwaukee, December 1988, p. 9. Providing another very interesting analysis, Mia Carter-Reis also discusses the maternal mise-en-scène of *Aliens* in "De-Feminizing the Future: Cleaning up the Outer Limits in *Aliens*," unpublished paper, University of Wisconsin-Milwaukee, 1987.

33. Doane, p. 9.

34. Kristeva, p. 77.

35. Of course, there are television shows that are also named after their female stars. The power of this reference to Cosby within "A Womb with a View" depends not only on the general currency afforded to his name, but more importantly, to both the place of this reference within the narrative structure of the text and to the way in which Cosby's name substitutes for any information concerning Baby Hayes's

actual new parents. Once again, granting the child a paternal heritage takes precedence over recognizing the mother.

36. For one such positive appraisal of the show, see, for example, John Fiske, *Television Culture*, p. 238.

37. Mimi White, "Crossing Wavelengths: The Diegetic and Referential Imaginary of American Commercial Television," *Cinema Journal* 25, no. 2 (Winter 1986), pp. 51–64.

38. Feuer, *The Hollywood Musical*, p. 84. See also Andy Medhurst's discussion of "The Musical" in *The Cinema Book*, ed. Pam Cook (New York: Pantheon Books/BFI, 1985), pp. 106–9.

39. Dyer, p. 188.

40. Sutton, p. 192.

41. Discussing the musical's "presumed address to a female, or at least feminine, audience," Andy Medhurst quotes, for example, film critic John Grierson who, in 1929, wrote of musicals: "They may have their place, but it is in the exclusively women's theatres which men may know how to avoid." Not only is the audience and the genre itself considered feminine, but, as Steve Neale points out in an article about male spectacle in the cinema, male musical actors/dancers are typically "feminized" when seen in this form. The need to erect some kind of masculine defense— here, through the assumption of the patriarchal name—is thus even more pressing for the male character in *Moonlighting*'s show. See Medhurst, pp. 109, 107; and Steve Neale, "Masculinity as Spectacle," *Screen* 24, no. 6 (November–December 1983), pp. 14–15.

42. *Look Who's Talking*, a Tri-Star Picture, was directed by Amy Heckerling and produced by Jonathon D. Krane/M.C.E.G. Kirstie Alley stars as the heroine, Molly, and John Travolta as the hero, James. While not actually a musical film, in many ways it mirrors "A Womb with a View" in this aspect too. The soundtrack plays an important role in supplementing the narrative, and it is made up of songs that play on the conflation of terms of romantic endearment and words that signify a parent/child relationship ("babe," "baby love," "my angel," "girl of my dreams," "daddy's home," etc.). In fact, the film as a whole conflates romance/sex with reproduction/parenting. While we never witness any sex in the film (it had a P.G. rating), the text offers the most blatant representation of reproduction that I have ever seen in a narrative film. As in "A Womb with a View," the specularization that typically defines the female star is literalized (as speculum) in an extraordinary way.

43. Not only does the film itself attempt to naturalize the hero's assumption of the paternal role, but the publicity for the film also attempts such a naturalization. On the release poster, the copy reads: "He's hip, he's slick, and he's only 3 months old. He's got John Travolta's smile, Kirstie Alley's eyes. And the voice of Bruce Willis . . . Now all he has to do is find himself the perfect daddy." By noting the attribute of the "father" that the child has "inherited" (and making it a priority by listing this before any mention of the mother), the publicity implies that Mikey is truly his father's own child—even though it goes on to indicate the gap that lies between father and son. Like the film itself, the release poster thus reveals the contradiction within its own paternal project.

44. It is interesting that in both of these texts, the presence of a grandfather takes on a crucial role. In other words, granting the child a paternal legacy is equally (or more) important than supplying him with a man to fill the role of father. As I explained in regard to *Moonlighting*, Cosby's name actually substitutes for any mention of Baby Hayes's new parents. In *Look Who's Talking*, Mikey's search for a father is the primary focus of the text, but significantly, it is the (paternal) grandfather

that actually brings the couple together, assumes the legality of their union, and initiates the scene in which James (the hero) will finally be recognized as the legitimate protector of the small child. While Molly's parents are seen near the beginning of the film, not only are they ineffectual (her mother dominates the father who, in contrast to Mikey, never speaks within the entire film—the "reason" for Molly's own independence and difficulty with men), but they drop out of sight once the hero's family is introduced.

TEN

Appropriating Like *Krazy*: From Pop Art to Meta-Pop

Jim Collins

Loretta Lynn guides my hand to the radio
Where would I be in times like these without the songs Loretta wrote?
'Cause when you can't find a friend you still got the radio
The radio, oh, listen to the radio

Nanci Griffith[1]

Why *not* Theolonius Monk goes country, or Sun Ra meets Hank Williams?

k. d. lang[2]

The "retro" phenomenon in the past decade has taken a number of different guises, ranging from simple revivalism to highly sophisticated forms of rearticulation that frustrate traditional notions of irony and parody. To dismiss these retro texts as mere nostalgia is to fail to appreciate the complicated set of issues they raise concerning the evolution of popular culture. "Mass" culture texts hitherto have been considered disposable commodities, but what happens when they not only get older and gain a certain kind of "classic" status, but continue to circulate and resonate decades after their original appearance, either through their continued transmission/ publication or through their intertextual citation by contemporary texts?

The quotation of mass media images has been a recurrent feature of "museum art"[3] for the past four decades, from the Pop art of the fifties and sixties, through the Appropriationist photographers of the late seventies and early eighties. A self-reflexive approach to the ideological, aesthetic, and psychological functions of popular culture has become a commonplace within the institutional frameworks that continue to delimit "high art" in America, but for the most part this creative work (and the critical work devoted to it) concentrates on the impact that the use of popular imagery has *within* and *on* those frameworks. The increasing self-reflexivity of popular culture coming from *within* popular culture remains to be fully explored. How do we account for texts that are so hyperconscious about their own history and their own discursive frameworks that the very basis of their textuality appears grounded not in representation, but in the appropriation of antecedent representation.

The two quotations that I have appropriated to introduce my argument represent two related but often opposing strategies used by popular artists to sort through the accumulated past of popular culture which, through technological developments (cable television, VCRs, "oldies" rock stations, etc.), now appears in a "suspended simultaneity." That simultaneity is either selectively rehistoricized in an ad hoc manner by popular texts anxious to demonstrate their allegiance to or departure from a particular "tradition," or it is just as selectively recombined in radically eclectic amalgamations that make a virtue of that simultaneity, thereby throwing into question the very category of tradition.

In the first quotation, Nanci Griffith situates herself quite explicitly as the inheritor of Loretta Lynn's brand of traditional country music, and at the same time the song valorizes the very technology that makes Lynn's continuing existence, and continuing relevance, possible. Listeners are encouraged to listen to the radio because it connects them with the music of the past, whereby listening becomes a form of meaningful communication that can take the place of friends "in times like these." What is especially significant about this intertextual reference is its ad hoc construction of a tradition in the very process of insisting on the connection. In the kind of intertextual referencing that Harold Bloom describes in *The Anxiety of Influence* (1973), a poet situates his or her work in relation to the already-established masterpieces (or the author as the producer of them), and literary history is, of course, filled with countless examples of poets and prose writers laboring to align themselves with various "Great Traditions." The particular case of Nanci Griffith's song, which epitomizes the historicist strategy in contemporary popular culture, is differentiated by the absence of the "always already" masterpiece status of the antecedent text, which is given its "classic" status only through the intertextual reference that valorizes in both directions at once, privileging the present text as an inheritor while it defines the wealth of the progenitor. Popular texts operating outside the confines of the academy and/or museum are deprived of the very institutional frameworks that secure canons and maintain traditions. Consequently, the intertextual reference, from simple quotation to elaborate "cover versions" of an antecedent song, remains one of the few consistently viable ways of conferring value to that antecedent text and of forging significant connections, even if such references fail to give the sort of stability to those relations that the academy or the museum might be able to ensure.

The other epigraph, a brief remark made by another contemporary country singer, suggests a rather different strategy, one which relishes that lack of stability, the outside-the-walls status of popular texts making them subject to virtually endless re-articulation because they are not "anchored" by the academy/museum. The singer in this case moves beyond the merely revivalist, reflecting the shifting nature of the "retro" gesture. Until quite recently, k. d. lang had "made a name for herself" by insisting that she was the reincarnation of Patsy Cline, naming her band the "Re-Clines," and having her own album produced by Cline's producer Owen Bradley in order to reconstruct the same sound for her album. This obsessive revivalist perspective is self-consciously retro, but the more current statement of the epigraph signals a very different sort of retro gesture that eschews simple revivalism just as self-consciously. Lang's statement is emblematic of this other strategy of re-articulation which has become so prevalent in texts like Jay Cantor's *Krazy Kat* (1987), Max Apple's *Propheteers* (1987), David Lynch's *Blue Velvet* (1987), Julien Temple's *Earth Girls Are Easy* (1989), Alan Moore's *Watchmen* (1986), and Frank Miller's *The Dark Knight Returns* (1986). According to these texts, the last thing popular culture needs to be is canonical; popular texts remain a source of attraction decades after their initial appearance because they continue to circulate, and therefore resonate, in diverse ways for heterogeneous audiences, both in their original forms and in their various reincarnations. One finds in these texts not the construction of a separate-but-equal canon, but the replacement of the canon with the eclectic paradigm which rejects the necessity of the canon as a means of organizing cultural production and evaluating its effects. This involves a similar kind of ad hoc development of hitherto unspecified intertextual connections, but here the goal appears to be not the acquisition of a certain degree of cultural *legitimacy*, but a far-reaching redefinition of what constitutes cultural *literacy*.

Mickey Is Taken to the Museum; Cindy Goes to the Movies

To understand the ongoing reconstruction of the history of popular culture and the reestimation of its current functions, I believe it necessary to discuss the historical development of both the appropriationist strategies used by primary texts and the critical work devoted to them. While the hyper-consciousness of popular culture in the eighties may not have "evolved" out of Pop art or "Image Scavenger" photography in any causal or teleological sense, comparing the recent work of Jay Cantor and Max Apple to Roy Lichtenstein and Cindy Sherman enables us to appreciate their points of contact, as well as their profound differences, which reflect the diverse set of personal motivations/institutional frameworks that inspire their different uses of popular images.

The first significant, widespread reevaluation of popular culture, specifically in regard to its binary relationship with "high art," occurred in Britain and the United States from the late fifties to the mid-sixties. The term "Pop art" was used to describe quite disparate techniques and perspectives on what was then considered "mass culture," i.e., homogeneous, mass-produced objects designed for immediate gratification/enslavement of their consumers. But the very appropriation of Pop imagery and mass production techniques by artists as different as Richard Hamilton, Andy Warhol, David Hockney, Claes Oldenburg, and Roy Lichtenstein meant that the popular could no longer be banished from the canvas or the museum. The definition of the avant-garde as that-which-is-not-mass-culture (developed and institutionalized by Theodor Adorno, Clement Greenberg, and company) was at that point held up to greater scrutiny because of the growing dissatisfaction with Abstract Expressionism as the official, hegemonic style of museum art. The aridity of that style (its self-enclosure, its removal from the realm of everyday experience, its Romantic fetishization of the originality of the artist's personal vision) and its institutionalization (the fact that it was not only hegemonic, but immensely profitable) led to a revaluation of the dichotomies that hitherto safeguarded its "integrity." The need to challenge this institutionalization is typified by Oldenberg's insistence that "I am for an art that is political-erotical-mystical, that does something other than sit on its ass in a museum. I am for an art that grows up not knowing that it is art at all, an art given the chance of having a starting point of zero."[4] The recognition that "art work" as a critical category had become, by the late fifties, a set of pernicious prohibitions and enclosures antagonistic to the original, radical gestures of the avant-garde led to the Pop attack on delimitation of that category. The mass production techniques adopted by Warhol and others were an affront to that most sanctified of categories—personal genius—that by the late fifties–early sixties was a form of product differentiation, a "name-brand" that guaranteed investment value: "That's probably one reason I'm using silk screen, so that no one would know whether my picture was mine or somebody else's."[5] Using image conventions and techniques developed within the realm of popular culture became a way of challenging the structures of that discursive formation that had "capitalized" on its prohibitions that were so completely institutionalized in its modalities and circuits of exchange.

Whether Pop artists were engaged in formulating a radical critique of the commercialization of Modernism, or simply "capitalizing" themselves by violating those prohibitions, has been debated since their first appearance. The initial criticism of Pop—that it wasn't "transformative" enough to be considered genuine art (i.e., that Lichtenstein, Warhol, et al., simply appropriated images without demonstrating the requisite level of personal manipulation of those images) reveals the exigencies of that discursive formation which demanded that any image "outside the walls" of that discourse had to be "converted" before entering the Holy City of the museum. The fetishization of the act of personal transformation was founded on a Romantic notion of creativity that remained firmly in place. Two decades later, to be "transformative" remains artists' highest priority, only now the term of choice is "oppositional" or "contestatory," reflecting the move away from personal creativity as transcendent value to a more "politicized" notion of creation as critical intervention. Andreas Huyssen's discussion of the cultural politics of Pop rests squarely on this division between the transformative and nontransformative potential. His historical overview of Pop centers on his own first encounter with it at the *Documenta* in Kassel in 1968, when he believed it might signal the beginning of a "democratization of art and art appreciation," but he then rejects it, arguing that "Pop artists took the trivial and banal imagery of daily life at face value, and the subjugation of art by the laws of a commodity-producing capitalistic society seemed complete."[6] The failure to be sufficiently transformative in this context means that capitalism necessarily subjugates art, but if truly transformative, then art subjugates capitalism. The absolute, either/or dichotomy leaves no room for ambivalence, for texts which might critique the mass-produced homogenization of mass culture, but which still acknowledge the force of popular images, especially in reference to the aridity of Abstract Expressionism. Huyssen modifies the rigid either/or alternatives in his conclusion, but even there he maintains, "the goal should still be a fictional transformation (Umfunktionierung) of false needs in an attempt to change everyday life."[7]

In his analysis of the origins of British Pop in the fifties, Dick Hebdige likewise acknowledges the inevitable absorption of Pop art into the language of commercial art, but argues that it played a crucial role in redefining the term "culture," throwing into sharp relief the tensions between the Arnoldian concept of culture ("the best that has been thought and said") and the more anthropological sense of the term (the ritual, images, and practices that form a "whole way of life"). Hebdige makes the crucial point that

> the dismissive critical response [to Pop] merely reproduces unaltered the ideological distinctions between, on the one hand, the "serious," the "artistic," the "political," and on the other, the "ephemeral," the "commercial," the "pleasurable"—a set of distinctions which Pop practice set out to erode. . . . Pop's significance resides in the ways in which it demonstrated, illuminated, lit up in neon, the "loaded arbitrariness" of those parallel distinctions, lit up the hidden economy which serves to valorize certain objects, certain forms of expression, certain voices to the exclusion of other objects, other forms, other voices by bestowing upon them the mantle of Art.[8]

Lichtenstein's comic strip paintings of the early sixties destabilized the parallel distinctions Hebdige cites; as such they helped inaugurate a process of redefinition of both the confines of popular culture and the critical presuppositions used to evaluate cultural production. But in order to appreciate the significance of Lichtenstein's work in relation to the more recent assaults on those parallel distinctions, we need to examine more closely what was and wasn't appropriated from popular culture in those paintings. Lichtenstein became interested in the subject matter and Ben Day dot patterns of the comic book because of the graphic possibilities they offered. In response to the criticism that the characters featured in his "action" comics (e.g., *Takka Takka* [1962], *Wham* [1962], *O. K. Hot Shot* [1963]) were militaristic, he argued that "the heroes depicted in comic books are fascist types, but I don't take them seriously in these paintings—maybe there is a point in not taking them seriously, a political point. I use them for purely formal reasons." "What I do is form, whereas the comic strip is not formed in the sense I'm using the word; the comics have shapes, but there has been no intent to make them intensely unified. The purpose is different, one intends to depict and I intend to unify."[9] Lichtenstein's appropriation of both the iconography and materiality of the comics represented an affront to both Modernism and the institution of the museum, but the emphasis on formal experimentation, in which Ben Day dots were yet another form of abstraction, made Lichtenstein's "radical" gesture easily recuperable by both. That the comics merely served as the raw material for a new minimalism becomes particularly conspicuous in Lichtenstein's subsequent homages to Cubism, Purism, and Surrealism, which feature the same Ben Day dots, but also figures appropriated from Picasso, Leger, and Dali. The comparability of the comic and Modernist "masterpiece" as sources for abstract experimentation/quotation emerges most clearly in his two Artist's Studio paintings. In the first, "Look Mickey" (1973), Donald Duck is the image on the wall, but in the later "The Dance" (1974), Matisse's masterpiece functions as the visual inspiration/antecedent for this work.

Recognizing this comparability of comics and Early Modernists as sources of appropriation in Lichtenstein's more recent work does not mean that his work does not destabilize the "parallel distinctions" to which Hebdige refers, but it does require a careful delineation of the object of the attack, of just what after all was being destabilized. Lichtenstein's comic book paintings of the early sixties were in a sense already "Artist Studio" paintings, in that the arena of conflict is still the specific discursive formation constituted by the gallery, the legacy of art history, the extended New York art scene, etc. Lawrence Alloway, in his perceptive study of Lichtenstein, argues that in paintings like *Reclining Nude* (1977), which quotes Henry Moore, Salvador Dali, and his own "Brushwork" series from 1966, Lichtenstein constructs the twentieth-century equivalent of the "gallery picture," comparable to Jan Brueghel's *The Sense of Sight*, or David Tenier's *Gallery of the Archduke Leopold William*; all "take culture itself as subject."[10] Alloway's analogy is convincing, but just how culture is constituted here is not fully explored. For the comic book paintings of the early sixties, "culture" might include the popular image, but it remains circumscribed by the institutional framework that produced those parallel distinctions. Two paintings in particular, *Masterpiece* (1962), and *M-Maybe* (1965) epitomize that sense of enclosure, of a calculated gesture made in reference to a very particular framework. In the former, the woman says, "Why Brad Darling, This Painting is a Masterpiece! My, Soon You'll Have All of New York Clamoring For Your Work," while in the latter, a lone woman says of an unspecified he, "M-Maybe He Became Ill and Couldn't Leave the Studio!" Arguably, the last phrase defines the scope of the attack—these paintings, these appropriations have force only so long as they remain, in a sense, within the studio, within the wholly artistic space defined by a particular circuit of production and evaluation. The use of the comic book creates a scandal only within that discursive space, and as such the iconoclastic dimension of the appropriation exists only within the world of museum art. Lichtenstein's pop appropriations may tell us a great deal about the limitation of that institutional framework, but they evidence little or no interest in the resonance of popular texts outside that realm, how they might capture the imagination of widespread publics, how they might affect us at a visceral level, forming the "stuff that dreams are made of."

The Appropriationist or "Image Scavenger" school that developed in photography of the late seventies–early eighties, specifically the work of Sherrie Levine, Barbara Kruger, and Cindy Sherman, also made appropriation a weapon in a similar series of attacks on the institutionalized notion of Fine Art Photography, but one also finds, particularly in the work of Sherman, a shift in emphasis, a fascination with the effects of the popular beyond the confines of that discursive formation. Levine's photographs of masterpiece photographs by Walker Evans and Edward Weston challenged the fetishized values of personal vision and the "aura" of the individual work in a medium capable of infinite reproducibility. Kruger's use of advertising images/file photos to which she affixes printed messages transforms the "found" image into a confrontational text. The openly discursive (in the Benvenistean sense of the term as well as the Foucauldian) nature of that confrontation in works such as *We Won't Play Nature to Your Culture*, *You Destroy What You Think Is Difference*, and *You Divide and Conquer* (all 1981–83) signals a crucial shift in the motivation for the appropriation. Here the exigencies of appropriation are not a matter of personal expression as formal experimentation, but a matter of taking control over an image-making process that, within a patriarchal order, has served only to exploit and subjugate women. The appropriation of the fashion image, coupled with the confrontational address to other women ("we") and men ("you"), foregrounds the connection between the construction of images and the construction of gender difference in both the "original" photo and in its re-articulations. Here Kruger broadens the scope of the appropriationist gesture, expanding the number of interested parties involved by that activity, and in so doing redefines the "stakes" by making the reception of popular imagery a vital critical issue. As such, Kruger's work marks a significant advance over the Pop art appropriationists because of its sensitivity to impact. This is not to suggest that Pop art was oblivious to or unconcerned with reception, or that it didn't involve a different relationship between artist and spectator. Carole Ann Mahsun argues, following Alloway, that in Pop "spectators are confronted with a self-contained entity removed from its familiar surroundings and challenged to do their 'own work of looking.' . . . Thus the pop artist avoids interpretation, 'message,' emotion, or personal style—avoids anything alien entering into the viewer's experience—and instead turns the viewer back upon his [sic] own sensory experience by thwarting conventional interpretive practice."[11] While Mahsun's characterization of that relationship may be accurate, the activity of the viewer is predicated on the relative silence of the artist, whose very disinterested neutrality on the subject of eventual impact allows that viewer to fill in the gap, as it were. But Kruger could hardly be called silent, nor does she avoid interpretation. Her second-person address emphasizes quite explicitly that the text is constructed in reference to that "you" who has already "interpreted" in regularized ways, so the appropriationist gesture is by ideological and semiotic necessity a discursive exchange.

The increased emphasis on the resonance of images outside the realm of museum art also distinguishes the work of Cindy Sherman, who, through her particular strategy of appropriation, conflates the concerns of personal expression and the cultural impact of popular media images. In her series of "Untitled Film Stills" (1977–80) and "Untitled" photographs (1981–85), Sherman poses herself as the heroine of a number of different genre films, enacting or "impersonating" the visual stereotypes those films produced and/or reiterated. By making herself into a series of icons, Sherman immerses herself in popular imagery and explores the connections between that imagery and personal gender identity. Where a Pop text like Richard Hamilton's $he (1958) may have presented a series of advertising images featuring women in the home (forming what he describes as "a sieved reflection of the ad man's paraphrase of the consumer's dream"),[12] Sherman's impersonations situate her as a performing artist within that world, thereby constructing the strange duality which is the foundation of her work. She is critical outsider, the director of an imaginary film, and character within the film, whose identity is enmeshed in and inseparable from that iconography. In her introduction to Sherman's photographs, Judith Williamson stresses the implication of the viewer in that work, arguing that Sherman's presentation of the multiple images of women "is such a superb way of flashing the images of 'Woman' back where they belong, in the recognition of the beholder. . . . Within each image, far from deconstructing the elision of image and identity, she very smartly leads the viewer to *construct* it; by presenting a whole lexicon of feminine identities,

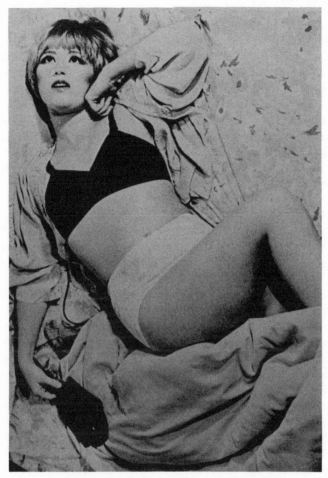

4. Cindy Sherman, "Untitled Film Still #6."

all of them played by 'her,' she undermines your little construction as fast as you can build them up."[13] Following Williamson's argument, one could say that Sherman is able to effect such a critique because she is the director, character, and beholder simultaneously, "Woman" looked at, but also a woman looking ambivalently at her self-image as cultural image. In this context, the act of appropriation is inseparable from the act of self-definition.

While the work of Kruger and Sherman invests the art of appropriation with broader significance by emphasizing the impact of popular images, as well as their modes of production, popular culture remains a category framed by the institution of museum art. This is not to suggest that either photographer wants to remain within that discursive context; like Pop, Appropriationist photography was initially considered an affront to all that was sacred about that context. But just as Pop was absorbed into the museum, the Post-Modernist photography of the early eighties has already been institutionalized. Abigail Solomon Godeau details this most recent absorption, pointing to the inclusion of these photographs in shows at galleries (Burden, Light, and White Columns) that specialized in showcasing Modernist and Official Art photography. "The appearance of Postmodernist photography within the institutional precincts of art photography signaled that whatever difference, much less critique, had been attributed to the work of Levine, et al., it had now been fully and seamlessly recuperated under the sign of art photography, an operation that might be called deconstruction in reverse."[14]

The cultural significance of the appropriation/citation of popular iconography may have been taken beyond the confines of museum art in the work of Kruger and Sherman, and in the process culture is defined as more than simply the best that has been shot and developed, but that activity remains a critique of popular image-making and Fine Art Photography from within the discursive formation of the latter, a formation that might steal images from the former, but must still keep its distance. That the critical component of that discursive formation continues to insist on a demonstrable distantiation, a discernible, oppositional "transformation" of the popular image is apparent in Solomon-Godeau's condemnation of what she labels the "second generation" of Post-modernist photographers (Frank Majore, Alan Belcher, Stephen Frailey), "whose relation to the sources and significance of their appropriative strategies (primarily advertising) seemed to be predominantly a function of fascination."[15]

To be fascinated appears to be the greatest sin of all, because it suggests a lack of respect for an institutional framework that may be challenged, but not jilted, especially by artists who have been seduced by mere popular culture. Making fascination antithetical to "critique" has been a stock-in-trade feature of avant-gardist self-promotion since its inception; fascination has been made to mean uncritical acceptance, promiscuity, lack of rigor, etc. Patrice Petro, in her brilliant study of Weimar cinema, makes the crucial point that distinctions between the popular and the avant-garde have been consistently linked to gender difference. "Mass culture is itself commonly personified as 'feminine,' having the capacity to induce passivity, vulnerability, even corruption. And as mass culture's opposite, modernism was often construed as masculine, as providing an active and productive alternative to the pleasure of mass cultural entertainment."[16] The disqualification of fascination as an acceptable response to popular culture reveals a series of interconnected problems, particularly the inability to account for pleasure,[17] except in terms of a negative category, that which the truly oppositional text will not allow, except in the form of a self-congratulatory detachment.

We Won't Play Other to Your Culture

The viability of fascination as a critical perspective distinguishes the most recent appropriationist texts like Max Apple's *The Propheteers* (1987) and Jay Cantor's *Krazy Kat* (1987), and fascination as a category is particularly useful in differentiating these works from earlier strategies of appropriation. Here the hyperconscious reflection on the nature of popular culture is not conducted from within a discursive framework that defines popular culture as its "Other," but in relation to the conventions, mythologies, and institutions of popular culture as another sort of discursive formation, or more precisely, a series of discursive formations. While these works are still aggressively appropriative in orientation, they are meditations on popular culture and how it resonates outside the walls of museum art. They are "transformative" in regard to the history of popular culture and its possible functions, challenging accepted opinions concerning its homogeneity, what it is capable of expressing, what factors shape its most recognizable forms, and how it circulates as a commodity.

In *The Propheteers*, Apple appropriates not just images or iconography of popular culture, but the entire personas of some of its major figures. Where Lichtenstein's artist's studio may have included Donald Duck, Apple's novel makes Walt Disney one of its major characters in this story of the development of Disney World, in which Disney's major foils are his evil brother Will, his rival Howard Johnson, and his sworn enemy, Marjorie Post Merriweather (and by extension her father C. W. Post, and her lover Clarence Birdseye). Unlike E. L. Doctorow's *Ragtime*, which features cameo appearances by historical figures like Emma Goldman and Henry Ford, Apple makes these figures his central characters, and instead of characterizing them in ways consistent with their historical images, he invents elaborate personal histories that he admits in his prefatory comments are "drawn entirely from my imagination. My only connection to the real names used in this novel is the frequent appearance of a number of them at my breakfast table." The reference to the breakfast table as the source or genesis of his inspiration is significant insofar as it functions as an image comparable to Lichtenstein's "Artist's Studio" paintings, but the disparity between the two sites suggests profound differences in their respective positions vis-à-vis popular culture. Where Lichtenstein's appropriation is a matter of bringing a "foreign" element into his discursive space, Apple's appropriation comes from within a world where Disney, Johnson, and Post form the fabric of everyday life.

Apple's imaginary history undermines a number of the most commonly held assumptions about mass culture, especially the binary, negative definition—i.e., that its mass-produced, corporation-based nature means that it can be neither folk culture (which was indigenous, spontaneous, of the people), nor genuine art (which is unique, of the individual artist). Folk culture and high art are united in this negative definition by their alleged authenticity and organicity, founded on the direct connection between produced and artistic producer. Apple's characters are among the most significant inventors of mass cultural existence, but their respective products, and the visions of America they entail, are represented within this novel as fundamentally authentic and almost maniacally organic. The novel opens with Howard Johnson endlessly roaming the highways with his assistant Milly, searching out locations for new motor inns. Johnson roams until he begins to know the territory:

> Howard knew the land, Mildred thought, the way the Indians must have known it. . . . Howard had a sixth sense that would sometimes lead them from the main roads to, say, a dark green field in Iowa or Kansas. . . . And before the emergency brake had settled into its final prong, Howard Johnson was into the field and after the scent . . . he felt some secret vibration from the place. Turning his back on Milly he would mark the spot with his urine or break some of the clayey earth in his strong pink hands, sifting it like flour for a delicate recipe. She had actually seen him chew the grass, getting down on all fours like an animal. . . . [18]

If the determination of the right place for his "houses" is described in terms of an organic folk-culture ritual, the inspiration for the orange roofs is characterized in terms of poetic inspiration comparable to genuine Art. In the course of their early travels, Milly and Howard visit Robert Frost, Howard's old poetry teacher. The two great men meet amicably, and then after leaving Frost, Howard and Milly stop for lunch, from which point Milly remembers:

> We stayed on that hilltop while the sun began to set in New Hampshire. I felt so full of poetry and of love. Howard only an hour's drive from Robert Frost's farmhouse. . . . I think the sun set differently that night, filtering through the clouds like a big paintbrush making the top of the town all orange. And suddenly I thought what if the tops of our houses were that kind of orange, what a world it would be. . . . The feeling we had about that orange, Howard, that was ours and that's what I've tried to bring to every house, the way we felt that night. Oh it makes me sick to think of Colonel Sanders, and Big Boy, and Holiday Inn and Best Western. . . . [19]

The connections that Apple makes between Johnson and the Indian (the natives who know nature most intimately) and Johnson and Frost (one of America's foremost nature poets), obviously suggest a high degree of both authenticity and organicity in his "oranging" of America. But the conclusion of Milly's reverie is just as notable, because it restricts those qualities to Johnson and depicts his rivals as their antithesis. Here "mass" culture is represented not as one homogeneous system of relations, but as a deeply conflicted, internally inconsistent collection of divergent envisionings of America. The conflict between authentic and inauthentic, organic and inorganic within popular culture recurs throughout the novel. Howard Johnson and Walt Disney come to represent (at least in the former's mind) polar opposites along exactly these lines. Their opposition becomes most explicit when Johnson stops in San Antonio and daydreams while contemplating the Alamo:

> Without too much effort he imagined himself, Milly, and Otis entrapped in that small clean fort while Walt Disney surrounded them with the engines of war. The Disney wolves and dogs growled at the walls, mice skirted the parapets. . . . Outside the fort were the Disneys, like bus tourists lined up before a gas station urinal. O smug one come out, they yelled from their pissoir, O eater of ice cream, longer for calm sleep, make way for us who are future.
>
> We have a thousand musicians synchronized to our movements and ten million carefully framed actions. All possibilities are predrawn. Already, five minutes from now our banner in 35-mm. color overhangs your roof. Your Alamo Lounge will become a wax museum, your 28 flavors a single gray Tastee Freeze. . . . As he tried to enjoy a quiet meal, the Disney creatures bombarded the walls with their popcorn machines and stormed the motel on ladders of pink and white peppermint sticks. Fess Parker led them singing the Davy Crockett anthem. . . . [20]

The conflict between Johnson and Disney, each representing different ways of capturing the hearts and minds of their public, culminates in the mid-sixties, and as such this novel could be considered a retro text, but the choice of this period is not motivated by a nostalgia (even a parodic one) for a bygone era. The choice of this period emphasizes its pivotal status in the history of popular culture due to the advent of television, the theme park, the superhighway, rising levels of disposable income, etc., all of which made for an increasingly mobile America where consumers begin to circulate as endlessly as the popular artifacts that surround them. At this point, American culture is "in transit" in a physical sense, but also in reference to what this new public considered to be pleasure or entertainment. Johnson sees his mission as providing comfort, a "house" (not a hotel) away from home, where "you were redeemed from the road,"[21] whereas Disney and company build an empire on the exhilaration of the road, the very foreignness, the fact that enjoyment comes from displacement. As Milly tells Howard, "The Disneys have made a happy little nightmare. Making nightmares, Howard, even good ones, is the opposite of what we've always tried to do."[22] The opposition between Johnson's travelers and Disney's vacationers represents the shifting geographic and psychological terrain. For the former, being in transit, the loss of connection with a sense of place, is a trial to be endured, but for the latter it becomes the maximum entertainment.

As a self-conscious meditation on popular culture, *The Propheteers* cultivates rather than avoids the category of "fascination." But in its appropriations the novel adopts a perspective that is neither uniformly condemnatory, nor uniformly celebratory, opting instead for a *critical* ambivalence. I use the term "critical" here because that ambivalence is not a matter of deadpan apathy, but alternation, its lack of consistency due to the very inconsistency of popular culture, which is made to appear both captivating and contemptible. This alternation is most explicit in the relation between Walt and Will Disney, which Apple constructs in terms of a popular culture doppelgänger, with Walt playing the role of the artist-visionary and Will the shameless huckster. Each envisions the nature (and eventual functions) of comic figures according to his own set of values. "An initial philosophical premise separated the brothers or cartoons throughout their lives. . . . To Walt Disney a mouse was always a mouse. Mouseness, not humanity, was the heart of his creation. The business Disney saw it otherwise. The mouse was only a cute disguise for the man who lurked within. If you put tits on girl mice, then Mickey could walk up and squeeze one and everyone would get a kick out of that."[23] Where Walt is lost in the joy of drawing, obsessed with refining the act of movement, Will hustles merchandise. One of his abortive projects is to sell biblical cartoons to the Sunday school market: "I'd say one good seven minute cartoon that we could put out for less than eighty thousand would revolutionize the Sunday Schools. . . . We talked to Stravinsky about the music and Vincent Price about the voice, but the Bishop said, 'No dice.' And this guy George Beverly Shea who does all the Billy Graham arrangements said it was too cute. Imagine a guy like him calling Walt Disney and Stravinsky too cute. Did anyone say De Mille's *Ten Commandments* was too cute?"[24] What happens to Walt's vision is the same thing that happens to Howard Johnson. "HJ felt the motions and the needs of travelers, and he translated his feeling into buildings and watering places. Now, his vision had become a large public corporation."[25] The opposition between individuals and corporations becomes the basis for the novel's ambivalence. Traditional notions of "mass" culture are rendered inapplicable because the visions of its creators are represented as entirely organic and personal, but the novel resists any kind of naive celebration of popular culture, because the popularization of those visions inevitably leads to their perversion when those visionaries shift from prophets to profiteers. Apple's own vision may be considered nostalgic, then, but only insofar as it privileges the precorporate moment of development when popular invention remains authentic, a manifestation of a kind of postindustrial "folk" culture that responds to the uniqueness of a newly mobile American culture without a nostalgia for the pretechnological past.

That the original inspiration for and eventual uses of popular invention are most often disconnected, or even contradictory, is most evident in the relationship between C. W. Post and Salvador Dali. Post conceives of his creation (breakfast cereal) not as a commodity, but as a distillation of his vision—in this case a world where cattle will not have to be slaughtered, because everyone will turn to a life of spiritual vegetarianism now that they have a nutritious alternative. Post's vision becomes most maniacal (and Apple's narration most parodic) when he tries to have meat dishes painted out of western art, first attempting to acquire some of the greatest masterpieces of European art, most especially *The Last Supper*, and then hiring Dali to replace the offending roasts with tasteful (and even more nutritious) fruit substitutes. This plan inspires an assassination plot directed at Post by his art dealer, and its completion remains a mystery. Not until Marjorie meets Dali years after her father's death does he make his rather startling confession. Initially expressing only contempt for the project, Dali later admits,

I was 20 years old. If you mentioned Rubens or Leonardo to me at that time tears still came to my eyes. . . . Great art, the glories of the past, the mysteries of every brush stroke—you know the whole story. It intimidates the young. There are your great-great-grandparents growing more powerful over the centuries, strengthened by death, accumulating a whole army of commentators and owners, each masterpiece becomes like a state over time, with its own citizens, its own language, it has rights and privileges. Then along comes your father, C. W. Post of Battle Creek, who recognizes none of this, is not affected by any worship of the past, considers it all idolatry. . . . Your father's commission cured me of worship of forms, of worship of the past. He didn't save the world from idolatry, but saved me from it.[26]

This reformulation of the relationship between the realms of popular culture and the avant-garde/high art is also foregrounded in Jay Cantor's *Krazy Kat: A Novel in Five Panels*. Like *The Propheteers* , this text is retro, appropriationist (abducting figures from the history of both popular and high art), and extrapolative (inventing entire new existences for popular icons, in this case the characters in George Herriman's legendary comic strip). As in Apple's novel, popular culture is the primary subject matter of the fiction, only here the hyperconsciousness is intensified further by the proliferation of discursive frameworks and the introduction of characters who are not just popular icons, but icons who are self-conscious about their own iconicity, obsessed with their own reception as they circulate through those frameworks.

The novel opens with Krazy Kat and Ignatz now in retirement from their strip career, but contemplating a return. Krazy sits reading trade papers, checking grosses, while Ignatz reads critical essays about them and ransacks novels looking for plots for their comeback. She muses over the tyranny of the box office and the technological changes that have occurred in storytelling, "from vaudeville to motion pictures, to radio, to television . . . and next? Computers? Video games? How would the next generation tell its stories?"[27] She also reflects on the current state of the comic pages, particularly the representation of cats. "They were Cute Cats, not Krazy Kats, sentimental Hallmark cards of cats tasting of cardboard sentiments cooked up on assembly lines by anonymous hands. . . . And with all the sentimentality, she thought, came its ghost, its ugly shadow—hardly its opposite!—obscenities like a book . . . *a book of things to do with a dead cat* . . . . It was a sick jaded audience that wanted—as these moderns did—to either drown in sugar or . . . poison mixed with amyl nitrate."[28] What is especially significant about Krazy Kat's reveries is the way Cantor represents popular culture—as the intersection of aesthetic, economic, critical, and technological factors that are in a constant state of refiguration.

That a popular icon is always in circulation is emphasized by the novel's aggressive eclecticism, in which different discursive formations, each giving different identities to Krazy and Ignatz, roll by like cylinders in a cultural revolver. In the first panel, the desert world of their comic landscape is invaded by the Los Alamos project, at which point the novel begins to mix "shoptalk" about a comeback with Krazy Kat's frustrated desire for Ignatz (and Robert Oppenheimer) along with scenes of nuclear holocaust. The second panel, "The Talking Cure," is a hilarious parody of Freud's correspondence, as Ignatz decides that their new career should be as analyst and analysand. In the third panel, "The Talking Pictures," the characters from the strip meet up with the Producer, with whom they discuss a cinematic comeback, the Producer throwing out one concept after another, featuring the pair in a western, a musical, a bio film, etc. The Producer is remarkably similar to Apple's Will Disney, demonstrating the same obsession with marketing, particularly tie-ins: "That's where the money is nowadays. You people are a potential K Mart full of franchised plastic."[29] In the fourth panel, "The Possessed," Krazy Kat and Ignatz meet the COMISALADS—the Comic Strip Artists Liberation Army, Division One, who call for the death of "Fascist Copyright Holders Who Suck the Brains of Avant-Garde Artists!"[30] This group, obviously a knockoff of the Symbionese Liberation Army (a link made even more explicit by the fact that Krazy Kat and Ignatz belong to "Mr. Hearst"), represents the inevitable conflation of radical politics and television culture, the former obsessed with media exposure, the latter driven by an insatiable appetite for the really new. "Media access sped like a drug through Mouse's blood. Getting on TV Ignatz said *was* the new avant-garde mass art form!"[31] In the last panel, "Venus in Furs," the couple now imagine themselves as human beings, inventing their "own" fantasy scenario, at which point the novel changes discourse again, now resembling, alternately, the psychoanalytic case study and hard-core pornography, in which the two try to come to terms with the inherent sadomasochism of Ignatz's brick-throwing, which Krazy sees as a gesture of love. The couple emerges from their ordeal as a wildly successful cabaret act, "Kat and Ignatz."

This eclecticism is not mere "pastiche" because the shifts from panel to panel are not simply stylistic variations, but changes in discursive formation—i.e., we see how each formation redefines their image as popular icons, as well as the love relationship between them in terms of its own discursive economy, now so wholly institutionalized. Where Lichtenstein's appropriations of popular culture were defined in terms of the institutional framework that was/is museum art, Cantor adopts a different strategy which does not, like the COMISALADS, seek to "liberate" the couple, but instead shows that they are in the "public domain," but as such they are subject to multiple articulations which anchor them in very specific ways. They circulate from discourse to discourse as mobile signifiers, but within the confines of each formation, both their identity and their desire are fixed values. In its juxtapositions of such different discourses, *Krazy Kat* resembles Manuel Puig's *Kiss of the Spiderwoman* (1978), but in Puig's novel, pulp romance and psychoanalytic theory, while quite literally adjacent and theoretically complementary, remain distinct, in two different regimes. In *Krazy Kat*, the couples cross the bar, as it were, and invade the theoretical discourse which has already appropriated and categorized their desire. Their very presence as operators of that discourse throws into question its sovereignty. Here appropriation ceases to be an entirely satisfying description of this circulation in that the preceding types of appropriation are abducted from x while firmly situated within y. But in *Krazy Kat*, the circulation of the characters, their ability to inhabit, even impersonate different discursive identities purposely obliterates any such fixed coordinates.

The traditional distinctions between popular culture and the world of the avant-garde/high art are destabilized in *Krazy Kat* due to this erasure of the coordinates previously used to measure their differences. Krazy and Ignatz argue repeatedly through the novel about the need to be more than "just a comic strip," which time and again leads to a discussion of flatness and roundness. For Krazy, "her art had been what she was—how could it have been otherwise?"[32] but Ignatz longs "to create the new rounder soul that we need for artistic greatness, that Americans need to be rounded, godlike individuals. Like in really good books. . . . Why not strut uptown to the mansion of high art, of roundness and say that our gift to America could rank with Eugene O'Neill's or Henry James's? America *needs* a truly democratic high art. America needs a rounded comic strip!"[33] Later, when they are living among the COMISALADS, Ignatz changes his model for artistic excellence to the avant-garde. When Krazy asks him, "But Ignatz, didn't people like us the way we were?" he responds, "That was false consciousness on their part. We have to shock and abuse them. They won't like it any more than they like twelve tone music. But our new work will awake them. . . . We're going to make the future. The future is our audience!"[34] But in the last panel, Krazy, in the form of Kate, the graduate student in art history, turns the tables on Ignatz when she shows him pictures of Pop art, specifically Jasper Johns's *American Flag*. Ignatz responds, " 'So high art wants to be flat?' Why did he suddenly feel so bewildered?"[35] Kate launches into her own tirade:

> The flag is what it is. So it has real presence. Fantasy = Reality. Art = Life. Just like in popular art where Hammett = Spade = Bogart. He's an icon like comic strip characters. Mickey Mouse, say, or Krazy Kat. Mickey isn't a drawing of Mickey. The drawing *is* Mickey. . . . The popular workers provided pleasure scenarios, liberated zones; the high arts stylized them and gave them back, as if they were a scandal. Trademark soup cans, flatness, same-same repetitions. But who were they shocking? Their own tuxedo dignity! Shock was spicy strychnine on the palette. The popular workers hadn't meant to shock, just to master a sorrow, improvise a pleasure.[36]

Kate's response to Ignatz stresses the variability of all evaluative criteria, that binary distinction between roundness and flatness can no longer serve as transcendent distinctions of equality when all values are functions of specific institutions. The rejection of Pop art appropriation of comic book figures like Warhol's, Lichtenstein's, or Fahlstrom's own "Krazy Kat" series (1963–65) is part of a wider indictment of the discursive formation of museum art, including its critical apparatus. While they read reviews of their cabaret act, Ignatz reacts in disgust, " 'This guy is like all the high brow critics you love so much. He's showing how smart he is by writing about us. See, he says, I *can* make something out of junk.' Ignatz didn't like these new magazines . . . their academic discourse peppered with jive talk. . . . This was not avant-garde popular art, but avant-people being ironic about a little uptown thrill."[37]

This dismissal, considered along with Kat's and Ignatz's "finding themselves" as a cabaret act (in which they make Cole Porter and Larry Hart songs *their own* by singing those songs which seem to illustrate perfectly the rather unusual nature of their desire), suggests that popular culture can continue to be vitally and personally meaningful for both its producers and its audiences if it achieves a kind of hybrid status that is neither an uncritical revivalism nor an avant-garde "wannabe." Cantor's rejection of the avant-gardist appropriation, and his advocacy of an eclectic but highly selective appropriation of antecedent forms of popular culture as a way of making affecting statements about the nature of desire in contemporary culture—instead of simply "holding a mirror up to a mirror"—leads to the simple but inevitable question: is a book like *Krazy Kat* still popular culture? Before we can answer that question, we must ask another: by what criteria can that question be answered satisfactorily? The most far-reaching ramification of the meta-pop hyperconsciousness of novels like *The Propheteers* and *Krazy Kat* is their purposeful complication of that question. Neither subject matter nor attitude toward popular culture can be the distinguishing criterion, since in *Krazy Kat*, cartoon animals are the main characters, and the novel concludes with a ringing endorsement of the possibilities of popular culture. Nor can the means of production and distribution serve as a litmus test in this case, since the book was published by a major trade press and sold in mall bookstores as well as university bookstores. If that very hyperconsciousness disqualifies it as popular culture, then certainly Ann Rice's bestselling vampire novels (in which vampires write their bestselling memoirs on word processors, discuss the future of myth, watch movies obsessively, become rock stars, etc.) and the Batman phenomenon in its various incarnations (which self-consciously foregrounds the re-articulation of super-hero narrative) must be excluded as well. Perhaps more appropriate questions are how we can *not* consider *Krazy Kat* popular culture, and what value is there in making exclusionary distinctions about whether any text is popular culture?

Delimiting popular culture continues to be a viable activity, but only for those who frame it as Other, as that which must be resisted, appropriated (only to be condemned or "transformed"), or dismissed as that which might tarnish the canon or collection. Hebdige's contention that Pop art erodes the "parallel distinctions" that cast popular culture in a negative light now seems accurate, but premature, more applicable to the meta-pop of the eighties. But in a sense, these more recent texts go even further; where Pop art challenges the "parallel distinctions," it still respects those binary oppositions in order to ensure itself the requisite parameters to read its challenge as a violation of the prohibitions, perpetuating them as it contests them. The meta-pop text of the eighties dismisses even the viability of such distinctions, except to expose them as obsolete—except, of course, for those discursive formations (like museum art or the National Association of Scholars) that have such vested interests in maintaining them.

This ongoing redefinition of popular culture by popular culture involves different strategies of appropriation—one which seeks to construct traditions through citation, and one which defies the very category of tradition through eclectic appropriation—but it also presupposes, implicitly or explicitly, different notions of cultural literacy which serve as the foundation for that redefinition. Where the former approach, exemplified by texts like Joe Dante's film *Gremlins* (1984) or Steven Spielberg's Indiana Jones cycle, posits a kind of separate but equal list of essential authors and titles guaranteeing a popular culture literacy, the latter approach involves the identification of names and titles, but also the recognition that "culture" is not just a "whole way of life," but an endlessly configurable assemblage of representations, the function, audience, and value of which are subject to constant re-articulation.

Notes

I would like to thank Jim Peterson for his generous contributions to the completion of this manuscript.

1. Nanci Griffith, "Listen to the Radio," *Storms*, MCA Records, 1989.

2. k. d. lang, quoted in "Uniquely inClined," by Robert Cross, *Chicago Tribune*, July 5, 1989, sec. 2: 4.

3. The term "museum art" here refers to "high art," but in the Foucauldian sense of a discursive formation, e.g., not just a particular set of styles, but their institutionalization as "art," secured by a series of interconnected apparatuses— some physical (the structure of the museum, network of galleries, etc.), some critical (in the form of journals, catalogues, and the like, which fix the significance of a given text, set evaluative standards for admission to or disqualification from the museum), some historical (the accumulated heritage of what constitutes fine art and fine art collecting).

4. Claes Oldenberg, "I am for an Art . . . ," in *Pop Art Redefined*, ed. John Russell and Suzi Gablick (New York: Praeger, 1969), 97.

5. Andy Warhol, Interview with G. R. Swenson, in *Pop Art Redefined*, 117.

6. Andreas Huyssen, "The Cultural Politics of Pop," in *Post-Pop Art*, ed. Paul Taylor (Cambridge: MIT Press, 1989), 47.

7. Ibid., 73.

8. Dick Hebdige, "In Poor Taste," in *Post-Pop Art*, 94.

9. Roy Lichtenstein, Interview with G. R. Swenson, in *Pop Art Redefined*, 93.

10. Lawrence Alloway, *Roy Lichtenstein* (New York: Abbeville Press, 1983), 93.

11. Carole Ann Mahsun, *Pop Art and the Critics* (Ann Arbor: UMI Research Press, 1987), 96.

12. Richard Hamilton, "An Exposition of $he," in *Pop Art Redefined*, 73.

13. Judith Williamson, "Images of Woman," *Screen* 24, no. 6 (1983): 102.

14. Abigail Solomon Godeau, "Living with Contradictions: Cultural Practices in the Age of Supply Side Aesthetics," in *Universal Abandon?* ed. Andrew Ross (Minneapolis: University of Minnesota Press, 1988), 201.

15. Ibid., 202.

16. Patrice Petro, *Joyless Streets: Women and Melodramatic Representation in Weimar Germany* (Princeton: Princeton University Press, 1988), 8.

17. For an in-depth discussion of this point see Tania Modleski, "The Terror of Pleasure: The Contemporary Horror Film and Postmodern Theory," in *Studies in Entertainment*, ed. Tania Modleski (Bloomington: Indiana University Press, 1986), 155–66.

18. Max Apple, *The Propheteers* (New York: Harper and Row, 1987), 6.

19. Ibid., 16–17.

20. Ibid., 112–13.

21. Ibid., 15.

22. Ibid., 39.

23. Ibid., 147–48.
24. Ibid., 160.
25. Ibid., 23.
26. Ibid., 261–62.
27. Jay Cantor, *Krazy Kat: A Novel in Five Panels* (New York: Collier Books, Macmillan, 1987), 5.
28. Ibid., 9.
29. Ibid., 119.
30. Ibid., 129.
31. Ibid., 150.
32. Ibid., 8.
33. Ibid., 61.
34. Ibid., 140.
35. Ibid., 213.
36. Ibid.
37. Ibid., 240.

ELEVEN

The Avant-Garde Finds Andy Hardy

Robert B. Ray

This piece originated as a talk given at Indiana University on the night of 21 March 1989, a date I remember not only as the first evening in a cool Midwestern spring, but also as my younger daughter's birthday, one she shares with the erstwhile pop-culture figure, Johann Sebastian Bach. For such lectures, academic custom typically offers only two choices: (1) the speaker who anticipates future publication will prepare a finished essay, fully dependent on the apparatus of the book, which he then must read to an audience convened (ironically) for an oral performance; (2) the speaker, on the other hand, who prefers immediate gratification, and who recognizes the occasion's fundamental "orality," will improvise an informal address which he subsequently must revise for appearance in print. In another culture (French, for example), we might want to label the first approach, with its postponed satisfactions, as "Protestant," and the second, with its propitiated hedonism, as "Catholic." In America, however, and particularly in this book, the more appropriate analogy arises from the coincidence of my daughter's birthday: if the written lecture is a kind of classical music, a performance controlled by a score, the familiar talk is a version of jazz, riffs derived from an outline.

Modernity's most characteristic symptom is the subjection of live event to representation. In "the age of mechanical reproduction," the dominant standard becomes the book, the shorthand term for the "written," worked-over, polished artifact against which we measure even immediate experience, itself decipherable only in terms of what we have "read." Almost no one, for example, encounters the actual Mona Lisa without having first seen copies of it, and as Glenn Gould observed, musical audiences accustomed to perfect recordings develop lower tolerance for concert hall "imperfections." As a corollary, even "live" recordings are now almost always revised by studio overdubs that correct faulty intonation, rhythm, and dynamics. The revision-for-publication of academic lectures, in other words, should seem merely business as usual.

The live event of most concern to academics is teaching, for which "the visiting lecture" amounts to an outwork, "a minor defensive position constructed outside a fortified area." These areas in question are our home institutions, both protecting (with tenure) and constraining (with curricula). Even as we near the end of the century, however, these institutions have still given little thought to how teaching might respond to those technological developments (film, radio, television, audio and video tape, computers, digital sampling) which promote what Walter Ong has called "a secondary orality." What should teaching be like, a classical concert or a jam session? Brian Eno has observed that classical music relies on trained musicians, defined as those who "will produce a predictable sound given a specific instruction [the score]."[1] Thus, in Eno's terms, a classical organization of music or teaching follows a prepared score and "regards the environment (and its variety) as a set of emergencies" to be neutralized or disregarded. The classical lecturer must pretend that he doesn't hear the murmurs of dissent or boredom emanating from his audience. The alternative approach assumes, again in Eno's words, "that changing environments require adaptive organisms" and hence takes "the irregularities of the environment as a set of opportunities around which it will shape and adjust its own identity" (p. 140).

This second description approximates what most teachers actually do and accounts for why individual classes that seem especially good almost always result from "emergencies"—unanticipated questions, misunderstandings, or disagreements that deflect us down paths less discoverable with conventional preparation. This kind of heuristic surprise is precisely what conventional lecturing, and most classical performance, forgoes; it is, by contrast, the raison d'être of jazz. But if our everyday classrooms resemble the small clubs where most pop music performances occur, the public lecture (in universities, at conferences) still takes place in the grand concert hall. Let us suppose, however, that rather than lagging behind normal pedagogy, the lecture might become precisely the site of greatest experimentation. With the exception of John Cage, almost no one has taken up this challenge.

In the piece that follows, I suggest that contemporary film studies might benefit from using the experimental attitude developed by the avant-garde arts. As I prepared the talk, I decided that I should also experiment, however slightly, with the lecture form itself, if only to follow Cage's example, which he explains as the intention "to say what I had to say in a way that would exemplify it; that would, conceivably, permit the listener to experience what I had to say rather than just hear about it."[2] I have, therefore, retained as much as possible the pattern of the original lecture in hoping that the reader (who now stands in the listener's stead) might have some sense of what it was like to be there.

I. Introduction

As I was working on this talk, I began to think about lectures and academics' reading papers and conferences and my own experience of those events, which I presume you probably share. I have seen, for instance, Derrida read for two-and-one-half hours a densely argued, closely reasoned essay to a packed room, with almost no one following a line of speculation that remains difficult even in print, with *its* chances for re-reading, stopping and starting. If we agree that such a lecture has, at best, an effect other than communicating knowledge (an effect probably related more to entertainment and the charisma of a superstar performer), we are still left with the question, what should a lecture be like?

We know that in the Middle Ages, when books were rare and in the care of priests, teaching consisted of readings from manuscripts regarded as too fragile (both physically and theologically) to be distributed to the students. We also know that now, when books have long since become commonplace, such teaching practice would be regarded as irresponsible. But although photocopy machines have, for a long time, made it possible to distribute any lecture to an intended audience, we continue to travel around the country reading carefully composed, *written* arguments to each other, while most people in the audience decide five minutes into the talk that "I'll wait for the article," the way our students skip the book and wait for the movie.

What, therefore, should this kind of academic talk be like? Since my subjects are, in no particular order, the movies (which are fun), the avant-garde (which is experimental), and representation (which is everything), I decided that the best model for this talk would be something like the Marx Brothers' *A Night at the Opera* as described by Roland Barthes: "the steamer cabin [the stateroom scene], the torn contract, the final chaos of opera decors," scenes which he called emblems of textuality, while prompting him both to praise "the preposterous" and to suggest how "the logical future" of criticism would be *the gag*.[3]

Now *this* was a challenge. Remember that when she was a little girl, Gertrude Stein had exactly this problem with her first writing attempt, a play whose initial stage direction read, "Enter the courtiers, making witty remarks"—a line which stopped her cold, since she couldn't think of any witty remarks.[4] If I decide to agree with Barthes about the value of the preposterous and the gag, I had better come up with something.

Given the responses of my colleagues at the University of Florida to this lecture title (which is also the title of a course I have been teaching), I do not have to work too much harder at coming up with something preposterous. Even my fellow teachers seem to snicker at the conjunction of the avant-garde and Andy Hardy, which, of course, is satisfying, since as Barthes argued, the pleasures of perversity should not be underestimated (p.63). (I began to think that if I really succeeded, I would become *identified* with the preposterous; something like this situation has transpired with my colleague Gregory Ulmer, to whom a recent request for a paper came in these terms: "Hi, we're organizing a conference on Nonsense, so naturally we thought of you.") I noticed in talking to my colleagues, however, that most of them confused the Andy Hardy series with either the

"Hey! Let's put on a show" Judy Garland–Mickey Rooney musicals *or* the Hardy Boys detective stories. But that confusion didn't deter me.

Having satisfied the preposterous requirement (and maybe the gag one, too), I still had to imagine a lecture style that would accommodate my subjects: the movies, the avant-garde, and representation. I decided from the start that I would speak in a way that would take account of our attention spans, designing this talk in discrete sections that would allow a listener to drop in and out of it without losing some single sustained train of thought. We are in the first section now, and if you don't like this one, you can stop listening until something else comes along in a few minutes that interests you more.[5]

One lecture style that interested me was John Cage's. In 1958, having been contracted to speak in Brussels on the "New Aspect of Form in Instrumental and Electronic Music," Cage gave a talk that consisted exclusively of thirty anecdotes, of which I will read only one:

> Staying in India and finding the sun unbearable, Mrs. Coomaraswamy decided to shop for a parasol. She found two in the town nearby. One was in the window of a store dealing in American goods. It was reasonably priced but unattractive. The other was in an Indian store. It was Indian-made, but outlandishly expensive. Mrs. Coomaraswamy went back home without buying anything. But the weather continued dry and hot, so that a few days later she went again into town determined to make a purchase. Passing by the American shop, she noticed their parasol was still in the window, still reasonably priced. Going into the Indian shop, she asked to see the one she had admired a few days before. While she was looking at it, the price was mentioned. This time it was absurdly low. Surprised, Mrs. Coomaraswamy said, "How can I trust you? One day your prices are up; the next day they're down. Perhaps your goods are equally undependable." "Madame," the storekeeper replied, "the people across the street are new in business. They are intent on profit. Their prices are stable. We, however, have been in business for generations. The best things we have we keep in the family, for we are reluctant to part with them. As for our prices, we change them continually. That's the only way we've found in business to keep ourselves interested." (*Silence*, pp. 263–64)

Now this tactic seemed such an appealing idea that I decided to try it myself. Here is an anecdote:

> When I was a boy, we lived in the country, twenty minutes outside of town, in a house on top of a hill, with a mile-long driveway that ran down the hill to the highway that led into town. Growing up, I remember my father always talking about a particular sports car that he had had when he was younger, his first car in fact. Because he had once been involved in rallies and road racing, my father kept photograph albums of his former cars the way most people do

of their children. But his favorite was his first, a red MG that he had wrecked a few months after his twentieth birthday (in a collision with a telephone pole) and which had been a total loss. For years afterward, he regularly scoured the want ads for a similar car. Finally one day he saw an ad for such a car, went to look at it, and found to his amazement (for it was twenty years later) that the car advertized was not merely one *like* his old car, but *was* his old car. He bought it on the spot. I remember the day he brought it home, or rather when the tow truck brought it, since the car was still a wreck and wouldn't run. We had at that time a large house with an enormous cellar that ran the length of the house. The tow truck arrived, we opened the trap doors to the cellar, and lowered the car into it. For years after that day, my father spent most of his leisure time in the cellar working on the car, taking it apart and putting it back together at least six times, straightening the frame (with weights hung from the ceiling), retooling the detail aluminum work on the dashboard, working on the engine. Occasionally, we would go into town with him to make exotic purchases of a special kind of leather for the steering wheel. The car became my father's trademark; everyone knew him for it. Finally after seven years, he declared that the car was ready. The tow truck came back, the trap doors opened, and the whole neighborhood stood around as the car came up the ramp my father had built for it. He looked around at the neighbor's children, smiled, and told them to hop in. The car was only a two-seater, and I got the privileged position in the front next to him, but six or seven other small kids piled into the rumble seat in the back, and off we went down the mile-long driveway that ran down to the highway, with wheatfields and haystacks on either side. A minute into the drive, with all of us singing and yelling and having a wonderful time, I noticed that my father was sweating profusely. "Is there something wrong?" I asked. He turned, looked at me, and without saying a word, simply handed me the steering wheel which had come off in his hands. Just ahead, our driveway made a sharp turn to the right; straight ahead was a small cliff with a twenty-five-foot drop to a ploughed field below. My father grabbed the steering column with both hands, and with all his strength managed to turn the car just enough to miss the drop and land us in the middle of a haystack just off the road to the right. When the car stopped, the kids cheered and said, "That was great! Can we do it again?"[6]

For the moment, I will leave it to you to decide what this anecdote has to do with my announced topic, but before leaving this section, I will tell one last anecdote by Cage:

What do images do? Do they illustrate? (It was a New Year's Eve party in the country and one of them had written a philosophical book and was searching for a picture that would illustrate a particular point but was having difficulty. Another was knitting, following the rules from a book she had in front of her. The rest were talking, trying to be helpful. The suggestion was made that the picture in the knitting book would illustrate the point. On examination it was found that everything on the page was relevant, including the number.) (*Silence*, p. 107)

II. Ways to Begin This Talk

That was the end of the first section; we are now starting the second section.

I might have chosen a more conventional way to begin a talk called "The Avant-Garde Finds Andy Hardy." Indeed, those who remember Calvino's *If on a winter's night a traveler*, with its multiple beginnings, can probably imagine dozens of other ways to start. Since today is the first day of spring, let us just say that if on a spring night a traveler came to Bloomington to speak about the avant-garde and Andy Hardy, he or she might begin in this way:

From 1939 through 1941. . . .

From 1939 through 1941, the Hollywood studio system, at the peak of its power and inventiveness, produced (among hundreds of others) the following movies:

Stagecoach
The Wizard of Oz
Wuthering Heights
Dark Victory
Gone with the Wind
Young Mr. Lincoln
The Hunchback of Notre Dame
Gunga Din
Goodbye Mr. Chips
Destry Rides Again
Ninotchka
Mr. Smith Goes to Washington
The Grapes of Wrath
The Roaring Twenties
Rebecca
All This and Heaven Too
The Mortal Storm
Pride and Prejudice
The Great McGinty
Citizen Kane
The Maltese Falcon
Woman of the Year
Sullivan's Travels
The Lady Eve
The Philadelphia Story
How Green Was My Valley

> *Meet John Doe*
> *The Great Dictator*
> *Dumbo*
> *Suspicion*
> *Fantasia*

During these same three years, the number one box-office attraction was not Gable, Garbo, Tracy, Hepburn, Garland, Stewart, Cooper, Davis, Power, Flynn, Bogart, Crosby, or Cagney. In 1939, 1940, and 1941, the most popular performer in the American cinema was Mickey Rooney.

While Rooney starred in a dozen movies during this period, his success rested primarily on a low-budget series initiated by MGM as a way of profiting from the surprising success of *Ah, Wilderness!* the studio's 1935 version of Eugene O'Neill's small-town comedy. The series, whose first film, *A Family Affair*, appeared in 1937, quickly came to focus on Rooney's character, Andy Hardy.

Between 1937 and 1946, MGM made fifteen Andy Hardy movies, seven in 1938 and 1939 alone. Working quickly and sticking to a formula, the filmmakers accidentally connected up with the main traditions of American culture. The Hardy movies belong to a group of films about American small-town families: *The Magnificent Ambersons, It's a Wonderful Life, Meet Me in St. Louis, Since You Went Away, The Human Comedy, Babes in Arms.* In many of these cases, the influences were explicit. From Booth Tarkington, O'Neill derived his own *Ah, Wilderness!* which in turn prompted the Hardy series. The Hardy movies influenced *Meet Me in St. Louis*, which starred Judy Garland, who had appeared in three Hardy films. *Meet Me in St. Louis* was based on stories by Sally Benson, who subsequently adapted Tarkington's *Seventeen* for Broadway (and who scripted the strangest of the small-town movies, Hitchcock's *Shadow of a Doubt*). The most important film of the group, *It's a Wonderful Life*, appears in hindsight as a dark Andy Hardy movie, summarizing and making overt themes which the Hardy series had swept under the rug: money, prostitution, suicide, hopelessness.

The Hardy films' success represents a phenomenon peculiar to modern life: a popular entertainment, made without aesthetic ambition, can gain an unprecedented hold on the collective consciousness. It would, in fact, be almost impossible to find someone who had reached movie-going age in the years 1937–46 who had not at least heard of Andy Hardy. Nevertheless, almost nothing has been written about the Hardy movies.[7] They continue to be mentioned, however, as the principal source of television's family sitcoms (from *Ozzie and Harriet* and *Father Knows Best*, the series most obviously derived from the Hardy movies, to *Family Ties* and *The Cosby Show*), but have themselves seemed beneath the attention of contemporary film scholars, ideological semioticians after bigger game.

This section of the talk has now ended; a new one begins here.

That would be one way of beginning this lecture, a way that corresponds to the protocols of academic teaching and writing that require a justification of method and subject matter: someone analyzing, for example, *Bleak House*, usually begins by arguing for the novel's significance (or neglect: the two often amount to the same thing). I have made such arguments about the Andy Hardy series, which in fact are a token gesture, designed to conceal my real reasons for speaking about them: first, for my own interest (does even my childhood liking for these movies bespeak a founding nostalgia? can a child be nostalgic?); second, for their ideological obviousness (demythologized by the passing of time alone); and third, for the scandal inherent in linking Andy Hardy with the avant-garde.

Here then would be another way to begin:

film studies is. . . .

If on a spring night a traveler came to Bloomington to give a talk called "The Avant-Garde Finds Andy Hardy," he might start by saying that film studies is dead. That would be the most dramatic way to put it, useful in an oral format perhaps, hyperbolic in writing, where I might put it this way: there is now an increasingly widespread sense that after nearly twenty years of exhilarating work, film studies has stagnated. The discipline whose beginnings coincided with the flowering of structuralist, semiotic, ideological, psychoanalytic, and feminist theory has evolved into another professional specialty (like Romanticism or eighteenth-century poetry), with all the routinized procedures of any academic field. Indeed, what "theory" overthrew (new critical interpretations based on close readings) film studies became. Cinema journals and conferences brim over with papers rounding up the usual suspects for hermeneutical interrogation. I recently wrote that the typical title in film studies has become "Barthes, Brecht, Bakhtin, Baudrillard, and all those other people, and *Robocop*." I thought at the time that I was exaggerating, but here are some typical titles from 1989's Society for Cinema Studies' conference in Iowa City:

"The Three Stooges and Derrida: Notes on Deconstructive Comedy"
"Oedipal Drama and the Post-Vietnam Hollywood Film"
"Hollywood and Vietnam: John Wayne and Jane Fonda as Discourse"
"*Cheers* and the Mediation of Cultures"
"Textual Pleasure and Transgression in *The Thorn Birds*"
"Female Desire in *All This and Heaven Too*"
"Masochism and Male Hysteria in *The Naked Spur*"
"Gendered Readings of *The Newlywed Game*"
"*Thirtysomething*, Polysemy and Intertextuality"
"Gender Relations and Popular Culture in Mayberry"

and Bingo!
"Ideological Crisis: *Robocop*, Video, and the Reconstitution of Subjectivity"

I want to make clear that I am not against theoretical analyses of popular culture; I am not against the application of sophisticated semiotic, ideological, and psychoanalytic methods to the study of popular forms. I am not against writing about *Mayberry RFD* or *The Newlywed Game*. My point is that, in effect, they already *have* been written about. The extraordinary contagiousness of contemporary theory lies precisely in its generalizing power: the old model of scholarship, which relied on a specialized, scrupulous coverage of a field of study, insisted that the right to speak about fiction or narrative accrued only to those who had read all the major novels in a given literature (hence such books as Wayne Booth's *The Rhetoric of Fiction*, which seems to mention every important English novel). Contemporary theory, on the other hand, finds its representative model in Barthes's *S/Z*, which uses one Balzac novella (and a minor one at that) to make an argument about narrative in general. Having seen that approach in action, academics have ignored its lesson and insisted on using it as a new model for case-by-case analyses. But if you understand Barthes's points about narrative, you do not need to see them worked out with a hundred other examples: that procedure may be useful for beginning students, as a way of apprehending Barthes's approach, but surely it should not be the model for advanced scholarly work that appears in journals, books, and conferences.

Why not? Simply because we know in advance where such analyses will lead, and thus even the most skilled of such efforts will achieve very little information, if we define information (as cybernetics does) as a function of unpredictability: the more predictable the message, the less information it contains.

How does this problem apply specifically to film studies? Having committed itself to a particular way of doing business (which we might call "semiotic," using that term to stand for this amalgam of structuralist, psychoanalytic, ideological, and feminist methodologies), film studies has, since 1970, constructed an enormously powerful theoretical machine for exposing the ideological abuse hidden by the apparently natural stories and images of popular culture. That machine, however, now runs on automatic pilot, producing predictable essays and books on individual cases.

New Criticism, which arose in the 1930s, maintained its dominance for over thirty years. Why has the semiotic paradigm grown stale so quickly? That question's answer also responds to those who while granting the staleness of much recent semiotic/ideological work on mass culture, insist on retaining the approach for political reasons. In fact, however, while the method originated in a political impulse coinciding with the 1960s' increased ideological sensitivity, the method now seems to serve more an immediate institutional politics of academic tenure and promotion. Thomas Kuhn, of course, would have predicted exactly this development: normal scientists, by virtue of their role, have far less intense commitment to their discipline's founding impulses than do its progenitors. Why? *Because they don't need such continuously conscious pledges of allegiance*: born into the paradigm, they take it for granted and pursue its immediate rewards. While Darwin, Newton, Einstein, et al. were devout missionaries, most biologists and physicists are just men and women with jobs, thinking about paychecks and day-to-day research puzzles. In an academic climate, whose vast oversupply of Ph.D.'s has fostered a concomitant oversupply of publications, *any* critical approach gets used up quickly by people for whom it amounts only to a means of getting, keeping, or improving a job.

As early as 1971, Barthes diagnosed this situation:

> the new semiology—or the new mythology. . . . it too has become in some sort mythical: any student can and does denounce the bourgeois or petit-bourgeois character of such and such a form (of life, of thought, of consumption). In other words, a mythological doxa has been created: denunciation, demystification (or demythification), has itself become discourse, stock of phrases, catechistic declaration. . . . [8]

Nearly twenty years ago, in other words, Barthes had intuited how redundant demystification had become, at least as an advanced theoretical practice. What else is there to do?

*****Just as chapters in long novels and detective stories often end with the unresolved, this talk uses questions to punctuate its rhythm. We are at the end of another section, and at a new starting point.*****

In talking about the story of "The Three Little Pigs," Jonathan Culler once suggested "that almost every *proper* question, such as 'What happened next?', will be critically less productive (less productive of critical discourse we find worth reading) than marginally improper questions, such as 'Why three little pigs?' "[9] The course I am presently teaching, "The Avant-Garde Finds Andy Hardy," which is an experiment, and for which this talk is a kind of lab report, presenting results achieved so far, requires its students to ask improper questions. The course, in other words, sets up a situation typical of contemporary film studies: we watch movies whose plots, characters, settings, and values seem *made* for the structuralist/semiotic/ideological/psychoanalytic/feminist that has become the coin of the realm among those whom one French writer identified as "les enfants du paradigme."[10] This course, however, explicitly *forbids* all such approaches. Instead, it requires students to ask "improper questions."

The importance of questions is illustrated by another anecdote from Cage's lecture on "New Aspect of Form in Instrumental and Electronic Music":

> A crowded bus on the point of leaving Manchester for Stockport was found by its conductress to have one too many standees. She therefore asked, "Who was the last person to get on the bus?" No one said a word. Declaring that the bus would not leave until the extra passenger was put off, she went and fetched the driver, who also asked, "All right, who was the last person to get on the bus?" Again there was a public silence. So the two went to find an inspector. He asked, "Who was the last person to get on the bus?" No one spoke. He then announced that he would fetch a policeman. While the conductress, driver, and inspector were away looking for a policeman, a little man came up to the bus stop and asked, "Is this the bus to Stockport?" Hearing that it was, he got one. A few minutes later the three returned accompanied by a policeman. He asked, "What seems to be the trouble? Who was the last person to get on the bus?" The little man said, "I was." The policeman said, "All right, get off." All the people on the bus burst into laughter. The conductress, thinking they were laughing at her, burst into tears and said she refused to make the trip to Stockport. The inspector then arranged for another conductress to take over. She, seeing the little man standing at the bus stop, said, "What are you doing there?" He said, "I'm waiting to go to Stockport." She said, "Well, this is the bus to Stockport. Are you getting on or not?" (*Silence*, p. 271)

OK. What kind of questions did I want to ask and where would they come from? I started with this one: Why, if given the choice, would almost everyone, including film studies students and professors, rather *see* a movie than read a critical article about it? As I thought about that question, it seemed a problem for the course and this talk. Others followed in its wake: Why do certain movies become popular? Why do individual scenes in otherwise forgettable movies fascinate us? Why have two decades of rigorous critique done very little to undermine the glamor and seductiveness of the movies? Why is someone willing to spend $165,000 to own only *one* of five pairs of slippers worn by Judy Garland in *The Wizard of Oz*?

Speaking at the University of Florida in Fall 1988, anthropologist Michael Taussig reported that when he asked Columbian Indians to account for imperialism's success, they replied, "the others won because their stories were better than ours." In a very real sense, Hollywood's stories have been better than film criticism's. If we want to match Hollywood's power without abandoning Habermas's "enlightenment project" (of critique and rational understanding), but want to achieve it by other means, might we begin by experimenting with the *forms* of criticism, which up until now has worked almost entirely with one kind of rhetoric: that of scientific realism, with its premise of a transparent language. What are the alternatives? What if we still want the hermeneutic effect, but feel we have exhausted hermeneutics as a possibility?

Taussig has insisted that what is at stake with such questions is "the issue of *graphicness*," a quality generally disdained by materialist critics who associate it with the enemies, commerce and mystification.[11] Confronted by enormously popular, powerful, mysterious representations (the movies, for example), criticism should, in Taussig's words, attempt "*to penetrate the veil while retaining its hallucinatory quality*," a process that "evokes and combines a twofold movement of interpretation in a combined action of reduction *and* revelation" (p.10). Where will we find the "improper questions" that might enable us to work in this way? The difficulty of that "proper" question derives from the historical condition diagnosed by Octavio Paz, who has observed that "the only Myth-Idea of the modern world" is Criticism: "From the 17th century onward," Paz writes, "our world has had no Ideas, in the sense in which Christianity had ideas during its time of apogee. What we have, especially from Kant on, is Criticism."[12]

Is there an alternative to criticism? Another source for improper questions? One place to look might be that branch of the humanities which, since the nineteenth century, has functioned as the equivalent of science's pure research: the avant-garde. If instead of thinking about the avant-garde as only hermeneutic self-expression, we began to imagine it as a field of experimental work waiting to be used (in the same way that pure science's exotica becomes another generation's technology), then we might begin to apply avant-garde devices for the sake of knowledge.[13]

III. The Avant-Garde

The very idea of using the avant-garde arts as a means to knowledge may seem strange indeed, since most people associate the avant-garde simply with tactics of shock, scandal, and ridicule. But from the start, the avant-gardists thought of themselves as practicing something like science. Zola and the Impressionist painters (perhaps the first real avant-garde) often cited Claude Bernard's call for a new attitude toward knowledge, one led by an allegiance to the scientific method; and Monet, Seurat, and Degas regularly spoke of doing a kind of "research." The most explicit use of the scientific attitude, however, appears with the surrealists, for whom the homonyms available in the words *expérience* (experience and experiment) and *recréation* (both fun and re-creation) are crucial. André Breton's *Manifesto of Surrealism* (1924) states the position which surely derived from his (and Aragon's) medical training: the *Manifesto* speaks repeatedly of knowledge, the failure of the old systems of reason and logic (which Breton thought had produced World War I), and the need to find new investigatory procedures:

We are still living under the reign of logic, but the logical processes of our time apply only to the solution of problems of secondary interest. The absolute rationalism which remains in fashion allows for the consideration of only those facts narrowly relevant to our experience. . . . In the guise of civilization, under the pretext of progress, we have succeeded in dismissing from our minds anything that, rightly or wrongly, could be regarded as superstition or myth; and we have proscribed every way of seeking the truth which does not conform to convention.[14]

Citing Freud as a model for new ways of doing research, Breton continues:

Perhaps the imagination is on the verge of recovering its rights. If the depths of our minds conceal strange forces capable of augmenting or conquering those on the surface, it is in our greatest interest to capture them; first to capture them and later to submit them, should the occasion arise, to the control of reason. [A key qualification, indicating the partial retention of the Enlightenment project.] The analysts themselves can only gain by this. But it is important to note that there is no fixed method a priori for the execution of this enterprise, that until the new order it can be considered the province of poets as well as scholars, and that its success does not depend on the more or less capricious routes which will be followed. (p. 66)

Breton's *Manifesto*, in other words, was a call, made sixty-five years ago, for different ways of working, for alternatives to Criticism, the West's one big Idea. The advantage of using the avant-garde as the source for such alternatives results from its capacity to give us two things: a new subject matter (just as Freud's psychoanalysis called unprecedented attention to dreams, slips of the tongue, forgotten names) *and* new means of presenting it.

This latter point is particularly important. If we say for the sake of argument (a locution which means, "Trust me on this one") that the avant-garde's current home is less in the fine arts than in contemporary theory, the striking point about our (meaning, "academics' ") use of this theory has been our rejection of its formal experimentation. Barthes's *S/Z, A Lover's Discourse*, and autobiography; Derrida's *Glas, Signsponge*, and *Spurs* are all strange books formally. Barthes and Derrida, of course, are using surrealism, deploying all of its favorite devices: collage, fragments, typographical play, puns, neologisms, development by motif rather than by logic. But for the most part, academics have merely cited their work (as if it appeared in conventional formats) and gone on writing straightforward essays. Why has an academic apparatus which has surrendered everything else (its canon, its new critical faith in art's autonomy) retreated to this Corregidor of style? What happens if we imitate the forms, too?

I designed my course as an experiment to see what would happen. I took the Andy Hardy films (and a few related MGM movies) as the course subject matter, estopped the students from pursuing conventional film studies approaches, and gave them a set of what my colleague Gregory Ulmer calls *inventios*: avant-garde practices from which they must extrapolate to produce texts about the Hardy cycle. This semester, the *inventios* are

John Cage's *Silence*
Julian Barnes's *Flaubert's Parrot*
Roland Barthes
Duchamp's readymades
Alexander Kluge's *The Battle* (a collage text about Stalingrad which performs Walter Benjamin's idea for *The Arcades Project*, a history written with found materials)
Surrealism, especially surrealist games
Derrida's *Signsponge* ("the signature experiment")
Hans Haacke's art projects
Brecht's theories of epic theater

I can show you how two of these extrapolations work. Let's begin with surrealism. While the surrealists gave us an array of work which might be used for other purposes, I am particularly interested in their games. Breton describes their origin:

> When conversation about current events and about proposals for amusing or scandalous interventions in the life of those days began to lose its vigor, we were in the habit of turning to *games*—written games at first, in which the elements of speech confronted each other in the most paradoxical way so that human communication, led astray from the start, caused the mind that registered it to run a maximum of adventures.[15]

Two aspects of the surrealist games prove most attractive: their automatic/collaborative nature, and their recreational (in both senses of that word) dimension. At the moment, the two games that most interest me are the exquisite corpse and the irrational enlargement of a film scene.

Most of you know the exquisite corpse, which works from a fixed syntactical structure:

What is a (noun)?
A (noun), (adjective) and (adjective).

The game requires four players, each of whom writes down (without consulting any of the others) his assigned part of speech (either noun or adjective). The result is a collaboratively produced metaphor: in Breton's words, "With the exquisite corpse we had at our disposal—at last—an infallible means of temporarily dismissing the critical mind and of fully freeing metaphorical activity" (p. 222). Since philosophy of science has shown that all knowledge systems rest on a few basic metaphors, and that a new paradigm always proposes a metaphoric shift, this game might have more profound consequences than at first appears.[16] At the least, it forces its players in directions that conventional research would not.

Here, then, is the assignment I gave to my class: Using the exquisite corpse game, generate with three other people twenty to twenty-five metaphors about either the Hardy films or *Meet Me in St. Louis* (a related movie). Pick the "best" five (i.e., the most suggestive, stimulating, memorable). Use two as topic sentences for paragraphs "about" the films; these paragraphs can be either analytical, speculative, anecdotal, conjectural, critical, narrative, or lyrical.

Here are a few samples, first on *Meet Me in St. Louis*, a more familiar movie than the Hardy series:

What is a trolley car?
A ballerina, still and massive.

What is the Halloween bonfire?
A window, hidden and electric.

What is a long-distance phone call from New York?
A knife, flippant and moonstruck.

What is Esther's (Judy Garland's) parasol?
A theology, measurable and courteous.

What is a trolley?
A painting, white and inky.

What are snowpeople?
Marshmallows, self-indulgent and empty.

What is Esther's perfume?
A reason, foreboding and whimsical.

What is John's Christmas present to Esther?
A riddle, clean and circular.

What is Garland's glamor?
A furrow, languid and furious.

And a few examples on the Hardy movies, with an occasional summary of the resulting paragraphs:

What is Polly Benedict?
A carriage, ethical and seductive.
     (Suggesting Polly's simultaneous old-fashionedness
     and sexuality.)

What is 1930s sexism?
A song, infantile and quiet.
> (Which accompanies the movies as background
> music.)

What is an Andy Hardy movie?
A disease, monochromatic and happy.
> (The Hardy films as symptoms of 1930s repression:
> "monochromatic" = black and white.)

What is a debutante [*Andy Hardy Meets Debutante*]?
A landscape, ignorant and elusive.
> (The deb, Daphne Fowler, as a screen for
> projection.)

What is poverty?
An echo, silent and persistent.
> (The Depression background just outside the series'
> frame.)

What is Polly Benedict?
A typewriter, vivacious and repetitive.

What is courtship?
A monologue, exhilarating and foreign.

What are Emily's Christmas packages [in *Love Finds Andy
Hardy*]?
Roads, silent and braided.

What is the hansom scene [with Mickey Rooney and
Judy Garland in Central Park, *Andy Hardy
Meets Debutante*]?
A park, bleak and inappropriate.

These sentences, and the assignment I made of them, may seem merely whimsical. To that objection, I can only make two responses. First, that this method is still in its infancy; we do not yet know how it works or how to use it most effectively. Second, that the surrealist games began as devices to enable them to approximate another research situation, one with its own strange, but strict, rules, one that from the outside appears as a kind of game: the psychoanalytic session. Here are Freud's instructions to a patient "beginning the treatment":

> What you tell me must differ in one respect from an ordinary conversation. Ordinarily you rightly try to keep a connecting thread running through your remarks and you exclude any intrusive ideas that may occur to you and any side-issues, so as not to wander too far from the point. But in this case you must proceed differently. You will notice that as you relate things various thoughts will occur to you which you would like to put aside on the ground of

certain criticisms and objections. You will be tempted to say to yourself that this or that is irrelevant here, or is quite unimportant, or nonsensical, so that there is no need to say it. You must never give in to these criticisms, but must say it in spite of them—indeed you must say it precisely *because* you feel an aversion to doing so. Later on you will find out and learn to understand the reason for this injunction, which is really the only one you have to follow. So say whatever goes through your mind. Act as though, for instance, you were a traveller sitting next to the window of a railway carriage and describing to someone inside the carriage the changing views which you see outside. Finally, never forget that you have promised to be absolutely honest, and never leave anything out because, for some reason or other, it is unpleasant to tell it.[17]

Although these instructions seem simple enough, they are, as Freud soon saw, extraordinarily difficult to follow, as are the corresponding "rules" for the analyst.[18] Indeed, this game, *like any other*, rewards practice: the more you play it, the easier it becomes. But at the beginning, it is a game so difficult to play that the surrealists invented *other* games as ways of learning it—games such as automatic writing and the exquisite corpse.

The other game with which I have been experimenting the surrealists called "irrational enlargement of a film scene," itself descended from an earlier game called "interrogation of the object."[19] This game involves from three to ten players, and when applied to the movies, requires the principal to ask such questions as these:

On *Meet Me in St. Louis* (with selected answers):

> What happened to Grandma?
>> She died a horrible death involving machinery.
>
> How is Mr. and Mrs. Smith's bedroom decorated?
>
> From where did the Truetts move?
>> Jay Gatsby's house.
>
> At what age will Tootie die?
>> She will live a long life, preoccupied by death.
>> At age five because she falls off a ride at the fair.
>
> Which four fatal diseases do Tootie's dolls have?
>
> Where in the house was the orchestra hiding?
>
> Who lives at 5134 Kensington?
>
> When Tootie cuts her lip, the doctor asks, "What is it this time, Tootie?" What was it the last time?
>
> What did Grandpa do for a living before he retired?
>
> What is Alonzo's major at Princeton?
>
> Where is Katie's [the maid's] family, and what relation is she

to the Bradys' maid, Alice?
Twins separated at birth.
Katie is Alice's mother, but Alice was adopted and
never knew.

What does Tootie become when she grows up?
A mortician.

What does John Truett do after the first party?
Goes home and practices turning on and off all the
lights in his own house.

What happened to Tootie to cause her fascination with
death?
She once saw a dead body on the
streetcar tracks in her quiet
suburban neighborhood.

Why doesn't Esther's singing wake her parents?
The house has thick walls.
They take sleeping pills.
It does, but they don't want to interrupt.

What was the case that Mr. Smith lost?

Would anyone famous have died if the trolley *had* gone off
the tracks?
Not anyone famous, but Elvis's grandfather was on
the trolley.

A few samples on the Andy Hardy movies:

from *Love Finds Andy Hardy*

What is the name of the road that Andy and Betsy
take to come home from the dance?
Magnolia Lane.
A road that winds back on itself and
becomes the same road.

Who does Mrs. Hardy meet on the airplane coming
home from Canada?

How does the boy who answers the ham radio call
get to the Forest farm?

When Polly Benedict first left home, how did she
travel?

What physical traits did Polly Benedict inherit from
her mother?
Blonde hair, blue eyes.
Straight teeth.

High cheekbones.
None, she's adopted—that's why we never
    see the mother.

What does Polly Benedict's bedroom look like?

What names did the Hardys consider before settling
    on Andy?

Whom does Polly eventually marry?
She never marries.
The hansom driver in Central Park [from *Andy Hardy
    Meets Debutante*].

Where is Carvel?
In Idaho.
In the Midwest.
Under Niagara Falls.
In Saskatchewan, off Highway 476 near
    Bolinda.

And five examples "about" *Madame Bovary*:

What should happen when Emma is in the attic
    contemplating suicide?
She turns into a lamp.
A sudden fire traps her in the attic and she
    burns to death.
The Ghost of Christmas Past tells her to
    shape up.
Knives float over her head in the shape of
    a pentangle.

What happens to Berthe [Madame Bovary's only
    child] in later life?
She becomes a nun.
She writes a book called *Madame Bovary*,
    filled with clichés.

What do bees symbolize in *Madame Bovary*?
The spread of disillusionment with reality.
The need to stay busy and focused on your
    own life.
The inadequate support for adultery.

What happens to Emma's dog, and why does he run
    off?
He realizes the hopelessness of the situation
    and chooses to leave with a circus.

What happens to the priest and the pharmacist when
    they fall asleep while sitting up with

Emma's corpse?
Each dreams he is the other.

What can we say about this game other than that it often yields funny answers? Several things:

1. These questions are often exactly the kind expressly forbidden by New Criticism, whose paradigmatic example of the improper question was "What did Hamlet study before the play begins?" New Criticism forbade these questions because the text, on which everything depended, could neither verify nor disprove any answer to them.

2. Such questions are precisely the kind that occur to us as the film unwinds, but which we suppress because the narrative shows them to be irrelevant. Their appeal represents a moment of delayed recognition on the viewer's part: we hear spoken, made explicit, something we wondered about without even realizing it, which we censored as irrelevant to the movie—exactly as Freud's patients censored fleeting thoughts for their apparent irrelevancy or indiscretion, thoughts which only a game (the psychoanalytic session and its rules) could retrieve.

3. These questions confirm how elliptical, how witty (in Freud's sense of condensation) cinematic realism is. We think after nearly two hours with the Smith family, or fifteen movies with the Hardys, that we know everything about them and their house and their neighborhood, but of course we know nothing, since the movies, like all realisms, work metonymically, giving us the part from which we can imagine the whole. When she worked as an advisor to the film crew making her own *The Return of Martin Guerre*, historian Natalie Davis tried to ensure authenticity by cramming the *mise-en-scène* with medieval details. The director explained, however, that they were unnecessary, since Hollywood worked on "the camel principle": if you want to suggest Egypt, you simply put a camel in the corner of a frame, and the audience does the rest. The irrational enlargement questions suggest specifically how that elliptical, metonymical process works by pointing at the places in the story where it struggles, where the viewer, however unconsciously, wants to know more.

As I said earlier, these games are still at a primitive stage of use. But they seem to have potential to effect a wholly different kind of research than the one established by semiotics.

IV. Flaubert's Parrot

I will mention one other model, Julian Barnes's *Flaubert's Parrot*, a hybrid, part novel, part Flaubert biography, part literary criticism. I have used this book with great success in classes. Nearly all of my students, from freshmen to graduate students, like it enormously, and at first, I used it primarily in world literature courses, usually with something by Flaubert himself. But

I have recently begun asking students to take the book as a manual suggesting different ways of writing.

As an *inventio*, *Flaubert's Parrot* has the advantage of resembling a catalogue of experimental styles. Each of the fifteen chapters works from a different principle: a chronology, an examination, a legal brief, a bestiary (based on metaphors Flaubert applied to himself). Reading the book, therefore, resembles watching television while switching channels: every chapter offers a fresh start, so if you don't like one, you don't have to wait very long for another completely different one to come along. As a way of presenting information, this style (which partakes of both collage and fragmentation) has enormous advantages. Students read this book with more pleasure than they would ever read a conventional biography of Flaubert, much less a critical study of his work. In effect, Barnes has found a story as good as Flaubert's own, one that is as much fun to read, but also one that never abandons the knowledge effect of criticism. In other words, Barnes has strategically adopted what Barthes called "the novelesque," a method of writing that draws on fictional resources: stories, images, details about the weather. This way of working, Barthes wrote, "subject[s] the objects of knowledge and discussion—as in any art—no longer to an instance of truth, but to a consideration of *effects.*"[20]

Barthes traced this "*third form*, neither Essay nor Novel," back to Proust, who had stood "at the intersection of two paths, two genres, torn between two 'ways' he does not yet know could converge . . . the way of the Essay (of Criticism) and the way of the Novel."[21] In *Flaubert's Parrot*, this form appears most strikingly in two chapters: "The Train-spotter's Guide to Flaubert" and "Snap!"

"The Train-spotter's Guide to Flaubert" consists of eleven brief, numbered sections, each having something to do with Flaubert and trains. At first, this approach, which is, after all, more poetic (organized around a motif) than expository (organized around an idea) or narrative (organized around a story), seems an incredibly oblique entry into Flaubert's life and works. For trains figure in no prominent way in any of his books, occurring only in *The Sentimental Education* , and there merely as a passing reference. But as the chapter proceeds, we learn how much Flaubert's affair with Louise Collet depended on the railroad (which enabled them to meet regularly at Mantes, halfway between Paris and Croisset); how much Flaubert regarded the railway as a symbol for all his hatred for bourgeois myths of progress. So when we learn in section 11 that the penultimate sentence of Flaubert's life, uttered as he sensed the onset of his fatal stroke, was "It's lucky it should happen today; it would have been a great nuisance tomorrow, in the train," we feel that trains *are* the key to Flaubert's life and works.

Which, of course, they are not. We can call the rhetorical principle organizing this chapter *paleontological*, for as with the reconstruction of dinosaurs, even the most unimportant part can be used to construe the whole. As a mode of presentation, this style has the advantages of both the list (which has enormous popular appeal: see the success of the various books of lists) and the gag (with a great punchline). More important, it provides a different research strategy. If the traditional model's predictability finds its visual representation in the worn index cards of certain research paths (the trail of the author, the trail of the "important theme"), the paleontological approach corresponds to the new searches made possible by computers, which can be instructed to highlight any word, no matter how "unimportant."

Here is a section using "The Train-spotter's Guide" from an undergraduate's paper:

Communication Breakdown

1. The doorbell rings, and Mrs. Hardy answers it. Telegram for Mrs. Hardy. She looks at Judge Hardy, terrified of the small slip of paper. "Oh, James, I can't read it," she cries, reconfirming her series-long fear of technology. "Telegrams always bring bad news." Reassured that her fears are groundless, and grasping onto Judge Hardy for support, she opens the envelope. Her mother has had a stroke and is in a coma. She must go to her.

Why are telegrams menacing in these movies, which appeared before World War II made their threat indexical? As both an advanced and retrograde means of communication, telegrams stand between the letter and the telephone. Comfortable only with the letter, which the telegram fatally imitates, Emily is made uneasy by the advance of civilization.

2. Thomas Edison's big break came when he saved a telegraph operator's son from being run over by a train, a mythic event transformed and doubled in *It's a Wonderful Life* by George's twin rescue of brother Harry and Mr. Gower's unseen patient. Eventually Edison found himself printing a newspaper leaflet called *The Weekly Herald*, containing advertisements, railroad information, and Civil War news received from railway telegraph offices along the line. Edison's experiments with the telegraph led him to inventing the stock ticker, the mimeograph, the phonograph, and improvements for the telephone. His inventions made him famous, prompting books and movies, one of which, *Young Tom Edison*, starred Mickey Rooney, Andy Hardy.

3. In *The Human Comedy*, L. B. Mayer's favorite film, Mickey Rooney plays Homer McCauley, the telegram delivery boy.

4. L. B. Mayer fired Judy Garland from *The Barkleys of Broadway* for constant tardiness, the first time she had ever been dismissed from a production. She got the news by telegram.

5. While filming at MGM, Mickey Rooney disguised himself as a Western Union messenger and walked into glamor girls' dressing rooms to deliver make-believe telegrams.

Mary Polino (Spring 1989)

The other chapter from *Flaubert's Parrot*, "Snap," is essentially a treatise on coincidences. In its second section, "Desert Island Discs," Barnes describes Flaubert's youthful summer romance with Gertrude Collier, an English girl with whom he maintained a lifelong, albeit intermittent, correspondence (he sent her a copy of *Madame Bovary*; she called it "hideous"). The section concludes with these two paragraphs:

> During the course of those long years (in 1847, to be precise, the year after Flaubert was recalling his Trouville sunsets to Louise) Gertrude had promised to love, honour and obey someone else: an English economist called Charles Tennant. While Flaubert slowly attained European fame as a novelist, Gertrude was herself to publish a book: an edition of her grandfather's journal, called *France on the Eve of the Great Revolution*. She died in 1918 at the age of ninety-nine; and she had a daughter, Dorothy, who married the explorer Henry Morton Stanley. [The coincidences here, by the way, start becoming eerie. Rooney played Edison-the-boy, but Edison-the-man was Spencer Tracy, who also played Stanley.]
>
> On one of Stanley's trips to Africa, his party got into difficulties. The explorer was obliged gradually to discard all his unnecessary belongings. It was, in a way, a reverse, real-life version of 'Desert Island Discs': instead of being equipped with things to make life in the tropics more bearable, Stanley was having to get rid of things to survive there. Books were obviously supernumerary, and he began jettisoning them until he got down to those two which every guest on 'Desert Island Discs' is furnished with as a bare, civilised minimum: the Bible and Shakespeare. Stanley's third book, the one he threw out before reducing himself to this final minimum, was *Salammbô*. (p. 71)

We might call this method "the paranoid sublime," for it consists in releasing information in a novelistic way that, by suppressing logical connections, produces the uncanny effect of universal relationships. It has the appeal of being anecdotal and mysterious, and thus makes use of precisely the proairetic and hermeneutic codes which Barthes saw as providing the forward momentum for all readerly narratives. Here are my last two examples, which allow me to end as I began, with an anecdote. The first is by a University of Florida graduate student; I wrote the second.

Peirce

Like the theory of evolution, structural linguistics has an uncertain parentage. But while Charles Darwin enjoys an unshakable prominence over his unfortunate doppelgänger Alfred Wallace, a man whose simultaneous and comparable work still goes largely unnoticed, it is difficult to speak of the modern study of signs without giving equal due to both of its founders. In fact, the discipline continues to be known by two different names. The one most common in Europe was coined by a Swiss academician named Ferdinand de Saussure. In his lecture notes, collected and published after his death by a group of loyal students, de Saussure describes what he considers a science yet unborn. "A science that studies the life of signs within society is conceivable. . . . " he writes. "I shall call it semiology." Unaware of de Saussure's work, an American named Charles Sanders Peirce developed his own theory of signification and called it "semiotics." His appellation remains current on this side of the Atlantic.

Again like evolution, like any truly revolutionary theory, semiotics remakes the world in a startling and controversial manner. Words, "signs," are arbitrary, it announces; they are by nature slippery, mutable, and untrustworthy. Yet we are utterly dependent on them, even as the connection between words and things becomes more and more tenuous, even if the physical and mental referents for our words, the meanings we intend and expect to convey, slide away and recede into an unreachable distance with every one we speak. Semiotics reveals human society as an endless world of talk, devoid of sure communication and shockingly unmoored from the material of existence. Or rather the material of experience turns out to be signs, less solid than the finest tissue, no more substantial than a penstroke or a breath of air. In the world of semiotics, we are all tightrope walkers working without a net.

Yet, as Thomas A. Sebeok and Jean Umiker-Sebeok have shown in an interesting essay, Peirce did not believe that the unreliability of words precluded making good guesses about the world.[22] Once his overcoat and watch were stolen when he inadvertently left them behind in a steamship cabin. The watch held great sentimental and professional value for Peirce, and he was determined to get it back. He immediately engaged a Mr. Bangs, head of the New York Branch of the Pinkerton Agency, to help him recover it. Peirce had already demanded a line-up of boat employees that he thought suspicious. On the basis of a sudden intuition, he had pulled one man aside and accused him of the theft. The man, of course, denied his culpability, but Peirce was certain of his guilt. The philosopher told Bangs that the case could be concluded through a brief surveillance of his suspect. In no time, the thief would attempt to pawn his ill-gotten gain, and when he did, an operative could arrest him on the spot. With the goods in hand, his intentions clear, the culprit could hardly escape conviction. Peirce would recover his property; the law would mete out swift justice.

Bangs, however, an experienced professional with the nation's most famous detective agency, had no intention of following the hunches of an innocent professor. He pursued his own line of investigation and soon reached a dead-end. True to the victim's intuition, the watch, missing its chain, showed up a few days later in a local pawnshop. The proprietor described the customer who had brought it in: there was no doubt; it was Peirce's man. Disgusted, Peirce convinced a detective to accompany him to the thief's apartment. The Pinkerton man was afraid to enter without a search warrant, but Peirce barged in and confronted the occupants. Though the suspect had gone out, Peirce found his wife. He announced that her husband was certainly going to jail, but that he had come to retrieve his overcoat and chain. By observing nuances of voice and gesture as he led the woman and a friend through the rooms, all the while questioning them about the whereabouts of his belongings, the determined philosopher quickly discovered both items. In his search, he had made only two stops. Each was entirely accurate.

Peirce would call the success of his investigation a product of "abduction," the third branch of logic (supplementing the classical forms of induction and deduction) which he had previously described in his papers. Others, less sophisticated, might just call it good detective work.

In 1921, seven years after Peirce's death, and a breadth of a continent away from this forensic adventure, Dashiell Hammett ended his own career with the Pinkertons. He had solved a case a day too soon. Had he not revealed the discovery he had made in a steamship smokestack until after he and the boat were at sea, he would have won a trip to Australia and a much-needed rest. Had he not quit immediately in self-disgust, he might have stayed on with the San Francisco branch indefinitely, or at least for as long as his health held out. Instead, he began writing detective fiction in earnest. By the end of 1922, he was breaking into print. By 1929, he had published his third novel, *The Maltese Falcon*, and was famous.

In this novel, his fictional detective, Sam Spade, tells an apparently trivial story about a man named Flitcraft who discovers that life isn't nearly as stable as he had previously thought. Flitcraft had been a moderately successful businessman and a reliable husband and father, but a near scrape with tragedy instantly revealed to him the precariousness of his existence. When a beam fell from several stories above him and landed next to him on the sidewalk, close enough to send a chip of concrete slicing into his face, it was as if "somebody had taken the lid off his life and let him look at the works." What Flitcraft sees in the box is absolute contingency, an arbitrariness of fate that seems incompatible with his staid way of living. He has believed in a version of the world that can't be true if this new experience is also true. He has been living a lie. Without a word, he leaves town, leaves his family, starts a new life. Eventually Spade goes looking for him.

What Flitcraft observes in his brief encounter with chaos is the world that a detective like Sam Spade lives with every day, a place of sudden violence and pervasive lies, of guesswork and inadequate explanation. The Flitcraft tale is a story within a story about stories; it is a microcosm of a world in which nobody's word is wholly trustworthy, and fictions compete for authority in the absence of reliable facts. This is the version of reality that Hammett articulates over and over in his writings.

As for Flitcraft, he eventually gravitates back to normal life, a normal job, a normal family. It is his habit, and habits are hard to break. But he hasn't forgotten his vertiginous glimpse of the abyss. By the time Spade catches up with him, he has chosen to call himself Charles Pierce (an inversion of the vowels in the philosopher's name).[23]

William C. Stephenson (Fall 1988)

In *Out West with the Hardys*, one of the series' most commercially successful entries (and, in fact, a top-five box-office hit in 1938), a scene occurs which, in the context of these movies, is exceptional for its explicit, albeit unexplained, emotional intensity. Emily has been frantically spring cleaning and seems overwrought. Since complaints from her are rare, her ill-temper is itself disturbing. She angrily announces that because she has no one to help her, dinner will consist only of bread and soup (the Depression meal), and the family warily gathers at the dinner table, attempting to reassure her while praising the qualities of what appears to be a very plain soup. Suddenly, the power fails, and the house is thrown into darkness and Emily into an unprecedented crying jag, utterly unmotivated in terms of the plot, and furthermore left unexplained. What is going on here? Why is this scene so troubling?

Partially, of course, because these movies attend so little to female characters or to the plights of domesticity, despite their family setting. Indeed, the Andy Hardy movies continue an American cultural tradition whose two 19th-century halves are Huck Finn (the complete non-conformist good-bad-boy) and Horatio Alger (whose heroes began as social outcasts, but end, by virtue of utter commitment to the norm, as successes). Andy Hardy is both Huck Finn and an Alger boy, but already before him, American culture had produced a figure in whom these two opposites had combined: Edison, a non-conformist from the West, who having been expelled from high school for mischief-making, had become the icon of success-through-hard-work. The myth of Edison was everywhere in early twentieth-century culture, appearing in ways that we no longer recognize. Baum's Wizard of Oz got his name (and his independent crankiness) from The Wizard of Menlo Park, and George Bailey's deafness in *It's a Wonderful Life* occurs in the same ear as Edison's. Judy Garland, who appeared in three Andy Hardy movies, starred in *The Wizard of Oz*, but more important, Mickey Rooney not only played Andy Hardy and Huck Finn; he also played Edison in *Young Tom Edison*, one half of a pair of 1940 MGM biopics completed by Spencer Tracy's *Edison the Man*.

And the lights in the Hardy dining room? When Edison died, President Hoover instructed America's cities to briefly shut off their power in memory of the man who had given them light and the movies.

Notes

1. Brian Eno, "Generating and Organizing Variety in the Arts," in *Breaking the Sound Barrier: A Critical Anthology of New Music*, ed. Gregory Battock (New York: Dutton, 1981), p. 130.

2. John Cage, *Silence* (Middletown, CT, 1973), p. ix.

3. Roland Barthes, *Roland Barthes*, trans. Richard Howard (New York: Hill and Wang, 1977), pp. 80–81.

4. Thanks to Gregory L. Ulmer for providing me with this story.

5. Thanks again to Gregory Ulmer for this idea. In one recent lecture, he experimented still further with this delivery style by simply announcing his intention to use it *without actually doing so*.

6. Although I did not say so at the lecture, this story did not happen to me but to a graduate student at the University of Florida, Lesley Gamble. I modified it only slightly.

7. Thomas Schatz's *The Genius of the System: Hollywood Filmmaking in the Studio Era* (New York: Pantheon, 1989), pp. 256–61, provides interesting material about several of the Hardy movies' scripting and production.

8. Roland Barthes, "Change the Object Itself: *Mythology Today*," in *Image Music Text*, trans. Stephen Heath (New York: Hill and Wang, 1977), pp. 166–67.

9. Jonathan Culler, "At the Boundaries: Barthes and Derrida," *At the Boundaries*, ed. Herbert L. Sussman, *Proceedings of the Northeastern University Center for Literary Studies*, volume 1 (1983), p. 28.

10. Robert Benayoun, "Les Enfants du Paradigme," *Postif* 122 (December 1970), pp. 7–26. My source for this phrase is David Bordwell, *Making Meaning: Influence and Rhetoric in the Interpretation of Cinema* (Cambridge, Mass.: Harvard University Press, 1989), p. 84.

11. Michael Taussig, *Shamanism, Colonialism, and the Wild Man: A Study in Terror and Healing* (Chicago: Chicago University Press, 1987), p. 369.

12. Octavio Paz, *Marcel Duchamp*, trans. Rachel Phillips and Donald Gardner (New York: Seaver Books, 1978), pp. 154, 153.

13. On the avant-garde as a source of ideas for criticism, see two articles by Gregory L. Ulmer: "The Object of Post-Criticism," in *The Anti-Aesthetic: Essays on Postmodern Culture*, ed. Hal Foster (Port Townsend, Wash.: Bay Press, 1983), pp. 83–110; and "Textshop for Post(e)pedagogy," in *Writing and Reading Differently: Deconstruction and the Teaching of Composition and Literature*, ed. C. Douglas Atkins and Michael L. Johnson (Lawrence: University Press of Kansas, 1985), pp. 38–64.

14. André Breton, *Manifesto of Surrealism (1924)*, in *Surrealism*, ed. Patrick Waldberg (New York: Oxford University Press, 1965), p. 66.

15. André Breton, quoted in Marcel Jean, ed., *The Autobiography of Surrealism* (New York: Viking Press, 1980), p. 222.

16. For discussions of metaphor's importance to knowledge, see *Metaphor and Thought*, ed. Andrew Ortony (Cambridge: Cambridge University Press, 1979).

17. "On Beginning the Treatment," *The Freud Reader*, ed. Peter Gay (New York: Norton, 1989), p. 372. This passage is echoed (whether deliberately or not I do not know) in Cage's "Lecture on Nothing":

As we go along
an i-dea may occur in this talk.
I have no idea whether one will
or not. If one does, let it. Regard it as something seen momentarily, as

though from a window while traveling.
If across Kansas, then, of course, Kansas.
Arizona is more interesting. . . .

(*Silence*, p. 110)

18. The technique . . . consists simply in not directing one's attention to anything in particular and in maintaining the same "evenly-suspended attention" (as I have called it) in the face of all that one hears. . . . as soon as
anyone deliberately concentrates his attention to a certain degree, he begins
to select from the material before him; one point will be fixed in his mind
with particular clearness and some other will be correspondingly disregarded, and in making this selection he will be following his expectations or
inclinations. This, however, is precisely what must not be done. In making
the selection, if he follows his expectations he is in danger of never finding
anything but what he already knows. . . .
    The rule for the doctor may be expressed: . . . "He should simply listen,
and not bother about whether he is keeping anything in mind." . . .
    It is not a good thing to work on a case scientifically while treatment is
still proceeding—to piece together its structure, to try to foretell its further
progress, and to get a picture from time to time of the current state of affairs,
as scientific interest would demand. Cases which are devoted from the first
to scientific purposes and are treated accordingly suffer in their outcome,
while the most successful cases are those in which one proceeds, as it were,
without any purpose in view, allows oneself to be taken by surprise by any
new turn in them, and always meets them with an open mind, free from
any presuppositions.

"Recommendations to Physicians Practicing Psycho-Analysis," *The Freud Reader*,
pp. 357–59.
    19. See The French Surrealist Group, "Data towards the Irrational Enlargement
of a Film: *Shanghai Gesture*," in *The Shadow and Its Shadow: Surrealist Writings on the
Cinema*, ed. Paul Hammond (London: British Film Institute, 1978), pp. 74–80. For
"interrogation of the object," see *The Autobiography of Surrealism*, pp. 298–300.
    20. *Roland Barthes*, p. 90.
    21. Roland Barthes, "*Longtemps, je me suis couché de bonne heure* . . . ," in *The
Rustle of Language*, trans. Richard Howard (New York: Hill and Wang, 1986), p. 281,
278.

    Proust's hesitation . . . corresponds to a structural alternation: the two
    "ways" he hesitates between are the two terms of an opposition articulated by
    Jakobson: that of Metaphor and Metonymy. Metaphor sustains any discourse
    which asks: "What is it? What does it mean?"—the real question of any Essay.
    Metonymy, on the contrary, asks another question: "What can follow what I
    say? What can be engendered by the episode I am telling?"; this is the Novel's
    question. . . . Proust is a divided subject . . . he knows that each incident in
    life can give rise either to a commentary (an interpretation) or to an affabulation
    which produces or imagines the narrative *before* and *after*: to interpret is to take
    the Critical path, to argue theory (siding against Sainte-Beuve); to think incidents
    and impressions, to describe their developments, is on the contrary to weave
    a Narrative, however loosely, however gradually. (pp. 278–79)

Elsewhere, Barthes observes how concrete, everyday details leaven a text, providing
it with sites for identification, transference, reverie:

    Why do some people, including myself, enjoy in certain novels, biographies,
    and historical works the representation of the "daily life" of an epoch, of a
    character? Why this curiosity about petty details: schedules, habits, meals, lodg-
    ing, clothing? . . . is it not the fantasy itself which invokes the "detail," the tiny
    private scene, in which I can easily take my place? . . .

Thus, impossible to imagine a more tenuous, a more insignificant notation than that of "today's weather" (or yesterday's); and yet, the other day, reading, trying to read Amiel, irritation that the well-meaning editor (another person foreclosing pleasure) had seen fit to omit from this Journal the everyday details, what the weather was like on the shores of Lake Geneva, and retain only insipid moral musings: yet it is this weather that has not aged, not Amiel's philosophy.

The Pleasure of the Text, trans. Richard Miller (New York: Hill and Wang, 1975), pp. 53–54.

22. Thomas A. Sebeok and Jean Umiker-Sebeok, " 'You Know My Method': A Juxtaposition of Charles S. Peirce and Sherlock Holmes," in The Sign of Three: Dupin, Holmes, Peirce, ed. Umberto Eco and Thomas A. Sebeok (Bloomington: Indiana University Press, 1983), pp. 11–19.

23. The relationship between Flitcraft and Peirce has been noted by Stephen Marcus in the introduction to Dashiell Hammett, The Continental Op (New York: Random House, 1974), p. xix.

TWELVE

███████████

The End of Mass Culture

Michael Denning

Reification and Utopia in the Reagan Years

The 1980s—the era of Reagan and Thatcher—produced a renaissance in the study of popular or mass culture in the universities of the United States and United Kingdom. Though this discovery of the "culture of the people" by intellectuals was by no means unprecedented (indeed a key text in the recent renaissance—Peter Burke's *Popular Culture in Early Modern Europe* [1978]—opened with an account of the first modern discovery of popular culture), it stood both as a symptom of our political and cultural situation and as a distinctively new interpretation of the terrain called variously popular, mass, commercial, or vernacular culture. This interpretation began from an impasse, a sense of an intractable antinomy in cultural criticism. Choosing one's term—"mass culture" or "popular culture"—was choosing a side. In the United Kingdom, the opposition was coded as one between structuralism and culturalism;[1] in the United States, between the Frankfurt critique of the culture industry and populism.[2] The attempt to transcend these oppositions dominated theoretical, historical, and interpretative arguments.

Perhaps the most influential formulations were two essays of 1979—Fredric Jameson's "Reification and Utopia in Mass Culture" and Stuart Hall's "Notes on Deconstructing 'the Popular.'"[3] Their central arguments—that mass cultural artifacts are at one and the same time ideological and utopian, and that popular culture is neither simply a form of social control nor a form of class expression, but a contested terrain—are by now commonplace, the opening moves in many recent discussions of popular culture.[4] The fixed poles of the late 1970s have lost their magnetic force; few left cultural critics or historians are driven to denounce or celebrate mass culture. No longer are considerations of popular culture merely occasions for jeremiads on cultural degeneration or a self-conscious cultural slumming. Rather the study of popular culture—understood as that contested terrain structured by the culture industries, the state cultural apparatuses, and the symbolic forms and practices of the subaltern classes—has become the center of cultural studies generally.

In this essay I want to consider the consequences of this shift. Is it simply the establishing of a new academic paradigm, a way of producing new research on formerly despised materials? Does it retain any connection to a wider critique of culture, let alone to a project of cultural reconstruction? Or is it, as skeptics and cynics put it, a way for left academics to find resistance and subversive moments in *Dallas* and *Dynasty*?[5] What is the relation of this rethinking of mass culture to considerations of working-class history and culture? I will begin by reconsidering the arguments of Jameson and Hall, and suggesting some reasons why these arguments found wide acceptance in the 1980s; I will then argue that we can best avoid the caricatures of the critics by integrating the analysis of commodity forms with that of class formations, and by resituating the study of popular or mass culture in a more comprehensive cultural studies.

At first glance, the essays of Jameson and Hall appear very different. Jameson's essay—a centerpiece in the launching of the journal *Social Text*—was addressed to literary, film, and cultural critics; Hall's essay—first delivered at a *History Workshop* gathering—to historians. Jameson's concerns revolve around the interpretation of cultural texts; Hall begins from the issue of periodizing cultural transformations. Moreover, left cultural discourse in the United States was largely bounded by the relatively recent translations of Frankfurt critical theory and Derridean post-structuralism; the quite different formation in the United Kingdom was symbolized by the furor over E. P. Thompson's attack on British Althusserianism. Nevertheless, despite the differences in address and situation, the essays by Jameson and Hall shared several key arguments. First, both stressed the political centrality of culture. One misunderstood contemporary society if one thought of culture as leisure, entertainment, escape—all that was not "real life." For, as Jameson put it, "we must ask the sociologists of manipulation . . . whether they inhabit the same world as we do. . . . culture, far from being an occasional matter of the reading of a monthly good book or a trip to the drive-in, seems to me the very element of consumer society itself. . . . everything is mediated by culture, to the point where even the political and the ideological 'levels' have initially to be disentangled from their primary mode of representation which is cultural."[6] Similarly, Hall's argument depended on his sense that popular culture was not simply "those things the 'people' do or have done. . . . Pigeon-fancying and stamp-collecting, flying ducks on the wall and garden gnomes." Rather, "popular culture is one of the sites where [the] struggle for and against a culture of the powerful is engaged. . . . it is one of the places where socialism might be constituted." "That," Hall concludes, "is why 'popular culture' matters. Otherwise, to tell you the truth, I don't give a damn about it."[7]

Second, Jameson and Hall sought to transcend the antinomies of social control and class expression, containment and resistance, incorporation and autonomy, manipulation and subversion, which had structured most ways of seeing popular culture. They did this not by ignoring the opposition but by relocating it. Thus, not only did they argue against the mutually exclusive positions that mass culture was *entirely* a manipulative industrial product or *entirely* an authentic cultural creation, but they also refused the proverbial separation of sheep from goats, of the progressive popular culture from the reactionary mass culture. Indeed, they argued that *neither* pole existed, that all cultural creation in capitalist society was divided against itself. As Hall writes, "if the forms of provided commercial popular culture are not purely manipulative, then it is because, alongside the false appeals, the foreshortenings, the trivialisation and shortcircuits, there are also elements of recognition and identification, something approaching a recreation of recognisable experiences and attitudes, to which people are responding."[8] Jameson also suggests "that the works of mass culture cannot be ideological without at one and the same time being implicitly Utopian . . . they cannot manipulate unless they offer some genuine shred of content as a fantasy bribe to the public about to be so manipulated . . . such works cannot manage anxieties about the social order unless they have first revived them and given them some rudimentary expression."[9]

But this does not merely "rescue" commercial culture; it throws into question any notion of a purely authentic popular culture. "There is no separate, autonomous, 'authentic' layer of working class culture to be found," Hall argues. "Could we expect otherwise?" he asks in a brief consideration of popular imperialism. "How could we explain . . . the culture of a dominated class. . . . which remained untouched by the most powerful dominant ideology . . . ?"[10] Jameson too argues that "the 'popular' . . . no longer exists," that even a "political art" is more a question than a prescription.[11]

It is the dialectic of containment and resistance, of reification and utopia which defines popular or mass culture for Jameson and Hall, though Hall emphasizes the battle surrounding the texts, artifacts, and performances— the "continuous and necessarily uneven and unequal struggle, by the dominant culture, to constantly disorganise and reorganise popular culture"[12]—and Jameson emphasizes the conflict within the symbolic forms themselves.

Finally, both Hall and Jameson throw into question the separation of high culture from popular culture, not by reversing the valuation or dissolving the distinction but by moving beyond what Jameson calls "the false problem of value." Jameson argues that mass culture and modernism are, in Adorno's famous phrase, "torn halves of an integral freedom, to which however they do not add up"; they share a social and aesthetic situation, and their responses to the dilemmas of form and of audience are complementary. Hall, on the other hand, focuses attention on the process of boundary construction, on the way that the dividing of Culture from nonculture is an exercise of cultural power that should itself be the object of scrutiny.

All of these are powerful and controversial arguments; my interest here is less in elaborating or defending them (or in discriminating between Jameson and Hall) than in suggesting several reasons why they won consent among socialist intellectuals in the 1980s. First, the regimes of Reagan and Thatcher closed the door on the period of boom and upheaval that followed the Second World War, the period that was now named postmodernism, the sixties, the American Century. Of course, the end had been in sight with the depression of 1973–74, and the collapse of the insurgencies of the late 1960s; nevertheless, the 1970s were marked by the continuing legitimation crisis that led to the fall of a second U.S. president (and a third if one counts the failure of Jimmy Carter to establish a hegemonic bloc) and saw victories to national liberation and socialist movements in Vietnam, Angola, Mozambique, Jamaica, Grenada, and Nicaragua. The success of the Reagan regime in constructing a new historical bloc, in giving new life to authoritarian regimes and counterrevolutionary forces, and particularly in forging a new national-popular ideology, a distinctive "populism," often perplexed left critics. The peculiar powers of the "Great Communicator," who seemed less Hollywood actor than broadcast host or television evangelist, demanded a cultural explanation. Whereas Richard Nixon's success seemed sufficiently explained by media debunkers detailing the "selling" of a president, Reagan confounded manipulation theory. There was that utopian promise in the Reagan narrative, that fantasy bribe, that element of recognition, and it is not surprising that the two finest interpretations of Reagan's regime—Garry Wills's *Reagan's America* and Michael Rogin's *Ronald Reagan, The Movie*—turn on the dialectic of ideology and utopia in popular culture. Similarly, Stuart Hall's theoretical discussion of popular culture gained its power by informing his influential account of the authoritarian populism of Thatcher's (and Reagan's) "Great Moving Right Show."

The crisis in feminism also provoked a reassessment of popular or mass culture. Like many insurgent movements, the women's movement emerged with an intransigent hostility to mass culture, denouncing, satirizing, and criticizing the popular paraphernalia of the feminine—beauty pageants, fashion, Hollywood cinema, and advertising. Feminist culture was avant-garde in sensibility, seeking new forms, new languages, new images for women's experience, and constructing new public spheres. By the 1980s, however, the political crises and successes of the women's movement—the mobilization of antifeminist women by the right, the dividing lines of race, class, and generation, and the popularization of an economic feminism among newly organized working-class women—led to a reassessment of commercial culture for women. Perhaps the most striking critical work in the renaissance of popular culture studies has emerged in the debates over popular romance novels and over Hollywood melodrama.[13]

Third, the interest in the essays of Jameson and Hall was a symptom of the recognition, naming, and acceptance of "post-modernism." Indeed postmodernism could be defined as the reevaluation of mass culture by artists, writers, critics, architects: a learning from Las Vegas.[14] In this light, Jameson might be seen not only as an analyst of postmodernism, but as an exemplary postmodernist theorist. If modernism and mass culture emerge together, "as twin and inseparable forms of the fission of aesthetic production under late capitalism,"[15] perhaps they come to an end together, recognizing their kinship, ceasing their hostilities, and fusing into the spools of magnetic tape that dominate our culture in what Paul Buhle has named "the age of the cassette."[16]

The changes in the culture industry in the last decade bolster this sense. Though the capital invested in culture is more concentrated than ever, cultural commodities appear less centralized, less concentrated, as the heyday of network television and the Hollywood studio system has passed. The technology of the cassette has changed American habits in consuming films, broadcast programs, and popular music, making contemporary capitalist culture look less like a mass culture and more like a series of elaborate, interlocking subcultures, each with their own market share. Though this vision of cultural pluralism is a far cry from a democratic or socialist culture, it has led to a reduction in the overt hostility to and fear of mass culture. However, the cultural battles have not ceased: one need only look at the battle over mass university education that has been waged over the slogan of the "canon" and the jeremiad of that typical product of American mass culture, Allan Bloom, or at the intense battles throughout the Reagan era over vernacular musics—like the attempts to censor rock lyrics and the moral panics over disturbances at rap concerts—which have been regularly reported by one of the best "little magazines" of the 1980s, Dave Marsh's *Rock and Roll Confidential*.

But the fact is that mass culture has won; there is nothing else. The great powers of broadcasting and mass spectacles are second nature. Think for a moment about the earlier moments of the mass culture critique: it began as a reaction to the novel and threatening powers of broadcasting and film, thought through the concepts of propaganda and manipulation, emblemized by the notorious panic provoked by Orson Welles's radio broadcast of *The War of the Worlds* on the eve of the Second World War. The second wave of mass culture critique was largely orchestrated around the postwar critique of Popular Front culture, the sense among the New York Intellectuals that the experiments in the popular arts that characterized the Popular Front were an integral part of a Stalinist (and capitalist) reduction of culture to kitsch. The third and most recent wave of hostility to mass culture largely derives from a hostility to the New Left and the coun-terculture; and this battle among memoirists and historians over the legacy of the 1960s has just begun. Thus it would be wrong to see the present flowering of popular culture criticism as the result of an academization of popular culture; for the academic industry—symbolized by the *Journal of Popular Culture* and the Popular Culture Association, which emerged in the early 1970s—has been a failure, never providing the theoretical or historical breakthroughs. Rather the recent breakthrough came out of the cultural criticism of the New Left, and particularly from the writers and readers associated with three journals: *Working Papers in Cultural Studies*, which was published by the Birmingham Centre for Contemporary Cultural Studies beginning in 1972; *Cultural Correspondence*, founded in 1975 with the subtitle "a strategic journal of popular culture"; and *Social Text*, founded in 1979. In Paul Buhle's account of *Cultural Correspondence*, he notes that it was "the first political journal of culture to assume that its readers (and writers) *watched* television."[17]

The work of these intellectual tendencies was not a clever game of finding subversive moments in each piece of pop culture, not a ritual in-vocation of a dialectic between the ideological and the utopian, let alone the progressive and the regressive. Rather it attempted to change the way we thought about culture generally. All culture is mass culture under capi-talism. There is no working-class culture that is not saturated with mass culture. The same historical transformations which produce a proletariat, labor power as a commodity, produce mass culture, culture as an "immense accumulation of commodities." There is now very little cultural production outside the commodity form.

Thus, the issue before us is twofold: first, how do we think the relations between commodity forms and class formations, between the omnipresent cultural commodities marketed by the cultural industries (and by the cul-tural apparatuses of the state) and the subcultures, class fractions, social movements that produce and consume them; and second, how do we think the relations between the wide variety of cultural forms and media, how may we get beyond the high/low dichotomy, the modernism/mass culture divide, the theories of brows, the canonic and noncanonic. It is not that these boundaries are not important, or without effects, but that we can no longer take them as starting points. We need a new conception of the spectrum of cultural forms.

Commodity Forms and Class Formation

How does the cultural critic or historian think about the relations between commodity forms and class formations? For the most part, they have seemed mutually exclusive, each the property of a distinctive kind of cul-tural studies. One powerful Marxist tradition of cultural studies depended on a notion of the relation between cultural products and social classes, enriching the foundational metaphors of base and superstructure with historical tropes that linked artistic genres and intellectual movements to the struggles between classes. It came to seem reductive, not only of the individual cultural products but of the cultural heterogeneity of class formations, and many of us cut our teeth on Sartre's celebrated complaint in *Search for a Method*: "Valery is a petit bourgeois intellectual, no doubt about it. But not every petit bourgeois intellectual is Valery." But it remained the central aspect of what was to become the "new" labor history, with its attempt to reconstruct and delineate working-class cultures.

Paralleling the new labor history was a revival of a Marxist cultural criticism which largely abandoned class categories, stressing instead the effects of the commodity form on culture. The code mediating between social structure and individual text shifted from class to reification, and, as is well known, a powerful hermeneutic arose which could read the scars capitalist reification had left on the sentences, brush strokes, and rhythms of modern art as well as of mass culture. In recent years, this hermeneutic has come to seem less a revelation than an exegetical exercise, not unlike the fall from Empson's startling, even mystic, revelation of seven types of ambiguity to the all-too-predictable contributions to the *Explicator*. Interpretation is finally an act of metaphor, and suffers the same ritualization to cliché. But the reification hermeneutic has also suffered from its lack of historical specificity; it too often looks like a Marxist version of the ideologies of modernism and modernization, like them dependent on a too-simple dichotomy of before and after.

Perhaps the most disturbing aspect of the commodity form argument is its paralyzing of cultural practice. Do any cultural forms escape the logic of the commodity? Is there a political or oppositional art? In the class model, cultural practice was relatively clear; one aligned oneself—in a variety of complex ways—with the rising class, the popular class. Was there a cultural practice in the face of reification? Jameson's work set the contradiction in plain view, at once arguing that there is "authentic cultural production" which draws "on the collective experience of marginal pockets of the social life of the world system," while recognizing that political art is a problem, not a choice, that "you do not reinvent an access onto political art and authentic cultural production by studding your individual artistic discourse with class and political signals."[18] I do not mean to solve the problem of a political art here, but the success and failure of our popular culture criticism hinges on this issue: the sense that interpreting a mass culture is not the same as changing it, that the new criticism of mass culture has not contributed to the creation of a new popular culture.

Thus, in recent years, we have seen several attempts to reintegrate the interpretation of commodity forms with the history of class formations, to situate the interpretation of the products of the culture industry with an account of the communities that use them. This is not merely a reprise of an older Marxism, because it begins not from an assumption that cultures are somehow attached to already constituted classes, but that cultural conflicts are part of the process of class formation, the forging of alliances among class fractions, social groups, and ethnic and racial communities. I want to mention briefly the two most promising and influential ways of rethinking class formations and commodity forms in cultural studies: the theories of the social construction of cultural value, and of hegemonic formations.

The first of these, the investigation of the social construction of cultural values, grows out of the battles in literary studies over the "canon," the resurrection of the almost moribund subdiscipline of sociology of culture, and the translation and appropriation of Pierre Bourdieu's *La Distinction*. In this work, one finds a turn away from judgments and interpretations of particular cultural works, and toward an exploration of the way cultural values, tastes, and hierarchies are established. What distinguishes this work from earlier sociologies of taste is its unwavering attention to the ideological consequences of taste, to the ways aesthetic distinctions are operations of domination and subordination. The relation between class formations and cultural commodities moves to the center, not because of some immanent or expressive class nature of particular cultural texts but because of the way they are mobilized as visible totems of class domination and as symbolic weapons in class conflict.

Consider the difference between the explanations of postmodernism offered by Fredric Jameson and Fred Pfeil: for Jameson, postmodernism is a stylistic dominant, a product of the "cultural logic of late capitalism," a new turn of the screw of reification. It is a new aesthetic, in the deepest sense: not only a new sense of rhythm and beauty and artistic value, but a new way of perception, of living the body, indeed a modification of the senses themselves in a world of simulacra and information, a society of cyborgs with amnesia, where human relations are not even relations between things but relations between the images of things. For Pfeil, on the other hand, postmodernism is the aesthetic, which is to say the cultural consumption habits, of a particular class generation, the youth of the U.S. professional and managerial classes. Though he occasionally does look to Talking Heads and Laurie Anderson as the Pascal and Racine of a rising class fraction expressing their "world view," he more often elaborates their cultural consumption as a marking of distinctions, a creation of a *habitus*, a life-style, as an example of the social construction of cultural value.

Though in many ways complementary to Jameson's work (Jameson takes architecture, surely the form most amenable to a logic of capital argument, as representative of postmodernism; Pfeil looks to the cultural commodities an individual buys, records and paperbacks, for his argument), Pfeil's work points to a powerful new opening in U.S. cultural criticism. This opening is already being explored by Janice Radway, especially in her analysis of the Book-of-the-Month Club; by Paul DiMaggio, in his explorations of high culture in nineteenth-century Boston; by Lawrence Levine, in *Highbrow/Lowbrow*; and by Richard Ohmann, Jane Tompkins, Lawrence Schwartz, and Pfeil himself in discussions of the cultural gate-keeping in the distribution of U.S. fiction. In all of this work, the processes of establishing cultural hierarchies, taste communities, and canons becomes the focus of cultural criticism. There are, however, several curiosities about this emerging body of work.

First, unlike Bourdieu, whose book depends on a powerful, if mistaken, articulation of a popular aesthetic, the elaboration of a working-class culture, the U.S. writers on the social construction of cultural value focus on the tension between fractions of the middle classes, and particularly on the cultural power of the emerging professional and managerial classes. The early failure of an aristocratic or patrician culture financed by a corporate elite, combined with the apparent failure of a distinctive working-class culture have given the subsumed classes a disproportionately central role in the construction of American culture. Thus we see a history of the cultural distinctions created by a sometimes radically anticommercial professional class, by the genteel tradition of a provincial middlebrow petit bourgeoisie, by the suburban culture that has been periodically chronicled in *The Lonely Crowd, The Feminine Mystique, The Culture of Narcissim,* and *Habits of the Heart* and, most recently, by postmodern yuppies. However, the U.S. version of the social construction of cultural values needs to move beyond a debunking of the authorized standards and judgments of taste and value to a mapping of the popular aesthetic and the cultural values of the working classes.

It is not clear, however, whether this is possible, whether, that is to say, the investigation of the social construction of cultural tastes can ever break free of debunking. For the attraction of Bourdieu's work to U.S. cultural critics owes something to his kinship with a classic American cultural critic, Thorsten Veblen. Like Veblen's attack on culture, Bourdieu's work cuts through the grease of most high cultural discourse; it is hard to take the rhetoric of the aesthetic disposition seriously after its uses as conspicuous consumption are so painstakingly unmasked. But like most powerful satires, it undermines the satirist as well. Whereas most of the attacks on the academic study of popular cultures are easily dismissed, the products of a populist or, more often, mandarin anti-intellectualism, it is more difficult to deny the power of Bourdieu's debunking:

> The struggles which aim . . . to transform or overturn the legitimate hierarchies through the legitimating of a still illegitimate art or genre, such as photography or the strip cartoon, or through the rehabilitation of "minor" or "neglected" authors etc., or to impose a new mode of appropriation, linked to another mode

of acquisition, are precisely what creates legitimacy, by creating belief not in the value of this or that stake but in the value of the game in which the value of all the stakes is produced and reproduced. . . . "middle-ground" arts such as cinema, jazz, and, even more, strip cartoons, science fiction or detective stories are predisposed to attract the investments either of those who have entirely succeeded in converting their cultural capital into educational capital or those who, not having acquired legitimate culture in the legitimate manner (i.e., through early familiarization), maintain an uneasy relationship with it, subjectively or objectively, or both. These arts, not yet fully legitimate, which are disdained or neglected by the big holders of educational capital, offer a refuge and a revenge to those who, by appropriating them, secure the best return on their cultural capital.[19]

By evacuating the content of cultural products and activities, by reading them as objects of consumption and markers in a symbolic class conflict, Bourdieu's work, far from providing a foundation for cultural studies or a reconstructive cultural practice, buries it. An investment theory of culture mimics the capitalist culture it critiques. If all cultural activity is a means of accumulating cultural capital, there is no place for a cultural politics. The consequences of "cultural studies" as a project are meager indeed.

The second major tendency that links class formations and cultural commodities offers a more persuasive account not only of the links between class and culture but between culture and politics: this is the theory of hegemonic formations and historical blocs. The revival of the work of Antonio Gramsci is no longer news: nowadays, everybody is a Gramscian. Nevertheless, the impact of Gramsci's work and the constellation of concepts he employed has been uneven, emerging quite differently in various national, disciplinary, and political contexts. Unfortunately, the recent debates over the concept of hegemony among historians of U.S. culture, particularly historians of labor, have not done justice to the richness and originality of the theory.[20]

There have been two very common misappropriations of Gramsci in the United States which continue to haunt these debates. First, the concept of hegemony has often been understood as a functional equivalent of commodification and reification. Reducing the work of both Gramsci and the Frankfurt School to a general notion of consumer society, this tendency has seen "hegemony" as domination through managed consumption and manipulated desire. Those persuaded by this view tend to be vehemently opposed to mass culture, and have drawn the fire of both socialist defenders of the utopian possibilities of the culture of abundance, like Warren Susman, and the defenders of consumer capitalism, like Walter Benn Michaels, the Daniel Boorstin of literary criticism. Second, the concept of hegemony has all too often appeared as a synonym for "consensus," and has led to a revival of consensus historiography (though from a point of view critical of the consensus). One sees this in Sacvan Bercovitch's provocative theories of the rhetoric of the American consensus, and, despite explicit disclaimers, in Jackson Lears's elaboration of a theory of "cultural hegemony." But as Eric Foner has noted of this "consensus/hegemony approach," "in adopting the notion of hegemony from Gramsci, American historians have often transformed it from a subtle mode of exploring the ways class struggle is muted and channeled in modern society, into a substitute for it. . . . Rather than being demonstrated, the 'hegemony' of mass culture and liberal values is inferred from the 'absence' of protest, and then this absence is attributed to the self-same 'hegemony.' "[21] It is this conception that Thomas Haskell satirized as "a feather pillow, perfect for catching falling Marxists."[22]

Jackson Lears's "The Concept of Cultural Hegemony" has been the focus of much of the recent debate, and it is a symptomatic essay. He moves beyond the early American appropriations of hegemony by turning from issues of mass commodity culture to the history of class formations and subordinate groups: "by clarifying the political functions of cultural symbols, the concept of cultural hegemony can aid intellectual historians trying to understand how ideas reinforce or undermine existing social structures and social historians seeking to reconcile the apparent contradiction between the power wielded by dominant groups and the relative cultural autonomy of subordinate groups whom they victimize."[23] Unfortunately, his concept (and this is characteristic of much of the U.S. discussion that followed, whether defending or rejecting a concept of hegemony) continues to be framed by the opposition between accommodation and resistance, attempting to define how victims are complicit in their own victimization, caught in the murky realms of consciousness and false consciousness. For Lears, the fundamental question remains: to what degree are the working classes incorporated? As George Lipsitz puts it well, "it is perhaps a measure of the inescapable irony of our time that Antonio Gramsci's ideas have gained popularity among scholars largely as a means of explaining the futility of efforts to change past and present capitalist societies."[24]

But Gramsci's concepts of hegemonic formations and historical blocs do not begin with the functionalist premise of Lears ("how ideas reinforce or undermine existing social structures"), which produces the characteristic deep freeze of contemporary accounts of hegemony. Rather they begin from the question of how social movements are organized among both the dominant and subordinate groups, how social formations are led. Precisely because the theory of hegemonic formations is a theory of action as well as structure, because Gramsci and Hall are politicians, educators, intellectuals in the widest sense, they formulate the issue not in terms of true or false consciousness, but in terms of a popular thought and culture that is shaped, reshaped, fought over. "Hegemonizing," as Stuart Hall put it, "is hard work." The building of hegemonic formations is not only a matter of "ideas," of winning hearts and minds, but also an issue of participation, in the sense of involving people both in cultural institutions—schools, churches, sporting events,—and in long-term historic projects—waging wars, establishing colonies, gentrifying a city, developing a regional economy.

The power of this conception for the analysis of popular cultural artifacts is that it provides the necessary complement to the analysis of the social construction of cultural value. If that work establishes that there are no intrinsic values in cultural objects, and no natural or expressive relation between classes and cultural practices, a theory of hegemonic formations provides the framework by which we may examine the historical articulations of class formations and commodity forms. No popular cultural practice is necessarily subversive or incorporated; it takes place in a situation, becomes articulated with a "party" in Gramsci's sense: an organized way of life, an alliance of class fractions, a conception of the universe, a historical bloc which creates the conditions for a political use or reading, the conditions for symbolizing class conflict.

The greatest difficulty in appropriating Gramsci's constellation of historical concepts for contemporary critiques of popular culture is that his work did not take full measure of "mass culture," of broadcasting, film, recorded music, mass spectator sports, and the explosion of cheap mass-produced symbolic commodities—McDLT's, Levis, and the fantastic array of plastic objects that are sold as children's toys and adult novelties. It is this absense that can make Gramsci look old-fashioned; Adorno's screech against radio music may not be appealing but it is recognizable. After all, for Gramsci, popular culture is figured by the Catholic church. Nevertheless, the advantages of Gramsci's framework may lie here as well: taking the Catholic church rather than network television as the representative instance may avoid the brief historical scope of most thinking about popular culture and the temptation of concepts like manipulation, propaganda, and deception that haunt the apocalyptic imaginations of modernists and postmodernists alike. Whereas a characteristic U.S. pragmatist socialist, Kenneth Burke, once suggested that socialists imitate advertisers, Gramsci would seem to argue that socialists imitate the clergy. Popular culture is more the product of long-term cultural organization and a symbolic community than a quick sale. Unfortunately, much of the recent revival of Gramsci's work for socialist cultural policies seems less Gramscian than Burkean.

Forms of Cultural Practice

We need a new way of thinking about the spectrum of cultural forms. If the theories of the social construction of cultural value give us a decoder of cultural hierarchies, boundaries, and canons, they remind us that no cultural form is fixed in the hierarchy: as Bourdieu argues, "the very meaning and value of a cultural object varies according to the system of objects in which it is placed."[25] It becomes less plausible to orchestrate cultural studies around those relational terms—high and low, mass and elite, popular and polite. Similarly, if the theories of hegemonic formations and historical blocs offer ways of articulating cultural commodities and class formations, they also remind us that cultural forms have no necessary class allegiance; they can't be ranked as capitalist forms or proletarian forms.

One possible and commonly suggested solution is to avoid ranking cultural forms altogether, to see them either as somehow equal—ballet and break dancing, Shakespeare and soap operas—or as so unalike as to make comparisons unnecessary. In either case, as an aesthetic and historical precept, there is no disputing taste. This is unsatisfactory; the refusal of discrimination often becomes the tacit continuation of established discriminations. The difficulty that haunts the Jameson essay with which I began haunts all significant cultural studies: how does one map the relations between the polite forms of high culture, the products of a commercial or mass culture, and the marginal or oppositional forms that seem to demand some adjective like "authentic" or "organic"?

One attempt was Raymond Williams's oft-cited distinctions between dominant, residual, oppositional, and alternative cultures, terms which he himself noted were provisional. I would suggest that we develop some of the categories in his subsequent book, *Culture*, to think about cultural forms in a way which privileges the "popular" in a specific sense. In his chapter on "Means of Production," Williams discusses the development of cultural forms in terms of the "inherent resources" of the species (beginning his account not from "literature" or the "novel" but from the social development of physical movement and voice in dance and song) and the degree of popular access to the form: "while anyone in the world, with normal physical resources, can watch dance or look at sculpture or listen to music, still some forty per cent of the world's present inhabitants can make no contact whatever with a piece of writing, and in earlier periods this percentage was much higher."[26] It is not surprising perhaps that the master art for Williams was the theater, the relatively simple development of the inherent resources of speech and movement for an audience that need have no special training in a notational system like writing. The great paradox of film and broadcasting has of course been that the genuine democratization of cultural audiences required such large capital investment and technical training as to have restricted greatly the production of films and broadcasts. Cultural studies, it seems to me, should take up the challenge of Williams's cultural materialism by exploring the social investments required by different cultural forms at different times—the investments of time, training, and capital required for production and for consumption of cultural forms.

Indeed any cultural studies worthy of the name should probably begin with those fundamental forms: song, dance, theater, and (the great absence in Williams's work) sport. Certainly any attention to working-class culture and aesthetics, which, as Bourdieu rightly argued, is a culture and aesthetic of necessity, would have to begin from these forms. And, I would argue, such an exploration would radically challenge a number of our common assumptions about working-class culture and popular culture, taken as they are from an undifferentiated sense of the mass media and consumer society.

For example, much of Bourdieu's conception of the "popular aesthetic" depends on his assertion of "the hostility of the working class and of the middleclass fractions least rich in cultural capital towards every kind of formal experimentation."[27] However, his evidence is drawn from studies of cultural forms where people "least rich in cultural capital" have restricted access to the codes which make experiment and code-breaking meaningful. If one looks to the forms where working people have elaborate bodies of knowledge, like popular sports, one finds an appreciation for experiment: think only of the way the formal innovations of such black artists as Rickey Henderson or Michael Jordan are elaborated on sandlots and playgrounds across the United States. Indeed the study of sports needs an entirely new perspective, which would break both from elaborations of the themes of Critical Theory—"sport as a prison of measured time," in one formulation—and from the functionalist modernization framework that structures most mainstream sports sociology and history. The writings of C. L. R. James on cricket stand as one of the few examples of a hermeneutic of sport, reading not sport or sports in general, but the ways of playing a sport, the moves, as symbolic actions.

After all, sport remains a cultural form whose training, equipment, and education is widely available, and whose preeminent artists are drawn predominantly from the working classes. Indeed, perhaps the most popular and significant *cultural* achievement of the U.S. feminist movement over the last two decades has been the enfranchisement of women as sports producers and consumers.

Similarly, vernacular song has long been recognized as a sensitive barometer of working-class cultures, and it is not surprising that the finest discussions of contemporary working-class cultures in the United States and the United Kingdom have come from cultural critics writing on music: one thinks of Paul Gilroy's discussion of the musics of the black diaspora, or the essays of Dave Marsh and George Lipsitz on the relations between postwar vernacular musics and the reshaping of the American working class. All three writers analyze not only the relations between popular audiences and industrial cultural production, but also the way cultural producers, in this case popular musicians, emerge from working-class communities, and serve as organic intellectuals in the formation of historical blocs.

If the study of popular culture is not to disintegrate into an antiquarian cataloging of fads and fashions or a postmodernist ransacking of retro styles, it must become part of a larger cultural studies. That cultural studies, I have argued, needs to be rooted in the exploration of the social construction of cultural value, the history of hegemonic formations, and the investigation of the material investments and constraints implied by various cultural forms. We have come to the end of "mass culture"; the debates and positions which named "mass culture" as an other have been superseded. There is no mass culture *out there*; it is the very element we all breathe.

Notes

1. See in particular Stuart Hall, "Cultural Studies: Two Paradigms," *Media, Culture and Society* 2 (1980); Richard Johnson, "Three Problematics: Elements of a Theory of Working Class Culture," in *Working Class Culture*, ed. John Clarke et al. (London: Hutchinson, 1979); Tony Bennett, "The Politics of the 'Popular' and Popular Culture," in *Popular Culture and Social Relations*, ed. Tony Bennett et al. (Milton Keynes: Open University Press, 1986).

2. See *American Media and Mass Culture*, ed. Donald Lazere (Berkeley: University of California Press, 1987). Despite its date, more than two-thirds of its essays were written in the 1970s.

3. I would also note the somewhat earlier essay by Gareth Stedman Jones, "Class Expression *versus* Social Control?" *History Workshop* 4 (1977): 163–70.

4. I will cite a version from my own study of U.S. dime novels as an example: "these popular stories . . . can be understood neither as forms of deception, manipulation, and social control nor as expressions of a genuine people's culture, opposing and resisting the dominant culture. Rather they are best seen as a contested terrain, a field of cultural conflict where signs with wide appeal and resonance take on contradictory disguises and are spoken with contrary accents" (Michael Denning, *Mechanic Accents: Dime Novels and Working-Class Culture in America* [London: Verso, 1987]).

5. For example, Jackson Lears recently noted that "left cultural historians have discovered traces of collective memory in Hollywood films, early network television programs, and other supposed citadels of social amnesia," and went on to say that he thought "such arguments may exaggerate the significance of the dissent embodied in mass cultural forms. There is too strong a tendency to elevate what is often a univocal, closed system of imagery into an elegant Bakhtinian conversation, where every neofascist utterance by Clint Eastwood implies a counterfascist critique of 'late capitalism' " ("Power, Culture, and Memory," *Journal of American History* 90 [1988]: 139). Similarly, Judith Williamson (like Lears an analyst of advertising) has recently complained of "left-wing academics . . . picking out strands of 'subversion' in every piece of pop culture from Street Style to Soap Opera," quoted in Meaghan Morris, "Banality in Culture Studies," *Discourse* 10, no. 2 (1988): 3.

6. Fredric Jameson, "Reification and Utopia in Mass Culture," *Social Text* 1 (1979): 139.

7. Stuart Hall, "Notes on Deconstructing 'the Popular,' " in *People's History and Socialist Theory*, ed. Raphael Samuel (London: Routledge and Kegan Paul, 1981), 234, 239.

8. Ibid., 233.

9. Jameson, "Reification and Utopia," 144.

10. Hall, "Notes on Deconstructing 'the Popular,' " 229.

11. Jameson, "Reification and Utopia," 134, 139–40.

12. Hall, "Notes on Deconstructing 'the Popular,' " 233.

13. On the romance, see Janice Radway, *Reading the Romance* (Chapel Hill: University of North Carolina Press, 1984); and Tania Modleski, *Loving with a Vengeance* (Hamden: Archon, 1982). On Hollywood melodrama see *Home Is Where the Heart Is*, ed. Christine Gledhill (Urbana: University of Illinois Press, 1987). Indeed, one of the first appropriations of Jameson's "reification and utopia" framework came in one of Radway's early essays on romance fiction.

14. A number of recent treatments of postmodernism make this argument; see in particular Andreas Huyssen, *After the Great Divide* (Bloomington: Indiana University Press, 1986); and Jim Collins, *Uncommon Cultures* (New York: Routledge, 1989).

15. Jameson, "Reification and Utopia," 133.

16. *Popular Culture in America*, ed. Paul Buhle (Minneapolis: University of Minnesota Press, 1987), x.

17. Ibid., xxiv.

18. Jameson, "Reification and Utopia in Mass Culture," 140.

19. Pierre Bourdieu, *Distinction: A Social Critique of the Judgement of Taste*, trans. Richard Nice (Cambridge, Mass.: Harvard University Press, 1984), 569nn81, 87.

20. The key intervention was Jackson Lears, "The Concept of Cultural Hegemony," *American Historical Review* 90 (1985): 567–93. The term also emerged in the controversy between Thomas Haskell and David Brion Davis over the relation between capitalism and abolitionism: see Thomas Haskell, "Convention and Hegemonic Interest in the Debate over Antislavery," *American Historical Review* 92 (1987): 829–78. More recently it has been the subject of an illuminating symposium on labor history and the concept of hegemony in the *Journal of American History* 75 (1988): 115–61.

21. Eric Foner, "Why Is There No Socialism in the United States?" *History Workshop* 17 (1984): 64.

22. Haskell, "Convention and Hegemonic Interest," 834.

23. Lears, "The Concept of Cultural Hegemony," 568.

24. George Lipsitz, "The Struggle for Hegemony," *Journal of American History* 75 (1988): 146.

25. Bourdieu, *Distinction*, 88.

26. Raymond Williams, *Culture* (London: Fontana, 1981), 93.

27. Bourdieu, *Distinction*, 32.

Contributors

CHRISTOPHER ANDERSON is Assistant Professor of Telecommunications at Indiana University. His writings have appeared in *Cinema Journal* and *The Village Voice*, and he is currently working on a book about the relations between the motion picture and television industries during the 1950s.

PATRICK BRANTLINGER is Chair of the English Department at Indiana University. Among his recent books are *Bread and Circuses: Theories of Mass Culture and Social Decay; Rule of Darkness: British Literature and Imperialism, 1830–1914;* and *Crusoe's Footprints: Cultural Studies in Britain and America.*

JIM COLLINS is Associate Professor of Communications at the University of Notre Dame. He is author of *Uncommon Cultures: Popular Culture and Postmodernism,* and of articles in *Screen, Cultural Studies, Discourse,* and *Iris.* He is currently at work on a book-length study of contemporary popular culture.

MICHAEL DENNING is Associate Professor and Director of American Studies at Yale University. His writings include *Mechanic Accents: Dime Novels and Working-Class Culture in America* and *Cover Stories: Narrative and Ideology in the British Spy Thriller.* He is at work on a book about the cultural politics of the Mercury Theater.

JANICE L. DOANE is Associate Professor of English at St. Mary's College in Moraga, California. With Devon Hodges, she is the author of *Nostalgia and Sexual Difference: The Resistance to Contemporary Feminism.*

JOHN FISKE is Professor of Communication Arts at the University of Wisconsin-Madison. Among his many publications are *Reading Television* (with John Hartley); *Introduction to Communication Studies; Television Culture; Understanding Popular Culture;* and *Reading the Popular.*

DEVON HODGES is Associate Professor of English and American Studies at George Mason University. She is author, with Janice L. Doane, of *Nostalgia and Sexual Difference.* She and Professor Doane are currently at work on a book-length study of feminist psychoanalysis from Klein to Kristeva.

LYNNE JOYRICH is Assistant Professor in the Department of English and Comparative Literature at the University of Wisconsin-Milwaukee. Her writings have appeared in *Camera Obscura* and in the collection entitled *Logics of Television.*

BARBARA KLINGER is Assistant Professor in the Film Division of Comparative Literature at Indiana University. Her articles have appeared in *Screen, Cinema Journal, Wide Angle,* and *The Yale Journal of Criticism.* She is currently at work on a book about Douglas Sirk and reception theory.

JAMES NAREMORE is Professor of English and Comparative Literature and Director of Film Studies at Indiana University. His writings on film include *The Filmguide to Psycho, The Magic World of Orson Welles,* and, most recently, *Acting in the Cinema.*

GEOFFREY NOWELL-SMITH is Director of Publications for the British Film Institute. He is the author of *Visconti,* and the coeditor, with Quintin Hoare, of Antonio Gramsci's *Prison Notebooks.*

RICHARD OHMANN is Professor of English and Director of the Center for the Humanities at Wesleyan University. His books include *English in America* and, most recently, *Politics of Letters.* He is on the editorial board of *Radical Teacher.*

ROBERT B. RAY is Associate Professor of English and Director of Film Studies at the University of Florida. He is the author of *A Certain Tendency of the American Cinema* and is currently at work on a book about the Andy Hardy films.

STEPHEN WATT is Assistant Professor of English at Indiana University. He is the author of *The Popular Theatres of James Joyce and Sean O'Casey*, and the coeditor, with Judith L. Fisher, of *When They Weren't Doing Shakespeare: Essays in Nineteenth-Century British and American Theatre*. He is at work on a book about postmodernism and contemporary American drama.

PETER WOLLEN, a writer and filmmaker, teaches in the Department of Film and Television at UCLA. He is the author of *Signs and Meaning in the Cinema* and *Readings and Writings*. With Laura Mulvey, he has made a number of films, including *Penthesilea, Riddles of the Sphinx,* and *Crystal Gazing*. His most recent film is *Friendship's Death*.

Index